The Food and Wine
of Greece

THE FOOD AND
WINE OF GREECE

Diane Kochilas

Illustrations by Vassilis Stenos

St. Martin's Press
New York

The publisher gratefully acknowledges permission to reprint the extract from "The Olive Groves of Thassos," which appeared in *Archaic Figure* by Amy Clampitt, copyright © Amy Clampitt, by permission of Alfred A. Knopf, Inc. Originally published in *The New Yorker*.

Seven savory Greek pie recipes were originally commissioned for publication in *Food & Wine* magazine.

Design by J. Dannecker

Library of Congress Cataloging-in-Publication Data
Kochilas, Diane.
    The food and wine of Greece / Diane Kochilas.
        p. cm.
    ISBN 0-312-05088-7
    1. Cookery, Greek. 2. Wine and wine making—Greece. 3. Greece—Social life and customs. I. Title.
TX723.5.K59 1990
641.59495—dc20   90-37197
                                                                          CIP

First Edition: November 1990
10 9 8 7 6 5 4 3 2 1

In memory of my dad, Thomas Kochilas, who gave us all so many unforgettable meals, and to Demeter, my guide.

For Vassilis.

Contents

Acknowledgments

How does one begin to thank all the people who make a book possible? I suppose more than anyone, I want to thank my mother, Zoe, who's always there, without question, when we need her. And to my sisters and their clans, Athena, Kostia, Paul, Trifon, George, Tom, Kristy, and Katherine. And maybe a special thanks to Athena and Paul, who made the mistake of first showing me Greece when I was young and impressionable.

This book could not have been written without the faith, support, and love of my husband, Vassilis, whose drawings illuminate these pages, and who tasted everything again and again, put up with me through piles of dishes and recipe rewrites, and who's taught me more about Greece than anyone in the world.

I can't begin to thank my in-laws, Georgios and Sappho Stenos, whose generosity, love, and faith have seen us through many difficult times.

I want to express my gratitude to John Mariani, who gave me that fateful push, and who's been a loyal friend and mentor. And to my agent, Diane Cleaver, who believed in this project from the start. Without my editor, Barbara Anderson, and her wit, enthusiasm, and turn of phrase, this book would not have taken shape. I also want to thank my copy editor, Joan Whitman, for her meticulous eye and patience with all the Greek words in the text.

To Constantine and John Boutari I am indebted and grateful and especially thankful for all of their support and goodwill toward this book. I want to thank Thrasybulus Anastasiades for trusting his instinct and Nicholas Manessis for encouraging me from the start and for helping me pair wine with food throughout the book. I owe special thanks to Yiannis Voyatzis, oenologist par excellence, for his encyclopedic knowledge of Greek wines and his invaluable advice with the wine chapter. And to Foteini Karageorge for all her help.

Also, I would like to express thanks to S.E.V.O.P. and to the Greek Wine Institute for the reams of information they provided, as well as to the Greek National Tourist Office and Hellenic Export Promotion Organization.

To the many friends whose encouragement and palates helped shape this book, and for whom it's always a pleasure to share a table, I'll be forever grateful. But especially to Stratis and Mary, for their openheartedness and generosity and, of course, friendship, and to Bea, fellow wanderer, who has a penchant for *skordalia* and lima bean casseroles and who understands why I like foreign shores so much. I owe many thanks to her dad, Ralph Sergiovanni, a teacher and inspiration always.

There isn't room here to thank all the great home cooks who pulled out their mothers' and grandmothers' recipe books and over whose pots I hovered, but they know who they are. A few stand out—Vassilis's grandmother, Ioanna Tsimbithou; Flora Mylona; Chryssoula Charachliani; Roussa Meleti; Irini Schiza; and Toula Vittoria. I also want to thank Marie Simmons, who helped develop some of the lamb recipes; and Agamemnon Tsilikas, who was so helpful in locating difficult-to-find historical material.

Sometimes good things come from having a foot in two cultures, and I hope this is one of them, because Greece is as much a part of me as New York.

Introduction

When I set out to write this book, my goal was to give a sense of Greece, of its culture and its way of life, through the country's food. I wanted to write a work that would encompass every aspect of Greek cookery, from its inherent healthfulness, based as many of the dishes are on a troika of olives, grains, and grapes; to its history, which began four thousand years ago when Crete first began cultivating the olive tree; to an extensive look at the wines and spirits and beverages of Greece, many of which are available but unknown in America; and finally, to the variety of Greek foods and flavors that most people—Greek-American and non-Greek alike—just don't realize exists.

When most people think of Greek food, what comes to mind are the few clichéd dishes served up in Greek diners across the United States: deadpan *moussaka;* cloying *baklava* preserved in, not merely flavored with, syrup; and skewers of grilled meat carved of anything but the tenderest spring lamb. The traveler might recall a salad of luscious tomatoes and pungent feta eaten in some tavern by the sea; or think of that trio of crisp cucumber, pickled octopus, and pearly ouzo that combine in a perfection of flavor and texture—irreproducible outside of summertime Greece; or yearn for a fresh, flaky fish seasoned with a drizzle of olive oil and lemon and a grinding between thumb and forefinger of oregano.

I've been an inveterate visitor to Greece for almost two decades, but it wasn't until I lived there that I gained a sense of how rich the cuisine is. The indigenous food of Greece—the rich warm stews, the myriad vegetable dishes, the sweets made possible by only the most skilled of hands—are rarely tasted beyond its boundaries and seldom sampled in any restaurant, even in Greece. Greek cuisine is country cookery at its best, home-based, dependent on the seasons, and often passed on in nothing more than a calligraphic hand in a ragged notebook from grandmother to mother to daughter.

Much of what Greeks eat is tied to the seasons: artichokes in spring; tomatoes and peppers in summer; legumes in winter. A large number of the basics needed to prepare many of the foods are still made at home. Many Greeks sun-dry their own tomatoes, slicing them in half, dousing them with sea salt, and leaving them to stiffen in the sun before stringing them like beads to hang in the kitchen. In many country villages, people cure their own pork and make their own wines, spirits, and beverages. Even working housewives still go to the bother of preserving their own fruits and pickling their own vegetables, which are, in the absence of a garden, bought at the farmers' markets that travel through city neighborhoods each day. And come fall, many urbanites march off to their native villages for the olive harvest.

It is this food, and the traditions, folklore, and culture that surround it, that I sought out in Greece. During the time that I lived there, I traveled the countryside, talking to cooks of all types—both home and professional—hovering over their pots, and observing their techniques. What I found was that the cookery, like the country, is a pastiche of old and new, East and West, and I have tried to reflect this mix of cultures and ideas in my recipes. Some of the dishes included here are my own renditions of traditional recipes culled from reading and travel; others are one cook's particular version of a classic; still others are specialties of a specific region or village.

In my travels through Greece, I came to appreciate these regional variations as being one of the most important aspects of Greek cuisine. Sometimes the changes were subtle from place to place, other times quite drastic. Most often I discovered that they had to do with ancient influences of culture or history or religion.

The Byzantines, for example, with their highly developed kitchen arts, have greatly influenced the modern cookery of Greece. That very Greek bread, the *vassilopitta,* or St. Basil's bread, served at New Year's, comes down to us from Byzantium, as does the *tsoureki* (but not its name), a sweetened loaf, plaited, egg-laden, and made especially at Easter.

The Eastern influences are innumerable, too, from the names of so many Greek foods—*boureki, dolma, loukoumi, soutzouki, kefte*—to the use of yogurt, raisins, and sesame. The spicy cooking of the Poli, or Constantinople, and the rich, perfumed cookery of Crete are both redolent of Eastern influences. A good number of Greece's pastry chefs and esteemed professional cooks hail from the city on the Marmara, now called Istanbul.

The Pontian Greeks, who lived around the Black Sea region, have a cuisine all their own and a skillful hand at pickling. Cabbage, leeks, and sardines—fresh and salted—are staples in their cookery.

The island cookery is by and large wholesome, simple peasant fare, rough and hearty and soul-warming, a cuisine shaped by paucity and spawned by ingenuity—making the best of what little Nature bequeathed to the land. But the Ionian islands are a slightly different story. Traditionally moneyed and cultivated, much of their cookery has

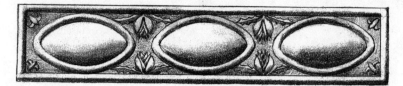

Italian or Venetian influences, claiming dishes with very non-Greek names like the Corfiot *pastitsatha*.

Ancient ways are alive in many Greek customs, such as placing a good-luck coin in bread or cake; slaughtering a lamb at Easter and spit-roasting it (a meal worthy of Homer's heroes); and preparing sweetened grain dishes such as *kolyva* and *polysporia*, either in remembrance of the dead or as offerings to saints, especially around holidays that fall near the harvest. The practice of serving *mezedes*, or appetizers, also has its base in ancient times.

In the pages that follow, I've tried to give a glimpse of the folklore, the traces of ancient ways, and the customs surrounding Greek cooking. I've tried to convey something about the way Greeks eat, the spirit of their cookery, their approach to life and to the seasons, and the growing and preparation of food. I've also tried to make the recipes a comfortable blend of the old and the new—geared to the American palate, but inherently Greek.

The book is divided into four parts, which I think represent the way Greeks eat and live: the basics—those elements upon which Greeks have thrived for generations, and sometimes millennia; the *mezedes*, which are really small plates of food, a smattering of almost anything that could accompany a glass of wine or ouzo, beer or whisky, or whatever the alcohol of the moment; the main courses; and finally, the sweets. The book begins with what's most fundamental to Greece regarding matters of the table—her wines, her olives, her herbs, and not least in stature, her breads.

Part I

THE ESSENTIALS OF GREEK CUISINE

Chapter 1

Wines, Spirits, and Other Beverages

Oínos efrénoi karthía
Wine pleases the heart

Wine, as these ancient words so succinctly put it, touches the core of the Greek psyche.

It would be an understatement to say that making it, drinking it, revering it are simply a part of Greek culture. Wine is as basic as bread to the way Greeks eat and live, and the history and myth of the vine in Greece are long ones.

— WINE IN GREEK MYTHOLOGY —

The myth, of course, begins with Dionysus, the god of wine, the god of living and growing things, of the movement of nature, of human emotions. In the pantheon of gods, Dionysus, or "twice born," was the son of Zeus and Semele. Zeus destroyed Semele after she asked him to reveal their child as a god, but saved the unborn child by sewing him into his thigh, from whence he sprang.

According to myth, Dionysus traveled through Asia, all the way to India, spreading en route the secret of the vine. When he returned to Greece to claim his place among the gods, he was rejected. Dionysus fled and was kidnapped by ransom-seeking sailors who mistook him for a nobleman. Asked where he wanted to go, the god answered Naxos, but the sailors set forth instead for Egypt. Suddenly, the boat stopped in mid-sea, and vines, burgeoning with fruit, enveloped the ship's mast. The air became laden with the scent of wine. Dionysus, wreathed in vine leaves, with tigers and panthers at his feet, finally had revealed himself. The crew was metamorphosed into dolphins, and the world forever changed, from one of reason and order into one of mystery and chaos.

To the ancient Greeks, Dionysus became identified with the very irony of nature itself—creative and fertile on the one hand, destructive and wild on the other.

—THE HISTORY OF GREEK WINE—

Krasi is the modern word for wine in Greek, and it derives from the ancient, meaning a mixture of wine and water, which was indeed the way wine was drunk in antiquity. *Oinos* is the ancient Greek word for wine, but its etymology is somewhat more of a puzzle. Athenaeus, in *The Deipnosophists,* writes that the ancient Greeks called grape vines *oinoi.* The author quotes Plato, who says the word comes from *oinous,* or "that which fills our brains with false impressions." Homer alludes to the derivation of the word as being *onesis,* or "benefit." In the *Bacchae,* Euripides tells us that Dionysus hails from Asia and, curiously, some scholars cite a Sanskrit root for the word *vena,* which means drink offering to a god. *Oinos* certainly is the root for many other words, including "wine" itself—as well as *vinum, vin, vino, oenology,* and *weim.*

The ancient Greeks enjoyed a reputation as great wine producers, and the history of the vine dates as far back as 5000 B.C., when wine may first have been brought to Greece from Asia. (Its origins are not definitely known; wine could have originated in Mesopotamia or in Egypt or Phoenicia.) The Greeks spread the vine all over the ancient world, east to the regions around the Crimean and Caspian Seas, and west all the way to Andalusia. The wines of Jerez, Málaga, and Sicily can trace their provenance to the Greeks, as can the vineyards up the Rhone valley.

It is known that the ancient Greeks were the first to label their wines with an appellation of origin, and that Greek wines were renowned on the world market up until the times the Venetians and Genoans sailed the seas. Resinated wine—what we know as the legendary retsina of Greece—was also made in the ancient world, as a way to protect against oxidation.

Wine has been made pretty much continuously all throughout the history of Greece and even during the Turkish occupation, but until recently there was little effort to control the quality of wine produced. The vine has always existed in ample supply in Greece, and wine has always been plentiful, an inherent part of the culture. But it was also something traditionally home-produced for personal consumption. Even commercially made wines, until recently, were by and large sold in bulk rather than bottled, but all of that is changing fast. Greek wines, and there are many that are very good, are getting better all the time.

The country's mild, dry climate and chalky soil are very favorable to the vine, and Greece holds a strong place in the world wine trade. The country is the ninth largest producer in Europe and the fourteenth worldwide.

The Greek wine industry is divided into three main areas: the small, individual producers, who make wine mostly for personal consumption (estate bottling exists at a very minimal level among some of the smaller vintners); the cooperatives, which account for about 40 percent of the total production (little of which is exported to America); and, finally, the 290 or so private companies, the largest of which make about 80 percent of the domestic wine consumed in Greece.

It is among the private companies that the most rapid progress has been made in modernizing Greece's wine-production facilities, and making its wines, especially for export, increasingly known for their high quality and consistent character year after year. The industry leader is probably J. Boutari and Sons, S.A., a Salonika-based concern and one of the oldest vintners in Greece. Boutari is best known for the wines it produces in Náoussa and Santorini, but the vintner also makes some excellent reds in other areas of Macedonia, namely Gouménissa and Amindaion. Next in line among the commercial vintners, in terms of quality wines, is a small Cephalonian producer, Calliga, known for its outstanding Robola. Tsantalis, with its Aghioritiko wine (which the company maintains is made with grapes from the Holy Mountain in Khalkidiki), is a popular brand in Greece. Achaia Claus, one of the oldest names in Greek wine making, is synonymous with the special Mavrodaphne. The company also produces lesser wines, such as Demestica. Porto Carras, based in Macedonia, is a small concern like Calliga that produces some excellent whites and some wines from French varietals. Botrys, Cambas, C.A.I.R., and Kourtaki make up the remainder of the major producers.

This handful of private concerns comprises the pantheon of chief Greek vintners, and in the last decade they have helped transform the country's wine industry into one of its major areas of export.

In the 1970s, the government began to regulate wine prices and to establish quality-control laws. Since 1976, Greece has been conforming with European Community legislation concerning wine production, and now, for the first time since antiquity, something akin to a luxury trade is beginning to take form. The Náoussa wines, especially Boutari's Grande Réserve and Náoussa; the wines of Cephalonia, like Calliga's Robola; the Aghioritiko wine in its stout bottle, made by Tsantalis; the bone-dry white Santorini wines also made by Boutari; and the dry white produced by Carras in limited amount make up the best of the Greek vintages. (Prices are still quite low compared with their European counterparts.)

There are twenty-eight appellations of origin, which account for about 12 percent of the total land under vine (some 75,000 acres). According to Greek law, all red appellations have to be aged for at least one year in barrels; "cava" reds must be aged a minimum one year in barrels, one year in tanks, and one year in the bottle; and "Grande Réserves" (there is only one, produced by Boutari) must be aged a minimum of two years in barrels and two years in the bottle.

Because of its mountainous geography, only about 20 percent of the vines in Greece are planted in open fields. Most are planted in steps sculpted neatly on mountain slopes. Greece's average annual production is about 140,000 U.S. gallons, some 2 percent of which is exported to America. Greeks, happy imbibers that they are, consume between fifty and seventy pints of wine per capita yearly.

Although there has been a move toward planting more commercially viable grape varieties, such as cabernet sauvignon, one of the most interesting aspects of the Greek wine trade is that most of the country's indigenous varieties aren't found outside its borders. Greece is home to more than three hundred native grape varieties (many of which have existed, even by the same name, since antiquity), and the country produces a surprising array of full-bodied, velvety reds, excellent dessert wines, and a range of whites and rosés. There is a revival afoot in the Greek wine trade. Export-minded vintners are realizing that their increasingly well-crafted wines offer the lure of the unknown to the foreigner. No discussion of Greek wine, however, could begin without first mentioning its most familiar, and perhaps disputed, vintage—retsina.

——RETSINA——

The wine we drank had a trace of resin, as if the
vineyard had merely been beside a pine-forest . . .
—*John Fowles,* The Magus

Retsina is usually a mysterious—and acquired—taste to most non-Greeks. It is made exactly as all white wines are made, except that it is lightly resinated; a small amount—about two parts per thousand—of pine resin is added to the must at the start of fermentation. Retsina is also a traditional appellation by law, that is, no other country in the world is allowed to produce it.

Adding resin to wine is a process that dates to antiquity, when either pitch, pine resin, or a combination of plaster and resin was used to make impermeable the clay vases (amphorae) in which wine was transported. The ancient Greeks observed that pine resin not only helped seal the amphorae from moisture, but also helped preserve the wine within. Pine resin may also have been used to squelch the scent of goat skin, in which wine was locally transported. (Cone wine is mentioned frequently in ancient Greek literature, and Dionysus is sometimes depicted with a pinecone at the end of his staff.)

The resin is collected from the Aleppo pine, or *calitris quadrivalis,* and it is thought that the best comes from the Attica region. There are two ways resin is gathered. The first is called the *thakri,* or "tear" method, in which the trunks are slashed and a small cup is hung to collect the clumpy, pastelike substance. The second is called the "pie," or *pitta* method, for the resin that trickles down naturally and clumps together with the pine needles and chips at the base of the tree, forming "pies," which are then collected.

About 85 percent of retsina is made from the *savatiano* and *rhoditis* grape varieties. The rest is made from local varieties around the country. Retsina accounts for almost 40 percent of total wine production in Greece. (That number has been declining slightly as more and more growers realize that this exotic and sometimes bitter-tasting Greek specialty is not always a welcome one to foreign palates. But, there has been a trend among vintners to produce lighter retsinas, well-crafted white wines with just a hint of resin.) Most retsinas come from the wine-growing regions that dominated the ancient trade: Euboea, Attica, Boeotia, and the Peloponnisos.

To the uninitiated, retsina might be considered harsh, and for many it's still an acquired taste. Yet, somehow, with the Greek climate and many of the grilled seaside dishes in the country's cookery, retsina is a delightful accompaniment.

Retsina should be drunk young, and should be drunk cool. The best comes specifically from the Attica region—Mesogeia, Koropi, Markopoulo, Mégara, Paeanea, Pallini, Pikermi, Spátha—and Boeotia.

── WINE REGIONS OF GREECE ──

── Macedonia and Thrace ──

Macedonia and Thrace have been known for the quality of their red wines since antiquity. Thásos, an island in the midst of the Thracian Gulf, was one of the most-prized vintages of the ancient world. In the early years of the twentieth century, the phylloxera destroyed much of the vineyards of Macedonia, but they were replanted and expanded, largely thanks to the industriousness of the Asia Minor refugees to Greece in the 1920s.

Though not the largest of the Greek wine-growing regions, Macedonia, with its ample rainfall and cool climate, is certainly the most favorable land in Greece for viticulture. The land under vine, from Thrace in the far east through Macedonia, and to Epirus in the northwest, comprises some 45,000 acres.

There are four appellations in Macedonia: **Náoussa, Amindaion, Gouménissa,** and the **Côtes de Meliton** in Sithonia, the middle neck of the Khalkidiki peninsula.

The **Náoussa** vineyards, on the luminous southeastern slopes of Mount Vermio, are among the most beautiful and distinguished in Greece. The region is closely associated with the Boutari family. The principal grape variety in Náoussa is the *xynomavro,* or "acidic black," with its big broad leaves and deep dense color. It is from the *xynomavro* that Náoussa's two excellent, dry, robust reds are produced: the Náoussa, and the Náoussa Grande Réserve, aged for at least four years. Both wines are potent, well-balanced, and brisk, or *brusco,* as the Greeks say. What characterizes them most is a kind of stubborn, quiet roughness, a balance of fruit and enduring tannins. If you ever stumble across an '84 Grande Réserve, snatch it up—it's one of the very best Greece has to offer.

Amindaion, northwest of Náoussa, at 2,000 feet above sea level, has a harsher climate than most of the rest of Greece. The vine ripens slowly here, and sometimes incompletely, and the region as a result produces a light red reminiscent of some northern European countries. The *xynomavro* variety also finds its home here, and besides reds, Amindaion produces some excellent rosés, some of which are sparkling.

Gouménissa, a small vineyard in the north-central part of Macedonia, produces only 500 tons of grapes annually. The principal grape varieties are the *xynomavro* and the mellow, velvety *negosca.* By law, the Gouménissa appellation is a blend of 70 percent *xynomavro* and 30 percent *negosca,* which are fermented together to produce the dry red vintage characteristic of this vineyard.

The **Côtes de Meliton,** a designated place name in Khalkidiki, is a relatively new vineyard—planted with both Greek and foreign varieties in the late 1960s under the direction of French oenologists. The region produces fresh and fruity white wines as well as some heady reds, and is closely associated with the Carras label. On the northern slopes of the mountain, some 750 acres are planted with the native white

Appellation Wines Produced in Greece, by Name and Region

— GREEK APPELLATIONS CONTROLLÉS —

Samos
Muscat of Patras
Muscat de Rion
Muscat of Cephalonia
Muscat of Rhodes
Muscat of Límnos
Mavrodaphne Patras
Mavrodaphne Cephalonia

— GREEK APPELLATIONS SUPERIEURES —

Macedonia and Thrace
Náoussa
Amindaion
Gouménissa
Côtes de Meliton
Epirus
Zitsa
Thessaly
Rapsáni
Anchialos
The Peloponnisos
Patras
Nemea
Mandinia
Attica
Kantza

The Ionian Islands
Robola Cephalonia
Crete
Arhanes
Dafne
Peza
Sitia
The Eastern Aegean Islands
Límnos
The Dodecanese
Rhodes
Cyclades
Páros
Santorini

AMINDAION

GOUMÉNISSA

NÁOUSSA

Thessaloniki (Salonika)

ZITSA

MACEDONIA

THRACE

Kavalla

EPIRUS

Corfu

Thásos

RAPSÁNI

CÔTES
DE MELITON

THESSALY

Vólos

ANCHIALOS

LÍMNOS

Ithaca

AEGEAN SEA

Lesvos (Mitilene)

CEPHALONIA

PATRAS

Euboea

Patras

*Zákinthos
(Zante)*

PELOPONNISOS

Athens

KANTZA

IONIAN SEA

NEMEA

ATTICA

MANDINIA

Andros

Chios

Sparta

Tinos

SAMOS

Syros

Mykonos

Ikaria

Naxos

Patmos

Kithira

PÁROS

SANTORINI

Kos

RHODES

CRETE

ARHANES

DAFNES

MEDITERRANEAN SEA

CRETE

SITIA

Karpathos

PEZA

Greek varieties of *assyrtico, athiri,* and *rhoditis;* the red variety *limnio,* named after the island of Limnos; and *cabernet sauvignon* and *cabernet franc.*

—— Epirus ——

Epirus, in the northwestern part of Greece, with its rigid mountainous terrain and harsh weather, is not by nature a wine-producing region. But **Zitsa,** in the far western corner, near the Albanian border, is home to the local white *debina* grape variety, which produces a surprisingly fine, elegant, and subtle vintage. Zitsa also claims one of the few sparkling wines in Greece, the light, fragrant Zitsa.

Métsovon, in the heart of the Pindus Mountains and famous for its smoked cheese, is gaining recognition for its experiments with cabernet sauvignon. The wine, one of the finest—and most expensive—in Greece, was developed at the Averoff estate in Katoi together with the Greek Wine Institute, a government agency.

—— Thessaly ——

Thessaly, in the center of mainland Greece, comprises four main wine-growing regions: **Tirnavos,** closely associated with the first productions of ouzo, **Kardhitsa, Rapsáni,** and **Anchialos.** Some of the varieties used in making local wine (most not found on the export market) are the black *messenikola* grape and the white *batiki,* both from Kardhitsa.

The vineyards of Anchialos, near the port city of Vólos, are planted at sea level and are situated along the Pagasitikós Gulf. The principal varieties here are the *savatiano* and *rhoditis.*

The most famous vineyards in Thessaly are situated at Rapsáni, on the slopes of Mount Olympus. The vineyards of Rapsáni are home to the *xynomavro,* as well as to the little known, strictly local, aromatic, and light *krasato* variety, and the *stavroto.* Most of the region's red wine is made from a blend of all three. The Rapsáni red is a vigorous, harsh wine when young. But it ages well and develops a mellow flavor and smooth bouquet with time.

—— The Peloponnisos ——

The Peloponnisos, the southern "hand" of Greece, separated from the mainland by the Gulf of Corinth, is the largest wine-producing region in the country, and some of the best Greek appellations come from here. About a quarter of all Greek wine is made in the Peloponnisos, and the area consists of three main place names: **Patras, Nemea,** and **Mandinia.**

Patras, one of the largest ports in Greece, is in the far north of the Peloponnisos, across the straits from Mesolóngion, where Lord Byron died. It is home to the *muscat, mavrodaphne,* and *rhoditis* grape varieties. Patras claims four appellation wines: the sweet white Muscat of Patras, a rich, golden dessert wine with a luscious bouquet and flavor; Muscat de Rion; plain Patras, which is light and dry and made from the *rhoditis* variety; and the sweet red Mavrodaphne.

Mavrodaphne, like retsina, is a special Greek wine. Deep, black-red in color, strong, heavy, and not unlike sherry, Mavrodaphne was most likely given its name in the nineteenth century by Gustav Claus, a Bavarian refugee who founded the Achaia Claus winery in Patras. Daphne was supposedly a beautiful dark-haired girl with whom he was in love. (*Mavro* means "black.") Some scholars, however, maintain that the wine, which is made in several parts of Greece, takes its name from the fleeting Daphne in Greek mythology, who prayed for help as she was being chased by Apollo and was transformed into a laurel just as the god was overtaking her. Mavrodaphne is strong, luscious, and sweet with unfermented sugar, 14 to 16 percent alcohol. The wine ages well and is best drunk at room temperature. Mavrodaphne of Patras is the most renowned, although a very good Mavrodaphne is also made in Cephalonia.

Nemea is a gentle sloping vineyard in the northeastern Peloponnisos, about an hour's drive from Corinth. The vineyard is famous for its Blood of Hercules (slayer of the dreaded lion of Nemea), made from the native grape variety called *agiorghitiko* (St. George). Don't confuse this with *agioritiko,* which comes from the Holy Mountain. The wine is dry, full-bodied, yet soft, and its color—rich dark red, almost black—is the key to its local nickname.

But Nemea, like Náoussa, also produces one of Greece's best dry reds from the *xynomavro* variety.

The vineyards of **Mandinia,** in the center of the Peloponnisos, lie at a height of 650 meters, around the ruins of the ancient town. Here, the *moschofileri* grape prevails, and it produces a supple, fruity white wine that is light and well balanced with a fine bouquet. The *moschofileri* is also used as a base in sparkling wines.

—— Central Greece ——

The areas of Attica, Boeotia, and Euboea, important in the ancient wine trade, comprise Central Greece. The region is mostly associated with the production of retsina. The dominant grape variety is the *savatiano*. The only appellation wines in Central Greece come from the vineyards at **Kantza,** in Attica, some twenty miles southeast of Athens. There the *savatiano* grape also dominates, but it makes not only resinated wines but also a supple, dry white that is one of the best in Greece.

—— WINE-PRODUCING ISLANDS —— OF GREECE

—— The Ionian Islands ——

Corfu, Cephalonia, Zákinthos, Ithaca, and Lefkada are the main islands in the Ionian group, and together claim some 25,000 acres of land under vine. From this part of Greece, especially from Cephalonia, come some of the country's finest wines.

Corfu, Greece's northwesternmost island and certainly one of its most verdant, produces several local wines of medium quality and one of the country's few excellent estate wines, the Theotoky, from the Ropa Valley. This dry white is produced in limited quantity—about 15,000 to 20,000 bottles annually. It is made from the Robola varietal and another local varietal named Kakotrigi, or "bad to harvest," a Corfiot grape of obscure origins that has been cultivated on the island for centuries and may have come from the Dalmation Coast.

Zákinthos produces mainly white wines. The native grape variety is the *verdea,* or "green" grape, which is also found on the western shores of the Peloponnisos, and is a relative of the *verdelho* found in other European vineyards. Zákinthos is also home to the *byzantis* variety, which has no appellation yet.

Lefkada claims the *vertzami* grape variety as native to its soil, which produces a dark, almost black, and opaque wine called Santa Mavra. In Lefkada, as on other Greek islands, the vines are cultivated on terraces.

Cephalonia, like Náoussa, Santorini, Crete, and Samos, is a special Greek wine-producing region. Apart from the well-known appellations, the muscat and Mavrodaphne of Cephalonia, the island produces another appellation, one of Greece's finest white wines, the full-bodied, well-balanced Robola of Cephalonia. Calliga, a small, family-run vintner, produces the finest and highest quality Robola on the island.

—— Crete ——

The fifth-largest island in the Mediterranean, Crete is also one of the region's oldest vineyards. The island accounts for about one fifth of

Greece's total wine production and is also the center for cultivating table grapes, sultanas, and currants. The austere mountains that divide the island also protect its vines from the hot southern winds that blow up at various times of the year.

Crete claims four different appellations: **Arhanes, Dafnes, Peza, and Sitia.** Among the native grape varieties are the *romeiko, kotsifali, mandilari, liatico,* and *vilana.*

Crete is renowned for its powerful reds, but it is here that the sweet topaz dessert wine known in the Middle Ages as Malmsey (also known as Malvasia, Malvoisie, and Malvasia) was probably first made, from the native *liatico* grape. (The wine took its name from Monemvasia, a port in the Peloponnisos, from where it was shipped all over Europe.) According to legend, Malvasia was made from a recipe given to King Minos by the Oracle of Delphi and was supposed to symbolize wisdom. Now, a sweet, similar wine from the *liatico* grape sometimes is still produced in Sitia and drunk by the locals as an aperitif. From the *liatico* variety also comes a robust fruity red.

Arhanes and **Peza** are the two Cretan appellations best known on the world wine market. The wines produced in these vineyards, like those of Gouménissa, are a blend—here, of the *kotsifali* grape (70 percent), native only to these two regions of Iráklion County, and the *mandilaria* variety (30 percent). The *kotsifali* grape easily develops a high sugar content and has a lucid red color; it lends to the wines of Arhanes and Peza their complex aroma and rich flavor. The *mandilaria* grape does not mature easily, but imbues the wines of this part of Greece with their exquisite ruby color and full body.

Another curiosity of Peza is the fruity white wine made from the strictly native *vilana* grape, which some oenologists believe is a relative of the German *sylvana,* whose provenance may very well be Asia Minor.

—— The Eastern Aegean Islands ——

Of the four most important islands in the Aegean—Límnos, Chios, Lésvos, and Samos—Samos houses the most reputed vineyards. (Lésvos and Chios are discussed in more detail in the spirits section of this chapter.)

Samos takes its name from the Phoenician word meaning "height," and it is one of the most mountainous islands in Greece. It is also one of the country's most important viticultural centers. When the Turks conquered Samos at the time of the fall of Constantinople in 1453, they denuded the island of its vines. But when the Greeks regained it in 1912, they found the vine flourishing, and the island's wines as good as ever.

Samos was one of the first appellations in Greece. The white *muscat* grape dominates the island, and Samos's microclimate is unique. The climate is generally mild, but the harvesting time is different on different parts of the island, beginning in August along the coast and ending in October in the high mountain reaches. The pale gold Muscat of Samos is one of the best-known wines in all of Greece. In addition to the naturally sweet muscat, Samos also produces dry and fortified sweet wines, and nearly all of them have the unique, pungent flavor and bouquet of the island's native grape.

The volcanic island of **Límnos,** home of Hephaistos, the god of fire, is one of the few places in Greece where the vine is cultivated not on mountain terraces but on large, wide plains. The island produces a bright red aptly called Limnio, from its native grape variety of the same name.

The *muscat of Alexandria* variety is also found on the island, and produces another appellation, the muscat of Límnos. Two other wines are made from this variety here, a dry, slightly muscat-scented white, and another golden, mellow liqueur.

—— The Dodecanese ——

Of the twelve islands that make up the Dodecanese, **Rhodes** is the most noteworthy in terms of wine production, and the island's main commercial vintner is C.A.I.R. The vine has been cultivated here since antiquity, and Rhodes was one of the most prominent exporters in the ancient world. Four vintages are legally recognized: the *attavyros,* cultivated on the flat, sandy southern side, which is swept by the hot Libyan winds; the white *athiri* and red *amorgiano,* both cultivated on the island's northern slopes and tempered by the cooling *meltemia* winds in late summer; and a muscat called *trani.* But more interesting is the dry white made from the indigenous *lindos* variety. The vineyard spreads gently under the ruins of the Acropolis of Lindos, where for two hundred years the Knights Templars had their commandery.

—— Cyclades ——

Páros and **Santorini** are the two most important islands of the Cyclades, both swept by the violent *meltemia* winds that whip through the Aegean from midsummer to early September. The islanders have developed as a result an unusual way of cultivating the grape.

On Páros, where the dry red *mandilaria* and white *monemvasia* varieties prevail, the vines are pruned very low. The Páros appellation is a dry, deep ruby-red wine, aged in oak barrels, with a developed bouquet and a velvet taste. Páros wine is made by law of one part *mandilaria* grapes and two parts must of the *monemvasia* variety.

Santorini, the black pearl of the Aegean, is one of the most ravishing terrains in all of the Mediterranean. Windswept and precipitous, virtually the entire island is a vineyard, and a blessed one, for Santorini's ecosystem—a synergy of soil, climate, and local grape varieties—creates what are probably the greatest white wines in Greece.

Santorini's microclimate is special. Her soil is an unpromising mixture of chalk and shale, cinders, ash, lava, and pumice. The island is very dry, and during the summer months, when the vines are ripening, the daytime temperatures are quite high. But the evenings are cool and humid. Santorini, like all of the Cyclades, is subject to the whipping north winds of July and August—the *meltemia*—which prevent moisture from accumulating on the grape during the day. But at night, the vineyards are dewy with humidity; the island's volcanic soil absorbs the evening's moisture, and with that nourishes the vine. All these factors enable the grape to ripen quickly on Santorini, but without sacrificing its acidity.

Santorini's indigenous grapes are as unique as her breathtaking beauty and singular microclimate. First, there are about ten varieties native only to the island, which have existed continuously since antiquity. But only a few are exploited to their fullest potential—the white, versatile *assyrtico,* which dominates the island, and the white, lightly muscat-flavored *aidani.* The vineyards themselves are as unusual as everything else about stunning Santorini. To shield their vines against the *meltemia,* the islanders have developed a method all their own. They prune the vines into a basket shape, with the grapes in the center surrounded by a wall of greenery. In the spring and summer, as the vines flourish, they look like scraggly, shapeless bushes springing from a thirsty earth.

The *assyrtico* is one of the most interesting varietals in all of the Mediterranean. The grape is characterized by a high level of acidity as well as a naturally high sugar content, which enable it to produce a wide range of excellent wines, from bone dry to quite sweet. The *assyrtico* imbues the native wines with a rich complicated taste, and with it the island claims two appellations, the dry Santorini, and the sweet, age-old Visanto.

The Visanto, a combination of the *assyrtico* and the *aidani,* is the island's traditional wine. (Although appellation class, it's available only locally.) It is a straw-colored *vin de paille* or *liasto,* as the Greeks say, made as the ancients made wine—by letting the grapes, once harvested, ripen in the sun.

The Santorini appellation, created by allowing the high sugar content of the *assyrtico* to ferment extensively, is an excellent, sun-colored, crisp, and complex wine, faintly redolent of flowers and as dry as the island from which it springs. The island's traditional white wine, high in alcohol content, is called Nichteri.

—— THE SPIRITS OF GREECE ——

—— Ouzo ——

The real Greek national drink is ouzo, a clear, unctuous, licorice-flavored liqueur distilled from the residuals of the grape after it is pressed for wine.

According to Achilles Tzartzanos, a philologist and scholar at the beginning of this century, the word was born in his hometown, Tirnavos, a small city in Thessaly.

In Tirnavos, sometime between 1878 and 1881, there lived three men: Stavrac Bey, an Armenian doctor of the Turkish army; Demetrios Doumenikiotis, who ran a general store and was something of a spirits afficionado and local connoisseur; and Andonis Makris, a textile merchant. At the end of the nineteenth century, Tirnavos was a town renowned not only for its fiery liqueurs but for the fine quality of its silks, the best of which were labeled USO Massalias, an integral part of our story and an indication of the fine silks' ultimate destination of Marseilles. (The term "USO" most likely was a transliteration of the Italian *uso,* which means use.)

Ouzo, or spirits similar to it but harsher and less flavorful, has been known in the eastern Mediterranean for centuries. The first distillation of the grape was called *souma,* or *hamiko,* but this generally had a putrid smell, a harsh flavor, and was extremely high in alcohol content. *Souma* was redistilled, and the second product was called *raki.* (*Raki* today still refers to the same fiery clear liquid, and it is still made from grapes, but also from other fruits such as figs. *Tsipouro* and *tsikoudia* are similarly diabolic distillations of the grape, or of other berries, such as arbatus and blackberries—harsh, sometimes unflavored, and generally produced locally in each region. The *tsipouro* of Crete is especially well known.) This second product was sometimes flavored with anise. It generally had a lower alcohol content and was therefore potable—but still quite potent. To make this liquid fire just a bit smoother on the palate, not to mention the stomach, it was sometimes distilled a third time and called *metavrasmeno raki,* or "reboiled" raki.

Demetrios Doumenikiotis was an expert in the production, and especially in the consumption, of all distillations of the grape. But it seems the doctor had a more discerning palate. Dr. Stavrac Bey suggested flavoring the third *raki* with other fragrances besides anise, and was especially fond of mastic, a natural gum with an almost smoky, incenselike flavor that comes from a rare shrub on the island of Chios. Doumenikiotis followed the advice of his imbibing partner and flavored a batch of *raki* with spices other than anise. When the three friends got together to test what the good distiller had done, none other than Andonis Makris, our textile merchant and expert in fine silks, declared, "This is as good as USO Massalias," USO, of course, being transliterated with alacrity to become what the world has since known as ouzo.

Anise, star anise, mastic, lime, coriander, and other spices are used to flavor ouzo. Some of the best still comes from Tirnavos (rather difficult to find in the U.S.), but the very best is said to come from Mytilini. If you're ever in Greece and lucky enough to spot the dark blue label of Barbayiánnis, or the yellow label of Pitsilladés, grab it, take it home, and savor it on some hot dry afternoon, preferably by the sea, with a salted cucumber and a grilled, plum-colored octopus as its worthy accompaniments.

Ouzo is drunk at room temperature, either straight up with water on the side, or mixed with a little ice water to cloud pleasantly both the glass and your senses.

Among the commercial brands, the best-known are these: Boutari; Ouzo 12; Sans Rival; Achaia Claus; Tsantali; and Ouzo Mini (Epom).

—— Mastiha ——

Another clear liqueur fermented from the resinous gum called mastic, mastiha derives from *Pistacia lentiscus,* a rare shrub indigenous to the island of Chios. The gum, still popular in Greece, was prescribed by Hippocrates as a remedy for coughs and colds. During the Middle Ages it was in great demand throughout Europe, but today the liqueur produced from it is really an acquired taste.

—— Brandy and Other Liqueurs ——

The name in Greek brandy is Metaxas, although Cambas and Botrys produce decent rivals. Metaxas produces three-, five-, and seven-star brandies. More interesting, however, is what Greek home cooks do to brandy. By flavoring it with the pits and skins of various fruits (apricot is a favorite, as are sour cherry and bitter orange) and letting it stand outdoors in the sun for forty days or more, they produce a variety of homemade liqueurs.

These liqueurs, like coffee, ouzo, and the spoon sweets, belong to a special part of Greek cuisine that centers on hospitality and the etiquette surrounding it. Liqueur is generally considered a "lady's" drink and Greek women make it part of their yearly repertoire of seasonal preparations. Here are two favorites.

Kyria Mylona's Apricot-Flavored Brandy

120 apricot pits,
    washed and dried
1½ quarts brandy
2 to 2½ cups sugar

Using a sharp knife, break open the tough outer shell of the pits. Gently slit the inner seed (the "almond" as the Greeks call it). Combine the white inner seeds with the brandy in a wide-mouthed glass jar and seal. Leave it, preferably in the sun, for 40 days. At the end of 40 days, melt the sugar (amount depends on desired sweetness) over low to medium heat, until it is completely liquefied. Cool it and add it to the brandy. Leave it for 2 or 3 days at room temperature and serve as desired.

Yield: About 2 quarts

Kyria Mylona's Sour Cherry–Flavored Brandy

2½ pounds sour
    cherries
5 cups sugar
1 cinnamon stick
4 to 5 whole cloves
Grating of nutmeg
1½ quarts brandy

Combine the cherries, sugar, and spices in a large wide-mouthed jar. Seal and store, preferably in the sun, for 40 days, shaking the mixture at least once a day. At the end of 40 days, add the brandy. Serve as desired.

Yield: About 2 quarts

——OTHER BEVERAGES OF GREECE——

——Teas, Tisanes, and Other Drinks——

There are too many herbal teas and infusions to list here—one for virtually every ailment. But there are a handful that Greeks drink frequently. Among them are the following:

Diosmo, or double mint, is the morning drink of choice for many Greeks. Boil 1 teaspoon of dried mint per cup of water. Strain and serve.

Fascomilo, or sage tea, is also popular. Bring as many cups of water as desired to a rolling boil. Add 1 to 2 teaspoons dried sage per cup. Cover and let stand 5 to 7 minutes before serving.

Hamomili, or chamomile, is said to calm the nerves and help insomnia and constipation. This is made the same way as mint tea.

Tilio, or lime blossom, similar in name to the French *tilleul,* is widely drunk in Crete, and is helpful for insomnia.

Canellada, an infusion made from boiling cinnamon sticks in water, is a popular iced drink in Crete. Serve plain or with sugar.

Vissinada, a dilution of sour cherry syrup and water, is one of the best-loved summer coolers in Greece. You can buy the syrup (or both syrup and preserves together) at most Greek and Middle Eastern specialty shops, or you can prepare it at home as most Greeks do (see recipe, page 291). To make the cooler, mix 1 to 2 teaspoons into an 8-ounce glass of ice water and stir.

Vanillia, made with vanilla paste, is another summer drink, a favorite with kids. Commonly, it's called *ipovrihio,* or "submarine," because a long spoonful of vanilla paste is submerged into a glass of ice water for a few minutes before drinking, until the water becomes laced with the essence of vanilla. (See page 294.)

Salepi. If you walk the streets of Athens at night in winter, especially around the central market, it's hard not to hear the drawn-out cries of the salepi vendors, a throwback from another era, who sell this mysterious age-old brew. The drink—white, warm, and viscous—is made by mixing the dried, pulverized root of a particular species of orchid, the purplish *Orchis mascula,* with water. For centuries, salepi was thought to be an aphrodisiac. Salepi vendors are fast disappearing, but the dried tuberous root can be found at spice shops and supermarkets around Greece.

——Coffee——

The last of the grandiose *cafeneia,* or coffee shops, replete with chugging ceiling fans, wall-size mirrors, and a *tambi,* or coffee master, have all but disappeared. But coffee drinking remains an almost mythical part of Greek popular culture, and the story of the *cafeneion* is one worthy of recounting.

The *cafeneion,* strictly forbidden to women, was a place where men went to congregate, play *tavli* (backgammon) or cards, read newspapers, and talk politics. The waiter knew the preference of every regular customer, and the *tambi,* standing behind the bar, prepared the coffee with almost ritualistic accuracy. First, he would choose the correct *briki,* a special small pot, usually made of brass or tin, with a wide bottom, a narrow mouth, and a long handle. He always worked with his back to the room. To his right were the sugar and coffee. To his left, the water. Measuring out the correct amounts of each with a special flat spoon, he then would roast the coffee, stirring it all the while, over a low open flame—or, as Cypriots sometimes still do, over burning embers *(steen hovoli).* If he was preparing more than one cup he would empty the *briki* a little at a time into each, so that the froth would top both. Usually, Greek coffee is served in small *flitzania,* or demitasse cups, but sometimes, and you find this more in the countryside, it's served in squat wine glasses or, for a double coffee, in heavy water glasses. Elias Petropoulos, in *Turkish Coffee in Greece,* reports that sailors sometimes add a shot of brandy to their coffee. Smyrna Greeks used to take it with a few drops of tahini, and a tradition on the Holy Mountain calls for mixing in a few drops of ouzo.

At the beginning of the century and up until the 1950s, when the *cafeneion* was the social center of the Greek underground, there were some fifty ways to prepare the Turkish brew. Each had its own name depending on the amount of coffee or sugar, as well as on the amount of time and the way in which it was boiled. Following is a list, quoted from Petropoulos's book, of the few surviving names one might still order in a Greek *cafeneion.* The recipes have been reworked for one demitasse cup and a standard teaspoon measure.

Me oligi (with a little): 1 teaspoon coffee, $\frac{1}{4}$ teaspoon sugar. According to Petropoulos, this is also called "yes-and-no."

Metrios (medium): 1 teaspoon coffee, 1 scant teaspoon sugar.

Metrios Varis (heavy medium): 1 heaping teaspoon coffee, 1 heaping teaspoon sugar.

Metrios Vrastos (medium boiled): 1 heaping teaspoon coffee, 1 heaping teaspoon sugar. To make this, lift the *briki* on and off the flame several times, until extrafrothy. This is also known as "boiled-and-not," or *vrastos-kai-ohi.*

Variglykos (heavy and sweet): 1 teaspoon coffee, $1\frac{1}{3}$ teaspoons sugar.

Polla variglykos (extra heavy and sweet): $1\frac{1}{3}$ teaspoons coffee, 2 teaspoons sugar.

Elafrys Glykos (light and sweet): $\frac{1}{2}$ teaspoon coffee, $1\frac{1}{3}$ teaspoons sugar.

Othomanikos: 1 teaspoon coffee, 2 teaspoons sugar, well-boiled with a lot of bubbles.

Glykivrastos (sweet and boiled): 1 teaspoon coffee, 2 teaspoons sugar. To make this you must lift the *briki* on and off the flame as soon as it begins to froth, several times, to make a lot of bubbles.

Varis se Miso: 1 teaspoon coffee, 2 teaspoons sugar, in half a demitasse cup of water. This coffee, according to Petropoulos, is as thick as yogurt.

Sketos (plain): 1 teaspoon coffee, no sugar.

To make Greek coffee, you'll need a *briki.* Combine any of the above recipes with one demitasse cup of water, unless otherwise instructed. Stir coffee continuously, but not fast, until it begins to froth up in the *briki.* Don't allow it to boil. Lift the *briki* up over the flame as soon as the coffee swells, and pour the coffee immediately into a squat demitasse cup. Serve piping hot with a glass of ice water.

Besides the traditional thickish brew enjoyed in Greece and through-out much of the Middle East, Hellenes of late have taken to drinking *frappe,* a cold shakerful of iced instant coffee, sugar, if desired, and milk (also optional). To make *frappe,* combine in a shaker 1 teaspoon instant coffee, sugar, 2 ice cubes, and 1 inch of ice water. Shake vigorously and pour into a tall glass. Fill with cold water until froth is just at the rim of the glass, then add milk to taste. Drink with a straw.

Chapter 2

The Basic Ingredients

Every ethnic cuisine has a core of basic elements—spices, herbs, techniques—that help to define it, or that appear and reappear in a variety of recipes within the cookery. Greek cuisine is a relatively simple one; it doesn't boast a repertoire of sauces, as do French, Chinese, and Italian. Give a Greek a healthy portion of olive oil, a shot or two of fresh lemon juice or good red wine vinegar, and a generous go at the garlic, and he will gladly mix or dribble them over everything from spring lamb to roasted potatoes to a simple cabbage salad.

What the cuisine does boast, though, are an unabiding loyalty to the seasons—a faithful and stubborn insistence that everything be fresh and "in its time"—and a reliance on the simplest, purest foods straight from nature. Olives and olive oil, honey, grapes, and a handful of herbs, spices, and nuts are so tied to the culture, so ancient in their uses and consumption, that Greek food just would not be the same without them.

There are elements, of course, that supplement nature's bounty. Cheese, milk, and yogurt are important in the cookery. Few of Greece's many dairy products are in fact known outside its borders; feta alone can count some dozens of varieties from all over Greece. There is also a wealth of seasonal preparations that add to the basics (and that are discussed separately in other chapters): dried or smoked meats; home-made sausages; sun-dried fruits and vegetables; grains; pickles; and preserves. Finally, as part of the essentials, are the native cooking utensils and methods—a variety of clay and metal crockery, and some age-old or idiosyncratic ways of baking and preparing food that impart an earthy flavor to true Greek cooking.

But of all the basics, the product of nature that is absolutely crucial to the cookery is the one that has shaped every Mediterranean culture since antiquity: the olive, and olive oil.

——THE OLIVE AND ITS OIL——

. . . their offspring a hidden
clustering of gray-green
worry beads that blacken
in October, after summer
people have all gone . . .
—Amy Clampitt, "The Olive Groves of Thasos"

Undoubtedly the best time to visit Greece is in the fall, when the summer people have all gone home, and when the olive harvest begins. In October, November, and December the weather is wet and damp, almost conducive to the wearisome toil of the harvest. The villages are filled with city dwellers, native sons and daughters who have returned to their families to help reap the fruit of the olive tree. Huge tarpaulins are spread beneath the trees to catch the countryside's harvest, and the work begins.

"I ate bread and olives with him," say the Greeks to denote good friendship. The branches of the olive tree are the symbol of peace; its fruits, like no other product of nature, are responsible for shaping an entire civilization. And, like the grape, the olive has a long and rich history and mythology.

According to legend, the olive tree was a gift of the goddess Athena, who, in contest with Poseidon to give the most useful offering to mankind, produced the olive tree. The tree probably originated in Asia, on the Iranian Plateau, and in Syria and Palestine, where it was developed into the rich, oil-yielding variety that spread all over the Mediterranean. The olive has been a part of Greece since 3000 B.C., when the trees were first cultivated on Crete. By 2500 B.C., the island was trading olive oil with Egypt and Asia Minor, and the first trees were planted at Mycenae in the Peloponnisos around 1700 B.C. But so well did the olive tree adapt to Attica soil that Athenian oil was considered the best in the ancient world (although Samos oil was renowned for its clarity).

The olive tree was considered sacred in antiquity. Special guards *(epimeletai)* were appointed to keep watch over them, and cutting one down was punishable by death. The olive tree had many uses in ancient

Greece. The birth of a child was announced by hanging an olive wreath on the door. Olive branches were used to crown the winners of the Olympic games, and the winner of the chariot race was awarded 100 amphorae (large oval jars or vases) of olive oil. The oil was used to light lamps and in cooking; it was in demand as a medicine and, with aromatic herbs, as a perfume and unguent. Homeric Greeks rubbed themselves with the oil, believing it bestowed longevity and good health when it penetrated the skin. (Waverley Root reports that olive oil contains salicylic acid, aspirin's active ingredient, but I've found no other evidence of that.) Nonetheless, its medicinal lore survives to this day. One reason why Greeks like their food so saturated in oil is the belief that it's "good for the system." And many a Greek swallows a spoonful of olive oil every morning, the way some people take a preventive aspirin.

In antiquity, though, the massive cultivation of the olive tree brought with it an unexpected result—deforestation. In the sixth century B.C., Solon outlawed the export of any other agricultural product besides olive oil. The landscape, once rich in fibrous-rooted trees that preserved the topsoil, was dessicated in favor of the deep-rooted, moisture-sucking, silver-green olive. Ancient Athens grew rich indeed on the olive's unctuous liquid, but it also came to depend so heavily on the crop that wheat and barley all but disappeared. The olive trade increased and the navy expanded—as did the empire itself—largely to meet the needs for basic foodstuffs and to defend the grain supply lines.

Yet somber as all that may seem, one just can't imagine Greece without her olive trees, gnarled, slow-swaying, silver-green flashes against the stark white light.

If you take a guided tour of Athens's more magical corners, some wily guide might point to an olive tree in Plaka (the old section of the city) and inform you that it's the very tree under which Plato sat to think great thoughts. It's not, of course, but the olive tree does have an exceedingly long lifespan—between 300 and 600 years. (Actually, there are ancient trees, the remains of an ancient grove that stretched to Eleusina, in what is now Colonos, a fairly industrial area of Athens.) What brings an olive tree to an untimely end is cold; the fruit is injured if temperatures drop below 28° Fahrenheit, and the tree itself is injured if the temperature dips below 10° F.

—— Buying Greek Olives in the United States ——

Greece produces dozens of different types of olives, and exports about ten varieties to the United States. Greek olives are distinguished from

Italian and Spanish olives by their strong flavor and pungent scent. In Spain and Italy, olives are treated with lye to remove the bitter glucoside called oleuropein, whereas in Greece they're simply packed in dry salt or brine in which they undergo a lactic fermentation. They may also be pickled in vinegar or preserved in olive oil.

If you've ever walked into a Greek or Middle Eastern specialty store, you're bound to have noticed the barrels, usually near the cheese counter, filled with olives and other pickled vegetables such as cauliflower and peppers. Loose olives, as opposed to those packed in tight jars or tins, have a fuller, richer flavor.

In choosing olives, remember that the fruit should be firm, not mealy, and the flavor should not be overwhelmed by the brine. Olives can be stored in a cool, dark place, in a sealed container, at room temperature in olive oil or brine for up to a year. Wash and drain the olives before serving. Greeks use olives in sauces and stuffings, pulverize them into a strong, grainy paste, add them to bread dough, and sometimes stuff them with almond slivers to serve as a *meze,* or appetizer. Most people know them in the ubiquitous Greek salad, as well as just plain, on a plate, with a little bread and cheese.

Greek olives most commonly found in the United States are the following:

Agriniou. Produced in Agrinio, where much of Greek tobacco is also cultivated, these olives range from golden green to flesh-colored. They are round, not quite as large as amphissas, but certainly as succulent. They stand on their own, with a bit of bread and cheese, as an excellent appetizer or addition to any table.

Amphissa. These fleshy, brown-black, juicy olives come from the Parnassus region on the mainland and range in flavor from subtle and sweet to bitter. Amphissas are great pitted and pureed with a little oregano, or pitted and chopped, or whole to use in bread.

Atalándi. Large, round, and purplish-green, atalándi, produced in the mainland town of the same name north of Athens, have a subdued, fruity flavor and are great in salads.

Kalamatas. The tautest of the Greek black olives, it must have been of kalamatas that Aristophanes was thinking when he wrote of virgins "with bodies firm as olives steeped in brine." The city of Kalamata is in the Peloponnisos, in the district of Messinia, and is famous for its wine-dark, almond-shaped, pungent olives. They are usually slit in one or two places *(haraktes),* then preserved in vinegar and olive oil. They are excellent in salads, stuffings, and bread. When choosing them, make sure they are succulent and not bitter, which would indicate underripeness.

Samos. The island of Samos makes wine and olives, and the olives that come from this place in the eastern Aegean are similar to throumbes. Wrinkled and slightly bitter, they, too, are allowed to mature on the tree and are then packed in salt water. Unlike the jet black throumbes, they're deep brown in color. Serve them plain or add them to salad.

Throumbes. Their name denotes not a place, but a type. Throumbes, deep black, small, and wrinkled, are harvested as late as December and January. They are allowed to ripen to maturity on the tree and then to dry on the branches. Tarpaulins are spread beneath the trees, just as they were in ancient times. The pickers then beat the branches with long poles until the olives fall off. They are collected from the tarpaulins and laid out to dry for a few more days. Traditionally, they're packed with salt into large clay vases and allowed to stand another few weeks. Throumbes can be either sweet or bitter. (Greeks like both versions.) They are oily and thick skinned, and ideally should be similar to prunes in their consistency. The best ones come from the island of Thásos. Eat them plain, as they are a wonderful *meze,* or add them to salads, such as tomato and potato.

Tsakistes, or Cracked Green Olives. Harvested mostly around Nafplion, also in the Peloponnisos, these can be either small and firm, or large and meaty, but firm. Green olives are harvested unripe and traditionally are cracked open with stones and cured in salt and water. You can find them in Greek food stores, where they are often sold in the barrel and flavored with lemon, garlic, and oregano. They make a nice addition to potato salad and are often eaten plain, as a *meze.*

Curing Your Own Olives. Most raw olives in the United States come from California. Look for olives that are firm and unbruised. Slit them to help draw out the bitterness. Place the olives in a large clay vase with enough water to cover, and change the water daily for 10 to 20 days, until they are no longer bitter. Prepare a brine of approximately 1 quart water and 2 cups salt for every pound of olives (the brine has the correct salt content if an egg floats upright in it), and store the olives in an airtight container in a dark cool place. To store them in oil, after the initial soaking, rinse them very well and soak them in vinegar for 24 hours. Drain them and store in glass or earthenware jars, covered with ample olive oil or a mixture, to taste, of olive oil and good red wine vinegar. Season them, if desired, with fennel (especially for green olives) or any combination of lemon, garlic, coriander, oregano, wild marjoram, or thyme.

Olive Oil

Greece is the third largest olive oil producer in the world, making some thirty thousand tons of oil per year, roughly a third of which is consumed domestically. Exports to the United States account for about seven hundred tons, encompassing many brands, the best of which come from Kalamata and Crete.

Greek olive oil is heavy, deep-scented, and rich. Like all olive oil, it is graded by the method of extraction and by its acidity. The best oils come from olives that are hand-picked and unbruised, and that are then stone-ground into a thick paste. (One of the oldest presses in the world, found on the island of Santorini, was made from the island's indigenous volcanic stone.) The paste is spread onto hemp or straw mats, which in turn are pressed either by hand or hydraulically to extract the liquid (it takes 1,300 to 2,000 olives to make one quart of oil). Cold pressing means that no cold water has been added to the paste to help extract the liquid. Greece has been slow to mechanize its olive production, and many olive oils are still hand-picked and cold-pressed.

Oil is made from about fifty varieties of olives, and like wine, its quality depends on where the olives are grown and how the oil is extracted. The ancient Greeks thought the best oil came from the slightly unripe olive. Next in quality was the oil from the green olive; and last the oil from the ripe olive that had already fallen off the tree.

The types and quality of olive oil can be divided into three categories: extravirgin, virgin, and pure. Extravirgin is the most expensive and the highest-quality oil. It contains no more than 1 percent oleic acid, and the best extravirgins are cold-pressed from the first pressing of the olive. There are about half a dozen varieties of extravirgin Greek olive oil available in the United States. Generally, extravirgin oils are golden green and assertive. They are excellent raw and have a fruity taste. Greeks call this oil *agourelaio,* or "raw oil." Extravirgin olive oil tends to smoke at relatively low temperatures, and is also expensive so avoid frying with it. But it is excellent for cooking and even better as a seasoning over salads, grains, vegetables, and fish.

Virgin olive oil has an acid content of 3.3 percent or less, and is also often cold-pressed, but the olives aren't always top quality. These oils are good for cooking, but avoid frying with them, as they smoke at relatively low temperatures.

Pure olive oil is the lowest grade and is generally made from the second and third pressings of the olives used to make extravirgin oil. Pure olive oil is also refined from the pits, skins, and pulp of the first cold-pressing. The oil is dissolved from the residue with solvents and then removed through distillation. The heat process makes it bland, and pure oil is often mixed with virgin to give it more flavor. It smokes at 400°F and is fine for frying and cooking, but can also be used raw.

Pirina, or crushed olive pits, is the fuel of choice for the wood-burning ovens of country bread bakers around Greece.

— HONEY —

Like the olive, the grape, and the salt of the sea, honey is deeply tied to Greece. To the ancients, it was a mysterious substance with unknown origins—a little bit of heaven fallen to earth. Aristotle said that "One cannot tell what is the substance the bees gather, nor the exact process of their work." Honey was used in religious rituals, as an offering to the gods, and as a beauty and diet agent. It was also thought to have medicinal qualities.

Honey was used in cooking and was, in fact, an important ingredient in ancient cuisine. The Greeks learned the art of domesticating bees from the Egyptians, although wild honey was most likely what they used. The best honey was thought to come from the thyme-scented slopes of Mount Hymettus, near Athens. The ancient Greeks made breads, cakes, and sauces with honey, and it was sometimes used as a sweetener for wine, or mixed with sweet flowers to make a kind of mortal man's nectar.

Today, honey is used mostly in making the syrupy sweets known throughout Greece and the Near East. Some people believe that the best honey still comes from Mount Hymettus, but Crete is probably the foremost source of honey in Greece, and the island's thyme-scented variety is well-known.

The flora—hundreds of species of wildflowers and herbs—and the sun and soil make Greek honey among the best in the world. Greeks consume about a kilo (roughly 2.2 pounds) of it per person annually, mostly in desserts and as a sweetener in coffee and tea. But it isn't a major export item. Only 10 to 20 percent of the ten thousand tons of honey produced annually is exported, and can be readily found in Greek and Middle Eastern food stores.

Greek honey is generally thick because the country's overwhelming sunshine reduces the natural moisture content of the honey. It's also left in the hive two or three days longer than its Western European and American counterparts, and is often distinguished by the subtle, redolent scent of thyme.

But thyme is not the only plant beekeepers allow their bees to feed on. Honey is produced from May to November, and each month marks a different feeding ground and different flavors. Beekeepers move their hives from place to place to take advantage of the changing flora.

May is for wildflowers, orange blossoms, and sage; June for thyme; July and August for fir trees and a later harvest of thyme. In September and October, bees feed on pine, and in November, on heather. These are, of course, general rules, especially in the commercial production of honey.

Crete, although rich in wildflowers and herbs, is especially known for its heavy, thyme-scented honey. Other islands abound in pine and heather. Honey that is predominantly scented with pine or fir is dark and rarely crystallizes. Thyme and orange-blossom honey is a medium golden brown, amberlike in color, and crystallizes slowly. Honey flavored primarily with wildflower blossoms and heather is light and thin and crystallizes easily.

—CHEESE—

The first time I tasted real Greek cheese, it came from a dripping white gauze sack, hung from the faucet of an old marble sink. It was goat's cheese from an island garden and the taste was pungent and earthy and delicious.

Cheese, like so many other things good for man (wine and olive oil, for example), came to us from the East with a stop in Crete. Fire-clay cheese strainers dating from the Neolithic and Early Bronze Age have been found on the island of Crete. At the Minoan Palace at Knossos, tablets dating to 3000 B.C. depict men making cheese from either goat's or sheep's milk.

Golden Age Greeks had a particular liking for cheese and were especially fond of cheesecakes. Ancient Greek wedding cakes are known to have been made of cheese, and the best purportedly came from a small shop on Samos. In Argos, the bride brought a gift of small honey-topped roasted cheesecakes to friends of the groom, and on Delos some of the island's currency depicted little cheeses.

Athenaeus, in *The Deipnosophists,* reports an ancient fondness for a particular cheesecake shaped like a woman's breast, and offers a recipe for another: "Take some cheese and pound it. Put it in a brazen sieve and strain it, then add honey and flour, best made of spring wheat, mix it all into one mass and heat."

The recipe sounds like the forebear of some of the sweetened cheese pies still made in modern Greece, *skaltsounia* in Crete and *melitinia* in Santorini, to name two. The ancients cooked cheese with honey and bulbs and also ate fish topped with cheese sauce, a dish that would be anathema to their modern descendents.

Today, cheese is produced all over Greece, but several areas have achieved distinction in the art: Dodoni in Epirus for feta; Metsovo, also in Epirus, for its wonderful *kapnisto,* or smoked cheese; Thrace, in the far northeast, for *feta telemes* (aged in tins); Thessaly for *manouri;* Crete for *anthotiro;* and Mitilini for its *lathotiri,* or oil cheese.

There are many indigenous Greek cheeses, some exported, some found only in Greece.

Anthotiro. This is a whey cheese, like soft *mitzithra* except that it contains a little salt. Similar to ricotta, *anthotiro* is excellent spread on bread with a little jam or honey.

Feta. This is the ubiquitous Greek cheese. Soft, white, and "pickled," it's the traditional cheese of Greek mountain shepherds. Greek feta is made only from goat's or sheep's milk. Feta produced outside Greece is made mostly with cow's milk. Its name derives from the way it is cut into blocks or large slices. (*Feta* means "slice.")

The cheese is made by heating fresh milk in large containers to about 95°F. Rennin (an enzyme that coagulates milk and that is obtained from the mucous membrane of the stomach of calves) is added, and when the cheese solidifies the curd is placed in a wooden barrel with a heavy cloth bottom, then left to drain. When the cheese firms sufficiently, it is cut into blocks and rubbed with dry salt. The blocks are turned and salted again, then cut into wedges, salted, and packed in either wooden kegs that hold between 100 and 170 pounds, or tins.

There are five basic kinds of feta: soft; medium; hard; *varrelisio,* or barrel feta; and *telemes* (tinned), which is made not with rennin but with yeast, and is generally mild. Feta varies in pungency and texture depending on where and with what it's produced. Ironically, one finds more varieties of feta in a Greek food shop in America than in a cheese specialty shop in Athens, because many producers export directly abroad. As a general rule, pure goat's-milk feta is very hard and piquant. Sheep's feta is less piquant.

Feta is produced in several countries besides Greece: Holland, France, Denmark, Bulgaria, and America. American feta is usually about one dollar a pound less than the imported variety, but it is highly salted and generally not of very good quality. One might also find a processed variety on the supermarket shelf, but this generally bears little resemblance to the creamy feta found in Greek specialty shops.

When making *tyropittes,* or cheese pies, most Greek home cooks, even in America, buy what is called *trimmata,* the crumbled feta at the bottom of the barrel, and that is usually about half the price of the regular variety.

Feta should be stored in the refrigerator. Some people store it in a bath of milk to keep it moist, but it must be consumed quickly if stored this way, or else its saltiness and flavor will leech out.

Commercially made *tyropittes,* especially in Greece, generally use a feta byproduct called *giza,* made by boiling the whey left over after the cheese is drained.

Graviera. This semihard yellow cheese is traditionally made from cow's milk. Corfu, Syros, Serres, Lárisa, Tinos, and Naxos all produce the cheese from cow's milk. Crete, Mytilini, Arta, Dodoni, and Kalpaki are producers of a sharper *graviera* made of sheep's milk. As a general rule, sheep's-milk *graviera* is whiter than that made from cow's milk.

Haloumi. A white Cypriot cheese made from goat's milk, *haloumi* is sometimes flavored with mint. Raw or pasteurized milk is curdled with powdered rennin, then cut into small pieces and stirred and cooked in whey until boiling. Salt and double mint, *diosmo,* are added and the cheese is placed in a whey brine. This is excellent grilled or (see *saganaki,* page 81) eaten as a table cheese.

Kasseri. This is a yellow, spun-curd cheese made from either ewe's or cow's milk. It resembles provolone in consistency and is generally eaten as a table cheese or grilled. (See *saganaki,* page 81.)

Kefalotyri. This sheep's-milk cheese is made in Cyprus, Syria, and, of course, Greece. It's a hard yellow cheese, eaten as a table or grating cheese or grilled. *Kefalotyri* is dry-salted and aged for at least three months. It gets its name from its shape—*kefali* means "head."

Lathotiri. This sheep's-milk cheese is produced in Mytilini and on Zákinthos and sold in Greek specialty food shops as small wax-covered balls or as barrel shapes. Its name translates as "oil cheese," because after it has matured for at least three months, it is submerged in olive oil, which imparts to it a delicious but heavy flavor. It's then sealed with wax.

Manouri. This is the most expensive of the soft white cheeses. Unlike *mitzithra, manouri* contains very little liquid, is salted, and is quite high in fat. The cheese was first produced in a village in Macedonia called Vlasti. Although difficult to find outside northern Greece, manouri Vlastis is generally harder and slightly saltier than its counterparts elsewhere in Greece.

Mitzithra. The word dates to the sixteenth century, when it referred to a kneaded cheese. This is a fresh, soft, white cheese very similar to pot cheese. It contains no salt and little fat. *Mitzithra* is a feta byproduct. The whey from the feta and fresh milk are combined in a vat and curdled for several days. Then the whey is removed and the residual curd is collected, drained, and pressed. *Mitzithra* is sold either soft, as a table cheese, or salted and pressed until rock-hard, and used as a grating cheese. The best comes from Crete.

Touloumi. This special cheese is difficult to find outside Greek mountain villages. It's made with fresh goat's milk and packed into a whole goat skin and left to age for several months. If you can find this wonderful, pungent cheese in Greece, hold your nose and try it.

— Other Dairy Products —

A Word on Yogurt. Greek yogurt, called *yiaourti,* is thick and creamy, made from either cow's or sheep's milk, and sold in two versions. There is unstrained, which is like plain yogurt in America but a bit smoother; and strained, *strangismeno,* or *sakoulas* if bought fresh in clay bowls from a cheese or sweet shop. It has many uses in the Greek kitchen. Yogurt is baked into sauces *(yiaourtava);* eaten on the side with rice and spicy meat dishes; served with honey and fruit or nuts as a dessert; made into a cool soup or summer drink; and consumed as an ingredient in cake. It's also a folk remedy for sunburn.

To make your own yogurt: You'll need a bit of store-bought yogurt to use as a starter. Have 2 to 3 tablespoons ready at room temperature. Heat 1 quart milk over medium heat for 2 to 3 minutes to bring it near the boiling point, being careful not to scorch the milk. Pour milk into a large clay or glass bowl. Cool it slightly, to between 105°F and 120°F, then stir in the 2 to 3 tablespoons of starter yogurt very thoroughly. Cover with a cloth, place it in an unlit oven or in a warm, draft-free place for about 8 hours; don't disturb it at all until the yogurt thickens. Store in the refrigerator for up to 5 days, and save a bit of starter for the next use. To make individual cups, follow the same directions but use about 1 teaspoon of starter per cup.

What is known in America as yogurt cheese is known in Greece as *strangismeno yiaourti,* or simply "strained yogurt." It's easy enough to make: Empty the contents of a cup (or more, if desired) of yogurt into a piece of doubled cheesecloth. Tie and let it drip for at least 2 hours, or until desired thickness is reached. Strained yogurt is generally not as thick as yogurt cheese.

Butter. Like yogurt, butter is made either from sheep's or cow's milk, the former generally considered better. Sheep's-milk butter, like sheep's-milk cheese, is whiter and more pungent. Fresh butter is sold loose in specialty shops in Greece, and one also finds clarified butter in jars.

——HERBS, SPICES, AND SPECIAL FLAVORS——

On the periphery of the central market in Athens, and tucked into several other spots around the city, are the tiny shops that sell *botana* (herbs) and spices. These are wonderful places, where bouquets of dried oregano are tied up garland-style around the entranceway, and where one can usually find more than three hundred different herbs and spices, mostly native to Greece but also imported from the world over. Despite the variety of available flavorings, however, Greeks are conservative when it comes to seasoning their food. Herbs are used as much for their homeopathic value—infusions of lemon balm for the heart; rosemary to help with diets; lime blossom *(tilio)* as a relaxant, for instance—as they are for flavoring. And no more than a handful of herbs and spices appear repeatedly in the Greek cooking repertoire: oregano, cinnamon, allspice, nutmeg, dill, parsley, double mint, and fennel. There are, of course, dozens more that show up here and there throughout Greek cookery; below is a brief description of them and their uses.

Allspice. This is known in Greek as *bahari,* and is used powdered and whole in béchamel sauce, minced meat sauce, and snail, rabbit, and beef stews.

Anise. Known as *glykaniso* to the Greeks, anise was used by their ancient ancestors and appreciated in aniseed bread, which was considered a great delicacy. Now anise is used in biscuits and as a flavoring in ouzo.

Ash. Known more mundanely as lye—*alisiva* to the Greeks—wood ash is boiled in water, which is then carefully strained and used to clarify and keep fruit firm for spoon sweets. The ash itself is discarded.

Basil. Considered a sacred herb in Greece, basil is found more often in a vase by a church altar than in a steaming pot of sauce. According to legend, Aghia Eleni (St. Helen), mother of Emperor Constantine, was told in a vision that she would find the True Cross in a place fragrant with perfume. She found it, as the story goes, under a patch of basil and the herb has held religious significance ever since. It is with basil that Greek Orthodox priests sprinkle holy water during the ceremony of the Epiphany; to the ancients, basil was a symbol of mourning. (Its name comes from the Greek for "kingly.") It's a telltale sign of spring, grown in virtually every household in Greece, but kept in the pot for its fragrant smell and for the common folk belief that it wards off insects.

Bay Leaf. *Vayia* or *Daphne* to the Greeks, bay leaf is one of their favorite seasonings. It's used in red sauces, meat stews, and with baked fish and poultry. Bay leaf is also used to flavor dried fruits such as figs and raisins.

Caper. Pickled and eaten by themselves, capers are also sprinkled into salads, used in stuffings, and favored as a topping on Greek pizza.

Cinnamon. This much-used Greek spice is known as *kanella,* which is also a feminine name. Greeks use it in tomato and meat sauces, meat stews, snail stew, rice dishes, and cheese pies. It's also a predominant flavor in many of the country's sweets—boiled whole in syrups, and sprinkled over everything from rice pudding to *halvah.*

Clove. Like cinnamon, nutmeg, and allspice, clove is a common seasoning in spicy red sauces and meat sauces. You'll notice the flavor frequently in *moussaka* and *pastitsio,* and it's common to decorate diamond-shaped wedges of *baklava* and other sweets with cloves.

Coriander. Although coriander has one of the longest recorded histories (its seeds have been found in Bronze Age ruins on Santorini) and was known and used readily in ancient Greek cooking, it has fallen out of favor today. The herb is found more commonly in Cypriot foods, especially pork dishes and potatoes. Its seeds appear regularly at spirits distillers, as it is, along with anise, a common flavoring in ouzo. Not to its advantage, coriander's name derives from the Greek word for bedbug, *koris,* with which the ancients held its odor to be similar.

Cumin. Both cumin powder and cumin seed are used as a seasoning in white and red sauces, in sausages, and in meat-stuffed vegetable dishes. It's also a common flavor in spice biscuits, especially on Crete.

Dill. Dill is used everywhere—in savory green pies, meat stuffings, red and white sauces, homemade pickles, and salads. Greeks use it fresh more often than dried, although it's easy to find dried dill in supermarkets.

Fennel. The Greek word for fennel is *marathon;* the site of the famous battle was so called because its fields were brimming with it. Greeks eat the leafy part not the bulb. Like dill, fennel is used in many dishes, but is especially liked in salads, green pies, and homemade pickles.

Garlic. "Garlic and onions, right and left," say the Greeks to denote how common are their uses. On Clean Monday, at the start of Lent, fresh garlic is a favorite food, and is eaten boldly, as a vegetable. It's a seasoner for meats, especially lamb, tomato sauces, and vegetables of every kind. Garlic is most often found in the company of lemon and olive oil.

Mahlepi. One of the stranger spices found in the Greek cookery, *mahlepi,* is a Turkish spice from the seeds of a plant by the same name. It is sold in seed or powder form, and generally boiled with a bit of water and used as a standard seasoning in *tsoureki,* or Greek Easter bread.

Marjoram. Waverley Root tells us that the ancient Greeks made a pomade with marjoram to anoint their hair and eyebrows. Bridal wreaths were made with it as a wish for happy marriage, and it was planted on graves to bestow a happy afterlife. It's known as *matzourana* in Greek and is used fresh in savory pies and dried in red sauces and with meats. It's also drunk as an herbal tea.

Mastic. From the rare shrub called *Pistacia lentiscus* indigenous to the island of Chios, mastic has several uses in Greek cookery. Sold in opaque crystals, then pulverized at home, it's a common flavoring in sweets, especially in the sweet Easter bread called *tsoureki*. It's consumed as a natural chewing gum, made into a sugar paste like *vanillia* (page 19), and also distilled into a fiery clear liqueur called *mastiha*.

Mint. Mint is to the Greeks what basil is to the Italians. *Diosmo,* or double mint, is used to flavor red sauces and all sorts of meat dishes, especially meatballs, or *keftedes*. It's a favorite ingredient in rice stuffings and in cheese pies, both sweet and savory. Boiled, it's the morning drink of choice for many Greeks. *Menta,* or spearmint, is usually drunk as a tea.

Nutmeg. Nutmeg may have entered Europe through Byzantium in the fifth century. The assertion, says a skeptical Waverley Root, is based on the fact "Aetius of Amida, a Byzantine physician . . . concocted a medicine which he called *suffimis gum moschatum,* but we are not sure it contained nutmeg." It may have indeed been nutmeg in the doctor's remedy, for the Greek word for nutmeg is similar—*moschocarido,* literally, musk, or fragrant, nut. Nutmeg is liked in Greece. Béchamel is flavored with it, as are red and white sauces, meat stews, and some sweets.

Orange-Blossom Water. Called *anthonero* in Greek, orange-blossom water is used only in sweets. *Kourambiethes, loukoumi, pastelli,* and almond truffles are among the more common delights that use this Eastern Mediterranean essence.

Oregano. Like dill, garlic, and mint, oregano is used in many Greek dishes and is usually found in the company of garlic and lemon. Meatballs *(keftedes)* are flavored with it; lamb is rubbed with it; fresh, it's used in savory pies; and it's the ubiquitous herb in Greek salad, red sauce, and baked fish. It's also a favorite in the countryside, where villagers dry figs and flavor them with oregano.

Paprika. A popular spice among *souvlaki* vendors, who sprinkle paprika liberally over skewered chunks of lamb or pork, it is also a main ingredient in the *tsimeni,* or spice paste used to flavor *pastourma,* dried beef (page 238).

Parsley. *Keftedakia,* salads, savory pies, fish dishes, and tomato sauces all find room for a bit of fresh parsley. It's also a standard component of *kolyva* (page 160), a memorial grain dish.

Pepper. Greeks generally like their food mild. Black pepper is used sparingly throughout the cuisine, and hot pepper is found mostly in dishes from northern Greece and Asia Minor. Red pepper is used as a seasoning in baked lima beans and sausages.

Rose Geranium. Called *arbaroriza* in Greek, geranium leaves are used frequently to flavor spoon sweets and preserves, especially quince.

Rosemary. To Greek villagers, rosemary is known as *arimari* (from a transliteration of the word). It is correctly known as *dendrolivano,* with just as interesting an etymology. The ancient Greeks called rosemary *livanotis*—supposedly after a young priest who was murdered and whose blood soaked and scented a bunch of the plant. Rosemary is used fairly often in Greek cookery, especially by the open-minded, who forfeit established oregano for it around a leg—or rack—of lamb. Sometimes it's drunk as a tea.

Rose Water. Known as *rothonero,* rose water is used only with sweets, and interchangeably with orange-blossom water. The petals, unsprayed and from one's own garden, are sometimes preserved in a spoon sweet.

Saffron. The most expensive spice in the world is called *crocos* by the Greeks. Saffron was used to a great degree by the Greeks of yore and has been cultivated in Greece and Asia Minor for some three thousand years. The ancient Greeks considered its color a symbol of royalty, and murals depicting the saffron harvest—an onerous task at best—have been found at Knossos on Crete. But saffron has gone the way of coriander as far as modern Greeks are concerned; like the spice of equally long record, it's now used mainly in the distillation of certain spirits, and that limited still to one small place—Kozani and its environs in north central Greece. There, the regal stigmas tint and flavor home-brewed *tsipouro,* a distillation not unlike ouzo. Perhaps because of its medicinal aroma, saffron is also thought to alleviate ailments of the belly.

Sage. Waverley Root reports that "the most unusual food use of sage is probably that of the Ionian island of Zante [Zákinthos], where the galls which develop on sage stalks when they are punctured by insects are mixed with honey and made into preserves." I do not know this to be true, and no Zantean I've met seems to know for sure, either. I do know that Greek beekeepers feed their hives on sage, and that the herb is used more for its medicinal than its culinary qualities, and is drunk as a tea. *Fascomilo,* as it is called by the Greeks, is sometimes used in pilafs and chicken dishes.

Salt. *Alas* to the ancients, *alati* to modern Greeks, salt is one of the most revered elements in all the country's cooking. Coarse salt is used to preserve vegetables, fish, herbs, meat, and olives. Salt is also used to flavor milk in many Greek villages. It is considered essential to life, and the Greeks consider sea salt best.

Sesame. Its seeds are commonly sprinkled over breads, biscuits, and certain sweet and savory cheese pies. Sometimes they are used in lieu of nuts to make *baklava,* as well as in the making of a favorite Greek candy, *pastelli,* or sesame brittle. Sesame seeds, like bay leaf and oregano, are also a popular addition to dried figs, especially in Kalamata. Tahini, or sesame paste, is used as a base in *hummus;* in another similar dip, made without chick-peas; in a certain *halvah;* and in a soup called *tahinosoupa.* In Cyprus, tahini is turned into a sweet pie, and elsewhere in Greece it's used in place of butter to make Lenten sweets.

Slaked Lime. Called *xino* in Greek, slaked lime is used in combination with water to preserve the color and texture of fruits in spoon sweets and preserves.

Thyme. This herb, native to the Mediterranean, made its way into history about the time of the Sumerians, 3500 B.C. It was believed to hold aphrodisiac powers by the ancient Greeks. Its Greek name— *thymari*—is close enough to the English to attempt a pronunciation, and it is, like oregano and dill, among the herbs Greeks love most. It's picked in flower and used interchangeably with oregano to flavor lamb, rabbit, and fish, as well as red sauces and a wide variety of vegetables, especially potatoes.

Vanilla. Greeks use vanilla mostly in a powdered form in sweets.

—BASIC SAUCES AND DRESSINGS—

The ancient Greeks had their *garum* (salted fish paste) and were fond of cheese sauces, of which there were many. It seems, too, from Athenaeus that the miscarried matrix of an unfortunate sow found its way quite often into a variety of condiments—from white sauce, which the ancients invented, to a pungent brine and vinegar sauce, to a dressing made from the "bitter gall of rue."

Several thousand years have tempered the palates of modern Greeks, and most of the country's cooks now concur that, when it comes to sauces, the simpler the better. Although honey, saffron, and silphium have disappeared from the menu, olive oil, vinegar, and eggs are still among the basic ingredients in many Greek dressings. Following are six of the most basic sauces and dressings, the ones that appear and reappear throughout the cuisine. Other sauces, including meat sauces, tomato sauces, and yogurt concoctions, which have more limited usages, can be found in other chapters throughout the book.

Avgolemono

(EGG AND LEMON SAUCE)

ONE of the fundamental flavorings and thickeners in soups (see *prassoselinosoupa*, page 130; *kotosoupa*, page 131; *mageiritsa*, page 132; *psarosoupa*, page 132; and *patsas*, page 140), *avgolemono* is a much-loved sauce in stove-top vegetable dishes such as stuffed cabbage and *dolmadakia*. *Avgolemono* is usually prepared just before the dish is served.

Beat the eggs until pale and foamy (2 to 3 minutes). Beating continuously, gradually drizzle in the lemon juice. Using a ladle or large spoon, very slowly add the hot pan juices or broth to the eggs, beating all the while, until the egg mixture is warm. Pour the *avgolemono* into the contents of the pot for which it is being made and heat very lightly—without allowing to boil—just enough for the sauce to thicken slightly. Remove and serve.

Yield: 1 to 2 cups

2 to 3 eggs (or yolks only, as preferred), at room temperature
Strained fresh juice of 1 to 2 large lemons
1 to 2 cups hot pan juices or broth, from the dish for which avgolemono is being made

Béchamel

2 tablespoons butter
2 tablespoons
   all-purpose flour
1 cup milk, at room
   temperature or
   slightly warmed
Salt and freshly
   ground pepper, to
   taste
Grating of nutmeg
1 to 3 egg yolks
   (optional)

BÉCHAMEL is favored, as is *avgolemono,* for certain stove-top vegetables, such as stuffed cabbage and *dolmades.* Enriched with eggs, it forms the top of *moussaka* (page 164) and *pastitsio* (page 144).

A medium-consistency béchamel, like this one, is used in most of the recipes calling for béchamel in this book. If a thinner consistency is desired, reduce the butter and flour to 1 tablespoon each per cup of milk; for a thicker sauce, increase the proportions to 3 tablespoons each of butter and flour per cup of milk. Sometimes grated cheese is also stirred into the béchamel at the end of cooking.

In a medium saucepan, melt butter over low heat; do not brown. Add flour and stir to blend with a wooden spoon or wire whisk. Cook over low heat for 3 to 5 minutes, until flour no longer tastes raw. Slowly add milk over low heat and stir continuously with a wooden spoon or wire whisk, until sauce is creamy, still liquid, but quite thick. (This will take 10 to 20 minutes, depending on the strength of the heat.) Remove from heat and stir in salt, pepper, and nutmeg. Cool slightly before beating in egg yolks with a wooden spoon.

Yield: 1 cup

Note: When increasing the amount of the recipe, increase all the ingredients proportionately, except for the eggs. One to three yolks—as desired—are the standard number. Egg yolks are generally included for baked dishes, such as *pastitsio* and *moussaka.*

Skordostoumbi

USE this pungent dressing as a condiment (besides the standard *avgolemono*) in *patsas* (page 140). *Skordostoumbi* is also served as an accompaniment to some of the innard and entrail dishes so well-liked by the Greeks.

1 to 2 cups strong red
   wine vinegar
5 to 10 garlic cloves
   (to taste), peeled
   and slivered or
   coarsely chopped
¼ cup ground walnut
   meats (optional)

Combine all ingredients in a glass jar or bottle and let stand 24 hours before serving.

Yield: 1 to 2 cups

Latholemono

A favorite marinade for fish and some meat dishes (sometimes with a touch of chopped garlic), *latholemono* is also a standard dressing for salads and greens.

Combine all ingredients and shake well. Use immediately.

2 parts olive oil (preferably extravirgin)
1 part strained fresh lemon juice
Oregano, chopped parsley, dill, or thyme, to taste
Salt and freshly ground pepper, to taste

Lathoxitho

THIS dressing is similar to *latholemono,* except that vinegar—good, strong red wine vinegar—takes the place of lemon juice. *Lathoxitho* is consumed more readily as a dressing than as a marinade.

Combine all ingredients and shake well. Use immediately.

2 parts olive oil (preferably extravirgin)
1 part (or slightly less) strong red wine vinegar
Oregano, chopped parsley, dill, or thyme, to taste
Salt and freshly ground pepper, to taste

Mayonnaise

Beat the egg yolks with a wire whisk until pale and creamy—just thick enough to coat a spoon. Add $\frac{1}{2}$ teaspoon of the lemon juice, salt, and pepper and beat continuously for 1 minute. Very slowly add $\frac{1}{2}$ cup of the olive oil—about $\frac{1}{4}$ teaspoon at a time—and whisk continuously until the mixture thickens and emulsifies. Then add, drop by drop and alternating between each, the remaining lemon juice and olive oil, beating constantly until a thick creamy mayonnaise forms.

Yield: About 1$\frac{1}{2}$ cups

2 egg yolks
$\frac{1}{4}$ cup strained fresh lemon juice
$\frac{1}{2}$ teaspoon salt
Dash of freshly ground pepper
1 cup olive oil

— UTENSILS —

Clay was the most common material used in making kitchenware in ancient Greece. Mortars, cooking bells, and portable ovens were often fashioned from clay, as were frying pans, cooking pots, casseroles, braziers, and water jugs. It is interesting to note that clay, a material of necessity to ancient householders and to the Greeks throughout most of their history, is today a material of choice.

Cooking stands and makeshift ovens were common in antiquity. They were usually vase-shaped with an opening at the bottom for putting in the fuel—either twigs or charcoal. The pan, be it a small casserole or a larger pot for making stews, sat over the top of the ersatz oven. In Greece today, especially in the eastern islands, there exists a similar clay oven for grilling fish, called the *fou-fou.*

Water is still kept cool in clay jugs, especially in remote parts of the country; wine is sometimes left to ferment in large clay vessels embedded in the ground; and olives are stored in a *kioupi,* a squat earthenware container.

In Cephalonia, a traditional clay baking vessel is called a *tserepa.* Horsehair is used in place of wire to bind the clay. In Ioannina, one will find a regional specialty: *heli steen keramida,* or eel baked in clay. Originally, and quite ingeniously, Ioanninans used the clay tiles so common to Mediterranean rooftops, plugging the ends of the U-shaped improvised dish with dough to keep the juices from streaming out. In other parts of Greece, most notably Epirus, the *gastra* is the most traditional of the utensils. It means clay flowerpot, and its mouth is often sealed with dough before baking to keep in flavors.

(In a slight aside, the technique of sealing a dish or a food to be baked—whether it be in a clay bowl topped with dough, *en croûte,* in wax paper, or in the *stamna,* a clay waterjug that one still encounters in the north—falls into the general category of *klepthika,* or "of thieves." Legend has it that during the Greek War of Independence, Greek women would surreptitiously bring water jugs filled with food to their men, who were called *klephts,* fighting in the mountains. They would in turn cook it in makeshift, covered ovens underground—to keep steam or scents that might divulge their location from escaping. Now food that is sealed and baked has taken on the name *klephtic.*

The *tavas* is another traditional pan, stout and round, of either clay or copper, and common for baked meat and poultry dishes. *Giouvetsi* is a popular food made mainly with orzo and meat or chicken, and is so called after the clay dish in which it is customarily baked.

Wood, too, is sometimes essential in the Greek kitchen. The ancients fashioned tree trunks into deep-welled mortars for pounding grain. The *pinakoti,* while not a mortar, is a hollowed-out piece of solid wood traditionally used in bread baking. It is a beautiful, earthy basin in which the bread maker kneads the dough and lets it rest to rise. And certainly the mortar and pestle, probably one of the most important traditional tools in the Greek kitchen, are almost always made of wood. "Take it home and rub it with olive oil," advises the man in an old housewares shop off Athinas Street near the Athens Central Market, in regard to the care of a newly bought mortar and pestle. Most women inherit theirs, already smooth and well-worn, from their mothers and grandmothers.

Wood, of course, is also the traditional fuel of the household oven in Greece, although one would be hard put to find a city Greek so endearing of old ways as to build an outdoor brick oven on the balcony or to cook over an open hearth. But one is very likely to find old ways alive in country villages. Many village people have outdoor ovens for baking bread. In northern Greece, especially in Epirus, I've encountered women who still bake their *pittas,* or savory pies, over slow-burning embers *(steen hovoli),* protected by a kind of cooking bell called a *sini,* placed over the embers to make an oven.

There isn't enough room here to describe all of the traditional cooking tools of Greece, but for anyone seriously interested in the country's cookery, I would recommend the following few items in addition to the standard collection of cooking utensils that outfit any decent kitchen:

• Ovenproof earthenware pans of various sizes, and at least one large round stout one

• Wooden spoons

• At least one mortar and pestle made of wood, but preferably several in different sizes, for grinding nuts and spices and especially garlic, and for making purées such as *melitzanosalata* (eggplant) and *skordalia* (garlic and potato or bread)

• A *saganaki* pan if you can find one (try Greek specialty food shops), which is a small, round, two-handled skillet for making fried cheese and eggs

Chapter 3

Bread

To the ancient Greeks it was *artos,* from *artio,* or "to flavor"; to the moderns it is *psomi,* which means "morsel." So crucial is bread to the culture that even the general word for cook in Greek, *mageiras,* takes its root from *maza,* meaning "that which is kneaded."

Bread is a sacred food, a utensil, a good luck charm, a folk art, a gift, a token to commemorate the milestones of life. Greeks don't eat without it. "They are the only people who'll sit down to a bowl of pasta with a chunk of bread in their hands," a friend jokes, and he's right.

But the amazing thing about bread in this culture is that so very little has changed since Greeks first began eating it in antiquity. The special breads for Christmas, New Year's, and Easter, the habit of inserting a coin or a miniature plough or a piece of straw into the New Year's bread, the sculpted breads given as gifts in celebration of births, baptisms, and marriages in certain parts of Greece, the very concept of bread as a gift and the superstitions surrounding it—all are habits that trace their roots to uncannily similar customs of the ancient world.

——THE ROLE OF BREAD IN—— ANCIENT GREECE

The ancient Greeks learned to leaven bread from the Egyptians and nicknamed them the "bread makers," so singular—and revolutionary—was the practice in the ancient world. From Herodotus we learn that the Egyptians did everything in a fashion "different from ordinary mortals." While other Mediterranean civilizations used religious and sanitary laws to help prevent the decay of their foods, the Egyptians, for unfathomable reasons, seemed to favor letting theirs rot. It is to them, of course, that we owe the discovery of the fermentation process.

But the art of leavening bread developed late in the daily life of the ancient Greeks. Perhaps their nomadic roots prevented them from adopting it sooner, for bread making demands patience and time, and long after they had settled the region in about 2000 B.C., the Greeks still embraced the values of their wanderers' past. Reay Tannahill, in *Food in History,* notes that the Egyptians had developed an easily leavened wheat that could be readily separated from its chaff and therefore threshed without preliminary toasting as had been the case before. The new wheat was rare, probably available only for the rich, and was not common in Greece until the fourth century B.C. The older method of heating the wheat in order to thresh it precluded or hampered the possibility of making flour that was easily leavened.

The ancient Greeks knew, as we do today, the differences between hard and soft wheat. They also shared our modern-day fondness for the whitest of breads—*polytelias,* or "luxury bread," as Greeks today call it. The ancients had an affinity for soft white bread, which was also a popular treat at the theater.

The finest wheat was imported from Sicily and Ethiopia, but the most common grain was barley. Greeks still use barley, but not to make the awful porridges that nourished the ancient world, nor to make anything akin to fresh bread. It's a grain used for the popular *paximathia,* large, rough, wedges of slowly baked toast that Greeks soak in water and olive oil to soften; the *paximathi,* a few olives, and perhaps some cheese have been the standard midday meal of Greek farmers for centuries, and the best barley *paximathia* come from Crete.

The goddess of bread was Demeter, goddess of the earth, of family, and of property. According to myth, Demeter avenged the loss of her daughter Persephone—who was plucked one fine day while gathering flowers in Sicily by the god of the netherworld—by making the earth unfruitful. Zeus, bowing to her will, sent a messenger to Hades to beg for their daughter's release, for without food for nourishment and immolation neither humans nor gods could exist. Persephone was granted her release, but because the unfortunate maiden had sampled the food of Hades, she was compelled to return for a quarter of the year—just as seeds must remain in the ground for a portion of the year.

The cult of Demeter was called the Bread Church of Eleusis. The goddess was commemorated every autumn, after the planting of the seed corn, with the Celebration of the Bread, one of the most important festivals of the ancient world. Without exception, anyone who spoke Greek, men and women, children and slaves, could take part in the procession from Athens to Eleusis, and among the offerings to the goddess—sculpted breads, baked ploughs made of wheat and honey, special cakes—the modern customs surrounding bread took root.

——DECORATIVE BREADS AND—— BREAD CUSTOMS

In the following pages, recipe by recipe, I've tried to serve up offerings of both food and folklore. Where recipe ingredients are symbolic of fruitfulness, good luck, fertility, or whatever, I've so described. There is, however, one area of bread baking that comes down to us from the ancients and that is, to the sadness of anyone fond of old country ways, dying fast. This is the tradition of making ornate, decorative breads to mark the milestones along one's passage through life.

In the flea market of Iráklion, Crete, one comes across the commercialized version of these breads, replete with machine-made dough designs and a varnish finish. But in the villages one might still find the groups of women whose nimble hands sculpt delicate dough likenesses of birds, snakes, lemon blossoms, berries, grapes, pomegranate seeds, laurel leaves, and worry beads, all to be laid onto the the bread rings called *kouloures* in celebration of an engagement or marriage or birth.

Similar sculpted breads are also made in northern Greece, in Khalkidiki, as well as in other parts of the country. In the Peloponnisos, sweet bread rings decorated with fresh flowers are made to celebrate wedding engagements, and the future bride and groom pull apart the ring, as is custom, in a mockery of who will have the upper hand. Up until fairly recently, farmers in certain parts of Greece, in Mani in the Peloponnisos, for example, made New Year's breads in the shape of their animals as a token of good luck for them in the coming year. If an animal was forgotten, it was believed it would fall ill and die during the course of the year.

The Maniotes have another wonderful bread custom—*lalangia*. These are crisp, fried pieces of dough made around Christmas and usually eaten with cheese. Traditionally, the *lalangia* were prepared on Christmas Eve, and folk belief had it that their delicious smell warded off the mischievous imps thought to wreak havoc on earth between November 14, the Feast Day of St. Phillip and start of the Christmas fast, and January 6, the Epiphany.

Mani is a trove of local customs. At Eastertime, godparents would give enormous decorated *kouloures,* or bread rings, to their godchildren. Sometimes they were as large as four feet in diameter, and they would diminish in size as the child got older and reached puberty, when the custom stops. For girls, the *kouloura* was traditionally ring-shaped, to symbolize the continuity of the family; for boys, it was shaped like a horseshoe, because men go off to war and work the fields, and often did both on horseback.

Bread is the most revered food in Greek life, inextricable from the daily meal, a staple on special tables, whether festive or commemorative, and the object of a wealth of local superstitions and folk beliefs.

A loaf left topside down brings bad luck—*grousouzia,* as the Greeks say. So does stabbing a loaf of bread (which symbolizes the body of Christ) with a knife and leaving it upright. Ages ago, women would put a little piece of bread in the pockets of their sons and husbands for good luck when they were going off either to war or to the fields. Folk beliefs dictate that placing a little piece of bread under the pillow of a newborn child wards off evil, and eating the "elbow" of the loaf, or the end, is supposed to make one's mother-in-law especially endearing.

Horiatiko Psomi

(VILLAGE OR COUNTRY-STYLE BREAD)

WHEN you approach the village of Raches in the northern part of a not-very-tourist-populated island called Ikaria, the bakery is the first sign of life that you see. But it's a sign from another era, a one-story white house with geraniums spilling from recycled olive oil tins and a huge wood-burning oven within—the largest, in fact, on the island, with capacity for 150 kilos of bread. The walls are whitewashed every now and then, but they turn brown quickly. Niko and Argyro run the bakery that feeds the several hundred families of Raches. They make *horiatiko psomi,* or "village" bread, one of two kinds of bread eaten in Greece daily.

Horiatiko is traditionally made not with yeast but with *prozymi,* or sourdough starter. Niko makes it the way most bakers do, whether commercial or at home: He saves a bit of fermented dough from the previous day's preparation, adds to it a tiny bit of yeast, and lets it stand overnight in a well of flour. By morning, the starter has risen and the day's bread is ready to be made. *Horiatiko* is coarse and hearty and slightly piquant, its texture quite distinguished from the other daily bread of the Greeks, a light, airy loaf called *polytelias,* or "luxury" bread.

---

2 cups warm water
7 to 8 cups bread flour
1 envelope active dry
  yeast (or **prozymi**;
  see Note)
1 to 2 teaspoons sugar
$\frac{1}{4}$ cup olive oil
2 teaspoons to 1
  tablespoon salt
3 tablespoons olive oil,
  for rubbing pans
  and dough

1. In a large bowl, combine 1 cup of the warm water with 1 cup of the bread flour, the yeast, and sugar. Cover mixture with a cloth and let stand in a warm, draft-free place to proof, at least 1 hour, or until the mixture is thick and pasty and has begun to swell.

2. Pour remaining 1 cup warm water and $\frac{1}{4}$ cup olive oil into yeast mixture. Slowly add 6 cups flour and salt, stirring with a wooden spoon until all ingredients are combined. Turn dough out onto a floured surface and knead, adding remaining flour if necessary, for 10 to 15 minutes, or until dough is soft and silky to the touch. Place in an oiled bowl, cover with a light towel, and let rise in a warm place until doubled in bulk, about 2 hours.

3. Punch down dough and knead for about 10 minutes, until silky and smooth. Rub with 1 tablespoon olive oil, place back in bowl, and cover. Let rise again until doubled in bulk, $1\frac{1}{2}$ to 2 hours.

4. Lightly oil two $9 \times 5 \times 2\frac{3}{4}$-inch loaf pans. Place a heatproof pan of water on the bottom of the oven and preheat oven to 450°F. Remove

dough from bowl and gently punch down to original size on a lightly floured surface. Divide dough into two portions with a knife and shape into loaves. Place loaves in prepared pans. Cover and let rise again in a warm place until almost doubled in bulk.

5. When dough has almost doubled in bulk, brush surface with water and gently draw a sharp knife down the center of each loaf. Bake for 35 to 40 minutes, or until bread is golden brown and bottom rings hollow when removed from pan and tapped.

Yield: 2 loaves

Note: To make *prozymi,* save a fistful of dough from the previous preparation of bread (I store mine sealed in the refrigerator) and dilute it in warm water as you do packaged dry yeast. Or, to prepare it from scratch, mix 1 part flour to 1 part water and add a pinch of salt and sugar. Cover and let it ferment for 3 to 5 days, depending on the degree of pungency desired. Either way makes for a dense, hearty loaf.

Paximathia

THESE are the coarse, thick, toasted wedges of bread sold in bakeries all over Greece and enjoyed with a bit of marmalade or cheese as the standard breakfast fare. They are usually baked overnight, when bakers' ovens—especially the traditional, wood-burning ovens—aren't fired up but are warm enough so that the wedges of half-cooked bread dry out slowly, hardening without turning so brittle that they crumble. The secret to good *paximathia* is to bake them slowly enough to achieve the same effect. They are excellent dampened and broken into salads.

In bygone times, women made bread every ten to fifteen days, and turned most of it into thick dry wedges of toast as a way to preserve it. The *paximathi* was the traditional bread of the Greek farmer, who would take it into the fields, soak it in some water and oil, and eat it, often with little more than a few olives and some homemade cheese.

In Greek specialty stores throughout the United States as well as in bakeries all over Greece, the best *paximathia* are from Crete, made with barley, or the *eptazymo,* made with chick-peas. To make *paximathia* at home:

Prepare either *horiatiko psomi* (page 48) or *eptazymo* (page 56). When bread is rising in the bread pan, let it swell to slightly more than double in bulk. Using a pastry cutter or sharp knife, cut a row of $1\frac{1}{2}$- to 2-inch wedges in each loaf. Bake as for either bread, but remove from oven when half done. Cool loaves in pan completely. When loaves are cool, preheat oven to 170°F. Break off the wedges, place them on an ungreased cookie sheet, and bake slowly for 6 to 7 hours, or until hard and golden brown. If a deep golden brown color is desired, remove *paximathia* from cookie sheet and place them on oven rack just before removing from oven. Raise temperature to 350°F and bake for 5 to 7 minutes longer, turning once on each side.

Yield: About 1 dozen

Thoxistiko Artos or Prosforon

(HOLY BREAD)

ALSO known in Greek as the *andithoron,* "in lieu of the gift," referring to Holy Communion, *prosforon,* or offering, is made by women and used during the Greek Orthodox liturgy. It is made in exactly the same way as *horiatiko* (page 48), except that the oil is omitted (replace it with $\frac{1}{4}$ cup water).

Traditionally, this is a round loaf of ordinary *horiatiko* scored in the middle before baking, almost forming two layers, which symbolize the dual nature of Christ. The bread is stamped with a holy seal (see illustration). When preparing, keep the seal firmly placed over top of bread while it's rising so that the design is embedded.

Psomi Polytelias

(DELUXE OR "LUXURY" BREAD)

THE distinction between grades of flour and types of bread dates to antiquity. A more refined flour, even though its nutritive value may be less, has always been the preference, hence more expensive. In commercial bakeries in Greece, *polytelias* is made with highly refined flour. The distinction in home-baked breads is usually in terms of what goes into the loaf. Here, milk makes this bread "deluxe."

*2 envelopes active dry
   yeast
2 tablespoons sugar
½ cup warm water
4 tablespoons olive oil,
   plus 2 teaspoons for
   oiling pans
2 cups milk, scalded,
   then cooled to warm
6 to 8 cups bread flour
2 teaspoons salt
1 egg yolk (optional)*

1. In a large bowl, dissolve yeast and sugar in the warm water. Cover with a cloth or towel and let rest in a warm place 30 minutes to 1 hour, until yeast begins to proof (you'll see little bubbles forming at the top).

2. Combine 3 tablespoons of the olive oil with the warm milk and add to yeast mixture. Add 6 cups flour and salt to liquid, stirring with a wooden spoon until you can't mix it any longer. Dough will be wet and sticky.

3. Turn out onto a floured surface and work in remaining flour, a little at a time, until dough is no longer sticky. Knead for at least 10 minutes, adding more flour if necessary, until dough becomes smooth and silky to the touch. Form into a ball.

4. With remaining 1 tablespoon olive oil, lightly grease a large glass bowl. Roll dough in bowl so that all surfaces are well oiled. Cover with a cloth or towel and place in a warm place to rise until doubled in bulk (about 2 hours).

5. Punch down dough to original size and knead slightly. Place back in bowl, cover, and let rise again until almost doubled in bulk.

6. With remaining 2 teaspoons olive oil, lightly grease two 9×5 ×2¾-inch loaf pans. When dough has risen for second time, punch down again and divide into two portions with a knife. Shape into loaves and place loaves in prepared pans. Cover pans and let dough rise again until almost doubled in bulk.

7. Preheat oven to 400°F. Make several small slits in surface of dough and brush with egg yolk (optional, for a shiny appearance). Bake for 40 to 50 minutes, or until bread is golden brown and bottom sounds hollow when tapped.

8. Remove pans from oven and immediately remove loaves from pans. Let cool on racks. Serve warm or cold.

Yield: 2 loaves

Mediterranean Pitta Bread

PITTA bread may be frozen after completely cooled.

---

1. In a small bowl, dissolve yeast and sugar in 1 cup of the warm water. Cover with a cloth or towel and let stand in a warm place for 10 to 15 minutes; it will bubble.

2. Combine 6 cups of the flour and salt in a large bowl. Make a well in center. Add remaining 1 cup warm water, melted butter, and yeast mixture; mix with a wooden spoon until a sticky dough forms.

3. Turn out dough onto a lightly floured surface and knead, adding more flour if necessary, until dough becomes soft and silky to the touch. Shape into a ball and let rise, covered, in a lightly oiled bowl until doubled in bulk, $1\frac{1}{2}$ to 2 hours.

4. Punch down dough and let it rest for 20 minutes. In the meantime, dust two or three baking sheets or individual 9-inch round pans with cornmeal.

5. Divide dough with a knife into 10 to 12 balls. Roll out each ball into an 8-inch circle and place circles on baking pans, leaving about 1 inch between them. Cover with a cloth or towel and let rest again for 30 minutes.

6. Preheat oven to 500°F. Put first sheet on bottom of oven and leave for 3 to 5 minutes, until *pitta* bread has expanded into a bubble. Transfer to rack in middle of oven and bake for another 3 to 5 minutes. Remove and repeat with remaining circles. Let *pitta* cool.

2 envelopes active dry yeast
1 teaspoon sugar
2 cups warm water
6 to 7 cups bread flour
2 teaspoons salt
5 tablespoons butter, melted
Cornmeal

Yield: 10 to 12 individual *pittas*

Whole Wheat Pitta: Dissolve yeast, sugar, and 1 teaspoon honey in $1\frac{1}{4}$ cups of the warm water; cover and let stand in a warm place for about 10 minutes. Follow directions from step 2 above, using 3 cups bread flour and 3 cups whole wheat flour and omitting salt. Substitute $\frac{1}{4}$ cup olive oil for butter.

Yield: 10 to 12 individual *pittas*

Eliopitta

(CLASSIC CYPRIOT OLIVE BREAD)

CYPRIOTS call this a *pitta* to denote its relative flatness, but it bears little resemblance to the savory pies Greeks refer to as *pitta*. This is bread, indeed. The olives are sometimes added unpitted.

$3\frac{1}{2}$ *to 4 cups flour (preferably bread flour)*

1 tablespoon baking powder

Salt, to taste

$\frac{3}{4}$ *cup water*

$\frac{1}{4}$ *cup olive oil*

1 tablespoon dried mint

1 cup finely chopped onion

2 cups rinsed, whole, pitted amphissa olives

1 egg yolk (optional; see Note)

1. Preheat oven to 375°F. Lightly oil a 10×2-inch round baking pan.

2. In a large bowl, sift together flour, baking powder, and salt. Make a well in center. Add water, olive oil, mint, onion, and olives. Stir with a wooden spoon until dough is formed, then turn out dough onto a lightly floured surface. Knead until dough is smooth, about 10 minutes. (Because of the moisture in the olives, the dough will be moist, but it shouldn't stick to your hands.) Cover dough and let rest for 10 minutes.

3. Shape dough into a ball and pat down gently with palms to fit evenly into baking pan. Bake for 50 minutes to 1 hour, or until surface is golden brown. Remove pan from oven and immediately remove bread from pan. Let cool on a rack before serving.

Yield: 1 loaf

Note: For a glossy crust, brush bread with egg yolk about 15 minutes before end of baking period.

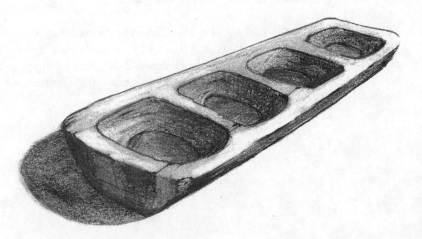

Olive Bread II

1. In a medium-size bowl, mix together warm water and yeast. Let stand 10 minutes.

2. In a large bowl, combine 3 cups each of whole wheat and bread flour, salt, orange rind, and thyme. Make a well in center.

3. Add yeast mixture, olive oil, orange juice, and ouzo to center of well. Add olives. Stir with a wooden spoon until all ingredients are combined, then turn out dough onto a floured surface and knead for about 10 minutes, adding some of remaining flour if necessary, until a smooth, silky dough is formed.

4. Lightly oil a large bowl and place dough in it. Cover and let stand in a warm, draft-free place until doubled in bulk, about 2 hours.

5. Preheat oven to 400°F. Lightly oil two $9 \times 5 \times 2\frac{3}{4}$-inch loaf pans. Gently punch down dough to original size and divide into two portions with a knife. Shape dough into two loaves. Place in prepared loaf pans, cover, and let stand again until doubled in bulk. Brush tops of loaves with water, gently draw a knife down center of dough, and bake for 45 to 50 minutes, or until golden brown.

6. Remove pans from oven and immediately remove loaves from pans. Let cool on wire rack.

Yield: 2 loaves

2 cups warm water
1 package active dry yeast
3 to 4 cups whole wheat flour
3 to 4 cups bread flour
2 teaspoons salt
1 tablespoon plus 1 teaspoon finely grated orange rind
2 teaspoons thyme
$\frac{1}{4}$ cup olive oil
1 tablespoon strained fresh orange juice
2 tablespoons ouzo
$1\frac{1}{2}$ cups rinsed, pitted, and coarsely chopped kalamata olives

Eptazymo

(CHICK-PEA BREAD)

SEVERAL years ago, when beginning the research for this book, an acquaintance in Athens who had helped in a study of cardiovascular disease in the Mediterranean sent me to a teacher and his family in a small village near Iráklion, Crete. There, she said, I'd find the most natural way of living she'd ever seen. I arrived unannounced one Sunday afternoon in early September when the family was just sitting down to dinner, and I had a meal that came straight from their garden. From the salad to the wine, to the very wheat used to make the bread we were eating, all was homegrown and pure. Like most villagers in Greece, the family had an outdoor wood-burning oven specifically for baking bread. It was here that the teacher's wife baked kilo after kilo of a bread I was to try for the first time but would never forget—*eptazymo.*

Eptazymo means "kneaded seven times" because traditionally it was made only at night when family and neighbors slept, and kneaded once every hour in a special room for bread baking, usually in the cellar of most village homes. Housewives never told anyone they were planning to make *eptazymo,* for fear that its difficult preparation would be jinxed. Hence, the reason for preparing it during the lonely hours between midnight and dawn. It's a bread unique to Crete and to Khalkidiki, in Macedonia, and is frequently made into *paximathia,* which can be found in most Greek and Middle Eastern stores throughout the United States. This recipe comes from a Cretan woman in Astoria, who manages to make an excellent *eptazymo* during the day, contrary to superstition, and in the gas-burning environment of a standard American stove. You will need a large ovenproof clay pot or bowl and a piece of woolen fabric large enough to wrap around it.

$\frac{3}{4}$ *cup dried chick-peas*
$2\frac{1}{2}$ *cups scalding water*
2 hot red peppers
10 to 12 cups bread flour
$\frac{3}{4}$ *cup hot, but not scalding, water*
1 heaping tablespoon salt
$\frac{1}{2}$ *teaspoon ground cinnamon*
$\frac{1}{4}$ *cup olive oil*

1. Preheat oven to 500°F at least 1 hour before you begin to prepare bread. Turn it off as soon as chick-pea mixture is ready, but oven must be hot.

2. Grind raw chick-peas to a coarse meal in the food processor.

3. Pour the scalding water into a clay bowl. Add hot peppers and ground chick-peas, mixing with a wooden spoon. Cover the bowl with its lid, wrap the bowl with a woolen blanket or cloth, and place inside hot but turned-off oven. Let stand for 7 hours.

4. After 7 hours (it's best to do this overnight), measure $1\frac{1}{2}$ to 2 cups bread flour into a large bowl and make a well in center. Remove clay pot from oven and discard the hot peppers. Add $\frac{3}{4}$ cup hot water along with chick-pea mixture to center of flour. Mix with a wooden spoon. Cover the flour bowl with a woolen cloth and let stand in a warm draft-free place until doubled in bulk, $1\frac{1}{2}$ to 2 hours. The mixture will be gummy, even as it rises.

5. Lightly oil two $9\times5\times2\frac{3}{4}$-inch bread pans.

6. In a large bowl, stir together 8 cups flour, salt, and cinnamon, making a well in center. Add olive oil and chick-pea mixture, and a little water if necessary. Turn out onto a floured surface (using remaining flour), and knead for about 10 minutes. Divide dough into two portions with a knife, shape into two even loaves, and place in bread pans.

7. Preheat oven to 375°F. Cover loaves with a loose cloth and let rise again in a warm, draft-free place until almost doubled in bulk, 1 to 2 hours. Brush with a little water and bake for 45 to 50 minutes, or until bread is golden brown and rings hollow on bottom when removed from pan and tapped. Remove at once from pans and cool on racks.

Yield: 2 loaves

Lagana

(FLAT, WIDE LENTEN BREAD)

LAGANA is a special Greek bread, flat and wide and eaten but one day a year, on Clean Monday at the start of Lent. Traditionally, *lagana* was unleavened, but now commercial bakers use yeast in its preparation. I learned to make this from a local baker in my neighborhood in Athens.

Lagana claims another tradition that also dates to antiquity—it's never cut with a knife, but broken off by hand, as iron connotes evil forces among superstitious Greeks.

---

3 envelopes active dry yeast
$\frac{1}{4}$ cup sugar
7 to 8 cups bread flour
$2\frac{1}{4}$ cups warm water
1 tablespoon salt
5 tablespoons butter or margarine, melted and slightly cooled
Olive oil
Sesame seeds

1. In a medium-size bowl, dissolve yeast, sugar, and $\frac{1}{4}$ cup of the bread flour in warm water. Cover with a cloth and let stand for about 15 minutes, until mixture begins to bubble.

2. In a large bowl, stir together 7 cups flour and salt, making a well in center. Pour melted butter into well and add yeast mixture. Stir well with a wooden spoon until mixture can't be stirred any longer and all ingredients are combined.

3. Dust work surface with some of remaining flour. Turn dough out onto floured surface and knead for about 10 minutes, adding more flour if necessary, until dough is smooth and silky to the touch.

4. Shape dough into a ball. Rub with olive oil. Place in a large bowl and cover with a cloth. Let stand for about 2 hours in a warm, draft-free place until doubled in bulk.

5. When dough has risen, remove from bowl and knead again on a lightly floured surface, down to original size, for 6 to 7 minutes. Dough should be soft—not sticky—and warm. Divide dough into 2 equal balls and shape each into a small loaf, about 6 inches in length.

6. Lightly oil 2 baking sheets. With a rolling pin (preferably a studded one), roll out each loaf into a flat oval shape about 15 inches long and 6 inches wide. Place on baking sheets. Brush with olive oil and sprinkle with sesame seeds. Cover and let rise until almost doubled in bulk, 45 to 50 minutes. Preheat oven to 450°F while dough is rising.

7. Bake each *lagana* for about 30 minutes, until deep golden brown on the outside. Remove baking sheets from oven and immediately remove loaves to a wire rack to cool.

Yield: 2 loaves

Koulouria Thessalonikis

(SESAME-COVERED BREAD RINGS,
SALONIKA STYLE)

THE equivalent of pretzels, these are the famous bread rings sold on street corners throughout Greece. They keep for several days.

---

1. In a medium-size bowl, stir together 1 cup of the flour, the sugar, salt, yeast, and warm water. Beat with a wooden spoon until a sticky mass has formed. Add ½ cup remaining flour and work into dough with hands. Sprinkle work surface with remaining ½ cup flour and turn out dough. Knead until all of flour is absorbed and dough is silky to the touch, 7 to 8 minutes. Cover and let rest for 5 minutes.

2. Mix together egg white and 2 tablespoons water.

3. With a knife, divide dough into quarters. Roll each quarter into a pencil-thin rod 20 to 24 inches long, being careful not to break dough. Cut into halves or thirds; shape each piece into a ring 7 to 8 inches in diameter. In the meantime, preheat oven to 375°F. Sprinkle several baking sheets with cornmeal. Place rings on baking sheets and let rise 20 to 25 minutes.

4. Brush each ring with the egg and water mixture and sprinkle generously with sesame seeds. (The entire surface should almost be covered with sesame seeds.) Bake for 15 minutes. Remove baking sheets from oven and immediately remove rings to a wire rack to cool.

2 cups bread flour
1 teaspoon sugar
1 teaspoon salt
1 envelope active dry
  yeast
⅔ cup warm water
1 egg white
2 tablespoons water
Cornmeal
Sesame seeds

Yield: 8 to 12 *koulouria*

Lalangia

(FRIED BREAD DOUGH)

A CHRISTMAS specialty from Mani, but also found in other areas of the Peloponnisos, *lalangia* probably date to antiquity.

Folklore has it that the pleasing scent that wafts up the chimney as the *lalangia* fry wards off the mischievous imps that inhabit the earth between the name day of St. Phillip on November 14 (the start of the pre-Christmas fast) and January 6, the Day of the Epiphany. The *lalangia* traditionally are made on Christmas Eve and either sprinkled with cheese and eaten with roasted meat or doused with honey and consumed as a sweet.

To prepare *lalangia,* you'll need a dough for *horiatiko psomi* (page 48). After the second rising, break off large pieces—about the size of a kiwi—and roll into pencil-thin strips 12 to 15 inches long. Tie into knots or nooses and deep-fry in ample, very hot oil until ruddy colored and crisp. Eat hot or cold.

Yield: 1 *horiatiko psomi* recipe yields about 3 dozen *lalangia*

Tsoureki or Lambropsomo

(EASTER BREAD)

THERE are many, slightly differing varieties of *tsoureki,* the traditional Greek Easter bread. The word is Turkish, and means "that which is kneaded," and the bread probably arrived in Greece via Constantinople. The red eggs that decorate it, a custom adopted in Byzantium, symbolize the blood of Christ, as well as eternity and fertility. Three long dough ropes, symbolic of the Holy Trinity, are traditionally braided, and sometimes the loaf is sprinkled with sesame seeds or almond slivers, or decorated with dough designs.

1. Heat the 2 cups milk to scalding then cool to warm. In a large bowl, stir together the warm milk, the yeast, 1 cup of the flour, and $\frac{1}{4}$ cup of the sugar. Cover and let proof in a warm place for about 1 hour.

2. In a large bowl, sift together 7 cups flour, salt, and remaining sugar. Add orange and lemon rind. Cut butter into flour with a fork or your fingers. Make a well in center. Add yeast mixture, eggs, *mastic*, and *mahlepi*. Stir with a wooden spoon until a dough begins to form. Turn out onto a lightly floured surface and knead, adding remaining flour a little at a time if necessary, for 10 to 15 minutes, until dough is soft and silky to the touch. Place in a buttered bowl, cover, and let rise until doubled in bulk, 1 to 2 hours.

3. Punch down dough to original size and remove a fistful of dough to be used for decorating *tsoureki*. With a knife, divide dough into 6 small balls and roll each into a strip 12 to 15 inches long and about $1\frac{1}{2}$ inches in diameter. Lay 3 strips side by side and pinch together at one end. Braid the strips, pinching them together at the bottom end, and then form the braid into a ring, pressing together both ends. Press dyed eggs into dough. Secure them from popping out by rolling little ropes of remaining dough and forming a ring around the base of each egg and over the top in the shape of a cross. Repeat procedure for second *tsoureki*. Place on a lightly buttered baking sheet, cover, and let rise until nearly doubled in bulk, about 2 hours.

4. While braids are rising, preheat oven to 375°F and stir together egg yolk and 2 to 3 tablespoons milk in a small bowl.

5. When *tsourekia* have risen, brush with egg yolk mixture. Bake for 40 to 45 minutes, or until rich golden brown and hollow sounding when tapped on bottom. Remove baking sheet from oven and immediately remove *tsourekia* to wire racks to cool.

Yield: 2 round loaves

Note: Mahlepi, mastic, and red dye can be found in Greek and Middle Eastern specialty shops.

2 cups plus 2 to 3 tablespoons milk

2 envelopes active dry yeast

8 to 10 cups bread flour

$1\frac{1}{2}$ to $1\frac{3}{4}$ cups sugar

$\frac{1}{2}$ teaspoon salt

Grated rind of 1 small orange

Grated rind of 1 small lemon

$\frac{1}{4}$ pound unsalted butter

5 eggs, very well beaten

2 teaspoons finely ground mastic (see Note)

2 teaspoons mahlepi, dissolved in $\frac{1}{4}$ cup boiling water and strained (see Note)

4 to 8 dyed red eggs (optional; see page 269)

1 egg yolk, slightly beaten

2 to 3 tablespoons milk

Vassilopitta

(ST. BASIL'S BREAD)

VASSILOPITTA is the Greek New Year's bread. A coin is inserted before baking, and whoever gets the slice with the coin is supposed to have good luck in the coming year. In some parts of Greece, such as Epirus, another ancient but still popular custom is to insert a piece of straw or a miniature plough into the bread, as well as a coin. Whoever gets the coin will, of course, have good luck for his person; whoever bites into the plough or straw will enjoy good luck for his crops.

There are dozens of slightly varying recipes for *vassilopitta* in Greek cookery. There is a distinction made between *vassilopitta moraitiko*, from the Peloponnisos, and *vassilopitta politiko* or *smyrnaiko*, from Constantinople and Smyrna, respectively. *Moraitiko* is flavored with orange and lemon, omitting the mahlepi and mastic found in the eastern versions. In Thessaly, the bread traditionally wasn't sweet at all; in other parts of Greece it was customarily a kind of meat pie. Sometimes Greeks just make an orange-flavored cake in celebration of the New Year. Most commonly, though, *vassilopitta* is similar to *tsoureki*, without the dyed eggs.

To make *vassilopitta*, follow the recipe for *tsoureki* (page 60) through step 2. Punch down to original size and knead for 5 to 7 minutes. The dough should be silky. Then divide the dough into 2 equal-size balls, form into 2 mounds, and spread gently into two large buttered baking pans. Let it rise again, brush with egg yolk and sesame seeds, and bake at 375°F for about 40 minutes, until deep golden brown in color.

Christopsomo

(CHRISTMAS FRUIT BREAD)

CHRISTOPSOMO is one of the most traditional Greek breads. Whole unshelled walnuts are sometimes used in decorating the bread, as are sesame seeds and almond slivers. Until not very long ago in Macedonia, the baker (usually the woman of the house) would make an imprint with her own hand on the top of the bread before baking

it and would tell her children that Jesus visited and blessed the loaf
while it was baking.

---

1. In a medium-size bowl, combine raisins, apricots, and figs. Cover
with water and let stand for 1 hour to soften.

2. Combine yeast, $\frac{1}{2}$ cup of the warm water, 1 teaspoon of the sugar,
and $\frac{1}{4}$ cup of the flour and let stand for 30 minutes to proof. Mixture
will be bubbly. In a separate bowl, sift together 6 cups of the flour and
salt and set aside until ready to use. Remove dried fruits with a slotted
spoon and have them ready for next step.

3. In a large bowl and with an electric mixer at high speed, beat the
four eggs until frothy. Add remaining $\frac{3}{4}$ cup sugar a little at a time and
continue beating. Pour in yeast mixture and blend well. Slowly add
1 cup milk and the butter, beating all the while. Add 2 to 3 cups of
the sifted flour in half-cup increments and stir to blend with a wooden
spoon.

4. Add pignoli nuts, chopped walnuts or almonds, orange rind, and
dried fruit to the egg mixture and stir with a wooden spoon. Continue
adding flour, stirring with a wooden spoon, and then kneading by hand
when a dough mass begins to form. Turn dough out onto a lightly
floured surface and knead, adding more flour as needed, until a soft,
malleable but silky smooth dough has formed, about 12 to 15 minutes.
(The dough will be quite dense, and you may want to divide it in half
and work with each half one at a time.) Place dough in bowl, rub with
1 tablespoon olive oil, turning to coat all sides, cover with a cloth, and
let rise in a warm, draft-free place until double in bulk, 2 to 3 hours.

5. Punch down dough to original size. Rub with remaining olive
oil and let rise again until almost double in bulk, about 1 hour. Lightly
oil two large baking sheets.

6. Punch down dough again and divide into two equal balls. Save
a fistful of dough from each ball for decorating the loaves. Shape each
large dough ball into a neat, round loaf, about 8 inches in diameter.
Press five unshelled walnuts in each of the doughs, at four points with
one in the center. Using leftover fists of dough, roll out thin ropes
about $\frac{1}{2}$ inch wide and coil around each of the walnuts to secure them.
Preheat oven to 350°F. Let dough stand, covered, for another 40 to 45
minutes.

7. In a small bowl and using a fork, beat together egg yolk and milk.
Brush over each of the loaves, and bake for 45 minutes to 1 hour, or
until golden brown. Remove loaves from oven and cool on wire racks.

Yield: 2 loaves, about 10 inches each in diameter

*1 cup combined dark
and golden seedless
raisins*

*$\frac{1}{2}$ cup chopped dried
apricots*

*$\frac{1}{2}$ cup chopped dried
figs*

*2 packages active dry
yeast*

1 cup warm water

*1 teaspoon plus $\frac{3}{4}$ cup
sugar*

*$6\frac{1}{4}$ to 8 cups
all-purpose flour*

1 teaspoon salt

*4 eggs, plus 1 yolk for
glaze*

*1 cup warm milk,
plus 2 tablespoons
for glaze*

*1 stick unsalted butter,
melted*

*$\frac{1}{2}$ cup lightly toasted
pignoli nuts*

*$\frac{3}{4}$ cup coarsely chopped
walnuts or blanched
almonds*

*1 tablespoon grated
orange rind, or
more to taste*

2 tablespoons olive oil

*10 whole, unshelled
walnuts for
decorating loaves*

Stafithopsomo

(RAISIN BREAD)

STAFITHOPSOMO is frequently sold in the form of buns or rolls in Greece, and is a favorite breakfast food. Here are recipes for two delicate loaves just as good for morning fodder.

1¼ cups warm water
1 envelope active dry yeast
5½ to 6½ cups bread flour
¼ cup plus 2 tablespoons sugar
2 cups dark seedless raisins
¾ cup milk, scalded, then cooled to warm
4 tablespoons butter, melted, plus 1 tablespoon for coating pans
2 teaspoons salt
Milk and 1 egg yolk for glaze (optional)

1. In a large bowl, combine warm water, yeast, 1½ cups of the flour, and 2 tablespoons of the sugar. Cover and let stand in a warm place to proof, about 1½ hours. Dust raisins with a little flour and set aside.

2. In a large bowl, combine warm milk, melted butter, ¼ cup sugar, and the salt. Add to yeast mixture. Add remaining 4 to 5 cups flour and raisins, a little at a time, and mix with a wooden spoon until dough begins to form.

3. Turn dough out onto a floured surface and knead for 10 minutes, or until it becomes smooth and silky to the touch. Place in a buttered bowl, cover with a cloth, and let rise until doubled in bulk, 2 to 2½ hours.

4. Lightly butter two 9 × 5 × 2¾-inch bread pans. Remove dough from bowl. Punch down to original size. With a knife, divide into two loaves. Place loaves in bread pans, cover with cloth or towel, and let rise until nearly doubled in bulk, 1½ to 2 hours. In the meantime, preheat oven to 400°F.

5. Brush each loaf with a little milk or a combination of milk and egg yolk (optional, for a shiny crust). Bake for about 45 minutes, or until bread is golden brown. Remove pans from oven and immediately remove loaves to a wire rack to cool. Cool before slicing.

Yield: 2 loaves

Part II

MEZEDES (APPETIZERS)

Chapter 4

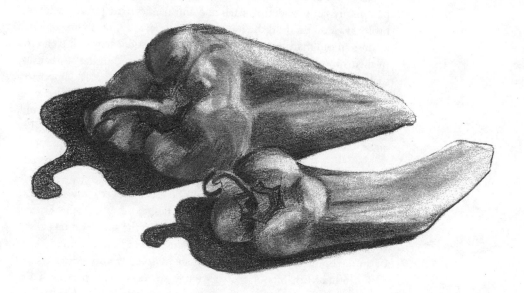

Introduction to the Meze

You're in Athens. Midafternoon. The city is hot and dusty and you're looking for a place that's quiet and silent and cool. What you want is on Pandrossou Street, in a refurbished stoa, past an artisan's model of a trireme and handcrafted pottery and embroidery. You head up the stairs to a small balcony, sit down, and lean against an old marbletop table. Newspapers rustle. Men with cigarettes in their mouths look at you once, to see if you're familiar to them. A surly waiter approaches and without speaking pours a clear, liquorice-scented liquid into your glass. A small dish accompanies it, filled with the crispest cucumber you've ever had, an olive or two, and a chunk of kasseri cheese pinned with a toothpick to a wedge of bread. The *meze*.

You're in Euboea, an enormous island that stretches along the coast of the Greek mainland, from Attica to Thessaly, walking by the fishermen's piers. On a clothesline outside nearly every taverna is an unlikely specimen for drying—the taut, flesh-colored octopus, its tentacles almost weblike as it basks and hardens in the sun. You take a seat by the sea. Out comes another surly waiter, soon bringing an icy beer, or an ouzo, or a chilled glass of resinated wine. He also carries a small plate dotted with bits of that octopus—so succulent—perhaps a luscious tomato flecked with sea salt, and a pungent dollop of *tzatziki*—yogurt mixed with cucumber and garlic. The *meze*.

It's winter and a blanket of snow has covered the village you are visiting. You've always wanted to spend a winter in an old town in the mountains. Pine-scented smoke billows from the chimneys. People are friendly and curious, but the streets are empty because of the cold, and you wander over to Niko's or to Christo's or to any of the homes of your new friends. A burlap bag hangs above the fireplace; a goatskin, rounded and seemingly stuffed, sits nearby; the pleasant smell of dough drifts from the oven; and a carafe of dark, rich wine waits on the table. You didn't come for any particular reason except to seek out some company as the winter fog begins to roll in and night starts to settle. Niko's wife removes a pinkish ball of cheese from the goatskin. It's called *touloumi,* a cheese. Niko slices off a bit of what's in the burlap bag—ham, smoking slowly, that will last the winter. The glasses are already on the table. A *pitta* is in the oven. You sit down, glad for the offerings and the company, indulging in what Greeks call a little *mezedaki.*

I can't illustrate what the real meaning of the *meze* is any better than with examples of how they are eaten. The word is actually Turkish, but the concept is quintessentially Greek. The *meze* is a tidbit of food, a bite-size offering of almost anything savory, from a simple salted cucumber to a bit of rich stew cut up into small pieces and served on a small plate. It's a sampling of food to help any game imbiber enjoy some wine or ouzo, and it's crucial to the table, for Greeks never drink without eating, and rarely drink without company.

There are *krasomezedes* and *ouzomezedes*—those that go well with wine *(krasi)* and those that counter ouzo nicely, but the difference is subjective. There is also the *bekri meze,* or "morsels for a hard drinker," which is usually a plate of red spicy stew cut up into small pieces. But more specifically, there are three categories of *mezedes* (plural) or *mezedakia* (plural and diminutive) served up on the Greek table: hot or cooked *mezedes;* dips and spreads; and salads, pickles, and vegetable *mezedes.* Cheese and olives and bread suffice if nothing else is in the cupboards, but usually there's a plateful of something on hand. And one may call any of the above by the Greek name for appetizer—*orektiko.*

Hot or Cooked *Mezedes:* The two most common to the Greek table are *tyropittakia*—little cheese triangles—and *keftedes,* or meatballs. Although one might find these at tavernas or ouzeries, they are more the domain of home cooks with the patience to fold up a tray's worth of *phyllo* strips for the cheese pies or to roll miniature meatball after miniature meatball and to fry them a few at a time. Shellfish, especially clams and mussels, are also popular *mezedes,* especially in Salonika and other parts of northern Greece. And *pitta,* or savory pie, although included in the main courses, really teeters between main meal and *meze.*

Dips and Spreads. There is a quartet of dips and spreads without which a night out at a taverna would be incomplete. They are *tzatziki,* a yogurt, garlic, cucumber, and dill mélange that appears in varying forms from the Balkans all the way to India; *melitzanosalata,* eggplant, garlic, olive oil, and lemon, and oftentimes more, pounded to a pulp, traditionally in a mortar but today usually whipped smooth in a blender; and *skordalia,* which falls between sauce and spread, depending on the predilection of the cook. It's a pungent puree of unbounded garlic—sometimes more than twenty cloves—potato or bread, olive oil and vinegar, and it's partnered at table with batter-fried cod or shark, boiled greens, or earthy beets. *Taramosalata,* or carp roe puree, completes the quartet. The last is grainy roe, mashed potato, ample olive oil, and lemon pureed in a blender. What results is the flesh-colored spread that is a tradition—eaten with scallions and fresh garlic—on Clean Monday at the start of Lent, but also a common dish all year. Of course there are many things to work up in a blender or with a mortar and pestle enjoyed by the Greeks as spreads. Olive puree is probably the province of new Greek cooks. *Htipiti,* a tart spread of strong feta and oregano, is territory for the diehards, as is *rengosalata*—a dip similar to *taramosalata* but made with the salty roe of a smoked herring.

Salads, Pickles, and Side-Dish Vegetables. I can't think of anything I like to eat more in Greece than fresh lettuce in the springtime, tomatoes in the summer, wild grilled mushrooms and sweet red peppers in the fall, and cabbage, shredded and smarting, in the winter. There is something about Greece's dry climate and overwhelming sunshine that makes her produce so luscious. And Greeks, sticklers that they are, adhere to the laws of the seasons, rarely eating anything out of its time. Their salads are fresh and many, but they also enjoy a seasoned hand at pickling. *Tursi* is the name for the briny concoctions of stuffed baby eggplant, whole-leaf cabbage, small green peppers, hyacinth bulbs and onions, and mushrooms that make up some of best-loved pickles. The city of Volos and its environs are famous for the art of pickling in Greece, and are also reputed to have some of the best ouzeries in the country. On Cyprus there is an interesting cauliflower pickle called the *mougra,* which is made by blanching the cauliflower, dipping it in a sour yeast batter, and storing it, with horseradish, in a jug of olive oil. My favorite, but unfortunately not included here, are the *tsitsiravla,* or the delicate, fennel-tinged pickle made from the blossoms of the wild pistachio tree, and which is a specialty of Volos.

In the pages that follow, I've given recipes and details about the many dishes that fall under the general heading of *meze*. There is no particular way to serve most of them, except to pick and choose the ones you like best and to lay them out at table, often together with the main course. Greeks like to eat a little of everything at once, and to drink and be merry, and enjoy life, mostly in the company of friends. "Food brings on the appetite," goes an old Greek saying, and that, to me, is the gist of the *meze*.

Chapter 5

Hot or Cooked Mezedes

Tyropittakia

(SAVORY CHEESE TRIANGLES)

A NOTE on *tyropittes:* The traditional recipe for this most Greek of *mezedes* is a simple combination of feta or mitzithra cheese (page 32), eggs, nutmeg, and sometimes mint. American Greeks use cream cheese in the filling, which is almost unheard of in Greece, and the use of several cheeses at once is a relatively new phenomenon. Also, the quantity of eggs may vary by one or two depending on the type and quality of feta used. Good Greek home economists, ever cautious of their pocketbooks, tend to buy *trimmata,* or the barrel residuals of the cheese, which are a little less expensive. I happen to like the softer variety of feta and fewer eggs, but with these recipes in particular, there is much room for experimentation.

Tyropittakia and *bourekakia* (page 72) are served piping hot just out of the oven or fryer. They're both Greek finger food—or toothpick food, at best—and should be passed around on a tray or platter. Both *tyropittakia* and *bourekakia* may be frozen and then baked or fried days later.

---

1. *For either filling:* Combine cheeses, pepper, herbs and spices, olive oil or butter, and well-beaten eggs in a large bowl. Blend very well with a fork or wooden spoon. Refrigerate, covered, for at least 1 hour before using.

2. *For packaged phyllo or strudel:* Preheat oven to 350°F. Unroll phyllo or strudel sheets and cut into thirds, lengthwise. Place a damp cloth over pastry to protect it from drying out. Remove one strip at a time. Brush with butter or olive oil. Fold right-hand side inward. Place 1 teaspoon filling in middle bottom of strip. Fold right corner up and to the left, forming a right angle. Fold the strip upward at right angles until you reach the end, to form a small triangle. Place on a cookie or baking sheet. Repeat with remaining pastry and filling, to create about 5 dozen triangles. Bake for about 20 minutes, turning each triangle once, until *tyropittakia* are golden brown.

Yield: About 5 dozen

Savory Cheese Pie may be baked whole in a pie dish or larger baking pan. Use either of the fillings above and follow the directions for making savory pie with either store-bought thin phyllo sheets, or homemade dough (page 112.)

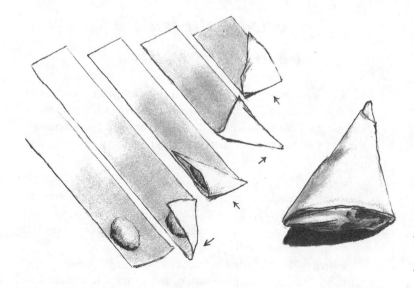

FILLING I
$\frac{3}{4}$ *pound feta, crumbled*
$\frac{1}{4}$ *pound Emmenthal or Swiss cheese, grated*
$\frac{1}{2}$ *cup grated Parmesan cheese*
$\frac{1}{2}$ *pound cream cheese*
Freshly ground pepper, to taste
Grating of nutmeg, to taste
Salt (optional, depending on saltiness of feta)
3 tablespoons olive oil or butter
3 eggs, well beaten
1 pound commercial phyllo pastry, or 1 recipe, doubled, for any homemade phyllo dough

FILLING II
$\frac{1}{2}$ *pound anthotiro*
1 pound feta, crumbled
$\frac{1}{4}$ *pound kefalograviera*
Freshly ground pepper
2 teaspoons dried mint
$\frac{1}{2}$ *teaspoon freshly grated nutmeg*
3 tablespoons olive oil or butter
2 to 3 eggs, well beaten
1 pound commercial phyllo pastry, or 1 recipe, doubled, for any homemade phyllo dough

Bourekakia

(FRIED, MINIATURE STUFFED DOUGHS)

*One recipe classic
phyllo dough (page
112; omit baking
powder), or 1 pound
commercial phyllo
pastry
Filling I or II for
tyropittakia (page
70), or filling for
spinach or meat pie
Olive or vegetable oil,
for frying*

If using store-bought phyllo, unroll sheets and prepare triangles with filling in exactly the same way as in *tyropittakia* (page 70). Heat oil to 360°F and deep-fry triangles, a few at a time, until they are crisp and golden brown.

If using homemade phyllo, divide dough into 4 to 6 equal balls and roll out each to a thin sheet. Using a round cookie cutter or glass, cut out circles 4 to 5 inches in diameter. Fill each with 1 teaspoon filling. Press closed to form crescents, pinching dough together either with wet fingers or a fork. Heat oil to smoking point and proceed as above. Place *bourekakia* on paper towels to rid them of excess oil.

Yield: About 5 dozen

Fried Keftedakia

(MINIATURE MEATBALLS)

*½ pound bread
1 pound lean ground
beef
2 tablespoons olive oil
1 cup finely chopped
onion
1 garlic clove, finely
chopped
3 to 4 eggs, slightly
beaten
¼ cup finely chopped
fresh parsley
3 tablespoons dried
mint
1 teaspoon oregano
¼ teaspoon cinnamon
¼ teaspoon grated
nutmeg
Flour
Olive oil, for frying*

... MORE Greek finger food. *Keftedakia,* be they of ground beef or lamb, chick-peas, fish roe, or tomatoes, make for an excellent *ouzomeze* (a tidbit that goes exceptionally well with the anise-flavored liqueur), but they are by no means limited to that. Serve with dry red wine, too.

1. To prepare bread (which preferably should be bakery bought), cut it into slices about ¾ inch thick. Run each slice quickly under the tap to dampen, then squeeze to wring out as much water as possible. Cut off crust if it's too hard.

2. In a large bowl, combine bread, meat, olive oil, onions, garlic, 3 eggs, parsley, mint, oregano, cinnamon, and nutmeg. Knead until all ingredients are well blended. If mixture seems dry (this might depend on the bread you use), add the fourth egg.

3. Shape 1 heaping teaspoon at a time of chopped meat mixture into small meatballs, about 1 inch in diameter.

4. Dredge meatballs in flour. Fill a large heavy skillet with about

an inch of vegetable oil and heat it almost to the smoking point. Fry *keftedakia,* a few at a time, turning constantly, until golden brown. Serve hot or cold.

Yield: About 100

Baked Keftedakia

FRIED *keftedes* are standard fare on any Greek party menu, but in the United States they've undergone a slight change. Many American Greeks, aware of the not-so-healthful aspects of fried foods, now bake their *keftedes.* This is a recipe that's become a traditional appetizer on my sister's Thanksgiving table.

1 recipe fried keftedakia (page 72)
¾ cup Parmesan cheese

1. Preheat oven to 375°F. Prepare the *keftedakia* through step 3.
2. Indent centers of each meatball with your thumb. Add a bit of grated cheese (about ¼ teaspoon) and seal into a ball again. Bake in a large ungreased pan for 12 to 15 minutes, turning the *keftedes* halfway through with a spatula or spoon. Remove pan from oven and place on a wire rack. Serve *keftedes* warm or cold.

Yield: About 100

Grilled Lamb Keftedes

1½ pounds minced lamb
1 egg, slightly beaten
3 tablespoons plain bread crumbs
2 cups finely chopped onion
2 garlic cloves, finely chopped
1½ teaspoons dried mint
1 tablespoon finely chopped fresh basil
3½ tablespoons finely chopped parsley
1 teaspoon ouzo, or ½ teaspoon anise extract
Salt and freshly ground pepper

1. Preheat broiler.
2. In a large bowl, knead together meat, egg, bread crumbs, onions, garlic, herbs, and ouzo until all ingredients are very well blended.
3. Take a tablespoon at a time and form patties about 2 inches in diameter. Place on a slotted broiler pan 6 to 8 inches from heat and grill for 8 to 10 minutes, turning once with a slotted spoon.

Yield: About 2 dozen

$1\frac{1}{4}$ cups peeled,
  chopped plum
  tomato (see Note)
$\frac{1}{2}$ cup finely chopped
  scallions
1 small to medium
  garlic clove, finely
  chopped
1 tablespoon finely
  chopped parsley
$\frac{1}{2}$ teaspoon oregano
$\frac{1}{4}$ teaspoon cinnamon
1 heaping teaspoon
  fresh mint
Salt and freshly
  ground pepper, to
  taste
1 cup all-purpose flour
1 teaspoon
  double-acting
  baking powder
Olive oil, for frying

Pseftokeftedes Santorini

(MOCK KEFTEDES, SANTORINI STYLE)

I LOVE this simple recipe for its color, which is like the crimson sunset of the island it hails from. Throughout the Aegean, one finds recipes similar to this, in which wild greens or onions or, as the case here, fresh tomatoes, are mixed with flour and herbs and fried into delicate, meatless *keftedes*. In the summer in Greece, it's one of the best *mezedakia* you can enjoy. Ouzo or a bone-dry Santorini white wine would be the perfect foil to the sweet but acidic tomato. Retsina, too, although an acquired taste to most, counters this dish nicely.

---

1. In a large bowl, combine tomatoes, scallions, garlic, herbs, and spices. Add flour and baking powder and mix together so that all ingredients are well blended and have the consistency of a thick batter (about as thick as pancake batter).
2. In a large heavy skillet, heat enough olive oil for frying. Taking a heaping tablespoon at a time, drop batter into hot oil and fry until golden brown and crisp.
3. Remove at once with a slotted spoon and drain on paper towels. Serve hot.

Yield: About 3 dozen

Note: In other islands, spinach or *horta* are often used instead of tomatoes. Follow instructions above, using $1\frac{1}{2}$ cups boiled, well-drained, chopped spinach, or any other greens.

$\frac{1}{4}$ cup tarama (carp roe)
$1\frac{1}{2}$ cups plain bread
  crumbs (see Note)
$\frac{1}{2}$ cup finely chopped
  onion
3 tablespoons finely
  chopped fresh
  parsley
1 tablespoon finely
  chopped fresh dill
1 heaping teaspoon
  dried mint
3 eggs
Flour, for dredging
Olive oil, for frying

Taramokeftedes

(FISH ROE KEFTEDES)

SOMEHOW, when one thinks of Lenten dishes, and this is a traditional one, retsina, light and subtle and chilled, should be in a glass nearby.

---

1. In a medium-size bowl, combine tarama, bread crumbs, onion, parsley, dill, mint, and eggs. Knead until all ingredients are well blended.

2. Taking a teaspoon at a time, shape mixture into little balls, $\frac{3}{4}$ to 1 inch in diameter. Dredge in flour.

3. Fill a large heavy skillet with about an inch of olive oil and heat to the smoking point. Add *taramokeftedes,* 6 or so at a time, and cook, turning constantly, until golden brown. Replenish oil if necessary.

4. Strain on a paper towel and serve warm, alone or with a side dish of *avgolemono* sauce (page 39).

Yield: About 3 dozen

Note: Two medium to large potatoes, boiled and mashed, can be substituted for the bread crumbs.

Revithokeftedes

(CHICK-PEA KEFTEDES)

CHICK-PEAS are a staple of the southern islands and of Cyprus. In Rhodes, they are used in these special *keftedes,* which are akin to Middle Eastern falafel.

1. Follow directions on package for soaking and softening chick-peas. Drain water and return chick-peas to pot. Sprinkle with baking soda and let stand for at least 15 minutes. Rub between fingers to remove husks, and rinse well with cold water.

2. Mix tahini with the hot water and work together with a spoon until tahini is softened, about 1 minute.

3. Grind chick-peas in food processor, a little at a time if necessary, to a coarse meal, 2 to 3 minutes. Add tahini mixture, chopped onion, and garlic and blend in food processor for another minute. Add egg, $\frac{1}{4}$ cup of the olive oil, the lemon juice, vinegar, paprika, cumin, dill, parsley, bread crumbs, salt, and pepper. Continue to blend in food processor until mixture is the consistency of a malleable paste.

4. A tablespoon at a time, form mixture into patties about $1\frac{1}{2}$ to 2 inches in diameter. (If desired, dredge with flour.) In a large heavy skillet, heat remaining $\frac{1}{4}$ cup olive oil to the smoking point, and fry chick-pea patties, flipping once, until golden brown.

Yield: About 3 dozen patties

Note: For convenience's sake, canned chick-peas may be used in place of dried. Rinse and drain well.

*½ pound raw
    chick-peas (see
    Note)*
*1 tablespoon baking
    soda*
½ tablespoon tahini
½ tablespoon hot water
*1 large onion, finely
    chopped*
*1 large clove garlic,
    finely chopped*
1 egg, slightly beaten
½ cup olive oil
*Strained fresh juice of
    1 lemon*
*½ tablespoon red wine
    vinegar*
1 teaspoon paprika
1½ teaspoons cumin
1 teaspoon dried dill
*3 tablespoons finely
    chopped fresh
    parsley*
*6 to 8 tablespoons
    plain bread crumbs*
*Salt and freshly
    ground pepper*
Flour (optional)

Salonika Mythia Yemista

(SALONIKA-STYLE STUFFED MUSSELS)

NOBODY quite knows why Salonika claims so many good *mezedes*—better seasoned, spicier, and more imaginative than their counterparts in other Greek cities. Here is one classic from Greece's "second city."

2½ to 3 pounds
   medium to large
   mussels
3 tablespoons olive oil
2 medium onions,
   finely chopped
   (about 1¾ cups)
½ cup whole-grain rice
Strained fresh juice of
   1 lemon
¼ cup dry white wine
1 large garlic clove,
   finely chopped
⅓ cup chopped fresh
   parsley
¼ cup finely chopped
   fresh dill
¾ tablespoon allspice
Pinch of sage
½ teaspoon dried
   marjoram
Salt and freshly
   ground pepper, to
   taste
1 pound baby shrimp,
   cleaned and shelled

1. Wash and scrub mussels very well to remove all sea matter from shells. In a large pot, bring 1 cup water to a boil. Add mussels. Cover and let simmer for 2 to 3 minutes, until shells have all opened and "the sea," as Greeks say, has been washed out. Remove at once, rinse, strain, and set aside.

2. Heat oil in a large heavy skillet. Sauté onions until translucent, 2 to 3 minutes, stirring frequently. Add rice, lower heat to medium, and continue to stir for another 3 to 4 minutes. Add half the lemon juice and half the wine. Stir in garlic, cover and simmer over low heat for another 5 to 7 minutes, until rice is softened but not cooked all the way through. Toss in shrimp, and add parsley, dill, allspice, sage, marjoram, salt, and pepper. Stir for another minute. Remove from heat.

3. Fill each mussel with 1 to 1½ teaspoons of rice stuffing. Close shells as much as possible, tying with thread if necessary. Place in skillet over remaining rice mixture. Pour in remaining lemon juice and wine, plus a little water if necessary. Simmer, covered, over low heat for 15 to 20 minutes, until rice is thoroughly cooked. Serve hot.

Yield: 6 servings

Mythia Pikantika

(PIQUANT MUSSEL STEW)

ALTHOUGH this recipe could easily be served as a main course, Greeks generally eat shellfish, especially mussels, as a *meze*. I've also found that it's the northern Greeks, particularly in Salonika, who relish mussels and clams, but the taverna that inspired this recipe happens to be in Holargo, a suburb of Athens.

---

1. Scrub shells with a hard brush and scrape off any debris. Rinse well in cold water. Place mussels in a large pot with enough water to cover. Cook on medium heat for 5 to 7 minutes, until mussels have opened. Discard water and rinse mussels well.

2. Heat olive oil in a large soup pot and sauté onion until translucent. Lower heat and add tomatoes, garlic, bay leaves, cinnamon, hot pepper, salt, pepper, and 1 cup water. Cover and simmer for 30 minutes, stirring occasionally.

3. After 30 minutes, stir in white wine. Uncover and simmer another 10 to 20 minutes, until sauce is thick. Stir in oregano and parsley. Stir mussels into sauce and cook for a few minutes, until hot. Place in a large bowl together with sauce and serve hot.

Yield: 6 to 8 servings

3 pounds mussels
3 tablespoons olive oil
1 large red onion, finely chopped (1 cup)
4 cups peeled, chopped plum tomato
3 garlic cloves, finely chopped
2 bay leaves
$\frac{1}{4}$ teaspoon ground cinnamon
1 to 3 hot red chile peppers, finely chopped, to taste (optional)
Salt and freshly ground pepper, to taste
1 cup white wine
1 tablespoon dried oregano
$\frac{1}{4}$ cup finely chopped parsley

Paradiso Stuffed Calamari

THIS dish comes from a favorite seaside taverna in Salonika. You will need toothpicks or a needle and thread to secure the stuffing.

---

3 pounds large whole squid (see Note)
¼ cup plus 1 tablespoon olive oil
1 cup finely chopped onion
1 large garlic clove, minced
1 pound feta cheese, crumbled or grated
1½ teaspoons oregano
½ teaspoon crushed red pepper (or more, to taste)
Strained fresh juice of 1 lemon
¼ cup finely chopped fresh parsley
Salt (optional, since feta is quite salty)

1. Heat grill or barbecue.
2. Clean squid thoroughly: Remove purplish outer sac from head and tentacles. Remove cartilage and sand bag on inside of squid and rinse thoroughly. Pull off mouth at other end and discard. Remove small tentacles and keep separate from squid body.
3. Finely chop tentacles. Heat 2 to 3 tablespoons olive oil in a skillet and sauté onion, stirring, until translucent. Add tentacles and garlic and sauté 4 to 5 minutes over medium heat, until onion is completely translucent and tentacles are softened.
4. In a medium-size bowl, combine feta, 1 tablespoon oregano, crushed red pepper, half of lemon juice, 1½ to 2 tablespoons olive oil, and parsley. Stir vigorously with a wooden spoon until feta is pasty and soft. Add onion mixture and combine well.
5. With a very small spoon or a butter knife, stuff squid, leaving ample room at top. (Squid will shrink under heat, so it's necessary to leave room in order to prevent them from bursting open.) Secure closed either with a toothpick or needle and thread. Place on a slotted broiler pan.
6. Stir together remaining olive oil, lemon juice, and oregano and brush over squid. Broil 8 inches from heat for 8 to 10 minutes, turning once, or until squid is soft and lightly browned on outside. Serve immediately.

Yield: 4 servings, about 4 stuffed calamari per person

Note: Cuttlefish, or *soupia* to the Greeks, can be readily substituted for the squid.

Htapothi Xithato

(PICKLED OCTOPUS)

THIS dish needs ouzo, a cool peeled cucumber, a few olives, and the sea. It's among what Greeks know as *ouzomezedes,* tidbits of food that go exceptionally well with the national drink, and it's a classic Greek appetizer.

1. Rinse octopus thoroughly and place in a large pot with no water. Cover and cook over low heat for 50 minutes to 1 hour (or slightly longer depending on the size and toughness of the octopus), checking so as not to burn, until the octopus is bright pink and tender and has exuded its liquid. Remove and cool.

2. Cut octopus into bite-size pieces, about 1 inch long.

3. Combine vinegar, water, olive oil, garlic, and oregano. Place octopus in a clean glass jar or bowl. Pour in liquid. Cover and shake gently a few times to combine well. Let octopus stand, either refrigerated or at room temperature, for at least 1 week before eating.

1 small to medium (about 2 pounds) whole raw octopus (see Note)
½ cup strong red wine vinegar
2 tablespoons water
½ cup extravirgin olive oil
½ garlic clove
1 teaspoon dried oregano

Yield: About 4 servings

Note: To ensure the tenderest possible octopus, Greeks pound it or slap it several dozen times against a hard surface such as marble or stone before rinsing and cooking it.

Sikotakia Tiganita

(FRIED LIVER)

THE Central Market in Athens, really the litmus test for the kinds of foods Greeks like to eat, is rife with stall after stall selling liver. All sorts of livers. From the not-too-pleasant-smelling pig's livers, to the tougher-than-desired beef livers, to the more delicate calf's and lamb's livers. Cut into chunks and fried or braised, with a generous dousing of fresh lemon juice afterward, liver is still a favorite Greek *meze*. Liver must be eaten hot and carefully braised so as not to dry out, and when done well, somehow it washes down perfectly with a stiff glass of brisk red wine.

---

1 pound calf's liver
All-purpose flour
Salt and freshly ground pepper, to taste
½ cup olive oil, or more, if necessary
1 to 2 garlic cloves (optional)
Strained fresh juice of 1 to 2 lemons
Parsley, for garnish

1. Rinse liver well and pat dry. Cut into small pieces, about 1 inch thick and wide and 2 inches long.

2. In a large dish or in a large paper bag, combine flour, salt, and pepper. Dredge liver in seasoned flour.

3. Heat olive oil in a large heavy skillet. Sauté garlic (if desired), then remove. Add liver, a little at a time, and brown until tender, turning frequently so as not to burn.

4. Drain on paper towels. Place in a serving dish, douse with lemon juice, and decorate with a few sprigs of parsley. Serve hot.

Yield: 4 to 6 servings

Saganaki

(FRIED CHEESE)

STANDARD fare in Greek *ouzeries* and one of the best-loved accompaniments to the anise-tinged drink, this simple *meze* gets its name from the small, two-handled pan it's made in. A small heavy skillet is an easy substitute for the traditional *saganaki* pan.

———————

1. Cut cheese into wedges about 3 inches long and $\frac{1}{2}$ to $\frac{3}{4}$ inch thick. Run each piece under the tap, then pat dry slightly.
2. Dredge cheese lightly in flour seasoned with pepper.
3. Heat olive oil or butter almost to the smoking point and add a few wedges of cheese at a time. Flip to cook on both sides, 2 to 3 minutes, and remove at once.
4. Sprinkle with lemon juice and serve hot.

Yield: 4 servings

$\frac{1}{2}$ pound haloumi, kefalotyri, or any hard, yellow cheese
All-purpose flour
Pepper, to taste
$\frac{1}{4}$ cup olive oil or butter
Strained fresh juice of 1 lemon

Dolmadakia Yialantzi

(RICE-STUFFED GRAPE LEAVES)

STUFFED grape leaves are probably synonymous with Greek cooking. *Yialantzi* refers to the distinct absence of meat in this dish. The stuffed grape leaves can be served both as a *meze* and as a main course.

---

*1 jar (16 ounces)
grape leaves, or $\frac{1}{2}$
pound fresh leaves*

*$\frac{1}{4}$ cup plus 2
tablespoons olive oil*

*1 medium red onion,
finely chopped
(about $\frac{1}{2}$ cup)*

*$\frac{1}{2}$ cup chopped
scallions*

1 cup long-grain rice

*2 garlic cloves, finely
chopped*

*1 teaspoon ground
cumin*

*$\frac{1}{4}$ cup plus 2
tablespoons finely
chopped fresh fennel*

*$\frac{1}{2}$ cup finely chopped
fresh dill*

*$\frac{1}{2}$ cup finely chopped
fresh parsley*

*1$\frac{1}{2}$ teaspoons dried
mint*

*Salt and freshly
ground pepper, to
taste*

4 to 5 cups water

*Strained fresh juice of
2 lemons*

*Plain yogurt
(optional)*

1. Rinse grape leaves well to rid them of briny taste. Bring enough water to cover grape leaves amply to a rolling boil, and drop the leaves in for 3 to 5 minutes to soften—whether using fresh or preserved. Remove and drain very well in a colander. Set aside to cool.

2. In a large heavy skillet, heat 2 tablespoons of the olive oil. Sauté onion and scallions until translucent. Add rice and sauté until very lightly browned, 3 to 5 minutes, stirring frequently with a wooden spoon. Lower heat. Add garlic, cumin, salt, pepper, and 2 cups water. Cover and simmer until rice is softened but not cooked and liquid has been absorbed. Remove skillet from heat and let cool. When the mixture is completely cooled, mix in fennel, dill, parsley, and mint, as well as 2 tablespoons olive oil or 1 raw egg, to keep rice moist while cooking.

3. Spread 1 to 2 tablespoons olive oil plus 3 tablespoons water on bottom of a heavy soup pot. Sort the grape leaves and spread ripped or unusable ones on bottom of pot, enough to cover the surface. Snip any hard stems from all the leaves before using.

4. Taking about 1 teaspoon at a time, place rice filling at center of leaf. First fold up the bottom portion of leaf, then the left then right edges, and roll upward to close (see drawing). Place 1 *dolmada* at a time, seamside down, on bottom of pot. Continue until all the filling is used. Sprinkle lemon juice over grape leaves. Add about 2 cups water. Place a plate directly on top of *dolmades* to keep them from opening, and then cover pot with lid. Place over medium heat and bring liquid to a boil. Reduce heat to low and simmer, covered, for at least 2 hours, until rice is cooked and grape leaves tender. Serve warm or cold, alone, with yogurt, or with béchamel.

Yield: About 5 dozen

Variation: Grape leaves may also be stuffed with minced meat. Use the meat filling for *lahanodolmades* (page 166) and prepare and cook as above.

Peinirli

(CANOE-SHAPED, BAKED, STUFFED DOUGH)

THIS is without a doubt tavern food. There are areas in the suburbs north of Athens, namely Drossia, that are lined with *peinirli* haunts. *Peinirli* (pronouned pay-neer-LEE) is fun food—boat-shaped dough vessels, spilling over with melted butter and cheese, and sometimes ham, *pastourma* (see Note), and sunnyside-up eggs.

---

1. Dissolve yeast in warm water and allow to proof, covered and in a warm place, for about 20 minutes.

2. In a medium-size bowl, sift together 4 cups flour and salt. Make a well in center and add yeast mixture. Mix in liquid with a fork until a mass begins to form, then turn out dough onto a lightly floured surface and knead until dough is soft and malleable, adding more flour to surface if necessary. (This dough should be slightly looser than bread dough.) Cover with a cloth and let rise in a warm place for about $1\frac{1}{2}$ hours, or until doubled in bulk.

3. Punch down dough and shape into 6 balls about the size of a medium peach. Cover and let rise once more until almost doubled in bulk, 30 to 40 minutes.

4. In the meantime, preheat oven to 450°F and lightly dust a baking sheet with cornmeal. Grate kasseri and mix with milk. Take one dough ball at a time and flatten into an oval, like a small *lagana* (page 58). The dough should be fairly thick—about $\frac{1}{8}$ inch. Add 2 to 3 tablespoons cheese mixture to center. Add *pastourma* or ham, or break an egg into center if desired. Pinch together ends of dough to form small "boats." Repeat with the rest of the dough balls.

5. Bake for 5 to 7 minutes. Remove baking sheet from oven and immediately dot *peinirli* with butter. Serve hot.

1 envelope active dry yeast
$1\frac{1}{4}$ to $1\frac{1}{2}$ cups warm water
4 to 5 cups bread flour, sifted
Salt
Cornmeal
$\frac{1}{2}$ pound kasseri
2 to 3 tablespoons milk
Pastourma (see Note), ham, or 6 eggs (optional)
Butter, as desired

Yield: About 6

Note: *Pastourma,* or spicy cured beef, can be found at Greek specialty food stores.

Chapter 6

Dips, Spreads, and Pureed Mezedes

Tzatziki

(YOGURT, CUCUMBER, AND GARLIC DIP)

SERVE alone with bread or crackers, or as an accompaniment to vegetable fritters and other fried food such as *keftedes* (pages 72–75) and squid.

---

1. Empty yogurt into a large square of doubled cheesecloth. Tie at the top and let hang to drip for 2 hours, until yogurt thickens and is strained. Place yogurt "cheese" in a medium-size bowl. You should have about 1½ cups.

2. Peel and grate cucumber. Taking a little at a time between the palms of your hand, squeeze as hard as possible until water is removed. Add to yogurt cheese.

3. Mix in garlic, dill, olive oil, vinegar, and salt. Combine all ingredients well. Refrigerate until ready to use.

Yield: About 2 cups

Note: In place of strained yogurt, use a mixture of ¾ cup plain, unstrained yogurt and ¾ cup sour cream, if desired.

1 container (32 ounces) plain yogurt (see Note)
1 large cucumber
3 garlic cloves, minced
1¼ tablespoons finely chopped fresh dill or fresh mint
3 tablespoons extravirgin olive oil
1¼ tablespoons red wine vinegar, or to taste
Salt, to taste

Makedonitiki Skordalia

(GARLIC AND POTATO PUREE, FROM MACEDONIA)

THE walnuts in this recipe are an addition special not only to Macedonia but also to Cephalonia. They impart an earthy, almost musty flavor to the garlic and potatoes, but may be just as easily omitted or replaced with almonds. A simpler version of *skordalia,* the one found most often in Greek tavernas, calls only for trimmed old bread, ample garlic, olive oil, and vinegar (see Note).

Serve *skordalia*—be it lima bean, potato, or bread—with deep-fried cod or shark fritters (page 217), wild greens, or beets.

Combine potatoes, garlic, walnuts, and salt in a food processor. Puree for 30 to 45 seconds, until ingredients are well blended. Slowly pour in lemon juice, olive oil, and vinegar, alternating among each, and continue pureeing for 2 to 4 minutes, until mixture is smooth and a little looser than mashed potatoes in texture. It will, however, be grainy because of the walnuts.

Yield: About 2 cups

Variation: For a simpler version, dampen and squeeze dry 4 or 5 two-inch wedges of stale Italian bread. Mash in a mortar with 5 to 10 garlic cloves (to taste). Drizzle in $\frac{3}{4}$ to 1 cup olive oil and $\frac{1}{4}$ to $\frac{1}{3}$ cup good red wine vinegar, pulverizing the mixture by hand with a pestle until it's loose and grainy. Add more olive oil and vinegar, if necessary. Serve in a small bowl garnished with parsley or an olive.

2 medium to large
  potatoes, boiled and
  peeled
4 to 8 garlic cloves (to
  taste), minced
1 cup finely chopped
  walnuts
Salt, to taste
Strained fresh juice of
  1 lemon
$\frac{1}{2}$ cup extravirgin olive
  oil
$\frac{1}{4}$ cup red wine
  vinegar

Lima Bean Skordalia

(LIMA BEAN AND GARLIC PUREE)

1½ cups dried baby lima beans
5 garlic cloves, minced
1 cup plus 1 to 2 tablespoons olive oil
Strained fresh juice of 3 lemons
¼ cup red wine vinegar
1 teaspoon salt
2 tablespoons grated Parmesan cheese

1. Soak lima beans overnight (or follow directions on package for quick soaking), then rinse and strain thoroughly.

2. Place lima beans in a large saucepan with enough water to cover by 3 or 4 inches. Bring to a boil, lower heat, and simmer until soft and cooked, 30 to 40 minutes. Remove saucepan from heat and drain off water. Cool beans slightly.

3. Place lima beans and minced garlic in a food processor. Puree, adding olive oil, lemon juice, and vinegar a little at a time. Add salt and grated cheese, and continue to puree for 15 to 30 seconds, until mixture is smooth and white.

Yield: About 2 cups

Melitzanosalata

(PUREE OF EGGPLANT)

2 to 3 medium eggplants (about 3 pounds total)
2 to 5 whole garlic cloves, peeled
¼ to ½ cup extravirgin olive oil (see Note)
2 to 3 tablespoons distilled white vinegar
1 teaspoon sugar
Salt, to taste
½ cup walnut meats, coarsely chopped (optional)
Black olive or parsley, for garnish

THIS spread should be earthy and pungent in flavor and pulpy in texture. Some people prefer to whip it all in a food processor or blender, which is certainly possible. I prefer the rough texture of this crushed version and the walnuts, which are an addition to be found in northern Greece and in certain of the Ionian islands.

1. Preheat oven to 375°F. Wash eggplant, pat dry, and puncture skin in several places with a fork. Bake whole in an ungreased pan for about 1 hour, until skin is shriveled and eggplant is soft to the touch. Remove from oven.

2. While eggplant is still hot, cut off stem and peel off skin. Cut lengthwise in half. Remove and discard as many of the seeds as possible.

3. Using a pestle, crush garlic, preferably in a wooden mortar. Add eggplant pulp to mortar and continue mashing. Slowly add olive oil and vinegar, alternating between each, and continue mashing. Add sugar, salt, and walnuts, and continue to pulverize. Place in a small

bowl, garnish with a black olive or parsley, and serve at room temperature.

Yield: About 2 cups

Note: The amount of olive oil, vinegar, and sugar may need to be varied slightly depending on the bitterness of the eggplant.

Taramosalata

(CARP ROE DIP)

WITH *skordalia* (page 85), *tzatziki* (page 84), and *melitzano salata*, *taramosalata* finishes the quartet of classic Greek dips. Made from the pink roe of the carp fish, *taramosalata* is a traditional food on Clean Monday at the start of Lent, when it's eaten with fresh onions and garlic. But it's also enjoyed throughout the year. Serve with bread, trimmed scallions, or stalks of fresh garlic.

The roe is usually sold in 10-ounce jars in the United States, but one might also find it loose. If buying it loose, look for the light pink version—"white" tarama as it's called in Greece. It's about double the price, but it's not mixed with food coloring and soy meal as the other version is.

Combine tarama, bread, potato, and scallions or onion, and pickled pepper in a food processor. Pulse on and off for about 30 seconds. Slowly add olive oil and lemon juice and continue pulsing until all ingredients are well blended and a creamy spread has formed. Serve chilled, garnished with parsley or an olive.

Yield: About 2 cups

5 ounces tarama (half a 10-ounce jar)
1 thick slice Italian or whole wheat bread (2 to 3 inches wide), drizzled with water and squeezed to remove excess moisture
1 medium boiled potato, peeled
4 scallions, or 1 medium onion, finely chopped
1 green pickled pepper, finely chopped (optional)
$\frac{1}{2}$ to $\frac{3}{4}$ cup olive oil
Strained fresh juice of 2 lemons

Htipiti

(PUNGENT FETA CHEESE SPREAD)

IS THIS really the creation of taverna owners in Salonika? Nobody knows for sure, but one of the best renditions of it I've had was at a seaside tavern in Greece's second city. It's served as a *meze,* but it also can be used as filling in stuffed grilled squid or raw green Italian peppers. *Htipiti* (pronounced *h-tee-pee-TEE* and translated as "that which is beaten") is the name Macedonians give to this tart feta spread. They give it punch as well, for nowhere else in Greece are hot peppers so adored. Elsewhere *htipiti* is known as *kopanisti.*

½ *pound feta*
3 tablespoons olive oil
*1 medium Italian
  pepper, seeded and
  finely chopped*
*2 small dried red chile
  peppers, finely
  chopped*
*1 pickled green pepper,
  seeded and chopped*
2 teaspoons oregano
Freshly grated pepper
*Strained fresh juice of
  ½ lemon*
*Black olive, for
  garnish*

In a medium-size bowl, mash feta with a fork or potato masher and slowly add olive oil, chopped peppers, oregano, and black pepper. Pulverize the mixture for about 10 minutes (less if you're doing it in a food processor), pouring in lemon juice a little at a time, until feta is smooth and creamy and "ignited," as the Greeks say (see Note). Cover and refrigerate at least 1 hour before serving. Serve cold.

Yield: About 1 cup

Note: The trick to this simple recipe is in the beating, for the longer the feta is whipped, the tarter it will be. The amount of lemon juice may vary slightly, depending on the texture and flavor of the feta.

Rengosalata

(SMOKED HERRING PUREE)

*1 smoked herring
  (about 1¼ pounds)*
*1 medium to large
  potato, boiled and
  peeled*
½ *cup olive oil*
¼ *cup strained fresh
  lemon juice*
Parsley, for garnish

1. To remove roe from smoked herring, hold fish from both the head and tail and place over a low to medium stove-top flame. Move the fish back and forth over the flame until skin cracks open and peels away easily. Remove skin and discard. Taking fish from the tail end, pull apart and split down the middle of body. Remove roe, being careful to pick away any small bones.

2. Place roe and boiled potato in a medium-size bowl and mash with either a pestle or potato masher, adding olive oil and lemon juice a little at a time. Puree by hand until fairly smooth.

3. Place puree in a serving bowl, garnish with parsley, and serve with bread and crackers.

Yield: About 1 cup

Black Olive Puree

With a mortar and pestle or in the food processor, blend all ingredients to a smooth paste. Spread evenly into a small bowl and let rest for at least 2 hours in the refrigerator before serving. Garnish with a few sprigs of parsley or with a green olive.

Yield: About ½ cup

*2 cups kalamata
  olives, rinsed,
  drained, and pitted*
*¼ cup finely chopped
  onion*
*1 tablespoon ground
  mint*
¼ teaspoon orange rind
1 teaspoon ouzo
1 teaspoon dried thyme
*Green olive or parsley,
  for garnish*

Potato and Caper Puree

THIS Greek dish was created by marrying the old with the new. Capers were well-known to the ancient Greeks, who introduced them to the Gauls around 600 B.C. The ancients ate them mostly as an appetizer, and they liked to pickle the very young buds. Potatoes, on the other hand, didn't arrive until the Greek revolution at the beginning of the nineteenth century, and when they did, they weren't welcome. Potatoes were brought to Greece by Ioannis Capodistriou, one of the leaders of the revolution, who tried to distribute them free to poverty- and war-stricken villagers in the Peloponnisos. To his surprise, nobody wanted the gratuitous tubers. Knowing his countrymen well and knowing, I assume, the value of the potato to a hungry young nation, Capodistriou decided to use a bit of reverse psychology. He put his suspicious imports under lock and key one night, to "protect" them. By morning, of course, they were gone, wily villagers letting curiosity get the best of them. They've been a part of Greek cuisine ever since.

Boil potatoes until soft, then peel. Puree warm potatoes, capers, olive oil, eggs, mustard, vinegar, and lemon juice, blending well but not for too long because potatoes will break down and become too starchy. Serve hot as a *meze* with meat, poultry, or fish, or as a side dish as one would mashed potatoes.

Yield: 6 to 8 servings

*2½ pounds small white
  potatoes*
1 cup capers
1 cup olive oil
2 eggs, slightly beaten
*1 tablespoon dry
  mustard*
*1 tablespoon vinegar
  (or more, to taste)*
*Strained fresh juice of
  2 large lemons*

Hummus

(CHICK-PEA PUREE)

*1 cup raw chick-peas,
    or 1 cup canned*
*1 tablespoon baking
    soda*
⅓ cup tahini
¼ cup cold water
*2 garlic cloves, finely
    chopped*
*½ teaspoon ground
    cumin*
¼ cup olive oil
*⅓ cup plus 1
    tablespoon strained
    fresh lemon juice*
*Salt and freshly
    ground pepper*
1 teaspoon paprika
Parsley sprigs
1 black olive

1. Follow package instructions for soaking and softening chick-peas. Once softened (either overnight or the quick way, in scalding water), boil until cooked, about 1 hour. Remove, strain, and cool. Place in a medium-size bowl and sprinkle with baking soda. (This makes it easier to remove husks.) Let stand 15 minutes. Rub chick-peas, a few at a time, between the palms of your hands to remove husks. Rinse and drain. (If using canned chick-peas, just rinse and drain well.)

2. In a medium-size bowl, combine tahini with cold water and stir vigorously with a fork to soften for 2 to 3 minutes.

3. Place chick-peas in a food processor and grind to a coarse meal. Add tahini, garlic, and cumin. Pulverize for about 45 seconds. Slowly add olive oil and lemon juice, alternating between each, and continue to process for about 5 minutes, on and off, until *hummus* becomes smooth and creamy. Season with salt and pepper. Remove to a serving bowl and sprinkle with paprika. Garnish with parsley and a black olive. Serve alone with bread or crackers, or as a counterpart to vegetable fritters such as fried eggplant or squash.

Yield: About 1½ cups

Tahinosalata

(TAHINI PUREE)

ALTHOUGH this isn't *really* Greek, it's a popular dish in Cyprus.

---

*1 cup tahini (sesame
    paste)*
¾ to 1 cup water
3 garlic cloves, minced
Salt, to taste
*Strained fresh juice of
    2 medium lemons*
¼ cup olive oil

In either a large bowl with an electric mixer or in the food processor, beat tahini with water to soften the paste. Add garlic and salt, and drizzle in lemon juice and olive oil a little at a time, beating vigorously, until a thick creamy spread forms. Place in a serving bowl and garnish with parsley or paprika and an olive.

Yield: About 1 cup

Pihti I

(JELLIED PORK)

*There were close at hand, on platters, whole hams
with shin and all, most tender, and trotters well
boiled.*

—Athenaeus quoting Pherecrates,
The Deipnosophists, *Book I*

THIS dish is traditionally made with pig's feet (trotters) and head,
boiled slowly for their gelatin, combined with vegetables and spices,
and then allowed to set. It's a classic at the Christmas table.

---

1. Wash the pig's feet and knuckles very well. Place in a large pot
with enough cold water to cover. Stud the onions with cloves and add
to pot. Add bay leaf, 1 cup of the vinegar, salt, and pepper. Cover the
pot and bring ingredients to a boil. Reduce heat to very low and
simmer very slowly for 4 to 5 hours, until the meat falls away from
the bones. Skim off any scum that might accumulate at the top of the
pot during cooking.

2. Remove the pig's feet and knuckles from the pot with a slotted
spoon and cut away meat from bones. Shred the meat or cut it into
very small pieces. Place in a large bowl or mold.

3. Crush or finely mince the garlic with a mortar and pestle and stir
well with remaining $\frac{1}{4}$ cup vinegar. Add the garlic and vinegar to the
pot liquids, stirring several times so that flavors are well combined.
Strain liquid in a colander or sieve, disgarding residue, and pour it into
bowl with meat, stirring well to combine. Place mixture uncovered in
the refrigerator for about 6 hours, or until it sets. Serve cold.

3 to $3\frac{1}{2}$ pounds pig's
   feet and knuckles
3 medium-size onions
6 to 9 whole cloves
1 large bay leaf,
   ripped
$1\frac{1}{4}$ cups strong white
   wine vinegar
Salt and freshly
   ground pepper, to
   taste
3 to 4 garlic cloves

Yield: 6 to 8 servings

Pihti II

THIS is a milder version of *pihti,* prepared not with pungent pig's feet and knuckles, but with veal shanks, and set with ample vegetables.

$2\frac{1}{2}$ to 3 pounds veal
   shanks
1 cup dry white wine
2 large onions
3 to 4 whole cloves
2 large bay leaves
4 to 5 allspice berries
Salt and whole
   peppercorns, to taste
2 to 3 medium-size
   carrots, pared and
   split in half
   lengthwise
2 medium-size celery
   ribs, cleaned and
   split in half
   lengthwise
2 tablespoons red wine
   vinegar
Strained fresh juice of
   $\frac{1}{2}$ large lemon
2 garlic cloves, minced
2 to 3 gherkins, rinsed
   and split in half or
   quartered
   lengthwise
1 to 2 tablespoons
   pickled capers,
   rinsed and drained
2 hard-boiled eggs,
   peeled

1. Wash shanks. Place in a large pot with enough cold water to cover and bring to a boil. Skim scum off the top of pot.

2. Add wine to pot along with whole onions studded with cloves, plus bay leaves, allspice berries, salt, and peppercorns. Cover the pot and bring ingredients to a boil. Reduce heat and simmer very slowly over very low heat for 3 to 4 hours, or until meat is very tender and falls away easily from bones. About 1 hour before removing pot from heat, add carrots and celery. Add more water, if necessary, to keep mixture moist during cooking.

3. Remove pot from heat. Remove meat, carrots, and celery from pot with a slotted spoon. Add vinegar and lemon juice to liquid. Stir several times and strain liquid through a sieve, discarding the residue. Add garlic to liquid. Cut meat away from bone, and chop meat into very small pieces.

4. Place meat in a large gelatin mold. Place carrots, celery, gherkins, capers, and whole eggs around sides and bottom of mold to make a design. Pour strained liquid into form and allow to set, refrigerated, for about 6 hours. Serve cold.

Yield: About 6 servings

Chapter 7

Salads, Pickles, and Vegetable Mezedes

4 plump tomatoes,
   cored and quartered
   or cut into eighths,
   depending on size
1 cucumber, peeled
   and cut into $\frac{1}{4}$-inch
   slices
2 green peppers, seeded
   and cut into thin
   round slices
2 to 3 salted anchovies
   (optional)
15 to 20 kalamata
   olives
1 large red onion,
   peeled and cut into
   thin round slices
$\frac{1}{3}$ pound feta cheese,
   either sliced into
   wedges or crumbled
$\frac{1}{4}$ cup olive oil, or
   slightly less, to taste
1 teaspoon dried
   oregano
Salt, to taste

Horiatiki Salata

(CLASSIC GREEK SALAD)

ANYONE who's been to Greece in the summer probably has a clear memory of picking luscious tomatoes out of a garden salad with the edge of a fork. Perhaps you even waited a few seconds before lapping them up, with fork before your eyes, contemplating their vermilion skin, savoring their dewy pulp. This is the classic "Greek salad"—found on Greek menus from Athens to Adelaide. Do it justice by choosing the best, the firmest and ripest, the plumpest tomato you can find; sprinkle it with sea salt, fleck it with dried oregano, and drizzle into it some gold-green olive oil.

Combine tomatoes, cucumber, peppers, anchovies, olives, and half of both the onions and the feta in a medium-size bowl. Strew remaining onions and feta over top of salad. Douse with olive oil and season with oregano and salt. Toss once more just before serving.

Yield: 4 to 6 servings

Vassilis's Paximathia and Tomato Salad

(BARLEY TOAST AND TOMATO SALAD)

2 to 3 thick barley, whole wheat, or eptazymo paximathia *(see Note)*
3 firm ripe tomatoes
1 medium onion
1 tablespoon finely chopped fresh basil or oregano, or 1 teaspoon dried
Salt and freshly ground pepper
Olive oil

1. Run the *paximathia* under the faucet to dampen and soften slightly. Break into chunks.
2. Combine the *paximathia,* tomatoes, onions, basil or oregano, salt, and pepper in a large bowl. Dribble generously with olive oil and serve.

Yield: 3 to 4 servings

Note: *Paximathia* are available in Greek specialty food stores. Or see recipe on page 50.

Tomato and Eggplant Salad

THIS recipe was inspired by a dish I tasted at Periyali, a Greek restaurant in New York City. I liked the idea of using an inherently Greek flavor like ouzo in a new way. Used sparingly, it makes this salad a wonderful side dish to grilled meats and kebabs.

1 large or 2 medium eggplants
$\frac{1}{4}$ cup olive oil
1 tablespoon ouzo
2 garlic cloves, finely chopped
Salt, to taste
2 medium to large plump ripe tomatoes, peeled and coarsely chopped
2 tablespoons chopped fresh parsley
Freshly ground pepper, to taste

1. Preheat oven to 450°F. Wash eggplant and pat dry. Puncture skin lightly with a fork and bake whole in an ungreased pan for about 25 minutes, or until soft and slightly shriveled. Remove and cool slightly.
2. Remove stems, cut eggplant in half lengthwise, and remove skin and seeds. Cut into strips about $1\frac{1}{2}$ inches wide, then cut strips in half. Place in a small deep bowl and marinate in olive oil, ouzo, garlic, and salt for at least 2 hours before using.
3. In a medium bowl, combine eggplants, tomatoes, and parsley. Toss well and season with freshly ground pepper. Serve at room temperature.

Yield: 4 servings

Kiousour

(TOMATO AND BULGUR SALAD)

BULGUR *(pligouri)* is used more on Cyprus, where this recipe comes from, than in Greece.

----

1. Bring water to a rolling boil. Add bulgur and olive oil; bring back to a boil, cover, and simmer over low heat until bulgur is soft and water absorbed. Remove from heat, fluff with a fork, and cool.
2. In a serving bowl, combine bulgur, tomatoes, onion, parsley, garlic, and olives.
3. *To make dressing:* Beat tahini with cold water to soften. Add lemon juice, olive oil, coriander, salt, and pepper. Pour over salad and toss. Serve either at room temperature or chilled.

Yield: 4 to 6 servings

$\frac{3}{4}$ cup water
$\frac{1}{2}$ cup bulgur
1 tablespoon olive oil
2 cups peeled, chopped
  plum tomato
1 medium red onion,
  finely chopped
$\frac{1}{4}$ cup chopped parsley
2 garlic cloves, finely
  chopped
15 kalamata olives
DRESSING
2 tablespoons tahini
1 tablespoon cold water
Fresh juice of 1 lemon
2 tablespoons olive oil
$\frac{1}{4}$ teaspoon ground
  coriander
Salt and freshly
  ground pepper

Angourosalata

(CUCUMBER SALAD)

EATING Greek garden cukes is an experience. They're as crisp as crackers and as refreshing as cool water. This is a simple summer salad that any visitor will find in tavernas and homes all over the country.

Peel and seed cucumbers. Cut in half across the width, then slice lengthwise into slender strips about $1\frac{1}{2}$ inches wide. Place in neat rows on an oval plate. Stud with olives. Season with olive oil, vinegar, oregano, salt, and crumbled feta, if desired. Serve cold.

Yield: 2 to 4 servings

Angourodomatosalata (Cucumbers and Tomatoes): Cut cucumbers into thin rounds and add 2 plump ripe tomatoes, washed, cored, and sliced, between rows of cucumbers. Season as above.

2 large cucumbers
10 kalamata olives
  (optional)
2 to 3 tablespoons
  extravirgin olive oil
1 to 2 tablespoons red
  wine vinegar
1 teaspoon dried
  oregano
Salt, to taste
2 tablespoons crumbled
  feta (optional)

Maroulosalata

(LETTUCE SALAD)

2 heads crisp romaine
    lettuce, shredded
5 to 6 scallions, peeled
    and chopped
$\frac{1}{2}$ cup finely chopped
    fresh dill
$\frac{1}{4}$ cup finely chopped
    fresh fennel
3 to 4 tablespoons
    olive oil
1 tablespoon strong
    red wine vinegar, or
    more, to taste
Salt, to taste

THIS is a simple spring salad. Lettuce is a seasonal produce in Greece, associated with spring and Easter, and made into a salad with fresh fennel and dill, scallions, and just a touch of olive oil. It's so tasty that in most locales not even salt is added.

Shred, wash, and drain lettuce well. In a large bowl, mix lettuce, scallions, dill, and fennel together. Toss with oil and vinegar and season with salt. Serve cold or at room temperature.

Yield: 4 servings

Horta

(WILD GREENS)

WILD greens, like ouzo or feta, are a characteristic element of the Greek table. The countryside is rich in greens and herbs, and Greeks collect all manner of "weeds" for their table: purslane *(anthrakla)*; curly endive *(andithia)*; a variety of sorrel called *lapatha*; black mustard leaves *(vrouva)*; rugula, or rocket *(roca)*; lemon balm *(melisohorta)*; chicory *(rathikia)*; dandelion greens; escarole; kale; collard greens *lahanitha*; and the leaves and stems of beets *(patzarohorta)*, to name but a few.

Black mustard tops, sorrel, escarole, chicory, dandelion greens, rocket, and beet stems and leaves are the most likely to be boiled, and one finds them easily enough both in ethnic markets in the United States and in local farmers' markets in Greece. Greens as subtle and difficult to find in cities as lemon balm or purslane—nicknamed *glistritha*, or "slippery," for the way its reputedly makes your mouth water, your tongue loose, and you talkative—are more likely to be used raw as ingredients in garden salads in the countryside. Sometimes greens are mixed together and boiled—dandelion and chicory, for example—but mostly they are boiled individually and served cold with a simple dressing of olive oil and vinegar or lemon juice. Greeks, and my family among them, are also in the habit of drinking the liquid after greens have been boiled, especially beet juice. Although an acquired taste, it's rather good.

To cook horta: Wash extremely well, making sure any sand and dirt are removed. Fill a large pot with cold water. Bring to a rolling boil. Add *horta,* keep the lid of the pot half on, and cook until soft, 25 to 40 minutes. Strain and cool. Serve with olive oil and vinegar or lemon juice. Keep in mind that, once boiled, *horta* is greatly reduced in volume; you'll need at least $\frac{1}{2}$ pound per serving. Eat it cold or at room temperature.

Variation: Use the juice of bitter Seville oranges (*nerantzia,* to the Greeks) in place of lemon juice or vinegar, as is often done in Cyprus.

Kolokithakia Vrasta

(COOKED ZUCCHINI)

THIS is a standard dish on spring tables in Greece, when zucchini is in season. Greeks tend to overcook their vegetables, and like their zucchini soft. It is best to choose zucchini that are small, firm, and all the same size. If using larger squash, quarter it down the middle lengthwise after it's been boiled.

Wash zucchini well and boil in salted water for 5 to 7 minutes. (They may also be steamed.) Remove and drain well. Dress with olive oil, lemon juice or vinegar, salt, pepper, and a little garlic, if desired.

Baby zucchini (see Note)
Olive oil, to taste
Lemon juice or vinegar, to taste
Salt and freshly ground pepper, to taste
1 garlic clove, crushed (optional)

Kounoupithi Vrasto (**Cooked Cauliflower**): Another favorite. Cut the cauliflower into florets, then steam or boil and dress as above.

2 medium zucchini
2 to 3 hard-boiled
  eggs, quartered
5 to 6 scallions,
  chopped
3 tablespoons finely
  chopped fresh dill
15 cracked green olives
2 teaspoons grated
  kefalotyri or
  Parmesan cheese
Latholemono *(page 41)*

1 pound green
  cabbage, shredded
5 to 6 scallions,
  chopped
$\frac{1}{4}$ cup chopped fresh
  dill
1 garlic clove, finely
  chopped
Salt and freshly
  ground pepper
3 tablespoons olive oil
Strained fresh juice of
  $\frac{1}{2}$ to 1 lemon

1 pound red cabbage,
  shredded
$\frac{3}{4}$ cup shredded carrot
$\frac{1}{2}$ cup diced celery
1 green bell pepper,
  seeded and sliced
1 chopped red onion
2 tablespoons chopped
  fresh dill
10 to 15 throumbes or
  any Greek olives
Salt, to taste
Olive oil and vinegar

Zucchini and Olive Salad

1. Wash and trim zucchini, then steam whole for 3 to 4 minutes, until bright green and firm. Cool, cut into rounds about $\frac{1}{4}$ inch thick, and quarter.

2. In a serving bowl, combine zucchini, hard-boiled eggs, scallions, dill, and green olives. Mix grated cheese into *latholemono* and pour over salad. Serve either at room temperature or cold.

Yield: 4 servings

Lahanosalata

(GREEN CABBAGE SALAD)

In a medium-size serving bowl, combine cabbage, scallions, dill, and garlic. Season with salt and pepper and toss with olive oil and lemon.

Yield: 4 servings

Variation: For a sharp version, shred 1 large white radish into salad as well. Instead of *latholemono,* or olive oil and lemon, Greeks also eat *lahanosalata* with a mayonnaise dressing. Use $\frac{1}{4}$ cup mayonnaise and toss well to combine.

Kokkini Lahanosalata

(RED CABBAGE SALAD)

In a medium-size serving bowl, combine cabbage, carrot, celery, pepper, onion, dill, and olives. Season with salt and dress with olive oil and vinegar, to taste. Toss and serve.

Yield: 4 servings

Patzarosalata

(BEET ROOT SALAD)

BEETS *(patzaria)* come to Greek markets in both the winter and spring. Their leaves are boiled for *horta,* and the juice from that boiling saved, refrigerated, and savored as a health drink for days afterward. To serve, the sliced beets are often spread in neat rows on an oval plate with the boiled greens surrounding them, and then seasoned.

---

1. Cut the greens off beet roots and set aside. (See *horta,* page 96, for how to cook them.) Wash and scrub roots thoroughly.
2. Place roots in a large saucepan with enough cold water to cover. Bring to a boil and cook until tender but firm, 20 to 25 minutes. Remove, drain, cool, and peel. Cut beets into round slices (halve or quarter slices, if desired). Toss with garlic, olive oil, vinegar, and salt. Serve cold.

Yield: 4 servings

1 large bunch fresh beets, greens included (2 to 3 pounds)
1 large garlic clove, finely chopped
3 to 4 tablespoons extravirgin olive oil (see Note)
2 teaspoons red wine vinegar (or more, to taste)
Salt, to taste (optional)

Patzaropatatosalata

(BEET AND POTATO SALAD)

TO MAKE this salad pretty, you might layer the beets, potatoes, capers, and anchovies in a clear glass bowl to form a design of choice.

---

1. Cut beet roots from leaves. Wash, scrub, and bring beets to a boil in enough cold water to cover. Boil until cooked but firm, about 20 minutes. Cool, peel, and cut into rounds about $\frac{1}{8}$ inch thick.
2. Boil potatoes until cooked but firm, 25 to 40 minutes, depending on their size. Cool, peel, and slice into rounds about $\frac{1}{4}$ inch thick.
3. In a serving bowl, combine beets, potatoes, capers, garlic, and anchovies, being careful not to crumble vegetables. Toss gently with olive oil and vinegar. Season to taste.

Yield: 4 to 6 servings

Note: In lieu of oil and vinegar, use 3 to 4 tablespoons mayonnaise, to taste.

1 bunch (6 to 8) large beets
1 pound new potatoes
3 tablespoons capers, rinsed and drained
2 garlic cloves, finely chopped
1 to 2 anchovies, deboned, split, and cut into 1-inch strips
3 to 4 tablespoons extravirgin olive oil (see Note)
1 tablespoon strong red wine vinegar
Salt, to taste

*2 pounds potatoes,
cooked, peeled, and
sliced into rounds,
then halved or
quartered (about 4
cups)
1 pound carrots,
cooked and diced
(about 2 cups)
1 cup cooked peas
2 dill pickles, chopped
2 to 3 hard-boiled
eggs, quartered
lengthwise
2 teaspoons capers
Salt and freshly
ground pepper
¾ cup mayonnaise*

Rossiki

(BOILED POTATO SALAD WITH MAYONNAISE)

ROSSIKI is at least as popular as Greek village salad (*horiatiki,* page 93). Every taverna in the country serves it, and it makes its appearance on party tables and as a *meze* all the time.

1. In a medium-size serving bowl, carefully combine potatoes, $1\frac{1}{2}$ cups of the carrots, the peas, pickles, half the eggs, 1 teaspoon of the capers, salt, and pepper, being sure not to crumble or break the vegetables.

2. Spread mayonnaise evenly on top of salad. Decorate with remaining carrots, eggs, and capers. Refrigerate until ready to serve. Mix just before eating.

Yield: 4 to 6 servings

*2 pounds small new
potatoes boiled,
halved and sliced
15 to 20 kalamata
olives, rinsed and
well drained
1 medium red onion,
thinly sliced into
rings
3 to 4 tablespoons
extravirgin olive oil
2 tablespoons quality
red wine vinegar
Salt and freshly
ground black
pepper, to taste
1 teaspoon dried
oregano or thyme*

Patatosalata

(TRADITIONAL GREEK POTATO SALAD)

1. In a medium-size serving bowl, combine potatoes, olives, and onion.

2. In a small jar, shake together olive oil, vinegar, salt, pepper, and oregano and pour over salad. Serve cold or at room temperature.

Yield: 4 servings

Variation: In the Peloponnisos, I found an interesting addition to this salad: oranges. Peel and thinly slice or chop 1 juicy navel orange. Pit and halve the olives, and combine with potatoes and oranges. Season with thyme. To make a prettier salad, serve in an oval dish with 1 slice of potato followed by a slice of orange, then onion, and stud with the pitted black olives. Drizzle olive oil, vinegar, thyme, salt, and pepper over the salad and serve.

Mavromatiki Salata

(BLACK-EYED PEAS AND TOMATO SALAD)

EVEN though many people associate black-eyed peas with days of hunger and food shortages—my father-in-law can't eat them because they remind him of the War—this salad is a family favorite. You can make it with any number of dried beans, and with baby limas it's especially good.

The peas should be cooked but firm. In a small serving bowl, combine peas, garlic, onion, tomato, and parsley. Season with olive oil, vinegar, salt, and pepper. Toss and serve at room temperature.

Yield: 4 to 6 servings

1 cup black-eyed peas, washed, soaked, and boiled
3 garlic cloves, finely chopped
$\frac{1}{4}$ cup chopped onion
1 cup chopped peeled plum tomato
2 tablespoons finely chopped fresh parsley
3 tablespoons extravirgin olive oil
2 teaspoons strong red wine vinegar
Salt and freshly ground pepper, to taste

Baby Lima Bean, Cucumber, and Radish Salad

1. Soak and boil lima beans according to package directions. They should be cooked but firm.
2. In a medium-size serving bowl, combine beans, cucumber, radishes, dill, olives, and onion.
3. In a small jar, shake together olive oil, vinegar, oregano, and salt. Pour over salad and toss. Serve at room temperature or cold.

Yield: 4 servings

1 cup dried baby lima beans ($\frac{1}{2}$ pound)
1 cup peeled diced cucumber
$\frac{1}{2}$ cup sliced and quartered red radishes
2 tablespoons coarsely chopped fresh dill
10 to 15 kalamata olives
1 medium red onion, coarsely chopped
3 tablespoons extravirgin olive oil
1 tablespoon strong red wine vinegar
1 teaspoon oregano
Salt, to taste

Shrimp and Caper Salad

*2 pounds medium
    shrimp, shelled and
    deveined
1 whole garlic clove,
    peeled
1 tablespoon salt
½ cup chopped
    scallions
1 garlic clove, minced
3 tablespoons capers
1 celery rib, chopped
Salt and freshly
    ground pepper, to
    taste
1 teaspoon dried
    oregano
2 tablespoons olive oil
2 tablespoons strained
    fresh lemon juice*

1. In a large pot, combine enough water to amply cover shrimp, whole garlic clove, and salt. Bring to a boil. Add shrimp and simmer for about 5 minutes, until bright pink. Remove pot from heat and immediately rinse shrimp in cold water. Drain well.

2. In a medium-size serving bowl, combine shrimp, scallions, minced garlic, rinsed capers, and celery. Add salt, pepper, oregano, olive oil, and lemon juice and toss. Chill for 30 minutes and serve.

Yield: 4 to 6 servings

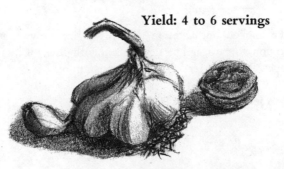

Piperies Florinis

(RED PEPPERS, FLORINA STYLE)

*Sweet red peppers
Extravirgin olive oil,
    to taste
Garlic, peeled and cut
    into slivers, to taste
Generous sprinkling
    of good red wine
    vinegar*

1. Preheat oven to 350°F. Wash peppers thoroughly and pat dry.

2. Place peppers, whole, on an ungreased baking sheet and bake at 350°F until their skin begins to blister. Turn peppers once in the oven so that they brown evenly, and be careful not to burn them. Remove and cool.

3. With a sharp paring knife, carefully peel the outer skin of each of the peppers and cut away their stems and seeds. Slice in half lengthwise, being careful not to tear them. Carefully scrape away seeds. Place on a large serving platter; douse with quality olive oil and dapple with garlic and vinegar.

Variation: Fried and grilled green peppers are also a summer and fall favorite. (Grilled peppers are a specialty of Mt. Pelion.) Wash and pat dry green Italian peppers. Either fry over medium heat in ample hot oil, until wrinkled and softened, or grill under a broiler or on a barbecue until done. Serve with *skordalia* (page 85), or eat plain as a great *meze*.

Volvi

(PICKLED BULBS)

I WAS in a mountain village on the island of Ikaria, where my family originates, the first time I tasted pickled bulbs. The unadulterated version of this dish calls for the bitter, flesh-colored bulb of the hyacinth (*volvi* in Greek), which are difficult to find in the United States. While hyacinth bulbs may certainly be used here, small white stewing pearl onions are a good substitute.

---

1. In a large pot, bring enough water to cover onions, plus 1 tablespoon of the salt, to a rolling boil. Add onions and simmer, uncovered, for 5 minutes. Remove pot from heat, discard water, and repeat with enough water to cover onions plus 1 tablespoon salt. Discard second water and repeat a third time, again in salted water, boiling the onions for about 10 minutes, until they just begin to turn translucent and to soften.

2. Drain onions and pat them dry with a lint-free towel.

3. In a small saucepan, bring the vinegar, garlic, chopped dill or fennel, and peppercorns to a boil. Remove pan from heat and cool slightly. Place onions in an airtight sterilized jar and pour vinegar mixture over them. Add enough olive oil to form a seal of about 1 inch of oil at the top of the jar. Cover with lid and let stand, refrigerated, for at least 10 days before eating. Serve in a small dish, by themselves, as a great *meze* for wine or ouzo.

3 tablespoons salt

2½ to 3 pounds small white onions (stewing onions), peeled and whole

2 cups distilled white vinegar

3 to 5 garlic cloves (to taste), coarsely chopped

2 tablespoons chopped fresh dill or fennel

½ teaspoon whole black peppercorns

Olive oil

Yield: About 1 quart

Melitzanakia Toursi

(STUFFED PICKLED BABY EGGPLANT)

THIS is an end-of-summer, early-fall treat, when the miniature eggplants are in season in Greece. It's also a specialty of Volos and a favorite *meze* for fiery ouzo, *raki,* or *tsipouro.*

2 to 2½ pounds baby or very small eggplants (not more than 3 or 4 inches long)
4 cups strong red or white wine vinegar
Salt
Celery ribs with leaves
3 to 4 medium carrots, scraped and diced
4 to 5 garlic cloves, finely chopped
Crushed red pepper or black peppercorns, to taste (optional)
¼ cup finely chopped fresh parsley
Olive oil

1. Remove stems from eggplants and make two or three incisions lengthwise in each eggplant. Bring to a boil enough water to cover eggplants, 1 cup of the vinegar, and 2 to 3 tablespoons salt. Drop in eggplants and simmer for 3 to 5 minutes, until they are softened. Remove pot from heat and immediately rinse and drain the eggplants completely. Let cool.
2. Drop celery ribs into boiling water for 1 to 2 minutes, just to soften. Drain and slit the celery lengthwise into strips about as thick as a medium strand of wool.
3. Combine carrot, garlic, hot pepper, and parsley. Taking one eggplant at a time, carefully fill each slit with carrot mixture. Wrap with softened celery strands and secure closed. Place upright in a large, airtight, sterilized jar and cover with remaining 3 cups vinegar. Pour in enough olive oil to form a seal of about 1½ inches of oil at the top of the jar. Store in a cool dry place for at least 1 to 2 weeks before eating.

Yield: About 1½ quarts

Manitaria Tursi

(PICKLED MUSHROOMS)

FROM about the end of October, after the first fall rains, until January or February, wild mushrooms abound in Greece. Generally the porcini or boletus mushroom is most common, but the woods hold dozens of varieties for the picking—by those who know. Greeks call wild mushrooms *manites* (no relation to the deadly *amanita*), and they either pickle them, grill them, or flour and fry them. Although the porcini is recommended here, the ordinary agaric will do just fine.

1. Gently wipe any dirt off the mushrooms. Trim the very bottoms off the stems if tough.

2. In a large pot, bring to a boil just enough water to cover mushrooms, plus salt. Pour in lemon juice and add mushrooms to blanch, 3 to 4 minutes. Drain the mushrooms and set to dry on a lint-free towel.

3. Place the mushrooms in a large jar, filling only about two thirds of it. In a small saucepan, bring the oil, vinegar, and peppercorns to a boil and remove immediately from heat. Pour into jar with mushrooms. Let the mushrooms rest at least a week in refrigerator before eating them, and keep stored in the refrigerator.

1 pound small even-size mushrooms
1 tablespoon salt
1½ tablespoons strained fresh lemon juice
⅓ cup olive oil
1 cup distilled white wine vinegar
5 to 6 whole black peppercorns

Yield: About 1 quart

Variation: Another method of preparing the mushrooms, and one that comes from an old expert in Raches, Ikaria, a part of the island covered with pine forests and rich with earthy mushrooms, is to split the mushrooms in half lengthwise (after they've been wiped and, if desired, trimmed). Season generously with salt and bake at 350°F for 10 to 15 minutes, tossing once or twice. Remove from oven and place in a jar with ample *lathoxitho* (page 41), tinged with oregano and peppercorns. Let them stand for several days, refrigerated, before serving.

Roasted Potatoes

1. Preheat oven to 450°F.

2. Place peeled quartered potatoes in a medium-size, preferably Pyrex, baking pan. Add remaining ingredients and combine well. Bake uncovered for 50 minutes to 1 hour. Toss in pan during baking and add more water, if necessary, during baking. When done, potatoes will be light golden brown and soft.

2 pounds large oval potatoes, peeled and quartered lengthwise
½ cup water
¼ cup olive oil
¼ cup strained fresh lemon juice
2 teaspoons dried oregano
2 garlic cloves, finely chopped
Salt and freshly ground pepper, to taste

Yield: 4 servings

Patates Antinaktes Kyprou

(CYPRUS-STYLE POTATOES WITH CORIANDER AND RED WINE)

ANTINAKTES means "shaken," and this is a classic Cypriot dish.

2 pounds small round
  fresh potatoes,
  unpeeled
¾ to 1 cup olive oil
¾ to 1 cup dry red
  wine
1 scant tablespoon
  ground coriander
  seed
Salt and freshly
  ground pepper, to
  taste

1. Wash and dry potatoes well.
2. Take a heavy object like a stone or a meat pounder and hammer potatoes once or twice each to break them open a little.
3. Heat olive oil in a large heavy pot. Add potatoes and sauté until lightly browned. Lower heat, cover pot, and cook potatoes 5 to 7 minutes. Add wine, coriander seed, salt, and pepper. Cover pot and cook over medium to low heat for about 1 hour, until potatoes are soft. Every 10 to 12 minutes, remove pot from heat and shake back and forth to further break up potatoes, but don't remove lid.

Yield: 4 to 6 servings

Fritters

(BATTER-FRIED VEGETABLES SUCH AS ZUCCHINI, ZUCCHINI BLOSSOMS, AND EGGPLANT)

SEASONED flour instead of batter may also be used to coat vegetables before frying.

BATTER (KOURKOUTI)
2 cups all-purpose
  flour
1 scant teaspoon salt
Dash of freshly
  ground pepper
¾ to 1 cup flat beer or
  water
Olive oil, for frying

1. In a small bowl combine 1½ cups of the flour, the salt, and pepper. Make a well in center and add beer or water. Stir with a fork until a thick batter forms. Refrigerate, covered, for several hours before using. Reserve remaining flour for dredging vegetables.
2. *For zucchini:* Wash zucchini and pat dry. Slice into rounds about ⅛ inch thick. Dip in flour, then in batter, and deep-fry in very hot oil.
For zucchini blossoms: Wash and drain the blossoms well. Dip in flour, then in batter. Fry them in very hot oil.
For eggplant: Wash and dry eggplants. Slice into either thin rounds or long thin strips. Salt, if desired, to rid them of any bitterness for 30 to 60 minutes. (If you do this, rinse them very well and pat dry.) Dip in batter and deep-fry in the same way as zucchini.

Prassosalata Pontiaki

(LEEK FRITTER SALAD, PONTIAN STYLE)

THIS is an interesting variation on a common theme—the fritter. Leeks are a kind of regional specialty among northern Greeks and *Pontiyoi*, Greeks who lived originally in the Black Sea areas of Asia Minor.

---

1. Use only the white part of the leek; slit it down the middle and wash and clean it thoroughly, making sure dirt and sand are removed from the inner layers.

2. Slice the leeks into fairly thin rounds—about $\frac{1}{8}$ inch wide. Bring a little more than enough water to cover them to a boil and add the leeks. Simmer until slightly translucent and softened. They should have some crunch to them—don't make them too mushy. Remove and drain the leeks very thoroughly, first in a colander, then by squeezing a few at a time between the palms of your hand to get out as much moisture as possible.

3. Combine flour, salt, and pepper. Dredge leeks, a few at a time, in the seasoned flour. Heat ample olive oil in a heavy skillet and fry leeks until pinkish brown and crisp. Remove to a serving plate and sprinkle with *skordostoumbi*. Serve warm.

Leeks
Flour
Salt
Pepper
Olive oil, for frying
Skordostoumbi
  (page 40)

Part III

THE MAIN COURSE

The Greek table is a welcome example of what it means to enjoy food. "We are a nation of *kalofagathes*," of "good eaters," a friend observes. The stately order of a proper meal doesn't really exist in Greece. There are no courses served, but dish after dish is spread out liberally, all to be had at once, with plenty to go around for all.

Greeks like to spend a goodly amount of time at the table. Even in tavernas, it's a rare waiter who'll swipe a plate from under you just as you put a last forkful of food in your mouth. Greeks like to fill their plates with a little *horta*, some warm *pitta*, a slice of meat, a spoonful of *tzatziki*, perhaps a mound of potatoes, and bread, without exception. The main meal of the day is still the afternoon one, followed by a nap. And at night Greeks take their meal late—often not before ten and more than likely around eleven or twelve.

Meals are to be shared. Wine is almost always served, and dialogue demanded. What we know as main courses fall into several categories: *pitta,* placed strategically first here, because it can be either—or both—*meze* and main plate; soups, which are more often than not main course fare; pasta and pilaf dishes come next, followed by the myriad vegetable and bean dishes, backbone of the country kitchen; next, in no particular order of importance, are the many chicken and game dishes, the always-loved bounty of the sea, meats of every kind and color, and the humble egg.

Chapter 8

Pitta (Savory Pies)

P*itta* is to the Greeks what pasta is to the Italians—food to warm
the soul. It is eaten as either main course or *meze,* hot or cold.
The classic Greek *pitta* is the ubiquitous spinach pie (*spanakopitta*), or, in the country, the *hortopitta,* a savory pie made with a variety
of wild greens, from lemon balm and leaves of the poppy plant, to the
more banal fennel and fresh, sea-sprayed dill. Mustard greens, dande-
lions, sorrel, and any number of other "sweet" greens find their welcome place between the crisp, olive-rich layers of homemade phyllo
all over Greece, but the capital of Greek *spanakopitta* is without doubt
Epirus, west of the Pindus mountains in the northern reaches of the
country, where greens were often all people had to eat. But like most
village Greeks, they are so appreciative of the flavors of their native
soil. I've met an Epirot woman who, in a feeble but valiant attempt
to cultivate some of those flavors far from home, grows "wild" greens
in tins along her balcony floor in grimy Athens. "So that my kids will
know what they're missing," she says wistfully.

Greens aside, there are myriad pies in Greek cookery. Some are as
odd as the liver and cinnamon pie called *tzoulama,* which is made only
in several southern villages of Crete. Another hails from Monodendri,
the first village one comes to in the Zagorohoria in northwestern
Epirus. Here, a small tavern, Kyria Kikitsa's—the only place to eat in
Monodendri—makes the best *tiganopitta* I've ever had. There's nothing
to it, really, just grilled dough and fresh feta, but the dish is crisp, truly
soul-warming, and absolutely unreproducible without the same homemade cheese and hand-milled flour. What's served up under *tiganopitta*

here is, I think, a respectable but humble essay, in deference, of course, to Kyria Kikitsa in the gray stone mountain village of Monodendri. Anyone who's ever traveled through Epirus knows the place.

— PHYLLO —

The Greeks have been wrapping their foods for millennia. The ancients were fond of a cheese pie wrapped in fig leaves, precursor to the modern-day *tyropitta,* and today Greeks make both sweet and savory pies using phyllo (the Greek word for "leaf"). It is a dough that, when store-bought, is similar to strudel pastry. The recipes in this chapter all call for homemade crusts. Traditionally, Greek home cooks use fresh yeast as the leavening agent in homemade phyllo. They place their bowls to proof near the fireplace or hearth in old country kitchens. These recipes call for baking powder in lieu of yeast, taking into consideration the time constraints for most American cooks.

The pies are earthy and the flavors inherent in homemade dough are incomparable to the store-bought variety of phyllo. The store-bought variety is, however, certainly fine to use, should you find yourself without time or rolling pin. It comes in one-pound packages and, unless otherwise indicated, look for the thinner variety. Always remember to brush between each layer of phyllo with a little olive oil and melted butter.

For the homemade versions, here are several to choose from. The recipes are ample for 10- or 12-inch round savory pies; if making a *tapsi* or large panful (12×15 inches), double the recipes.

Classic Phyllo Dough

2 to 2½ cups bread flour
1 teaspoon salt
2 teaspoons baking powder
¾ cup water (see Variations)
3 tablespoons extravirgin olive oil

1. In a medium-size bowl, sift together 2 cups of the flour, the salt, and baking powder. Make a well in the center and add water and olive oil. Stir with a fork until all ingredients are combined.

2. Turn dough out onto a lightly floured surface and knead until smooth and silky to the touch, 5 to 7 minutes, adding remaining flour if necessary.

3. Refrigerate dough, covered, for 1 hour (or up to 3 days).

4. *General directions for rolling out phyllo dough:* Remove dough from refrigerator 30 minutes before ready to use. To roll, divide into two equal balls (unless stated otherwise in recipe). Keep dough balls cov-

ered. Roll out each one on a lightly floured surface to a thin, usually 12-inch circle. Always brush bottom sheet—or, if using multisheets or store-bought phyllo, each layer—with olive oil. When layering phyllo, brush each sheet with olive oil. Follow individual directions for making savory pies.

Variations: Greek cooks sometimes replace the water with any of a number of other liquids.

For a springier dough, replace $\frac{3}{4}$ cup water with club soda, seltzer, or beer, or a combination of water and any of the preceding liquids. Try also yogurt or milk in place of half the water, for a malleable but somewhat heavy dough.

In making meat pies, replace 1 tablespoon water with 1 tablespoon red wine vinegar. *Spinach, greens, and leek pies* go especially well with 1 tablespoon ouzo added to the phyllo.

For bourekakia or fried pastries, omit the baking powder.

Classic Phyllo Dough II: Follow directions for classic phyllo dough, using 2 cups all-purpose flour, $\frac{1}{2}$ teaspoon salt, and 2 teaspoons baking powder. Cut 3 tablespoons vegetable shortening into flour, then make a well and add $\frac{1}{2}$ cup water. Eliminate the olive oil.

Whole Wheat Phyllo Dough: Follow directions for classic phyllo dough, using $\frac{3}{4}$ cup whole wheat flour, 1 to $1\frac{1}{4}$ cups bread flour, $\frac{1}{2}$ teaspoon salt, 2 teaspoons baking powder, 3 tablespoons to $\frac{1}{4}$ cup olive oil, and $\frac{3}{4}$ cup warm water. If desired, replace olive oil with $\frac{1}{3}$ cup vegetable shortening and use $\frac{1}{2}$ cup plus 1 tablespoon cold water instead of $\frac{3}{4}$ cup warm water.

Arnopitta

(LAMB PIE)

1½ *pounds ground lamb*

3 *tablespoons ouzo*

1 *tablespoon olive oil, plus 1 teaspoon for brushing pan*

1 *large onion, coarsely chopped (about 1¼ cups)*

1 *garlic clove, minced*

1 *small to medium apple, peeled, cored, and grated*

3 *tablespoons golden seedless raisins*

2 *eggs, slightly beaten, plus 1 yolk for crust*

¾ *cup chopped blanched almonds*

¾ *cup finely chopped parsley*

1 *tablespoon dried mint*

Salt and freshly ground pepper, to taste

One recipe classic phyllo dough flavored with ouzo (page 112)

1. In a medium-size bowl, combine uncooked lamb with ouzo and let stand, covered, in refrigerator for 1 hour.

2. Preheat oven to 350°F. Lightly oil a 10-inch pie dish.

3. In a large skillet, heat the 1 tablespoon oil and sauté onion until translucent. Add garlic, lamb, grated apple, and raisins; sauté, stirring constantly, until lamb is lightly browned. Remove skillet from heat and immediately drain off excess fat. Cool slightly.

4. In a large bowl, combine lamb mixture, beaten eggs, almonds, parsley, mint, salt, and pepper. Mix well.

5. Follow general instructions for rolling out and filling phyllo dough (see pages 112–113). Bake lamb pie for 50 minutes to 1 hour, or until crust is golden brown. (You may have to pour off fat drippings from top of pie, depending on how fatty the lamb itself is.) Serve hot.

Yield: 4 to 6 servings

Serving Suggestions: Ouzo, to match that in the pie filling and dough, would complement this dish nicely. Serve with *horta* and traditional Greek potato salad.

Kolokithopitta me Bobota

(ZUCCHINI AND CORNMEAL PIE)

THIS dish is found most frequently in the northern parts of the country, especially Epirus. *Bobota* is the word for cornmeal.

---

1. In a medium-size pot, boil zucchini until soft but not mushy, 7 to 10 minutes. Drain off all water, cut zucchini into $\frac{1}{4}$-inch slices, and press through a food mill, or mash by hand. Place in a colander or sieve and drain off excess water very well. Set aside and let cool. In the meantime, preheat oven to 375°F. Lightly grease a 10×15×3-inch baking pan.

2. Mix cornmeal and salt together in a large bowl and make a well in the center. Set aside.

3. In a medium-size saucepan, bring milk and water to a boil. Remove saucepan from heat and pour mixture into center of cornmeal. Add yogurt, well-beaten eggs, onion, 3 tablespoons olive oil, zucchini, and spices. Vigorously work liquid into the cornmeal, preferably with a wooden spoon, until a smooth, thick batter is formed.

4. Pour batter into prepared baking pan. Sprinkle with grated cheese and bake for about 45 minutes, or until mixture is soft but solid and golden brown on top. Remove pan from oven and let pie cool in pan for at least 30 minutes before serving. Serve warm.

Yield: 6 to 8 servings

Note: See page 33 for instructions on making strained yogurt, or use 1 cup plain unflavored yogurt and 1 cup sour cream to replace the strained yogurt.

3 pounds zucchini
3 cups yellow cornmeal
1 tablespoon salt
6 cups milk
2 cups water
2 cups strained yogurt (see Note)
3 eggs, very well beaten
1$\frac{1}{2}$ cups finely chopped onion
3 tablespoons olive oil, plus 1 teaspoon for oiling pan
$\frac{1}{4}$ teaspoon ground cumin
$\frac{1}{4}$ teaspoon nutmeg
Coarsely ground green peppercorns or black pepper, to taste (optional)
1$\frac{1}{2}$ cups grated kefalograviera or Parmesan cheese

Classic Kolokithopitta

(SAVORY SQUASH PIE)

*One recipe phyllo
  dough, preferably
  with yogurt (page
  113)*
5 tablespoons olive oil
*5 pounds mixed hard
  squash, peeled,
  seeded, and chopped
  or shredded*
*1 large red onion,
  chopped*
1 cup chopped scallions
*½ cup finely chopped
  fresh parsley*
*¼ cup finely chopped
  fresh dill, packed*
*2 to 3 tablespoons
  finely chopped
  fennel leaves*
*½ pound feta cheese,
  crumbled*
*¼ cup grated kefalotyri
  or Parmesan cheese*
*1 to 2 eggs, slightly
  beaten*
*1 tablespoon chopped
  fresh mint*
*Salt and freshly
  ground pepper, to
  taste*
*Plain bread crumbs
  (optional)*
*1 egg yolk for
  brushing crust*

KOLOKITHOPITTA is one of those seasonal preparations, a specialty in summer and fall, that people look forward to all year. In Greece, it's most often made with zucchini or pumpkin, but may be made with a mix of any squashes, hard and soft.

---

1. Preheat oven to 375°F. Lightly oil a 10½-inch pie dish. Remove phyllo dough from refrigerator.

2. Heat 2 tablespoons of the olive oil in a large heavy skillet and sauté squash until softened, 5 to 7 minutes. Remove skillet from heat, drain squash in a colander, and cool.

3. In a separate skillet, heat 2 tablespoons olive oil and sauté onion and scallions until translucent. Remove skillet from heat.

4. In a large bowl, combine squash and onions, parsley, dill, fennel, cheeses, beaten eggs, mint, salt, and pepper. If mixture is at all liquid, add plain bread crumbs, a tablespoon at a time, but try to avoid this step by draining squash extremely well.

5. Divide phyllo dough into two equal balls. On a lightly floured surface, roll out first half to a 12½-inch circle. Place carefully in pie pan and brush with remaining 1 tablespoon olive oil. Spread filling evenly over dough. Roll out top half of phyllo and carefully place over filling. Trim excess dough, leaving about 1 inch hanging over rim. Press top and bottom layers together and roll inward to form a thick rim. Make several small incisions on surface of dough with a sharp knife. Brush with egg yolk and bake for 35 to 40 minutes, or until crust is golden brown. Remove pan from oven and cool on a wire rack. Serve hot or cold.

Yield: 6 to 8 servings

Serving Suggestions: Intense, pungent retsina would nicely counter the simple, down-home flavor of squash here. Accompany this with a wedge of feta, drizzled with olive oil and sprinkled with oregano, and some hearty bread.

Athena's Classic Spanakopitta

(SPINACH PIE)

THIS is probably *the* ubiquitous Greek *pitta*. The recipe that follows was inspired by my sister, whose spinach pies have graced our table for many a holiday.

─────────────

1. Remove phyllo dough from refrigerator. Preheat oven to 375°F. Lightly oil a 10½-inch pie plate.

2. Wash and chop spinach and squeeze dry thoroughly, then drain very well. Heat 2 tablespoons of the olive oil in a heavy skillet. Sauté scallions and leek for 5 to 7 minutes over medium to low heat, until the green part of the leek is bright and softened and scallions are almost translucent. Add the spinach and stir until wilted, 5 to 7 minutes. The spinach will exude liquid. Remove spinach together with scallions and leeks to a colander, and let drain completely. Set aside and cool.

3. In a large bowl, combine spinach, dill, parsley, scallions, and leek. Add egg, ¼ cup olive oil, feta, kefalotyri, spices, salt, and pepper. Mix thoroughly, preferably with a wooden spoon.

4. Divide phyllo dough in half. On a lightly floured surface, roll out first half of dough to a circle about 12 inches in diameter. Carefully place in oiled pie plate. Brush with remaining 1 tablespoon olive oil. Spread spinach filling evenly over dough.

5. Roll out remaining dough to a 12-inch circle. Carefully place over filling. Gently press top and bottom pastries together and cut away excess, leaving about ½ inch hanging over rim of pie plate. Roll top and bottom pastries together toward inner edge of rim to form a border crust. Make four small incisions in center of pie with a sharp knife. Lightly beat egg yolk and milk and brush pie crust with the mixture. Bake for about 40 minutes, or until crust is golden brown. Serve warm or cold.

Yield: 6 to 8 servings

Serving Suggestions: Classic *spanakopitta* is simple fare that needs a fresh, basic table wine such as Boutari's Lac des Roches.

One recipe phyllo dough of choice (page 112)
Oil, for greasing pan
1½ pounds fresh spinach
¼ cup plus 3 tablespoons extravirgin olive oil
½ pound scallions (white part as well as 2 to 3 inches of green), finely chopped (about 1 cup)
1 large leek (white part as well as 2 to 3 inches of green), coarsely chopped
2 large bunches fresh dill, chopped, or 1 bunch fresh fennel and 1 bunch dill
1 large bunch parsley, chopped
1 egg, slightly beaten
¾ pound feta cheese, crumbled or chopped
2 tablespoons grated kefalotyri or Parmesan cheese
¾ teaspoon ground nutmeg
½ teaspoon ground cumin
Salt and freshly ground pepper
1 egg yolk
2 tablespoons milk

Vasso's Kreatopitta me Béchamel

(GROUND BEEF AND BÉCHAMEL PIE)

THIS might very well be a Greek-American invention. The recipe comes from an excellent home cook and family friend, who serves it on her holiday tables.

*One recipe classic
phyllo dough (page
112)
2 tablespoons olive oil,
plus extra oil for
brushing dough
2 cups finely chopped
onion
1 pound ground beef
1 cup peeled, chopped
plum tomato
1 teaspoon cinnamon
1 teaspoon nutmeg
1 teaspoon ground
cumin
2 bay leaves
½ teaspoon sugar
1 to 2 dried red chile
peppers, crushed
(optional)
15 to 20 whole black
peppercorns
Salt, to taste
1 tablespoon strong
red wine vinegar
1 egg, slightly beaten
2 to 3 cups béchamel,
enriched with 2 egg
yolks (page 40)
2 to 3 tablespoons
grated kefalotyri or
Parmesan cheese,
for sprinkling in
dough*

1. Remove phyllo dough from refrigerator. Divide into four equal balls and let rest, covered, at room temperature while you prepare the filling for this *pitta*.

2. In a large skillet, heat olive oil. Add onion and sauté for 3 to 5 minutes over medium heat until slightly translucent and coated with oil. Add ground beef and sauté, stirring constantly and making sure meat doesn't stick, until beef begins to brown.

3. Add tomatoes, cinnamon, nutmeg, cumin, bay leaves, sugar, hot peppers, peppercorns, and salt. Lower heat and simmer, covered, until liquid has been absorbed, about 15 minutes. Occasionally skim off any fat if meat is not lean. Add a little water, if necessary, to keep from burning or sticking to pan. About 5 minutes before meat is done, add vinegar. When liquid is completely absorbed, remove skillet from heat and let cool for about 20 minutes. Once cooled, mix in slightly beaten egg.

4. While meat is cooling, preheat oven to 375°F. Lightly oil a 9-inch bundt pan.

5. Prepare béchamel sauce.

6. On a lightly floured surface, roll out first dough ball into a circle large enough to fit into bundt pan and hang over its sides by about 4 inches. Place dough in pan gently, being careful not to rip it. The dough has to be loose enough inside the pan so that the weight of the filling won't tear it. Leave at least 2½ inches of dough hanging over the sides of pan. Brush dough with olive oil and sprinkle with grated cheese. Make a small incision in the dough where it rests over center of bundt pan; pull slightly so that there is some extra dough hanging over the middle. This will be pinched together with dough hanging over the sides to form the bottom of the pie. Roll out second dough ball in exactly the same way, place in pan, and brush with oil.

7. Pour béchamel into pan, making sure it's evenly distributed. Add meat mixture. Bring the dough hanging over the outer and inner sides of the pan together and pinch carefully closed.

8. Bake at 375°F for 45 minutes to 1 hour, or until dough is golden brown. Remove from oven and cool in pan for at least 25 minutes before serving. Turn upside down and release gently onto serving platter.

Yield: 6 to 8 servings

Serving Suggestions: This rich dish needs a robust wine to match. Try a dark, full-bodied Nemea, and serve with fried green Italian peppers and hearty *horiatiko* bread.

Roussa Meleti's Three-Meat Cephalonian Pie

1. With 1 teaspoon olive oil, lightly oil a 12-inch round pie pan and set aside. Remove phyllo dough from refrigerator.

2. Heat 2 tablespoons olive oil in a large heavy skillet. Add onion and sauté until translucent, 3 to 5 minutes, stirring frequently with a wooden spoon. Add rice and stir for 1 to 2 minutes, until it begins to brown very lightly. Add meats to skillet and sauté with rice and onion, stirring constantly, until meat begins to brown. Lower heat and add garlic, tomatoes, cinnamon, and nutmeg to skillet. Add a little water, if necessary, to keep meat from sticking and burning. Cook, stirring frequently, for 10 to 15 minutes, until liquid is absorbed and rice softened. Remove skillet from heat and let cool slightly.

3. Preheat oven to 350°F. In a large bowl, combine cooled meat mixture, beaten egg, grated cheese, salt, pepper, and parsley.

4. Divide phyllo dough into four equal balls. On a lightly floured surface, roll out each ball, one at a time, into a thin circle about 14 inches in diameter. Place bottom layer in pie dish and brush lightly with a little of remaining 2 tablespoons olive oil. Place second phyllo sheet over bottom layer and brush with oil. Spread filling evenly over dough. Repeat with top layers, brushing between each with olive oil. Brush top phyllo with egg yolk and bake for 50 minutes to 1 hour, or until crust is golden brown. Remove pan from oven and let cool on a wire rack. Serve warm or cold.

Yield: 6 to 8 servings

Serving Suggestions: Robola Calliga from Cephalonia, to match the place where this pie is from, or a light, crisp, intensely fruity rosé sec by Boutari, are compatible with this fragrant meat pie.

5 tablespoons olive oil
One recipe classic phyllo dough, or one with yogurt or vinegar (page 112)
1¼ cups finely chopped red onion
¼ cup long-grain rice
¼ pound shredded lamb
½ pound shredded pork
¾ pound shredded beef
3 garlic cloves, finely chopped
1½ cups peeled and chopped tomato
¼ teaspoon cinnamon
¼ teaspoon nutmeg
1 egg, slightly beaten
½ cup grated kefalotyri or Parmesan cheese
Salt and freshly ground pepper, to taste
½ cup chopped fresh parsley, packed
1 egg yolk (optional), for brushing crust

Prassopitta

(LEEK PIE)

LEEKS, although cultivated throughout Greece, are especially esteemed in Macedonia and among the Pontian Greeks, who make a number of dishes with them. The leek, like straw to Americans, is the Greek epithet for describing straight hair.

6 tablespoons olive oil
One recipe phyllo
  dough of choice,
  preferably flavored
  with ouzo (page
  112)
2½ pounds leeks
⅓ cup finely chopped
  fresh parsley,
  packed
½ cup finely chopped
  fresh dill, packed
¼ pound feta cheese,
  shredded or
  crumbled
¼ cup grated kefalotyri
  or Parmesan cheese
¾ teaspoon ground
  nutmeg
½ teaspoon sugar
¼ teaspoon ground
  allspice
Salt and freshly
  ground pepper, to
  taste
1 egg, slightly beaten
1 egg yolk, for
  brushing crust

1. Preheat oven to 375°F. Using about 1 teaspoon olive oil, lightly oil a 10½-inch pie plate. Remove phyllo dough from refrigerator.

2. Wash and clean leeks very well, being sure to remove any dirt from between layers. Remove roots. Use white parts and 3 to 4 inches of greens. Cut each leek in half lengthwise and chop into ⅛-inch pieces.

3. Heat 2 tablespoons of the olive oil in a large heavy skillet. Add leeks. Lower heat, cover, and cook for 5 to 8 minutes, checking so that mixture doesn't stick to bottom and burn. Leeks will be bright and soft when they are done. Remove pan from heat and let cool.

4. In a large bowl, combine cooled leek mixture, parsley, dill, feta, 3 tablespoons of the kefalotyri, nutmeg, sugar, allspice, salt, and freshly ground pepper. Toss lightly. Add beaten egg and 2 tablespoons olive oil and combine well so that mixture is moist.

5. Divide phyllo dough into two equal balls. Roll out one at a time on a lightly floured surface to a circle slightly larger than pie plate. Place first half of dough in lightly oiled pie plate, brush with 1 tablespoon olive oil, and spread leek mixture evenly over bottom layer of dough. Sprinkle remaining tablespoon of kefalotyri over top of filling. Place second half of dough over pie.

6. Cut away excess dough, leaving about 1 inch hanging over edge. Seal edges by pressing top and bottom together with thumb and forefinger, and rolling toward inner edge of pie plate. Make four small incisions on top layer of dough with a small, sharp knife. Brush with egg yolk and bake for about 40 minutes, or until crust is golden brown. Remove pie from oven and cool on a wire rack. Serve warm or cold.

Yield: 6 to 8 servings

Serving Suggestions: This is a pungent, spicy dish that needs a soft, medium-dry wine. Try Makedonitiko or Aghioritiko, both by Tsantalis. Serve with *keftedes* and feta or *htipiti*.

Kotopitta me Feta

(CHICKEN AND FETA PIE)

1. Preheat oven to 350°F. Using about 1 teaspoon olive oil, lightly oil a 10½-inch pie plate. Remove phyllo dough from refrigerator until ready to use.

2. In a large bowl, combine diced chicken breast, scallions, dill, celery, pepper, and herbs. Sprinkle feta and grated cheese over mixture and mix again. Add eggs, 2 tablespoons olive oil, and ouzo and toss gently until all ingredients and flavors are thoroughly mixed.

3. Divide phyllo dough into two equal portions. On a lightly floured surface, roll out bottom half of dough to a 12-inch circle. Carefully place in pie dish. Brush with 1 to 2 tablespoons olive oil. Spread chicken mixture evenly over bottom dough.

4. Roll out top half of dough, again to a 12-inch circle. Place over filling. Press top and bottom layers together around edges and trim excess, if necessary. Roll top and bottom edges toward inner rim to seal. Make several small incisions in top of dough with a sharp knife. Brush with egg yolk (optional, for a glossy dough), and bake for 45 to 50 minutes, or until crust is golden brown and chicken tender. Remove pan from oven and let cool on a wire rack. Serve warm or cold.

Yield: 6 to 8 servings

Serving Suggestions: Try a Boutari Lac des Roches or a Robola Calliga with this *pitta*.

¼ cup olive oil, or more if necessary
One recipe phyllo dough of choice flavored with ouzo (page 112)
2 boneless chicken breasts, diced
1 cup chopped scallions
¼ cup chopped fresh dill, packed
½ cup finely chopped celery
Freshly ground pepper, to taste
2 teaspoons dried thyme
Pinch of sage
Pinch of dried mint
½ teaspoon marjoram
½ teaspoon tarragon
⅓ pound feta cheese, crumbled
2 tablespoons grated kefalotyri or Romano cheese
2 eggs, slightly beaten
½ teaspoon ouzo
1 egg yolk (optional), for brushing crust

Anginaropitta

(SAVORY ARTICHOKE PIE)

THIS is a Cephalonia-inspired dish, but without the cinnamon that often tinges this specialty and makes it taste like chocolate.

One recipe classic or whole wheat phyllo dough (pages 112–113)

2 tablespoons olive oil

8 large artichoke hearts, quartered then halved (see page 183)

3 pounds plum tomatoes, peeled, cored, and chopped (about 4 cups)

2 garlic cloves, minced

$\frac{1}{2}$ cup chopped fresh parsley, packed

1 teaspoon dried marjoram

1 tablespoon chopped fresh basil

Salt, to taste

15 to 20 crushed black peppercorns

1 egg, slightly beaten

3 tablespoons grated feta cheese

1. Remove phyllo dough from refrigerator and set aside, covered, until ready to use. Preheat oven to 375°F. Lightly oil a $10\frac{1}{2}$-inch, preferably clay, baking dish.

2. Heat olive oil in a large heavy skillet. Add artichokes, tomatoes, and garlic. Lower heat, cover, and simmer 40 to 50 minutes, stirring occasionally and adding a little water, if necessary, until artichokes are tender and sauce thick. Remove skillet from heat, cool slightly, and add parsley, marjoram, basil, salt, peppercorns, egg, and feta to mixture just before placing in pie plate.

3. Divide the phyllo dough into two equal portions. On a lightly floured surface, roll out half of dough into a 12-inch circle. Place carefully in pie pan and lightly brush dough with oil. Spread artichoke mixture evenly over dough. Roll out remaining half of dough and carefully place over filling. Press top and bottom layers together and roll inward to form a thick rim. Press with prongs of a fork to form serrated design, if desired. Make one or two sharp incisions in top of crust. Bake for 30 minutes, then reduce heat to 350°F and continue to bake for another 20 to 30 minutes, or until crust is golden brown. Remove pan from oven and place on a wire rack to cool. Serve warm or at room temperature.

Yield: 6 to 8 servings

Serving Suggestions: Artichokes are difficult to pair with wine. I would suggest a Náoussa red here or a rich, aromatic Cava Boutari to counter the complex flavors in this *pitta*. Serve *anginaropitta* with a simple bulgur pilaf and a hearty tomato and barley-toast salad.

Lagopitta

(SAVORY RABBIT PIE)

LIKE savory artichoke pie and cod fish pie, this is a traditional Cephalonian dish.

———

1. Marinate rabbit meat with wine, tomatoes, garlic, parsley, mint, marjoram, rosemary, olives, and 2 tablespoons of the olive oil for 3 hours.
2. After rabbit has been marinated, preheat oven to 375°F. Remove phyllo dough from refrigerator and lightly oil a 10½-inch round baking dish.
3. Heat remaining 2 tablespoons olive oil in a large heavy skillet. Sauté onion until translucent. Add rice and sauté until lightly browned, stirring constantly so as not to burn. Add rabbit and marinade mixture to rice, lower heat, and simmer, covered, for 5 to 7 minutes, until most of juice has been absorbed. Set aside to cool slightly.
4. Divide phyllo dough into two equal portions. On a lightly floured surface, roll out half of dough into a 12-inch circle and fit into baking dish. Brush lightly with olive oil. Spread rabbit mixture evenly over dough. Roll out remaining half of dough and carefully place over filling. Press top and bottom layers together and roll inward to form a thick rim. Make one or two small sharp incisions in top of dough. Place in oven and lower heat to 350°F. Bake for about 45 minutes, or until dough is golden brown. Remove pan from oven and place on a wire rack to cool slightly. Serve warm.

Yield: 6 to 8 servings

Serving Suggestion: Rabbit goes with Grande Réserve, no ifs, ands, or buts.

1 medium-size rabbit, cleaned, deboned, and meat shredded
⅔ cup dry red wine
3 tomatoes, peeled, cored, seeded, and chopped (with juice)
4 garlic cloves, minced
3 tablespoons finely chopped fresh parsley
1 teaspoon dried mint
½ teaspoon dried marjoram
Pinch of dried rosemary
5 to 10 black olives, rinsed, pitted, and chopped
5 tablespoons olive oil
One recipe classic phyllo dough (page 112)
1 large white onion, finely chopped
¼ cup long-grain rice
Salt and freshly ground pepper, to taste

Tzoulama

(SWEETENED LIVER PIE)

KYRIA Evanthia is from Vorrous, a small village in the southern part of the county of Iráklion, Crete. She and other locals make *tzoulama* with a layer of mitzithra, a special soft white cheese (page 32). Traditionally, this dish is a carnival specialty, prepared toward the end of *Apokries,* as carnival is called in Greece. It is admittedly one of the oddest dishes in the country's culinary catalog.

**Double recipe of
classic phyllo dough,
to make one large
dough (page 112)**
Butter
2 cups long-grain rice
**2 to 2$\frac{1}{2}$ pounds
chicken livers, diced**
4 cups chicken broth
**$\frac{3}{4}$ cup dark seedless
raisins**
1 cup chopped walnuts
1 to 1$\frac{1}{2}$ cups sugar
**1 pound mitzithra
cheese**
**1 to 2 teaspoons
cinnamon**
$\frac{1}{4}$ cup olive oil

1. Preheat oven to 375°F. Lightly grease an 11 × 15 × 3-inch baking pan. Remove phyllo dough from refrigerator.

2. Heat 3 to 4 tablespoons butter in a large heavy skillet. Add rice and sauté until very lightly browned, stirring constantly so as not to stick. Add livers and sauté until brown. Add broth, bring to a boil, reduce heat, and simmer, uncovered, until liquid is absorbed. Remove skillet from heat and cool slightly. In a medium-size bowl, combine livers and rice with raisins, walnuts, and half the sugar. Set aside until ready to use.

3. Divide phyllo dough into six equal balls. Roll out first ball on a lightly floured surface. Place on bottom of lightly greased baking pan. Brush lightly with oil. Roll out second dough ball and place it on top of the phyllo in the baking pan. Brush lightly with oil.

4. Spread half the mitzithra evenly over the phyllo. Add chicken liver mixture and spread evenly over cheese. Dot with butter and sprinkle with half the cinnamon. Roll out and add another two layers of dough, brushing each lightly with oil. Spread remaining mitzithra then chicken liver mixture evenly over dough, then dot with butter and sprinkle with cinnamon. Roll out remaining dough circles, brushing each lightly with oil. Bake for 50 minutes to 1 hour, until dough is golden brown. Remove pan from oven and let cool slightly. Serve warm.

Yield: 10 to 12 servings

Tiganopitta Epirou

(SKILLET PIE FROM EPIRUS)

THIS will never be the same simple pie one gets for about a thousand drachmas in Kikitsa's little stone taverna in Monodendri, up in the Zagohoria, the northwest reaches of Epirus. The flour is different; the cheese, homemade, certainly is different; and the result here is my humble attempt to reproduce perfection.

1. In a medium-size bowl, sift together flour and salt. Make a well in center and add warm water and 2 tablespoons olive oil. Mix until a dough forms and knead in bowl for 5 to 7 minutes, or slightly longer, until dough is smooth and silky to the touch.

2. Divide dough into several balls, and roll out each on a lightly floured surface to a $\frac{1}{2}$-inch-thick circle a little smaller than the base of the skillet. Dot with feta, fold into a crescent, and flatten with rolling pin or fingertips to a circle about as large as the base of the skillet. Heat remaining $\frac{1}{4}$ cup olive oil in a large heavy skillet. Fry until golden brown, flipping to cook on both sides. Repeat with remaining dough. Serve warm.

1 cup sifted all-purpose flour
$\frac{1}{2}$ teaspoon salt
$\frac{1}{4}$ cup warm water
$\frac{1}{4}$ cup plus 2 tablespoons olive oil
$\frac{1}{2}$ cup grated feta cheese

Yield: About 4 servings

Serving Suggestions: *Horta,* olives, and a high-acid Zitsa white wine, from Epirus, would match this simple recipe perfectly. Try a Kourtaki Apelía, a plain white table wine, or Kourtaki Kouros, too.

Hirinopitta

(GROUND PORK PIE)

One recipe classic
   phyllo dough (page
   112)
2 tablespoons plus 2 to
   4 teaspoons olive oil
1 large onion, coarsely
   chopped (about $1\frac{1}{2}$
   cups)
$\frac{1}{2}$ cup long-grain rice
2 to 3 garlic cloves,
   minced
1 cup finely chopped
   celery
1 pound lean ground
   pork
$\frac{1}{2}$ cup water
$\frac{1}{2}$ cup dry white wine
2 eggs, slightly beaten
1 scant teaspoon finely
   minced orange rind
2 heaping tablespoons
   finely chopped dill
Salt and freshly
   ground pepper, to
   taste
1 egg yolk, for
   brushing crust

1. Preheat oven to 375°F. Lightly oil a $10\frac{1}{2}$-inch pie dish. Remove phyllo dough from refrigerator and let stand, covered, at room temperature until ready to use.

2. Heat the 2 tablespoons olive oil in a large skillet over medium heat and sauté onion until translucent. Add rice and stir constantly for 2 to 3 minutes, being careful not to let rice stick to skillet, until it begins to brown very lightly. Add garlic, celery, and pork and toss together until ground pork also begins to brown. Add water. Continue stirring until rice mixture has absorbed most of the liquid, about 5 minutes. Pour in white wine and let simmer for 3 to 5 minutes longer, until all of liquid is absorbed but mixture is moist. Remove skillet from heat and let cool.

3. In a large bowl, combine pork mixture, beaten eggs, orange rind, dill, salt, and pepper. Mixture should be moist but not liquid.

4. Divide dough into two or four equal-size balls, one for the bottom, one for the top; or two for the bottom, two for the top, as desired. On a lightly floured surface, roll out each ball, one at a time. Place bottom layer or layers in pan and brush each lightly with oil. Spread filling evenly over phyllo, cover with top one or two sheets, again oiling between layers. Leave about 1 inch of dough hanging from rim of pie dish. Cut away excess and pinch top and bottom layers together. Roll up dough around inside rim of dish to form a border. Brush with egg yolk. Make a sharp incision in center of pie. Bake for 50 minutes to 1 hour, or until crust is golden brown. Remove pan from oven and cool slightly. Serve hot.

Yield: 6 to 8 servings

Serving Suggestions: I would go with a Robola Calliga here, or a Boutari demi-sec rosé.

Bakaliaropitta

(FILLET OF COD PIE)

THIS recipe was inspired by an old Cephalonian Lenten specialty and by a chef who is a native of the island. *Pitta*, meatless and without dairy products or olive oil, is traditional fare on the island during Holy Week before Easter. With olive oil, eggs, and cheese, this obviously wouldn't qualify as a Lenten specialty, but it's great nonetheless. Serve with generous portions of *skordalia* (page 85).

---

1. In a large pot with enough water to cover, soak cod at room temperature for 24 hours, changing water every 6 to 8 hours. Remove cod and drain well.

2. Place cod in a large pot with enough water to cover and bring to a boil. Reduce heat and let simmer, covered, over medium heat for $\frac{1}{2}$ hour, until fish is soft and falls apart easily. Remove cod from water and drain well.

3. While cod is boiling, heat 2 tablespoons olive oil in a large skillet. Add scallions and sauté over medium heat until nearly translucent. Add rice and sauté, stirring constantly, for 3 to 5 minutes, until rice begins to brown very lightly. Add tomatoes and continue stirring until most of juice is absorbed. Pour in water and $\frac{1}{2}$ cup white wine and stir mixture, again, until liquid is absorbed. Remove skillet from heat. Cool.

4. Preheat oven to 350°F. Lightly oil a 10$\frac{1}{2}$-inch pie dish. Remove phyllo dough from refrigerator and keep covered until ready to use.

5. Remove any bones from cod and break apart meat into small chunks (not more than about $\frac{1}{2}$ inch in length or width). Place in a large bowl. Add cooled rice mixture, eggs, parsley, mint, marjoram, allspice, grated cheese, salt, pepper, and 2 tablespoons olive oil; combine well.

6. Divide phyllo dough into two equal balls. On a lightly floured surface, roll out first half into a circle 12 to 13 inches in diameter. Carefully place in prepared pie dish, leaving at least 1 inch hanging over the rim. Brush with remaining teaspoon olive oil and spread cod filling evenly over dough. Sprinkle remaining 4 teaspoons white wine over filling.

7. Roll out second half of dough. Place over filling, again leaving at least 1 inch hanging over rim. Cut off any excess. Pinch and roll top and bottom layers together around rim of pan. With a sharp knife, make several small incisions in top of dough. Brush with egg yolk and bake for about 45 minutes, or until crust is golden brown. Remove pan from oven and place on a wire rack to cool slightly. Serve warm.

1 pound salted cod fillet
$\frac{1}{4}$ cup plus 2 teaspoons olive oil
1 cup coarsely chopped scallions
$\frac{1}{2}$ cup whole-grain rice
$\frac{1}{2}$ cup peeled and chopped plum tomato
$\frac{1}{4}$ cup water
$\frac{1}{2}$ cup plus 4 teaspoons dry white wine
One recipe phyllo dough of choice (page 112)
2 eggs, slightly beaten
$\frac{1}{2}$ cup finely chopped parsley
1 teaspoon dried mint
$\frac{1}{2}$ teaspoon marjoram
Dash of allspice
$\frac{1}{4}$ cup grated kefalotyri or Parmesan cheese
Salt and freshly ground pepper, to taste
1 egg yolk, for brushing crust

Yield: 6 to 8 servings

Serving Suggestions: Cod in any shape or form needs retsina. Serve *skordalia* and wild greens *(horta)* with this.

Melitzanopitta Thessalias

(THESSALY EGGPLANT PIE)

MY mother-in-law was the first to describe this dish to me. It's an old recipe, native to the area around Vólos.

---

2 tablespoons olive oil, plus 3 to 4 teaspoons for oiling pan and dough

One recipe classic or whole wheat phyllo dough, flavored with ouzo (page 112)

4 medium eggplants, about 2½ pounds

Strained fresh juice of 1 lemon

Salt

½ cup coarsely chopped scallions

2 garlic cloves, minced

½ cup finely chopped walnuts

¼ cup finely chopped parsley

2 eggs, slightly beaten

1 cup grated kefalotyri or Parmesan cheese

2 teaspoons ouzo

1 teaspoon oregano

Pepper, to taste

3 to 5 tablespoons semolina, depending on looseness of mixture

1 egg yolk, for brushing crust

1. Lightly oil a 10½-inch pie plate and set aside. Remove phyllo dough from refrigerator and let stand at room temperature, covered, until ready to use.

2. Bring a large pot of water to a boil. Drop in eggplants and simmer for about 10 minutes, or until skins are brownish, softened, and slightly wrinkled. Remove eggplants from water; rinse and drain. Let cool.

3. Peel eggplants carefully. Discard skins. Cut each in half lengthwise. In a large bowl, cover eggplants with cold water, lemon juice, and generous salt; let sit for at least 30 minutes. Drain very well and run cold water over them to ensure that salt is removed. Squeeze, in colander, so that eggplant is pulpy and as much water as possible has been removed.

4. In a large bowl, combine eggplant pulp, scallions, garlic, walnuts, and parsley. Add beaten eggs, 2 tablespoons olive oil, and grated cheese. Mix thoroughly. Add ouzo, oregano, and pepper and combine well.

5. Because eggplant will continue to ooze water, add semolina, a tablespoon at a time, until all liquid has been absorbed. The mixture should be moist. Preheat oven to 375°F.

6. Divide phyllo dough into four equal balls and keep covered. On a lightly floured surface, roll out one ball at a time into a paper-thin, almost transparent sheet (about as thick as a dime). Place first sheet in lightly greased pie plate, leaving about 1 inch hanging over rim. Brush lightly with about 1 teaspoon olive oil. Repeat with second dough ball. Spread filling evenly over dough. Repeat dough procedure with top two layers. Pinch and roll top and bottom doughs together to form a border on inside rim of pie plate. Brush with a beaten egg yolk for a glossy surface. Make a small incision in center of pie with a sharp knife and bake for 50 minutes to 1 hour, or until crust is a golden brown. Remove pan from oven and place on a wire rack to cool slightly. Serve warm.

Yield: 6 to 8 servings

Serving Suggestions: The eggplant is almost as filling as meat would be in this pie. Serve it with a rich, oak-barrel–aged Cava Boutari, or a Náoussa, or even a dry, mellow Gouménissa red.

Chapter 9

Soups

Greek soups have come a long way from the pork, blood, vinegar, and salt concoction called black broth *(melas zomos)* that was the mainstay of the ancient Spartans; or from the barley gruel that fed most of ancient Athens.

Soups in Greek cookery are rich and filling, a main meal. There isn't a great variety, but there are some regional variations for the handful of vegetable and legume, fish, innards, and meat soups that do exist.

A *hortosoupa* (greens and vegetables) in northern Greece might be distinguished from its counterpart elsewhere by the addition of fiery red peppers. A *patsas* (tripe) in Salonika might take only *skordostoumbi* (vinegar and garlic) as its choice for tartness; in Epirus, walnuts are sometimes added; and in the Ionian Islands, sometimes tomato might color—and flavor—the brew.

Fresh fish soup in Greece is worth traveling for, and the world's most famous fish soup, bouillabaisse, got its start here, descendent of the ancient *kakavia*.

Avgolemono, or egg and lemon sauce, is by far the most common flavor in Greek soups, and finds its way into many, from fish and chicken, to any number of vegetable and innards soups.

Soups also play an important part in the folk and religious life of Greece. *Bourani,* which is now really a pilaf dish, may first have appeared as a steaming cauldron of rice and spinach broth, prepared in villages in Thessaly on Clean Monday, before Lent, and fed to the poor. *Tirozoumi,* literally "cheese broth," is a traditional meal made with herbs and cheese and served on *Tirini Deutera,* or Cheese Monday, also a pre–Lenten holiday. *Zoumi,* the word for broth, is prepared from fish, meat, or vegetables and is sometimes the only reminder of practices long gone by: During Easter, and during the commemorative Saints' Days on the Orthodox calendar, it was customary in many villages to prepare meat (often goat) and broth in the village square and to give it out as charity to the poor. Everyone usually shared the meal together, outdoors in the bench-strewn streets around the square. It was a practice against poverty and malnutrition—people could eat meat at least one day a year regardless of their economic circumstances. Now, at *pani-gyria,* or religious festivals, throughout the countryside, *zoumi* is often the only part of the meal still distributed free—growing affluence has made the gratuitous meat no longer a necessity. Last, of course, there is the Greek Easter soup, *mageiritsa,* a lamb innards and *avgolemono* soup eaten after the midnight service on Holy Saturday to break the fast.

There are Greek soups to please vegetarian and carnivore alike, rich meat soups and thick meat pottages, but unlike the soup cookery of other countries, few Greeks use stock as a base. It's plain water that usually starts the pot.

Prassoselinosoupa Avgolemono

(LEEK AND CELERY SOUP WITH EGG AND LEMON)

$\frac{1}{4}$ cup olive oil

3 pounds leeks, tough upper greens cut off, and cut into $\frac{1}{8}$-inch rounds

1 pound celery (including leaves), washed and finely chopped

8 cups light stock or water

Salt and freshly ground pepper

$\frac{1}{4}$ teaspoon ground cumin

2 to 3 eggs, at room temperature

Strained fresh juice of 1 to 2 large lemons

1. Heat 2 tablespoons of the olive oil in a large soup pot. Add leeks and celery and stir with a wooden spoon until leeks are translucent. Add stock or water, salt, pepper, and cumin. Cover, bring to a boil, reduce heat, and simmer over low heat for about 1 hour, until vegetables are soft.

2. Remove vegetables from pot with a slotted spoon and puree, together with remaining 2 tablespoons olive oil, either in a food processor or blender. Return to pot and simmer over low heat for 7 to 10 more minutes. Remove pot from heat.

3. In a medium-size bowl, beat together egg and lemon until frothy. Very slowly add 4 to 5 ladlefuls (2 to 3 cups) of hot soup to egg mixture, beating vigorously with a whisk to keep egg from curdling. Pour egg mixture into soup and stir well using a wooden spoon. Serve warm or chilled with a grating of pepper.

Yield: 6 to 8 servings

Serving Suggestions: This creamy, tart soup needs a wedge of feta along with olives, bread, and a crisp, complex wine—either Santorini Boutari, Chateau Matsa, or Robola Calliga.

Kotosoupa Avgolemono

(CHICKEN SOUP WITH EGG AND LEMON)

WHY are we always so enamored of our mother's chicken soup? Mine makes a tangy, creamy one with nothing more than broth, rice, and *avgolemono*. This one is similar except that bits of chicken meat are incorporated into the soup.

1. Bring chicken, onion, and water to a slow boil. Skim foam off top frequently. Add salt to taste and simmer, covered, for 2 to 3 hours, until chicken meat comes away from the bones.

2. Turn off heat and remove chicken and onion from pot with a slotted spoon. Discard onion and debone chicken, shredding or chopping meat fine. Put chicken meat back in pot, bring to a boil, and add rice, bulgur, or *trahana*. Simmer, with cover ajar, adding more water if necessary or desired, until grain is cooked.

3. In the meantime, in a medium-size bowl beat together egg and lemon until frothy. Very slowly add 4 to 5 ladlefuls (2 to 3 cups) of hot soup to egg mixture, beating vigorously with a whisk to keep egg from curdling. Pour egg mixture into pot and stir well with a wooden spoon. Serve immediately. Season individual bowls with freshly ground black pepper.

Yield: 6 to 8 servings

1 medium roasting chicken, 3 to 4 pounds
1 large onion, unpeeled and studded with 2 cloves
2 to 2½ quarts water
Salt, to taste
1 cup long-grain rice, bulgur, or **trahana** *(see page 150)*
2 to 3 eggs, at room temperature
Strained fresh juice of 1 to 2 large lemons
Freshly ground pepper, to taste

Psarosoupa Avgolemono

(FISH SOUP WITH EGG AND LEMON SAUCE)

*8 to 12 cups fish broth
(page 233)
¾ cup long-grain rice
or bulgur
2 to 3 eggs, at room
temperature
Strained fresh juice of
1 to 2 large lemons*

1. Bring broth to a boil in a large soup pot. Add rice and simmer, partially covered, 20 minutes or so, until rice is tender.

2. Beat together egg and lemon until frothy; when rice is cooked, remove pot from heat and slowly add several ladlefuls (2 to 3 cups) of hot soup to egg mixture, beating vigorously to keep egg from curdling. Pour egg mixture into soup, stir well, and return pot to heat for 1 minute. Heat gently but do not allow to boil or egg will curdle. Serve hot.

Yield: 4 to 6 servings

Serving Suggestions: This soup, like all *avgolemono* soups, needs a crisp white wine to stand up to its tartness. Try a delicate, complex Santorini Boutari, a Calliga Robola, or even a Porto Carras Réserve, sometimes hard to find in the States. Serve with *psari Vrasto, horta,* and bread.

Mageiritsa

(EASTER LAMB SOUP)

MAGEIRITSA means whatever the cook can come up with from what's leftover of the main ingredients of the Easter meal, namely roasted lamb or goat. No part of the animal goes to waste. Some people even use the tripe and feet. *Mageiritsa* is prepared on Holy Saturday and is eaten, with *tsoureki* (page 60) and dyed eggs (page 269), to break the fast after the midnight mass. This recipe comes from Ikaria, and the addition of lemon balm *(melissohorto)* might be said to be a local specialty.

1. Wash all innards extremely well and chop heart, lungs, and liver. To prepare intestines, first cut into lengths of 1 to 3 feet to make them easier to handle. Attach each piece to the water faucet and run warm

water through them until they are very clean, squeezing them between thumb and forefinger, if necessary, to force out any impurities.

2. Drop the intestines and head into boiling salted water (enough to cover the head). Remove intestines with a slotted spoon after 2 to 3 minutes, but continue simmering the head for another 25 to 30 minutes, skimming off the scum from the top of the pot as often as necessary to make for a clear broth. Remove and set aside (some people eat it).

3. Cut intestines into small pieces, about ½ inch long. Heat olive oil in a skillet and sauté liver and scallions until wilted. Return intestines to pot and add remaining meats, including shredded lamb, if you're using it, as well as the lettuce and herbs. Add more water, if necessary, and simmer for 50 minutes to one hour. Add rice and continue simmering until soft.

4. In the meantime, in a medium-size bowl, beat together egg and lemon juice until frothy. Very slowly add 4 to 5 ladlefuls (2 to 3 cups) of hot soup to egg mixture, until egg is tempered, beating vigorously with a whisk to keep egg from curdling. Pour egg mixture into pot and stir well with a wooden spoon. Simmer for 1 minute, but don't allow to boil or egg will curdle. Serve hot, seasoned with freshly ground pepper.

Yield: 8 to 10 servings

Serving Suggestions: Only a deep, red Náoussa, which is versatile and delicate, would stand up to this unique Greek soup. For serving ideas, see the Easter menu (page 330).

Intestines, heart, lungs, liver, and head (optional) of 1 lamb
Salt
10 to 12 cups water
¼ cup olive oil
6 to 7 scallions, finely chopped
1 pound boneless lamb, shredded or finely chopped (optional)
½ to ¾ cup shredded lettuce (optional)
1 to 1½ cups chopped fresh parsley
½ cup chopped fresh dill
2 tablespoons chopped fresh mint
½ cup chopped fresh fennel
1 to 2 tablespoons chopped fresh lemon balm, if available
⅓ cup long-grain rice
2 to 3 large eggs, at room temperature
Strained fresh juice of 1 to 2 large lemons
Freshly ground pepper

Kakavia

(CLASSIC FISH SOUP)

½ cup olive oil
¾ cup coarsely chopped
    scallions or leeks
1 medium white onion,
    finely chopped
2 to 3 garlic cloves,
    chopped
3 to 4 ripe plum
    tomatoes, peeled,
    cored, seeded, and
    chopped
1 celery rib, with
    leaves, coarsely
    chopped
3 tablespoons chopped
    fresh fennel
¼ cup chopped fresh
    parsley, packed
8 to 10 cups water
Salt and fresh
    peppercorns, to taste
2 to 3 sprigs fresh
    oregano or thyme
4 to 6 pounds whole
    fish (bass, cod,
    trout, haddock,
    halibut, whiting,
    pollack, snapper,
    trout, grouper, etc.),
    cleaned
1 to 2 pounds mixed
    shellfish (shrimp,
    scallops, mussels,
    lobster), cleaned and
    in shells
¼ cup strained fresh
    lemon juice
Paximathia (page 50)

THIS is, by all accounts, the precursor to modern-day bouillabaisse. It made its way from Greece to Marseilles (Massalia) in about 600 B.C., where it evolved into bouillabaisse. Both soups are named for the pot in which they're cooked—the *kakavi* in Greek, the *bouillet* in French—and both can be made with any number of fresh fish and shellfish. There are many renditions of *kakavia* in Greece; of the two offered here, one is rich, filled with vegetables and herbs, and the other Spartan, made of little more than the sea itself.

---

1. Heat olive oil in a large soup pot and sauté scallions or leeks and onion until wilted. Add garlic, tomatoes, celery, fennel, and parsley; stir once or twice with a wooden spoon. Pour in water; season with fresh oregano or thyme; bring to a rolling boil, and simmer over medium heat until vegetables are almost cooked. Season with salt and pepper.

2. Add fish. Bring to a boil, covered, and simmer over low heat for 15 minutes. Add shellfish, and simmer for 5 to 7 minutes, pour in lemon juice and remove pot from heat. Serve with thick *paximathia* in each bowl.

Yield: About 8 servings

Serving Suggestion: Wine would play second fiddle to this traditional, flavorful soup; try a simple white table wine like Boutari's Lac des Roches, Aghioritiko by Tsantalis, or Apelia or Kouros by Kourtaki.

Rozino's Traditional Ikarian Fisherman's Kakavia

THIS recipe comes from a day spent in an ancient village on the north side of Ikaria, waiting for the spearfishermen to come home. They did, with more than a lucky catch. Then Rozino, our host, made us the simple *kakavia,* served as I think it should be—on a deserted hillside in an old gray stone cabin with no light except the fire and the sun.

To make this *kakavia* you'll need exceedingly fresh fish—any poaching fish (see preceding recipe) will do—cut into large slices, plus some shellfish; enough water to cover the fish, plus ½ cup (or to taste) sea water (the Aegean tastes better than the Atlantic); ¾ to 1 cup olive oil; salt and pepper, to taste; plus ample fresh strained lemon juice—count on using 3 to 4 lemons for 4 pounds of fish.

Bring enough water to cover the fish by 3 or 4 inches, plus sea water and olive oil, to a rolling boil; add the fish and simmer gently until the fish is cooked and tender. Add ample lemon juice to taste, plus salt and pepper, and serve piping hot with fresh bread torn into it in chunks.

Serving Suggestion: Retsina alone would counter this hearty, simple soup.

Yiaourtosoupa Thessalias

(THESSALY COLD YOGURT SOUP)

THIS recipe is from my mother-in-law, who remembers it from her childhood in Vólos. In some parts of Greece, yogurt is made into a refreshing summer cooler. Try this with sheep's-milk yogurt, if it's available. But goat's-milk yogurt will do, too. Strained Greek yogurt may be found in Greek specialty food stores.

In a medium-size bowl, combine yogurt, garlic, cucumber, ground walnuts, 2 tablespoons of the mint, and salt. Refrigerate, covered, for 2 hours. Before serving, thin with ice water or milk and garnish with remaining mint and a thin slice of cucumber, if desired.

Yield: 2 to 3 servings

1½ cups strained Greek yogurt (page 33)
1 garlic clove, crushed
1 cucumber, peeled and shredded, plus 1 thin slice with peel per bowl, for garnish
2 tablespoons ground walnuts
¼ cup chopped fresh mint
Salt, to taste
¾ cup ice water or cold milk

3 tablespoons olive oil
6 scallions
3 pounds plum
    tomatoes, peeled,
    cored, seeded, and
    chopped
8 to 10 cups water or
    light stock
1 whole garlic clove
Salt and freshly
    ground pepper
½ cup long-grain rice,
    bulgur, or trahana
    (page 150)
¼ cup chopped fresh
    parsley
2 to 3 teaspoons red
    wine vinegar

10 to 12 cups water
2½ pounds beef bones
1 to 1¼ pounds beef
    shoulder, cut into
    large wedges
1 unpeeled onion,
    studded with 4 cloves
Salt and freshly
    ground pepper
2 large white
    potatoes, peeled
1 celery root,
    julienned (see Note)
2 cups chopped celery
2 cups diced carrots
5 medium onions,
    peeled and chopped
2 plump tomatoes,
    peeled and chopped
1 cup bulgur or trahana
¾ cup chopped parsley
Grated kefalotyri or
    Parmesan cheese

Domatosoupa Náoussas

(RICH TOMATO SOUP FROM NÁOUSSA)

THICKER than the usual Greek tomato soup, this is an excellent choice with brusco Náoussa red wine.

---

1. Heat olive oil in a large stockpot. Sauté scallions until translucent. Lower heat and add tomatoes, 8 cups water, garlic, salt, and pepper. Simmer, covered, 20 to 25 minutes over low heat.

2. Add rice, cracked wheat, or *trahana,* and more water if necessary. Simmer, covered, over low to medium heat another 25 to 30 minutes, or until grains are tender. Five to 7 minutes before removing soup from heat, add parsley and vinegar and leave uncovered.

Yield: 4 to 6 servings

Serving Suggestions: Only a wine from the same place as this soup would hold up to its richness. Try a Náoussa or Cava Boutari, and serve with wild greens, an array of dips like *melitzanosalata* and *htipiti,* and, of course, bread.

Kreatosoupa me Pligouri

(BEEF SOUP WITH BULGUR)

1. In a large soup pot, bring water, bones, beef, and studded onion to a boil. Season with salt. Lower heat and simmer, covered, skimming off foam frequently, for 2 hours. Remove bones, beef, and onion from stock with a slotted spoon; set meat aside.

2. Add vegetables to stock. Simmer, covered, over low heat for another 1 to 2 hours, adding water, if necessary. Season with salt and pepper. Add bulgur during last 30 minutes and simmer until tender. Ten minutes before removing from heat, stir in parsley. Serve hot, sprinkled with grated cheese.

Yield: 6 to 8 servings

Note: To prepare celery root, peel and dip in water and lemon juice to keep from browning.

Serving Suggestion: An earthy Nemea red, deep and dark, would be the perfect foil to this filling soup.

Faki

(HEARTY LENTIL SOUP)

I HAVE secretly wanted to write a cookbook ever since the days I watched my father, the family cook, keeping vigil over an enormous pot of lentil soup. The Greeks have an expression when someone does something very well, and with love. *"Kendai,"* they say ("He [or she] embroiders"), and that's just what my dad would do whenever he boiled the lowly lentil. This isn't his recipe—he left no written traces of the countless dishes he knew—but I think it's a worthy homage.

The lentil *(faki)* gets its name from *fakos,* or lens, with which its shape has been compared. The legume has been a Greek food since ancient days, although it was considered the poor man's mainstay. The philosophers ate it, says Waverley Root, to prove that they were above worldly pleasures, and the modern Greeks eat it to prove they really know a worldly pleasure when they taste one, because this soup warms plebeian and prince alike on chilly winter days.

---

1. In a large soup pot, heat the $\frac{1}{4}$ cup olive oil and sauté 2 of the onions until translucent. Add lentils and carrots and sauté 2 to 3 minutes, stirring constantly with a wooden spoon. Add garlic, tomatoes, parsley, 6 cups water, bay leaf, salt, pepper, and hot peppers (if desired). Cover, bring to a boil, reduce heat to low, and simmer for 1 to $1\frac{1}{2}$ hours, or until lentils and carrots are very tender. Add more water during cooking, if necessary.

2. Five to 7 minutes before removing soup from heat, pour in vinegar. Serve topped with remaining raw onion and a dribbling of remaining olive oil.

Yield: 6 to 8 servings

Serving Suggestions: *Faki,* among the heartiest of Greek soups, needs the powerful taste of retsina as a balance. Serve this with little else besides feta and bread.

$\frac{1}{4}$ *cup plus 2 tablespoons olive oil*

3 medium white onions, coarsely chopped

2 cups dried baby lentils, rinsed

2 medium carrots, scraped and chopped (about $\frac{3}{4}$ cup)

2 garlic cloves, finely chopped

4 to 5 plum tomatoes, peeled and squeezed (with juice)

$\frac{1}{4}$ *cup finely chopped fresh parsley*

6 to 8 cups water, or more if necessary

1 large bay leaf

Salt and freshly ground pepper, to taste

2 small hot red peppers (optional)

$\frac{1}{4}$ *cup strong red wine vinegar*

½ *pound dried*
chick-peas
2 *teaspoons baking*
soda
½ *cup olive oil*
2 *medium onions,*
finely chopped
3 *large ripe tomatoes,*
peeled, seeded, and
coarsely chopped
1 *large bay leaf*
2 *garlic cloves, sliced*
thin lengthwise
Salt and freshly
ground pepper, to
taste
6 *to 8 cups water, or*
more if necessary
Strained fresh juice of
1 *lemon*

Revithatha

(TANGY CHICK-PEA SOUP)

IT MAY be the nemesis of any child forced to eat it during Lent, but to me this simple soup encompasses all I love about Greek cooking, and that is the ability to make a meal—and a good one, at that—of nature's humblest products.

1. Wash and soak chick-peas according to package directions. Drain and sprinkle with baking soda. Let stand 15 minutes. Remove husks by rubbing chick-peas between thumb and forefinger. Rinse well and drain.

2. In a large soup pot, heat olive oil and sauté onions and chick-peas, stirring with a wooden spoon, until onions are translucent. Add tomatoes and stir over low heat for 2 to 3 minutes with a wooden spoon. Add bay leaf, garlic, salt, pepper, and 6 cups water to start. Cover, bring to a boil, lower heat, and simmer, stirring occasionally, for 1 to 1½ hours, or longer, until chick-peas are tender. Add more water during cooking, if necessary.

3. Remove from heat, discard bay leaf, and stir in lemon juice. Serve warm.

Yield: 4 servings

Serving Suggestion: As far as wines go, only retsina would do here.

¼ *cup olive oil*
2 *onions, diced*
2 *carrots, diced*
1 *celery root, blanched*
in acidulated water
and julienned (see
Note)
2 *celery ribs, plus*
leaves, diced
10 *to 12 cups water*
½ *pound (1 cup) baby*
lima beans, rinsed
and soaked to soften
6 *to 8 plum tomatoes,*
peeled and chopped
Salt and freshly
ground pepper
Strained fresh juice of
½ *lemon*

Fassolatha

(BABY LIMA BEAN SOUP)

1. In a large soup pot, heat ¼ cup olive oil. Sauté onions, carrots, celery root, and celery for 3 to 5 minutes, stirring frequently with a wooden spoon, until onions are translucent.

2. Add water, beans, tomatoes, salt, and pepper, and bring all ingredients to a rolling boil. Lower heat and simmer 2 to 2½ hours, adding more liquid if necessary, until beans are tender. Turn off heat and pour in lemon juice.

Yield: 4 servings

Note: To blanch celery root, cut away tough outer crust; drop into boiling, salted water; after 3 minutes, remove and drop immediately into ice water.

Serving Suggestions: Serve this with wild greens, fried green peppers, or *volvi* (pickled onions). Simple wines like retsina, Lac des Roches, or Kourtaki Apelia go nicely here.

Hortosoupa

(CLASSIC GREEK VEGETABLE SOUP)

1. In a large soup pot, heat olive oil and add onions. Stir with a wooden spoon over medium heat until coated with oil and wilted, 4 to 5 minutes. Add cabbage to pot and stir until cabbage is softened and almost translucent, another 3 to 4 minutes.

2. Toss in diced carrots and celery and stir until coated and slightly softened, 5 to 7 minutes. Add potatoes, stir for 2 to 3 minutes, and cover the pot for 2 to 4 minutes, keeping the heat on low.

3. Pour in stock or water and bring the mixture to a boil. Reduce heat, cover, and simmer for 10 to 12 minutes. Add the chopped tomatoes and their juices. Season with salt. Keep the pot covered and simmer the soup over low heat for 1 hour. Ten minutes before removing pot from heat, stir in parsley. Remove from heat and season individual portions with ground black pepper and grated cheese. Serve hot.

Yield: About 6 servings

$\frac{1}{2}$ cup olive oil
2 large onions, peeled, halved, and diced
1 cup shredded cabbage
3 medium carrots, pared and diced
2 to 3 celery ribs, with leaves, diced
2 to 3 medium potatoes, peeled and diced
8 to 12 cups stock or water
3 to 4 medium tomatoes, peeled, cored, and chopped (with juices)
Salt, to taste
$\frac{1}{3}$ cup chopped fresh parsley
Freshly ground pepper, to taste
Grated Parmesan or kefalotyri cheese, to taste

Patsas

(TRIPE SOUP)

ONE either loves or hates *patsas*. If one happens to be of the former inclination, one goes so far as to travel to the dark and sultry central market in Athens, after 2 A.M. and perhaps in an inebriated state, to take some sobering liquid—a steaming bowl of this age-old soup. Salonika, the real capital for this controversial dish, brims with *patsatzithika*, unadorned eateries whose specialty is tripe soup. The differences are nominal between the Salonika versions and those found in the rest of Greece. The soup is made either with *avgolemono*, or served with a pungent condiment called *skordostoumbi*, basically garlic—lots of it—marinated in red wine vinegar, or, sometimes, made into *patsas protoyiahni*, a dish that falls somewhere between soup and stew and made, distinctly, with tomatoes.

---

1 honeycomb tripe and 1 to 2 lamb or beef feet, cut into thick pieces by the butcher
Salt
1 whole, peeled onion
Avgolemono *(page 39),* **skordostoumbi** *(page 40), or 1 cup chopped, peeled fresh tomatoes*

1. Wash the tripe very well and cut it in half. Wash the feet very well, too. Place both in a large soup pot with enough salted water to cover by 3 or 4 inches. Add the onion and bring to a slow boil. Skim off the foam that forms at the top of the pot. You may have to do this several times. Leave the pot cover slightly ajar and simmer for about $1\frac{1}{2}$ hours, until the tripe is soft and the meat falls away from the bone on the feet.

2. Remove the tripe and feet with a slotted spoon. Cut tripe into small (about $\frac{1}{2}$-inch) pieces and clean the meat away from the bone on the feet. Place the cut-up tripe and meat back in the pot. Bring to a boil again. Simmer over low heat for 30 minutes.

3. At this point, depending on the kind of *patsas* you wish to make, do one of the following:

For patsas with avgolemono: In a medium-size bowl, beat together 2 eggs and the juice of 1 to 2 lemons, to taste. Very slowly add 2 to 3 cups of the soup to the *avgolemono*, drizzling it into the bowl a little at a time and beating all the while. Pour the *avgolemono* back into the soup pot, heat for a minute without allowing it to boil, and serve hot. Garnish, if desired, with parsley.

For patsas with skordostoumbi: The garlic for the *skordostoumbi* (see page 40) should be allowed to marinate in the vinegar for several hours before the mixture is sufficiently flavored. After removing soup from heat, serve it in individual bowls and liberally sprinkle in *skordostoumbi*.

For patsas protoyiahni: Prepare the tripe and feet as for the soup. After skimming the foam off the top of the pot, add $\frac{3}{4}$ to 1 cup tomatoes. Simmer uncovered, so that the liquid will be reduced. After removing the tripe and feet to chop and clean away meat from bone, return them to the pot and season with chopped garlic, to taste, and $\frac{1}{4}$ cup chopped fresh parsley. Simmer uncovered for another 35 to 40 minutes, until the mixture is thick. Serve hot with, if desired, a sprinkling of *skordos-toumbi.*

Yield: 4 to 6 servings

Serving Suggestions: *Patsas* needs only two things: bread and retsina.

Lamb's Head Soup

1 lamb's head, skinned
   and clean, with
   brains and eyes
   intact
Salt, to taste
1 to 2 medium carrots,
   pared and whole
1 to 2 celery ribs
$\frac{1}{2}$ to $\frac{3}{4}$ cup long-grain
   rice
2 egg yolks
$\frac{1}{4}$ to $\frac{1}{2}$ cup strained
   fresh lemon juice
Coarsely crushed black
   peppercorns

1. When you get the head from the butcher, it will be split slightly, lengthwise down the middle. Wash the head thoroughly and scrape away any blood clots.

2. Place head in a large pot with enough salted water to cover by 3 to 4 inches and bring to a slow boil, uncovered. Skim off the foam from the top of the pot. Add carrots and celery. Cover and simmer for 1 to $1\frac{1}{2}$ hours, until the meat and vegetables are tender.

3. Remove head from pot. If desired (see Note) cut away and chop all the meat, including the brains, sweetbreads if there are any, and tongue (you'll have to cut away the rough outer part) and put them back into the pot. Add enough water or stock to make 8 cups. Bring the liquid to a slow boil, add rice, cover, and simmer over low heat until rice is cooked, about 20 minutes.

4. When rice is cooked and soup done, add *avgolemono:* In a medium-size bowl, beat egg yolks with lemon juice. Very slowly and stirring constantly, add a ladleful at a time of hot lamb soup to egg yolk mixture until egg is tempered. Pour *avgolemono* into pot and stir over low heat for 1 minute, without allowing to boil. Serve immediately.

Yield: About 6 to 8 servings

Note: Head may be served separately, in which case you'll have stock with vegetables, rice, *avgolemono,* but no meat.

Serving Suggestion: This almost musky but tart soup requires a simple, fresh wine such as Lac des Roches, or even retsina.

Chapter 10

Pastas and Pilafs

ommon belief has it that the noodle made its way into Europe
via China and Marco Polo. But the Greeks were eating whole
wheat noodles long before Marco Polo set sail.

There is no doubt that the earliest recorded word for noodle in the
Mediterranean is Greek, and that word is *itria,* reports Charles Perry
in *Petits Propos Culinaires* (volume 9, October 1981). *Itriyah* is also the
word for noodle in both Arabic and Hebrew, he writes, and both
languages borrowed it from Aramaic, which in turn lifted it from the
plural of the Greek *itrion.* So it very well may have been the Greeks
who were the first noodle makers.

Even the word macaroni may be derived from the Greek, *makaria,*
a grain product eaten to honor the dead; or from the Greek *maccare,*
which means "cut up, sharply." *Laganum,* the Latin word that may be
the origin of present day *lasagne,* may have been borrowed from Greek
as well. In ancient Rome, *laganum* meant a boiled paste; to the ancient
Greeks, it was a "light bread, not a food." Today, *lagana* refers to a
flat bread eaten before Lent.

Grain is still the basic sustenance for the modern Greeks, although
for them it's mainly in the form of bread, not pasta. There are, however, a few native Greek macaroni products, and not a few ways to
prepare them. Greeks like their pasta soft and traditionally boil it in
broth or sauce, not water. Some of the older recipes, like *manti,* still
call for that.

One type of pasta is the *hilopitta,* a simple egg noodle, still made at
home, especially throughout the countryside. The word translates as a

pitta (any flat dough in Greek is called *pitta*) made from batter, *hilos.* Another traditional pasta is *trahana,* a hard, pebblelike grain product similar to couscous. *Trahana* (which means means crispy or crunchy in Greek) is made at the end of every summer all over Greece with either plain or sour milk (*xynogala*—creamy soured milk, thick like yogurt), yogurt, or tomatoes. It was long a country way of preserving milk and eggs. *Kritharakia,* which is a small, rice-shaped pasta like orzo, isn't homemade any longer, but it's much loved in *giouvetsi,* a dish of meat or chicken and *kritharakia* baked in a special clay dish. *Pligouri,* or cracked wheat, is a staple in the south and northeast of Greece, and *hondros* is a Cretan grain product similar to *trahana* but slightly larger.

Although wheat is the most revered grain among the Greeks, with a long history and deep ties to the country's religious and cultural life, rice, a relative newcomer, enjoys more diversity in the kitchen. Short and medium grain, as well as slightly polished rice are popular among Greek cooks. (The recipes in the following pages call for long-grain rice.) Brown rice or wild rice are almost unheard of. Rice is cooked with meat to make the myriad stuffed and rolled vegetable dishes so admired in the country's cookery; it's boiled into soups and mixed with vegetables and herbs to make some of the *lathera,* or oil-based dishes, such as *spanakorizo* (page 158), *domatorizo* (page 157), and *prassorizo* (page 158); it's cooked with beans and legumes, especially lentils, and combined with minced meat to make *yuverlakia* (page 259); and, cooked up with raisins and nuts and sometimes sweetened with cinnamon, it becomes the *pilaffi tis nifis,* or bride's pilaf, which is served at village weddings all over Greece.

Pastitsio

(CLASSIC BAKED PASTA CASSEROLE)

ITS name is unquestionably Italian in origin, but the practice of baking pasta with meats reflects a Near Eastern influence. With *moussaka,* a similar dish but made with eggplant, *pastitsio* is probably the best known Greek food.

$\frac{1}{4}$ *cup olive oil*
3 medium onions, finely chopped
1$\frac{1}{2}$ pounds ground lean beef
1 large garlic clove, minced
3 cups peeled and chopped plum tomato
1$\frac{1}{4}$ teaspoons cinnamon
1 teaspoon ground nutmeg
6 to 8 whole cloves
1$\frac{1}{4}$ teaspoons allspice
15 to 20 crushed black peppercorns
Salt, to taste
2 to 3 eggs, slightly beaten (optional)
1$\frac{1}{2}$ pounds thick spaghetti
Grated kefalotyri or Parmesan cheese
6 to 8 cups medium béchamel (page 40)

1. In a large skillet, heat 2 tablespoons of the olive oil. Add onion and sauté until translucent, 5 to 7 minutes, stirring frequently with a wooden spoon. Add meat and continue stirring until meat begins to brown. Add garlic, tomatoes, spices, peppercorns, and salt. Stir well to combine all ingredients. Lower heat and simmer, covered, for 35 to 40 minutes, until liquid has been absorbed and meat is cooked (add water if necessary). Remove pan from heat, let meat cool slightly, then add beaten eggs (optional).

2. While meat is simmering, bring a large pot of water to a boil and cook pasta until it is almost done. (It should be just a little firmer than normal.) Remove and drain. Toss with 1 to 2 tablespoons olive oil and grated cheese in a large bowl to keep it from sticking.

3. Preheat oven to 350°F. With remaining olive oil, lightly grease an 11 × 15 × 3-inch baking pan.

4. Make béchamel, adding 3 well-beaten egg yolks, allspice, nutmeg, and grated kefalotyri to sauce, beating vigorously with a wire whisk.

5. Spread half the spaghetti evenly across bottom of baking pan. Pour in meat sauce, spreading evenly over pasta. Sprinkle with 1 to 2 tablespoons grated cheese. Add remaining pasta. Pour béchamel sauce over pasta, making sure it's evenly spread over top of pan. Sprinkle with 2 tablespoons grated cheese. Bake for about 45 minutes, until béchamel thickens and swells and a golden brown crust forms on top.

Yield: 8 to 10 servings

Serving Suggestions: A robust Nemea red would blend well with this rich dish, and with the one that follows. Serve with a green salad such as *maroulosalata.*

Aliki's Politiko Pastitsio

(PHYLLO-WRAPPED BAKED PASTA)

THIS pasta dish comes from the mother of a family friend who's Greek from the Poli (Constantinople). It's similar to the preceding *pastitsio*, but it's slightly sweeter and enveloped in phyllo leaves, as was the tradition in Asia Minor.

---

1. Preheat oven to 350°F. Lightly oil a 9 × 12 × 3-inch baking pan.
2. In a large heavy skillet, heat the olive oil. Add onion and sauté over medium heat until coated and pearly. Add chopped meat and sauté, stirring frequently, until lightly browned. Add tomatoes, salt, pepper, bay leaves, cinnamon, sugar, and peppercorns. Lower heat and simmer, uncovered, stirring frequently with a wooden spoon, for 5 to 7 minutes, until liquid is almost absorbed. Pour in red wine and tomato paste, and continue to simmer over low heat until liquid is gone. Remove skillet from heat and cool slightly. Remove bay leaves.
3. Bring a large pot of water to a boil and cook pasta until almost done. Remove and drain well. Return pasta to pot and combine with meat mixture.
4. While pasta is boiling, make béchamel. Fold in feta and enrich the béchamel, when slightly cooled, with 2 egg yolks.
5. Pour about two thirds of béchamel into meat and pasta mixture and combine well. Reserve one third for top.
6. Layer 4 to 5 sheets of phyllo in baking pan, brushing each layer lightly with butter and oil. Spread meat and pasta mixture evenly over phyllo. Spread remaining béchamel over mixture. Top with 3 to 5 sheets of phyllo, lightly brushing between each with butter and oil. Brush top with egg yolk and milk. Score into serving-size portions and bake for 45 to 50 minutes, or until béchamel has set and phyllo is golden brown.

Yield: 6 to 8 servings

2 tablespoons olive oil
2 medium onions, finely chopped (about 1 cup)
1 pound lean ground beef
¾ cup peeled, chopped plum tomatoes
Salt and freshly ground pepper, to taste
2 bay leaves
1 cinnamon stick
½ teaspoon sugar
10 to 20 crushed black peppercorns
¾ cup semisweet red wine
2 teaspoons tomato paste
1 pound ziti
4 to 6 cups medium béchamel (page 40)
¼ pound feta cheese, grated
1 egg yolk plus 2 to 3 tablespoons milk for brushing top of phyllo
1 pound thin, store-bought phyllo
⅓ cup olive oil and butter combined, for brushing phyllo

Kalamarakia Macaronatha

(PASTA COOKED IN SQUID SAUCE)

THIS dish is traditionally made with octopus. The version here came about quite by accident, but we liked it better than the real thing. To substitute octopus for squid, see the variation.

2 pounds fresh squid,
  cleaned and cut into
  1-inch rings
½ cup olive oil
2 large onions, peeled,
  cut in half
  lengthwise, and
  finely sliced
3 large garlic cloves,
  chopped
2½ cups canned or
  fresh peeled and
  chopped plum
  tomato (with juice)
1 cup dry red wine
2 bay leaves
1 teaspoon oregano
1 teaspoon ground
  cinnamon, or 1
  small stick
½ teaspoon sugar
Salt and freshly
  ground pepper, to
  taste
4 cups water
1 tablespoon tomato
  paste
½ cup finely chopped
  fresh parsley,
  packed
1 pound ditali (pasta)

1. Wash and clean squid. Using your index finger, clean inside of squid thoroughly, removing cartilage. Remove purplish outer membrane, as well as mouth and eyes. Rinse well and cut into 1-inch rings.

2. In a large pot, heat ¼ cup of the olive oil. Add onion and sauté until translucent, about 5 minutes. Add garlic and squid. Stir once or twice, then reduce heat to low. Add tomatoes, wine, bay leaves, oregano, cinnamon, sugar, salt, and pepper. Add ¾ cup water. Cover, bring to boil, and simmer over low heat for 50 minutes to 1 hour, until squid is very tender.

3. Add 3 cups of remaining water. Keep covered but raise heat and bring mixture to a slow boil. Add tomato paste and parsley and stir once or twice with a wooden spoon. Liquid should still be boiling. Uncover, remove bay leaves, add ditali, and stir continuously with a wooden spoon so that pasta doesn't stick together. Add more water if necessary. Continue to boil for 7 to 10 minutes, until pasta is cooked al dente. The sauce should be thick. Remove and serve immediately.

Yield: 4 to 6 servings

Htapothi Macaronatha (**Octopus and Pasta**): Wash a medium-large octopus (about 2½ pounds) in cold water, removing the hard center. Cut into bite-size chunks, about 1½ inches in length. Place octopus in a saucepan without water. Cover and simmer for 15 to 20 minutes over low heat, until all its liquid has been exuded. Add ½ cup of the wine and simmer another 10 to 15 minutes. Add oil, onions, and garlic, and stir once or twice to combine. Add the tomatoes, wine, bay leaves, oregano, cinnamon, sugar, salt, pepper, and ¾ cup water. Bring to boil, lower heat, and simmer for 50 minutes to 1 hour, until tender. Add tomato paste, if necessary, to thicken the sauce, but omit the parsley. Boil the pasta separately and serve topped with octopus sauce.

Serving Suggestion: Although seafood, this dish is meatlike in its richness and needs a brisk, strong red wine such as Náoussa Grande Réserve.

Macaronia me Kima

(SPAGHETTI WITH MEAT SAUCE)

Bring a pot of salted water to a rolling boil and add pasta. Cook to al dente. Combine or top with meat sauce, sprinkle with grated cheese, and serve hot.

Yield: 4 to 6 servings

Variation: Add 1 or 2 hot crushed red peppers to meat sauce, if desired.

1 pound spaghetti
Meat sauce for either version of **pastitsio** *(pages 144 and 145)*
Grated kefalotyri or Parmesan cheese

Macaronia me Domatosaltsa

(PASTA WITH TOMATO SAUCE)

1. In a medium to large saucepan, heat 2 tablespoons of the olive oil. Sauté onion until translucent, stirring with a wooden spoon. Add tomatoes and garlic and stir with onions over medium heat. Add water, 1 cup at first, more if necessary, cinnamon stick, bay leaf, oregano, hot peppers (optional), sugar, salt, and pepper. Cover, bring to boil, then simmer over low heat for 2 hours, checking occasionally so that sauce doesn't burn, and adding water if necessary. During last half hour of cooking, add wine or vinegar and let simmer with lid half covering pot. Remove cinnamon and bay leaf. If desired, drizzle in remaining tablespoon of olive oil when sauce comes off heat.

2. While wine is simmering in sauce, prepare pasta according to package directions. When pasta is cooked, drain well and top with sauce. Serve hot.

Yield: 4 to 6 servings

3 tablespoons olive oil
2 medium onions, finely chopped
3 to 4 cups peeled and chopped plum tomato
2 garlic cloves, minced
2 to 3 cups water
1 small cinnamon stick
1 large bay leaf
1 teaspoon dried oregano or thyme
1 to 2 small hot red peppers, crushed (optional)
$\frac{1}{4}$ to $\frac{1}{2}$ teaspoon sugar
Salt and freshly ground pepper, to taste
$\frac{1}{2}$ cup dry red wine, or $\frac{1}{4}$ cup good red wine vinegar
1 pound spaghetti or other pasta

Macaronia me Saltsa Elias

(MACARONI WITH OLIVE AND TOMATO SAUCE)

THIS is by no means a traditional recipe, but one that has popped up on menus in the last few years in a small but important new wave in Greek cooking—an attempt to utilize some of the cuisine's native ingredients in new ways.

---

2 tablespoons olive oil
1 medium red onion,
  finely chopped
2 to 3 cups chopped
  and peeled fresh
  tomato
4 to 5 thin curls of
  grated orange rind
  (about ½ teaspoon)
1 garlic clove, finely
  chopped
1 to 2 cups water
½ cup dry red wine
1 cup rinsed, pitted,
  and sliced amphissa
  or kalamata olives
2 scant tablespoons
  capers, rinsed
3 tablespoons chopped
  fresh parsley
1 teaspoon dried
  thyme or several
  fresh sprigs
¼ teaspoon crushed
  fennel seed
  (optional)
Salt and freshly
  ground pepper, to
  taste
1 pound macaroni

1. In a heavy saucepan, heat olive oil. Add onion and sauté until translucent, stirring with a wooden spoon. Add tomatoes, orange rind, and garlic. Stir well. Add about 1 cup water, lower heat, and simmer, covered, until sauce thickens, adding more water, if necessary. About 30 minutes before removing sauce from heat, add wine, uncover pot slightly, and continue simmering. Add olives and capers 15 minutes before removing sauce from flame. Stir in herbs, salt, and pepper 10 minutes before sauce is done.

2. While wine is simmering in sauce, prepare pasta according to package directions. When pasta is cooked, drain well and top with sauce. Serve hot.

Yield: 4 to 6 servings

Rizi or Hilopittes me Yiaourtava

(RICE OR NOODLES IN YOGURT SAUCE)

YIAOURTAVA, or yogurt sauce, is a popular condiment in parts of Macedonia and generally among Asia Minor Greeks. Sometimes rice is actually cooked in yogurt, but this works best with homemade yogurt. Commercial yogurt imparts a harsh and very tart flavor to the rice. Here is a simpler version of *yiaourtava.* Try this with sheep's-milk yogurt if you ever come across any, or with the easier-to-find goat's-milk yogurt.

In a medium-size bowl, stir together all ingredients except rice or pasta. Pour over cooked rice or pasta.

Yield: 2 to 4 servings

2 cups plain yogurt, strained for 30 minutes in a double thickness of cheesecloth

1 egg, slightly beaten, at room temperature (optional)

1 teaspoon dried mint, or 3 teaspoons chopped fresh mint

1 garlic clove, finely chopped

$\frac{1}{2}$ to 1 teaspoon cumin

Salt and freshly ground pepper, to taste

1 cup long-grain rice, wild rice, or $\frac{1}{2}$ pound egg noodles, cooked

Trahana

(DRIED, HOMEMADE PASTA PEBBLES)

AT THE end of every summer, Greek women all over the country make this cereal, which is a typical and age-old preparation for winter. There are several versions of *trahana*. Traditionally it is made with what Greeks call *xynogala,* a thick, soured milk, similar in consistency to yogurt. Regular milk is also used, as is yogurt, and tomato pulp and other mashed vegetables sometimes replace the dairy products to make a Lenten version of this homemade grain product. I've eaten a northern Greek version of Lenten *trahana* in Sithonia, Khaldiki—made with ground chick-peas and dried tomatoes—and it was absolutely delicious.

In order to make *trahana* you'll need an outdoor space, and dry hot weather. You can also buy *trahana;* sweet *trahana* (made with whole milk); tart, or *xyno, trahana;* and Cretan *hondros,* a similar product but larger cut, ready made in Greek and Middle Eastern specialty shops. Generally *trahana* is the size of small granules or pebbles. On Cyprus and sometimes in Crete (where it's called *hondros,* or "fat") it's made into larger amorphous chunks. But, all over Greece, it's savored, like rice and pasta, in soups and stews, or fried.

---

1 cup warm milk (whole or low-fat)

3 envelopes active dry yeast

1 teaspoon sugar

½ cup all-purpose flour

12 to 14 cups semolina flour

2 tablespoons salt

8 to 10 eggs, slightly beaten

5 cups strained or unstrained plain yogurt (page 32)

1. In a medium-size bowl, combine warm milk, yeast, sugar, and all-purpose flour. Cover and let stand in a warm draft-free place until doubled.

2. In a very large bowl, stir together semolina flour and salt and make a well in center. Add swollen yeast mixture, eggs, and yogurt. Mix with a fork until a dough begins to form. Turn out dough onto a lightly floured surface and knead for 15 to 20 minutes, until smooth. Cover and let stand in a warm place for 8 to 12 hours (overnight), until the dough is swollen and has soured slightly.

3. The next morning, spread a white cotton or linen cloth in a hot dry place, preferably outdoors in the sun. Break off pieces of dough the size of kiwifruit, flatten into patties about ½-inch thick, and lay out on the cloth for 8 to 10 hours, turning once. Press the semidried patties through a food mill with a large-hole grater, or grate by hand so that dough becomes the size of small pebbles. Leave to dry, turning every so often, for several more days until the dough is rock-hard. If *trahana* is left to dry in the sun, take it indoors at night, and avoid outdoor

drying in polluted areas. Store all winter in a cotton sack, away from humidity and moisture.

4. *For fried trahana:* In a large heavy skillet, heat 3 to 4 tablespoons olive oil. Sauté 1 large coarsely chopped onion until translucent. Add 1 chopped garlic clove and stir in skillet once or twice. Pour in 1 cup *trahana* and stir around pan with a wooden spoon—over medium-low heat—until lightly browned. Add $1\frac{1}{4}$ cups water or stock, season with salt, pepper, and $\frac{1}{2}$ teaspoon dried mint, and simmer over low heat, uncovered, for about 30 minutes, until *trahana* has absorbed the liquid and is tender. Add, if necessary, slightly more water during cooking. Serve sprinkled, if desired, with grated cheese.

For trahana in savory pies: Use $\frac{1}{2}$ to $\frac{3}{4}$ cup as an addition to savory pies. Sauté the *trahana* first in 2 to 3 tablespoons olive oil to soften, then add to pie filling, especially spinach, leek, and squash.

Yield: 10 cups dried *trahana*

Lenten *Trahana*: Omit yeast, dairy products, and sugar in above recipe. Weigh the flour you will use. Prepare an equal weight, combined, of tomatoes, carrots, and peppers as follows: Peel and seed the tomatoes, scrape the carrots, and seed the peppers. Chop all the vegetables. Bring the carrots and peppers to a boil in barely enough water to cover them, until soft and cooked. Strain and puree together with tomatoes. Combine semolina flour and salt and make a well in center. Add pureed vegetables and knead until a dough mass begins to form, adding a bit of water or slightly more flour if necessary. Follow directions for *trahana,* leaving the patties overnight, then grating and drying. This version is wonderful in soup. Use 2 tablespoons per cup of water or broth.

Hilopittes

(HOMEMADE EGG NOODLES)

2 cups semolina flour
1 teaspoon salt
2 large eggs
¼ cup milk, at room
    temperature
2 tablespoons olive oil
Cornmeal

1. In a medium-size bowl, stir together semolina and salt and make a well in center.

2. Add eggs, milk, and olive oil. Using a fork, incorporate flour into liquid by stirring from the center outward, until a ball of dough is formed. Knead on a lightly floured surface for about 10 minutes, until dough is silky to the touch but firm.

3. Cover dough and allow to rest for 1 hour before rolling.

4. Using a knife, divide dough into four equal balls. (See Note.) On a lightly floured surface, roll out each ball into a paper-thin sheet. Sprinkle lightly with cornmeal and roll gently into a scroll. With a sharp knife, cut into strips about ¼-inch wide. Sprinkle a tray lightly with cornmeal. Place noodles on tray and cover. Let dry for at least 30 minutes before boiling.

5. Bring a large pot of water or light stock to a rolling boil. Add noodles, separating carefully to keep them from sticking together. Boil for 3 to 5 minutes. Remove and drain well. Drizzle with 1 or 2 tablespoons olive oil to keep from sticking. Serve with sauce of your choice.

Yield: 4 to 6 servings

Note: If you own a pasta maker, use this recipe and follow machine directions for making noodles.

Manti

(CRESCENT-SHAPED STUFFED PASTA FROM ASIA MINOR)

THIS is a wonderful Asia Minor dish, akin to dumplings, and an old specialty among Constantinople and Smyrna Greeks. Despite the fact that it's time-consuming to prepare, and a recipe from days gone by, it is, like other traditional foods, gaining new popularity. I've found one restaurant in Athens that serves it, whose owners are descended from Asia Minor Greeks. This recipe comes from the mother of a friend who grew up in the Poli, and I think the homemade version is better than any you might stumble across in a restaurant or taverna.

---

1. *To prepare manti:* In a large bowl, sift together flour and salt and make a well in center. Add eggs and water to well and, with a fork, work liquid into flour, stirring from the inside toward the walls of the bowl, until all liquid has been absorbed and a stiff dough forms. Turn out on a lightly floured surface and knead for at least 10 minutes, until dough is silky to the touch but firm. Cover and let rest for at least 1 hour before using (see Note).

2. *To prepare filling:* While dough is resting, in a large bowl, combine chopped meat with onion, parsley, salt, and pepper. Knead to mix thoroughly.

3. Using a knife, divide dough into four equal balls. Roll out each, one at a time, on a lightly floured surface, to a sheet that is thinner than a dime but not translucent. Using a cookie cutter or glass, cut out as many 3-inch circles as possible. Set circles aside and cover. Repeat with remaining dough, reworking scraps of each sheet, so as much dough as possible is used.

4. Fill each circle with about $\frac{1}{2}$ teaspoon filling and fold over to form a half-circle. Seal edges by pressing tightly together with fingertips. Wet fingers a little if necessary, to help seal the dough.

5. In a large pot, bring stock to a rolling boil. Drop in *manti,* a few at a time, and boil for about 5 minutes, until dough is the consistency of a dumpling. Remove with a slotted spoon and set in a large serving bowl. Continue until all *manti* are boiled.

6. While manti are boiling, combine yogurt and garlic.

7. When all manti are cooked, pour a little stock over manti in bowl. Top with chopped fresh tomatoes and yogurt and garlic mixture. Serve hot.

Yield: 6 to 8 servings

Note: Manti can be made in advance and frozen until ready to cook.

Serving Suggestion: Boutari's Grande Réserve, perhaps the best commercially made red wine in Greece, counters this strong-flavored dish perfectly. But a Nemea or Gouménissa red would go nicely here.

MANTI

3 cups all-purpose flour

1 teaspoon salt

2 eggs, slightly beaten

$\frac{1}{2}$ cup water

FILLING

$\frac{3}{4}$ pound chopped lean ground beef or lamb

$\frac{1}{2}$ cup finely chopped onion

$\frac{1}{2}$ cup finely chopped fresh parsley, packed

Salt and freshly ground pepper, to taste

ASSEMBLY

10 cups light stock

3 cups yogurt, preferably strained (page 33)

4 to 5 garlic cloves, finely chopped

3 cups peeled and chopped plum tomato

Cypriot Ravioli

PASTA
**2 cups all-purpose
flour**
½ teaspoon salt
2 large eggs
**1 to 2 tablespoons
olive oil**
¼ cup milk
**Olive oil for frying or
water for boiling**

FILLING
**¾ pound manouri
cheese (see Note)**
**3 tablespoons chopped
fresh mint, or 1
heaping teaspoon
dried**
**¼ to ½ teaspoon
cinnamon, to taste**
Freshly ground pepper
2 eggs, well beaten

1. *To prepare pasta:* In a medium-size bowl, mix together flour and salt. Make a well in center and pour in eggs, olive oil, and milk. With a fork, moving in a circular motion from center of well outward, work flour into egg and milk until all ingredients are combined and a dough begins to form. Turn out dough on to a lightly floured surface and knead for about 10 minutes, until dough is firm but silky to the touch. Cover and let dough rest at room temperature for 1 hour before using.

2. *To prepare filling:* While dough is resting, in a medium-size bowl, combine *manouri* with mint, cinnamon, pepper, and eggs and stir vigorously with a fork or wooden spoon until all the cheese is evenly seasoned. Refrigerate for 30 minutes.

3. Using a knife, divide dough into four equal balls. On a lightly floured surface, roll out each ball into a thin sheet, about the thickness of a dime. Using a cookie cutter or glass, cut out as many 3-inch circles as possible. Place on a large plate or tray, preferably sprinkled with cornmeal to keep them from sticking, and keep covered. Repeat with remaining dough.

4. Fill each circle with about ½ teaspoon filling and fold over to form a half-circle. Seal edges by pressing tightly together with thumb and forefinger, or with the prongs of a fork to form a serrated design. (The ravioli can be frozen at this point until ready to cook.)

5. To cook: Bring a large pot of salted water to a rolling boil, drop in ravioli, and cook for about 5 minutes. Remove with a slotted spoon and drain well. Serve with peeled, chopped fresh tomatoes and a dribbling of olive oil. Or, deep-fry the raw ravioli in hot oil until lightly brown, 1 to 2 minutes, and serve piping hot.

Yield: About 100 ravioli

Note: Manouri, a soft white cheese, can be found in Greek specialty markets. Substitute fresh farmer cheese if manouri is unavailable.

Serving Suggestions: This sounds like a daring combination, but to balance the pungent sweetness of the cinnamon and mint, I'd recommend a rich, sweet Mavrodaphne from Patras or Cephalonia.

Lahanorizo Thrakiotiko

(SPICY CABBAGE AND RICE PILAF, FROM THRACE)

THRACE, in the far northeastern corner of Greece, is home to some excellent dishes. There are many different influences in northern Greek cooking, and one unusual combination found in several dishes is that of cabbage—either pickled or plain—and raisins.

---

1. In a heavy stewing pot, heat butter and sauté onion until soft, 2 to 3 minutes. Add cabbage and sauté over medium heat, stirring frequently with a wooden spoon, until soft and translucent, 3 to 5 minutes.

2. Add tomatoes and water and bring mixture to a gentle boil. Add rice, raisins, almonds, cinnamon, and salt. Lower heat and simmer, uncovered, stirring frequently, until liquid is absorbed and rice cooked.

3. Place mixture into a lightly buttered mold and allow to set for 8 to 10 minutes, then turn out onto a platter. Or toss gently in serving bowl. Serve warm.

Yield: 4 servings

Serving Suggestions: This is another exotic, sweet dish with Eastern overtones that I'd pair with Mavrodaphne from Patras or Cephalonia.

2 tablespoons butter
1 cup coarsely chopped onion
$3\frac{1}{2}$ cups washed, thinly shredded green cabbage
1 cup peeled and chopped plum tomato
$2\frac{3}{4}$ cups water
1 cup long-grain rice
$\frac{1}{2}$ cup dark seedless raisins
$\frac{1}{2}$ cup finely chopped blanched almonds
$\frac{1}{4}$ teaspoon cinnamon
Salt, to taste

Bourani

(BAKED CINNAMON-TINGED RICE AND TOMATO)

YEARS ago, it was a tradition on Clean Monday, in Tirnavos, Thessaly, that a huge cauldron of *bourani* be made in the main square of the village. It began as a simple Lenten dish, a soup of spinach and rice seasoned only with a touch of vinegar, no oil. The pot would be set up in the morning and villagers would gather around to sing baudy songs and engage in a little innocent ribaldry. Now, *bourani* is better known as a rice dish that can be either boiled or baked. Here is a baked version, the combination of several sources.

---

3 tablespoons olive oil
2 medium onions,
  finely chopped
1½ cups long-grain
  rice
1 green Italian pepper,
  finely chopped
2 garlic cloves, finely
  chopped
½ cup chopped fresh
  parsley
3 cups peeled and
  chopped fresh
  tomatoes
2 cups warm water
1 small cinnamon
  stick
Salt and freshly
  ground pepper, to
  taste

1. Preheat oven to 375°F.

2. In a large heavy skillet, heat 2 tablespoons of the olive oil and sauté onion until translucent. Add rice and sauté until slightly softened, being careful not to burn and stirring constantly with a wooden spoon. Remove skillet from heat after rice has cooled for 3 to 4 minutes.

3. In a clay or Pyrex casserole dish, combine rice and onions with remaining ingredients and bake, uncovered, for 45 to 50 minutes, or until rice is tender. Check occasionally and add more water, if necessary, during baking.

4. Remove from oven and cover with a towel or cloth for 15 minutes. Serve warm.

Yield: 4 servings

Serving Suggestions: Despite the tomato in this dish, I would serve it with a crisp, clean wine such as Calliga's Robola. A wedge of a spicy meat pie of rabbit or lamb and a bowl of simple greens counter this nicely, too.

Domatorizo

(TOMATO AND RICE PILAF)

THIS dish (and the three that follow it) falls somewhere between pilafs and *lathera*, a category of stove-top vegetable and legume dishes that translates literally as "oily," because traditionally olive oil made up the basis of their flavor. The recipes here have been modified.

1. In a heavy skillet, heat olive oil and sauté scallions, stirring constantly with a wooden spoon until softened, 2 to 3 minutes. Add rice. Stir continuously with a wooden spoon until the rice is very lightly browned, about 2 minutes.

2. Pour in water and add garlic, bay leaves, salt, and pepper. Lower heat and simmer, uncovered, for 3 to 5 minutes. Add tomatoes and wine. Stir with a wooden spoon gently but continuously for 15 to 20 minutes, until liquid is almost all absorbed (some will be absorbed by rice after it is removed from heat) and rice is cooked. Add parsley and mint 8 to 10 minutes before removing from heat.

3. Remove skillet from heat and place *domatorizo* in a large bowl or mold. Serve warm, sprinkled if desired with grated cheese.

Yield: 4 servings

Serving Suggestions: Retsina or a simple white table wine would both go well with this homespun country dish.

2 to 4 tablespoons olive oil
$\frac{1}{2}$ cup finely chopped scallions
1 cup long-grain rice
$1\frac{1}{4}$ cups water
1 garlic clove, minced
2 bay leaves
Salt and freshly ground pepper, to taste
1 cup peeled, seeded, and chopped plum tomatoes
$\frac{3}{4}$ cup dry white wine
3 tablespoons chopped fresh mint, or 2 scant teaspoons dried mint
$\frac{1}{4}$ cup finely chopped fresh parsley

Spanakorizo

(SPINACH AND RICE PILAF)

SPANAKORIZO is a typical Greek country dish, often eaten warm or cold, and topped with a sunnyside-up egg. Serve with feta and an extra helping of lemon, too.

4 tablespoons olive oil
1 cup finely chopped
    onion
1 cup long-grain rice
1 garlic clove, minced
2½ cups water
8 cups chopped fresh
    spinach (about 1
    pound)
½ cup chopped fresh
    dill, packed
½ teaspoon cumin
Salt and freshly
    ground pepper, to
    taste
Strained fresh juice of
    2 lemons
1 tablespoon quality
    red wine vinegar

1. In a large heavy skillet, heat 2 tablespoons of the olive oil. Add onion and sauté until soft, 2 to 3 minutes. Add rice. Stir with a wooden spoon over medium to high heat until it begins to soften, 2 to 4 minutes. Stir in garlic. Pour in water and stir to keep rice from sticking. Add spinach, dill, cumin, salt, and pepper. Reduce heat to low and simmer, covered, stirring occasionally until all liquid is absorbed and rice is cooked. Add lemon juice 3 minutes before end.

2. Remove skillet from heat and turn *spanakorizo* into a medium-size serving bowl. Pour vinegar and remaining 2 tablespoons olive oil, preferably extra virgin, into mixture. Toss and serve.

Yield: 4 servings

Serving Suggestions: A simple white wine—Tsantali Aghioritiko, Boutari Lac des Roches, or retsina—would best match this humble, earthy dish.

Prassorizo (**Leek and Rice Pilaf**): Omit the spinach, onions, vinegar, and lemon in *spanakorizo*. Use 3 pounds leeks, white part only, chopped. Sauté in 3 tablespoons olive oil until slightly translucent. Add the rice and continue stirring until very lightly browned, 2 to 3 minutes. Pour in water and stir to keep rice from sticking. Add dill, cumin, and ½ teaspoon sugar and simmer over low heat, covered, until rice is cooked and leeks tender. Add a bit more water during cooking, if necessary. Remove skillet from heat and turn *prassorizo* into a medium-size serving bowl. Drizzle in 1 to 2 tablespoons olive oil. Toss and serve.

Moutzientra

(LENTIL AND RICE PILAF, FROM CYPRUS)

1. In a medium-size saucepan, bring lentils and water to a rolling boil over high heat. Add bay leaf, hot pepper, garlic, and tomatoes. Lower heat to medium-low and simmer, covered, for about 35 minutes, stirring occasionally with a wooden spoon, until lentils are softened but not cooked through.

2. While lentils simmer, heat 2 tablespoons of the oil in a large heavy skillet and sauté onion until translucent.

3. When lentils are softened, add rice and onions to pot and simmer for about 20 minutes longer, until rice is cooked. Add more water, if necessary, and stir occasionally to keep mixture from sticking to bottom of pot.

4. Remove pot from heat. Discard bay leaf and mix in remaining 2 tablespoons olive oil. Cover with a cloth for 10 to 15 minutes to retain moisture. Serve warm.

1 cup dried lentils, washed
4½ cups water
1 bay leaf
1 small chile pepper, finely chopped (or less, to taste)
1 garlic clove, finely chopped
1 cup peeled and chopped plum tomato
¼ cup olive oil
1 cup finely chopped red onion
¾ cup long-grain rice

Yield: 4 to 6 servings

Pligouri Pilaffi

(BULGUR PILAF)

BULGUR, *pligouri* to the Greeks, is eaten in soups and stews, and is coming back as a grain used to make simple, hearty pilafs. It can also be used in salads.

In a large pot, bring the salted water to a boil. Add olive oil and bulgur. Reduce heat to low, cover pot, and simmer until water is absorbed and bulgur soft, about 20 minutes.

1½ cups water
Salt, to taste
1 to 2 tablespoons olive oil
1 cup bulgur

Yield: 4 servings

Kolyva

(SWEETENED GRAIN)

KOLYVA in ancient Greece was the name given to small coins and to small round sweets. Today, *kolyva* falls into the general category of symbolic sweet preparations called *polysporia,* or "many grains," because it is made from a combination of wheat or corn and other legumes. Perhaps because wheat is symbolic of life and regeneration, *kolyva* is traditionally served at funerals and memorial services for the dead, as well as on certain saints' days and on *Psychosavato,* or All Souls' Day.

But *kolyva* can also be a vegetarian's dream dessert. In some parts of Greece, it is made from a combination of broad beans, chick-peas, limas, whole wheat, and other legumes boiled together and sweetened with honey or sugar. In Epirus and Thessaly, corn is used as the main grain; in Thrace, wheat with sugar and raisins are the main ingredients. In Macedonia, on December 14, the saint's day of Aghios Moristos, protector of animals, *kolyva* is thrown to the earth and given to animals as a wish for good health; and in Crete, at the port town Aghios Nikolaos, sailors take a bit of *kolyva* with them in their pockets for protection as they go off to sea. This is one of the most significant and symbolic dishes in Greek folklore and religion.

---

4 cups whole wheat
Salt
1 cup sesame seeds,
   lightly toasted
1½ to 2 cups ground
   walnuts
2 cups ground
   almonds
1¼ to 2 cups golden
   seedless raisins
½ cup finely chopped
   fresh parsley
½ to 1 cup
   pomegranate seeds
   (optional)
3 to 4 tablespoons rose
   water (optional)
2 to 3 teaspoons
   cinnamon
½ to ¾ cup sugar or
   honey, to taste
2 to 3 cups
   confectioners' sugar,
   for garnish
Dragées (small silver
   balls for decorating
   cakes), rose petals,
   or blanched whole
   almonds, for
   garnish

1. In a large pot, bring ample, lightly salted water (enough to cover kernels by 3 to 4 inches) to a boil and add whole wheat kernels. Simmer, uncovered, for 1½ to 2 hours, until tender, stirring occasionally to keep wheat from sticking to sides and bottom of pot.

2. Drain the kernels thoroughly and spread to dry on a lint-free cloth or towel.

3. In a large serving bowl, combine whole wheat with the walnuts, almonds, raisins, parsley, pomegranate seeds, rose water, and cinnamon. Add ½ to ¾ cup sugar or honey, tossing to mix well.

4. To serve *kolyva* as a commemorative dish, cover a large serving tray with paper napkins or doilies. Spread the *kolyva* over the napkins or doilies, forming a gentle mound toward the center of the tray. Sift the remaining confectioners' sugar over the *kolyva* and pat down to pack with a large sheet of wax paper or rubber spatula so that sugar forms a kind of icing on top of the *kolyva.* Make a stencil out of cardboard of a Greek cross and the initials of the deceased. Use the

stencils to make a simple design with the silver dragées, rose petals, or almonds on top of *kolyva*. When this is served in church, it's scooped into little bags or onto napkins and distributed at the end of the liturgy. Eat *kolyva* with your fingers or with a spoon.

Yield: About 16 cups or enough for about 50 servings

Chapter 11

Vegetables and Legumes

The essence of Greek food is nature itself—the vegetables and legumes people cultivate in their own gardens and, in the cities, the fresh produce one finds in the traveling farmers' markets. *Laiki agora,* they're called in Greek, literally, "people's market." The name is apt since what has generally been the mainstay of most Greeks is the food that comes directly from their sun-blessed soil.

Of course poverty—or at least scarcity—has dictated most of the Greeks' herbivorous tendencies, but ingenuity and a love of the land and of what it gives have commanded the ways that nature's bounty should be cooked. There is a wealth of vegetable and legume dishes in the country's cookery. Some of those dishes are wholly disagreeable: cauliflower boiled to the point where human teeth become superfluous, or the tenderest zucchini served up in much the same flaccid way. But by and large Greek vegetable cookery is an act of delicate synergy: Nature does her part by providing produce that is nearly always perfect, and the cook does his or her share by preparing it simply and well.

Vegetable cookery falls into two large categories: the *gemista* dishes—stuffed or rolled vegetables—and the *lathera,* literally "oily," referring to the myriad stews and stove-top casseroles where olive oil traditionally is poured without restraint and provides the basic flavor to the dish.

Ground meat (lamb, beef, and sometimes pork), rice, pine nuts, raisins, onions, herbs, and eggplant or squash pulp are all to be found in one place or another among the stuffed and rolled vegetables. In Crete, a land not wanting in metaphors, meatless stuffed vegetables are called "orphans." Zucchini flowers, whole pickled cabbage leaves, and short tubular leeks filled with rice or meat are the most exotic of the *gemista*.

While dishes willingly labeled "oily" might seem anathema to the American palate, the *lathera* stews and casseroles are among the most delicious dishes in Greek cookery. They include some that aren't in this chapter, that are placed instead among the pilafs—*spanakorizo, domatorizo,* and *prassorizo.* But artichokes, sweet peas, okra, and eggplants cooked in a gentle bath of gold-green olive oil with onions, garlic, tomatoes, and herbs will change your mind forever about their misleading epithet. The *lathera* recipes have been toned down here— calling for a quarter or a half cup at best of olive oil to the pot.

As for the legumes, they're plentiful, too, with lima beans, split peas, and lentils leading the list. They're baked into casseroles alone; or cooked into stews with the help of eggplant or spinach; or simmered into culinary purgatory—somewhere between soup and solid—as is the case with the green and yellow split pea. It's boiled to a smooth puree, topped with ample raw onions, and doused, unrepentingly, with a healthful dose of olive oil.

——MOUSSAKAS AND BAKED——
VEGETABLE DISHES

Moussaka

(BAKED EGGPLANT WITH GROUND MEAT AND BÉCHAMEL)

6 to 7 pounds large
eggplants, sliced
lengthwise

Salt

Olive oil

$\frac{1}{2}$ cup plain bread
crumbs (optional)

4 to 6 cups béchamel
sauce (page 40)

1 cup grated kefalotyri
or Parmesan cheese

MEAT SAUCE

Olive oil

4 to 5 medium onions,
coarsely chopped

2 pounds lean chopped
meat

3 cups peeled and
chopped plum
tomatoes, with juice

3 garlic cloves, finely
chopped

7 to 8 whole cloves

1 small cinnamon
stick, or $\frac{1}{2}$ teaspoon
ground

2 small bay leaves

Pinch of allspice

Salt and freshly
ground pepper, to
taste

3 tablespoons tomato
paste

$\frac{1}{2}$ cup dry red wine

INVARIABLY mispronounced with the accent on the second instead of the last syllable, *moussaka* is probably *the* Greek national dish to many foreigners, although its origins are thought to be Asian. Reay Tannahill, in *Food in History,* reports that *moussaka* is the descendent of the Asian *maghmuna,* a "layered dish of mutton, onions, and aubergines." But *moussaka* isn't limited to eggplants; it can refer to any layered vegetable dish baked with ground meat and topped with béchamel.

Moussaka is made everywhere in Greece and most people are familiar with the rendition below, with eggplants. A light summertime version, especially in the islands, is made with potatoes and squash; artichokes are also popular.

———

1. *To prepare eggplants:* In making moussaka, the eggplants are traditionally fried in order to soften them. There has been a move away from such heavy cooking in Greece of late, but should you want to fry them first: Wash eggplants and cut off stems and tips. Cut lengthwise into large oval slices, about $\frac{1}{3}$ inch wide. Place in a large bowl and douse with ample salt. Allow to rest in salt for 45 minutes. Rinse slices very well, drain thoroughly, and pat dry. In a large skillet, heat 2 teaspoons to 1 tablespoon olive oil for every two slices of eggplant. Sauté slices lightly and drain on paper towels.

Or, brush salted, rinsed eggplant slices on both sides with oil and place on an ungreased baking pan. Broil until golden brown and soft.

In either case, remove and cool slightly before using.

2. *To prepare meat sauce:* In a large heavy skillet, heat 2 tablespoons of olive oil and sauté onion until translucent. Add chopped meat and brown lightly. Add tomatoes, garlic, cloves, cinnamon, bay leaves, allspice, salt, pepper, and a little water, if necessary. Lower heat, cover, and simmer for 45 to 50 minutes, adding more water, if necessary. About 5 minutes before turning off heat, add tomato paste and wine.

Keep cover off and simmer until all liquid has been absorbed. Remove skillet from heat and cool slightly.

3. While sauce is simmering, make béchamel. Cover and have ready to use.

4. Preheat oven to 350°F. Lightly oil an 11 × 15 × 3-inch baking pan or Pyrex dish large enough to hold *moussaka.*

5. Sprinkle bread crumbs (optional) on bottom of baking pan. Place a layer of eggplant slices over bread crumbs. Spread meat mixture evenly over eggplant and cover with another layer of eggplant. Gently pour béchamel over top layer. Sprinkle with grated cheese and bake for 45 minutes to 1 hour, or until béchamel is thick and golden brown on top. Serve warm.

Yield: 8 to 10 servings

Moussaka with Zucchini and Potatoes: Cut 2 to $2\frac{1}{2}$ pounds medium-to-large zucchini lengthwise into $\frac{1}{8}$-inch slices. Peel 2 pounds large oval potatoes, peeled and cut lengthwise into $\frac{1}{8}$-inch slices. In a large heavy skillet, heat 2 tablespoons olive oil and sauté vegetables, a few slices at a time, until softened and lightly browned. Add more oil as needed. Remove and drain on paper towels. Assemble and cook as for *moussaka,* using potatoes and zucchini in place of eggplants.

Moussaka with Artichoke Hearts: Wash 18 to 20 whole large artichoke hearts well and submerge in lemon juice and water to keep from blackening. (Four or five 9-ounce boxes of frozen, cut artichokes may be used instead; follow package directions for defrosting.) Bring enough water to cover the artichokes to a rolling boil and parboil the hearts to soften slightly. Remove and drain. Cool slightly and cut in half, if desired. Layer them as you would eggplants.

Serving Suggestions: Any of the Náoussa, Páros, or Nemea dry reds would match the richness of this dish.

Briam

(BAKED MIXED VEGETABLES)

THIS baked vegetable dish is light and easy to prepare. It is a favorite spring and summer meal throughout Greece.

2 tablespoons plus ¼ cup olive oil

3 medium onions, sliced

1¼ pounds small white potatoes, peeled and halved or sliced into thick rounds

1½ pounds zucchini, cut into ⅓-inch rounds

6 to 8 plum tomatoes, peeled and coarsely chopped

2 large bell peppers, seeded and sliced into thin rounds

2 to 3 garlic cloves, finely chopped

1 teaspoon dried oregano

¼ cup chopped fresh parsley

2 tablespoons chopped fresh dill

Salt and freshly ground pepper, to taste

¼ to ½ cup water, or more if necessary

1. Preheat oven to 350°F.

2. In a large heavy skillet, heat the 2 tablespoons olive oil and sauté onion until translucent. Remove skillet from heat.

3. In a medium-size baking pan, combine sautéed onion, vegetables, herbs, salt, pepper, ¼ cup olive oil, and some of the water. Bake for 1½ to 2 hours, until potatoes are tender and vegetables completely cooked. Add a little water during baking, if necessary, and check occasionally to prevent burning. Remove pan from oven, cool slightly, and serve.

Yield: 4 to 6 servings

Serving Suggestions: A table wine such as Boutari's Lac des Roches or a semidry wine like Tsantali's Aghioritiko would go well with *briam*.

——STUFFED VEGETABLES AND—— DOLMADES

Lahanodolmades

(STUFFED, ROLLED CABBAGE LEAVES)

GREEKS have been wrapping their foods since antiquity. In the ancient world, the fig leaf was a much admired delicacy and used to stuff foods similar to the Eastern *dolma*. Today, the green cabbage and the grape leaf are by far the most commonly filled foliage. But there are others, as the next few recipes indicate.

1. Carefully cut out hard core of cabbage and gently separate leaves, being sure not to rip them. Wash thoroughly. Bring a large pot of

water to a boil and submerge cabbage leaves for 2 to 3 minutes, until slightly softened. Remove at once, drain well, and cool.

2. *To prepare meat filling:* In a large heavy skillet, heat 2 tablespoons olive oil and sauté onion until translucent. Add rice and stir until rice begins to brown very lightly. Add chopped meat and stir until lightly browned. Lower heat and add garlic, herbs and spices, salt, pepper, and ½ cup water (more if necessary) to meat mixture. Stir to mix thoroughly, cover, and simmer over low heat until meat is almost cooked and rice softened but not done, 15 to 20 minutes. Add more water, if necessary, to keep meat from sticking to skillet, but liquid should be completely absorbed when mixture is removed from heat. Cool slightly. (When mixture is cool, you may add beaten egg to keep filling moist during remainder of cooking.)

3. Cover the bottom of a large soup pot with 2 tablespoons of the olive oil. Using whatever cabbage leaves are too small to roll or that have ripped or are irregular, cover bottom of pot. Taking one leaf at a time, place about 2 teaspoons of filling (slightly more or less, depending on the size of each leaf) in bottom center of cabbage leaf. Fold over left and right sides, then roll up gently from the bottom toward the top of leaf. Carefully place in pot, seam side down. Repeat process until all filling and leaves are used. Pour ¾ to 1 cup water (enough to come up about 1½ inches in bottom of pot), remaining 2 tablespoons olive oil, and juice of 1 lemon over stuffed cabbage. Place a plate over rolled leaves to press them down. Cover the pot, bring liquid to a boil over medium heat, then reduce heat to low and simmer *dolmades* for 2 to 2½ hours, until leaves are very tender and almost translucent. Add more water to pot, if necessary, during cooking time.

4. There should be at least 1½ cups liquid in pot to use for *avgolemono* sauce (see Note). Remove pot from heat before making *avgolemono* sauce. In a medium-size bowl, beat together the 2 or 3 eggs and remaining lemon juice until frothy. Very slowly add about 3 ladlefuls (1½ cups) of broth to egg mixture, beating vigorously with a whisk to keep egg from curdling. Pour sauce over *lahanodolmades* and serve immediately.

Yield: 4 to 6 servings

Note: *Lahanodolmades* may also be served with béchamel or plain strained yogurt or sour cream in place of *avgolemono* sauce.

Serving Suggestion: To make prosaic cabbage more elegant, I'd serve this with Calliga Robola, a soft white wine with a long finish.

1 large green cabbage
¼ cup olive oil
Strained fresh juice of 2 or 3 lemons
2 to 3 eggs, at room temperature
MEAT FILLING
2 tablespoons olive oil
¾ cup finely chopped onion
½ cup long-grain rice
½ pound ground beef, lamb, or pork
1 garlic clove, finely chopped
¼ cup finely chopped fresh dill, packed
¼ cup finely chopped fresh parsley, packed
1 teaspoon ground cumin
1 teaspoon dried mint
Salt and freshly ground pepper, to taste
1 egg, slightly beaten (optional)

Yiaprakia

(STUFFED PICKLED CABBAGE)

YIAPRAKIA are stuffed cabbage leaves, much like the preceding recipe, except that the cabbage is pickled. *Yiaprakia* are part of the traditional Christmas meal in Macedonia.

**1 whole pickled
   cabbage (see Note)
Meat filling for
   lahanodolmades
   made with ground
   pork (page 166)
$\frac{1}{3}$ cup olive oil
Strained fresh juice of
   1 large lemon**

1. Separate the leaves of the cabbage carefully and rinse extremely well to wash away as much of the salty brine as possible. Drain thoroughly.

2. Prepare the meat and rice filling as for *lahanodolmades*.

3. Pour 2 tablespoons olive oil and 2 tablespoons water on the bottom of a large stewing pot. Cover the bottom of the pot with the ripped or otherwise unusable leaves of the cabbage.

4. Taking one cabbage leaf at a time, fill with meat filling as for *lahanodolmades* and roll in the same fashion. Place the stuffed pickled *yiaprakia* seam side down in the pot. Repeat process until all filling and leaves are used. Pour in remaining olive oil and lemon juice, as well as $1\frac{1}{2}$ to 2 inches of water. Place a plate over rolled leaves to press them down, cover the pot, and simmer over low heat for about 2 hours, or until the cabbage is tender and the meat and rice cooked.

Yield: 4 to 6 servings

Note: Whole pickled cabbage can be found in Greek specialty food shops. Because the pickled cabbage is inherently salty, use salt sparingly in the filling.

Maroulodolmades

(STUFFED, ROLLED ROMAINE LETTUCE)

"I WOULD sell you the cabbage you want, but it's been sitting in those crates for three months, and I wouldn't recommend it for stuffing," my favorite *manavi*, or local vegetable vendor, confided one spring morning as I set out to make *lahanodolmades* for company. I was lucky that morning, it seems, because he confided something else: his wife's best dish—*maroulodolmades*, otherwise known as stuffed lettuce leaves. You can use the stuffing for *lahanodolmades* (page 166) or the rice stuffing below.

---

1. To prepare rice stuffing: In a large heavy skillet, heat 2 tablespoons olive oil. Add scallions and sauté until translucent. Add rice, lower heat to medium, and sauté, stirring constantly, until very lightly browned, being careful not to burn. Pour in water, cover, and simmer until liquid is almost absorbed and rice softened but not cooked. About 5 minutes before removing skillet from heat, add dill, parsley, mint, garlic, fennel, pine nuts, salt, and pepper; stir well to combine. Remove skillet from heat and cool.

2. Bring a large pot of salted water to a boil. Cut off the base of the lettuce and separate the leaves carefully so as not to rip them. Wash well. Submerge a few at a time into boiling water for about 1 minute, until softened, but watch them because if they're too soft they will fall apart. Remove carefully with a slotted spoon and drain very well in a colander.

3. Lightly oil the bottom of a large soup pot. Take whatever leaves are either too small or too irregular to stuff and place them, open, on bottom of pot. With a sharp paring knife, lightly draw an incision down the hard center vein of each leaf that will be used for stuffing, cutting just enough so that leaf can bend to be rolled without breaking.

4. Place 1 teaspoon stuffing in center bottom of leaf. Fold sides inward, and roll up from the bottom toward the top. Place seam side down in pot. Repeat with remaining stuffing and leaves, layering the rolled *dolmades* in the pot, if necessary. Pour juice of 1 lemon, 2 tablespoons olive oil, and about 1 cup water over *dolmades*. Place a plate on top of the *dolmades* to hold them in place, cover pot with lid, and cook over low heat for 1 to 1½ hours, until rice is completely cooked and lettuce is soft.

5. Prepare *avgolemono* sauce: In a medium-size bowl, beat together the 1 or 2 eggs and remaining lemon until frothy. Very slowly add 4 to 5 ladlefuls (2 to 3 cups) of pot juices from step 4 to egg mixture, beating vigorously with a whisk to keep egg from curdling. Pour *avgolemono* over cooked *maroulodolmades,* heat for 1 to 2 minutes over low heat in the pot, without allowing to boil, and serve immediately.

Yield: 4 to 6 servings.

Seskoulodolmades **(Dolmades with Swiss Chard):** Follow the directions for *maroulodolmades, avgolemono* and all, replacing the romaine with 3½ to 4 pounds Swiss chard, cut, washed, and parboiled just like lettuce.

Serving Suggestions: Boutari Santorini, with its depth and crispness, matches these two dishes well. And so do the delicate Chateau Matsa from Savatiano grapes, also by Boutari, and Robola Calliga.

---

2 tablespoons olive oil
½ cup finely chopped scallions
¾ cup long-grain rice
1½ cups water
½ cup finely chopped fresh dill
¼ cup finely chopped fresh parsley
2 tablespoons finely chopped fresh mint
1 garlic clove, finely chopped
1 tablespoon finely chopped fresh fennel (optional)
4 to 6 tablespoons lightly toasted pine nuts (optional)
Salt and freshly ground pepper, to taste
3 heads romaine lettuce
3 to 4 tablespoons olive oil
Strained fresh juice of 2 or 3 lemons
2 to 3 eggs, at room temperature

Grape Leaves Stuffed with Lentils and Rice

DOLMADES stuffed with lentils and rice might turn out to be a vegetarian's dream. It's certainly not a standard dish in Greek cookery, but it is a delicious deviation.

---

35 to 40 grape leaves, fresh or packed in brine (see Note)
8 cups water, scalding
½ cup plus 2 tablespoons olive oil
2 medium onions, finely chopped
3 garlic cloves, finely chopped
½ cup long-grain rice
½ bunch chopped fresh parsley (20 to 25 sprigs)
⅔ cup cooked lentils
1 large, soft, ripe tomato, peeled and chopped
1 teaspoon dried mint
Dash of ground cloves
Salt and freshly ground pepper, to taste

1. If using grape leaves packed in brine, rinse them very well. Submerge either fresh or pickled leaves in scalding water for 4 to 6 minutes to soften. Remove with a slotted spoon, being careful not to rip the leaves. Rinse well several times and drain in a colander.

2. In a large, heavy skillet, heat 3 tablespoons of the olive oil. Add onions and sauté, stirring occasionally with a wooden spoon, until translucent. Add garlic and stir for 30 seconds. Add rice, lower heat, and sauté, stirring constantly, for 5 to 7 minutes, until rice is very lightly browned and softened. Mix in chopped parsley and stir for another minute. Remove skillet from heat.

3. In a medium-size bowl, gently mix cooked lentils, rice mixture, chopped tomato, mint, cloves, salt, pepper, and 3 tablespoons olive oil. Separate grape leaves that are too small or too irregular to roll. Pour 2 tablespoons olive oil on bottom of a medium-size saucepan. Layer 4 to 5 imperfect leaves over oil.

4. Taking one leaf at a time, snip off any remainder of a hard stem. Place 1 teaspoon rice mixture in center bottom of leaf (see illustration). Fold the left and right sides over filling and roll up, gently but tightly, from bottom to top, until a bite-size little log is formed. Place seamside down over leaves on bottom of pot. Repeat with remaining stuffing and leaves. Pour remaining olive oil and ½ cup water over rolled *dolmades*. Place a dish over *dolmadakia* so they don't loosen when cooking. Cover pot with lid and cook over low heat for 45 minutes to 1 hour, or until leaves are tender and rice thoroughly cooked. Serve warm or cold.

Yield: 4 to 6 servings

Note: Grape leaves are usually stuffed with the meat filling used in *lahanodolmades* (page 166), or with rice, as in *dolmadakia yialantzi* (page

82). If using the *lahanodolmades* meat filling for this recipe, divide the filling in half for 35 to 40 grape leaves, or double the number of grape leaves. Use fresh or pickled leaves, and follow directions above for softening.

Fisekia

(STUFFED LEEKS)

THIS old Macedonian recipe is named for the cylindrical shell of a rifle or cannon, to which some imaginative gourmet noticed a resemblance.

---

2 large firm leeks
½ cup olive oil
1 medium onion,
*   finely chopped*
½ cup long-grain rice
½ pound chopped meat
Salt and freshly
*   ground pepper, to*
*   taste*
1 cup finely chopped
*   fresh parsley,*
*   packed*
1 teaspoon dried mint,
*   or 3 teaspoons fresh*
Strained fresh juice of
*   1 lemon*

1. Cut off tough upper greens and roots of leeks, enough so that there are 8 to 10 inches of the vegetable left. Cut in half across the width, to make cylinders 4 to 5 inches long. Taking a sharp knife, carefully and gently draw it lengthwise down the center of each leek cylinder, to split it open, one or two layers at a time. Gently remove each layer of leek. (They will form self-closing cylinders.) Wash thoroughly. Chop the tight inner core to use in stuffing.

2. In a large heavy skillet, heat 2 to 3 tablespoons olive oil and sauté onions and chopped inner core of leeks over medium heat, until coated with oil and wilted. Add rice and sauté for 2 to 4 minutes, stirring constantly with a wooden spoon and being careful not to burn, until rice begins to brown lightly. Add chopped meat and brown. Add salt, pepper, and 1 cup water. Reduce heat and simmer, half covered, until liquid is absorbed and rice is softened but not thoroughly cooked. Remove skillet from heat, toss in parsley and mint, and cool slightly.

3. On the bottom of a large stewing pot, spread 2 to 3 tablespoons olive oil and 2 to 3 tablespoons water. Gently spread 1 to 1½ teaspoons filling along the lengthwise "trough" inside each leek. Don't overstuff because the rice will expand when cooked. The curve of the leeks will cause them to curl naturally into long rolls. Carefully place leeks side by side in neat rows on bottom of pot, making several layers, if necessary. Pour lemon juice over them and cover them with a plate to keep them from opening. Add enough water just to keep the bottom of the pot moist. Cover the pot, reduce heat to low, and simmer the *fisekia* for about 30 minutes, or until the leeks are tender and the stuffing is cooked. If necessary, add more water during cooking. When *fisekia* are done, drizzle in remaining olive oil. Serve warm or cold.

Yield: About 3 dozen

Variation: Make the *fisekia* with the vegetarian stuffing for *maroulodolmades* (page 168).

Serving Suggestion: I love this dish—it's so delicate—and I think it needs a complex wine to match. I'd place it with Chateau Matsa or with Calliga's Robola.

Kolokithakia Yemista

(STUFFED ZUCCHINI)

1. Wash zucchini and cut off about 1 inch from top. Taking either a teaspoon or a potato peeler, gently scoop out inside of squash, being careful not to puncture shells. Set aside hollowed shells. Chop removed flesh and set aside.

2. In a large heavy skillet, heat 2 tablespoons of the olive oil. Sauté scallions until translucent. Add rice and cook, stirring with a wooden spoon, for 3 to 4 minutes, until very lightly browned. Reduce heat, add chopped zucchini, garlic, cumin, salt, pepper, and raisins. Stir to combine all ingredients. Add $\frac{1}{2}$ to 1 cup water, if necessary, to keep rice from burning. Simmer, covered, over low heat until rice is softened but not cooked. Remove to a medium bowl and cool slightly. When stuffing has cooled, add egg and herbs and combine well.

3. Gently fill each hollowed zucchini shell with stuffing, leaving about $\frac{1}{2}$ inch near opening for rice to expand (see Note). Pour remaining 2 tablespoons olive oil and $\frac{1}{2}$ to 1 cup water into a pot large enough to hold squash tightly upright. Place squash, open side up, in pot. Cover and simmer over low heat for 40 to 45 minutes, or until squash is tender and rice cooked. Remove and serve warm or cold, topped, if desired, with béchamel sauce.

Yield: 4 to 6 servings

Note: If any filling is left over, shape it into balls or small cigars shapes and cook along with stuffed squash. Zucchini may also be stuffed with the meat filling used in cabbage *dolmades* (page 166).

Serving Suggestion: Try a simple table wine with this dish—Apelia by Kourtaki, Lac des Roches by Boutari, or even a subtle retsina.

10 to 12 medium zucchini
$\frac{1}{4}$ cup olive oil
4 to 5 scallions, finely chopped
1 cup long-grain rice
2 garlic cloves, finely chopped
$\frac{1}{2}$ teaspoon ground cumin
Salt and freshly ground pepper, to taste
$\frac{1}{4}$ cup dark seedless raisins (optional)
1 egg, slightly beaten (optional)
$\frac{1}{4}$ cup chopped fresh parsley, packed
2 tablespoons chopped fresh mint
2 tablespoons chopped fresh dill
1 to 2 cups béchamel sauce (page 40; optional)

Kolokithokorfathes Yemistoi

(STUFFED ZUCCHINI BLOSSOMS)

THE blossoms of the zucchini are sold at farmer's markets throughout Greece at the end of May and beginning of June. The sight of them is lovely—large, fragile yellow flowers jutting from crates or scattered along large tables. They come attached, sometimes just tenuously, to the squash itself. This is an exotic dish in Greece and one that displays the deftness of the cook because the flowers tear easily and dry out very quickly. They should be as fresh as possible before making.

Kolokithokorfathes may be either baked or prepared in a large heavy pot, such as a Dutch oven.

---

15 to 20 zucchini
  blossoms, attached
  to the squash
6 tablespoons olive oil
1 cup finely chopped
  scallions or white
  onions
$\frac{1}{2}$ cup long-grain rice
1 cup chopped fresh
  tomato
1 to 2 garlic cloves (to
  taste), finely
  chopped
$\frac{1}{2}$ to 1 cup water or
  dry white wine
2 tablespoons finely
  chopped fresh fennel
  leaves
3 tablespoons finely
  chopped dill
3 tablespoons finely
  chopped fresh
  parsley
2 tablespoons finely
  chopped fresh mint
Salt and freshly
  ground pepper, to
  taste

1. Place the zucchini (with blossoms attached) upright in a small vase or bowl, and soak the stems in cold water overnight. Don't wet the flowers. The blossoms absorb moisture very quickly, and soaking the stalks helps keep them soft.

2. When ready to use the flowers, make the stuffing: In a large heavy skillet, heat 3 tablespoons olive oil and sauté scallions until translucent. Add rice and sauté 2 to 4 minutes, stirring with a wooden spoon, until it begins to brown very lightly. Add tomato and garlic. Stir well to combine all ingredients. Add $\frac{1}{2}$ cup water or wine. Reduce heat, cover skillet, and simmer for 10 to 12 minutes, adding more water, if necessary, until rice is softened but not thoroughly cooked and liquid is absorbed. Remove skillet from heat; toss in herbs, salt, and pepper; cool the mixture slightly.

3. Pour remaining olive oil in bottom of a stewing pot.

4. Gently cut off each blossom from zucchini, being sure not to tear flower or make a hole in its base. Take one blossom at a time and gently fill with about $1\frac{1}{2}$ teaspoons rice stuffing. Fold the top of the blossom over to close it. Place each flower on its side in the stewing pot. Gently pour in barely enough water to cover about half the blossoms.

5. Place a plate over the blossoms to keep them from opening. Cook, covered, over low heat for about $1\frac{1}{2}$ hours, or until the blossoms are tender and the rice is done, checking every 20 minutes to see if more water is necessary. Serve warm.

Yield: About 4 servings

Serving Suggestions: This, like stuffed leeks, is one of the truly special dishes in Greek cookery. I'd serve it with one of the country's delicate, complex white wines: a dry Santorini or a Chateau Matsa. A hearty *spanakopitta* or even squash pie *(kolokithopitta)* would accompany the stuffed blossoms nicely, as would a stunning plate of *piperies florinis* (roasted red peppers).

Yemista Orphana

(MEATLESS OR "ORPHANED" STUFFED VEGETABLES)

10 to 12 large, firm, ripe tomatoes, or any mix of tomatoes, bell peppers, zucchini, and eggplants (see Note)

¼ cup olive oil

5 to 6 scallions, finely chopped

1 cup long-grain rice

2 garlic cloves, finely chopped

1 small cinnamon stick (optional)

⅓ cup dark or light seedless raisins

⅓ cup lightly toasted pine nuts

¾ cup water, or more if necessary

Salt and freshly ground pepper, to taste

¼ cup chopped fresh parsley, packed

2 to 3 tablespoons chopped fresh mint

1 cup béchamel sauce (page 40), or 12 stuffed grape leaves (both optional)

"ORPHANED" is the epithet used on Crete, where this recipe was obtained, to describe meatless stuffed vegetables. Tomatoes are probably the most commonly stuffed vegetables, and like *moussaka* and *pastitsio*, are probably among the handful of foods that evoke Greece to most visitors. Meatless stuffed vegetables are also called *nistisimes*, or Lenten, regardless of the season. *Yemista* simply means "stuffed."

On Crete, raisins are a staple in rice stuffing; they are common, actually, throughout the country, and are frequently found in the company of pine nuts or almonds. To make this a truly Cretan dish, crown the sumptuous vegetables not with their own severed caps, nor even with a generous ladling of stiff béchamel, but with an earthy stuffed grape leaf as a stopper. *Yemista* are also sometimes topped with a mixture of coarse plain bread crumbs and crumbled feta.

The most common way to prepare this dish is with stuffed peppers and eggplants in the same pan. On Sundays in Greece, bakeries are open only for the public use of their ovens (for a small fee), and even today, when most people—in the cities at least—have their own ovens, one sees husband after husband carrying large round pans to and from the bakeries. The tradition is that Sunday is the woman's day off, although it always seemed to me a lot more work to stuff a tray full of vegetables than to carry a laden pan to the local baker's oven. . . .

---

1. Wash the vegetables. Take a very sharp knife and slice off the top of each tomato and/or pepper. Seed the pepper. Keep each vegetable and "cap" together, since the tops will be fit back on when vegetables are stuffed.

2. With a teaspoon, gently scoop out the pulp of each tomato, being careful not to tear the outer skin. Leave a shell thick enough (about ½ inch) to hold stuffing. Remove seeds, chop pulp, and place, with juices, in a large bowl.

3. In a large heavy skillet, heat 2 tablespoons of the olive oil and sauté scallions until translucent. Add the rice and stir frequently until very lightly browned, 3 to 4 minutes. Add tomato pulp, garlic, cinnamon stick, raisins, pine nuts, and water. Reduce heat, cover skillet, and simmer for 5 to 7 minutes, until rice is softened but not cooked and

most of liquid is absorbed. (The mixture should be moist.) Remove
cinnamon stick; season stuffing with salt and pepper; toss in herbs.

4. Preheat oven to 350°F. Stuff the vegetables with rice filling and
crown either with their own caps, a stuffed grape leaf, or a generous
ladling of thick béchamel. Place in a baking pan. Add a little water to
pan (about $\frac{1}{4}$ cup), drizzle remaining 2 tablespoons olive oil over the
yemista, and bake for 50 minutes to 1 hour, until vegetables are soft
and blistery (for tomatoes and peppers) and rice cooked. Baste with pan
juices during baking, if necessary. Serve warm or cold.

Yield: 4 to 6 servings

Note: If using eggplants in this recipe, keep them whole. Cut off the
stems and scoop out the pulp. Finely chop the eggplant pulp, discarding
as many of the bitter seeds as possible, and sauté it together with
scallions and rice.

Variation: To make meat-stuffed tomatoes and peppers, use the meat
filling for *lahanodolmades* (page 166). Substitute cinnamon for the
cumin, and use the tomato pulp and raisins and pine nuts, if desired.

Serving Suggestions: Almost any wine could go well with stuffed
tomatoes, peppers, and eggplants. Try the simple white table wines, like
Lac des Roches, or even a more robust Nemea red. Make sure feta—as
well as bread and olives and an array of tart dips—is on the table when
you serve this dish.

Anginares Yemistes

(STUFFED ARTICHOKES)

2 cups water
3 to 4 lemons
12 large artichokes
Meat stuffing for
   lahanodomades
   (page 166)
½ cup crumbled feta
   cheese
Béchamel (page 40) or
   avgolemono *(page*
   39)

1. Have ready a large bowl of 2 cups cold water mixed with the juice of 2 lemons. Cut off stems and tough outer leaves and chop off 1 to 1½ inches from top of artichokes. Open flowers and, using a teaspoon or potato peeler, scrape out choke. Rub each artichoke with lemon as soon as you clean it and then submerge it immediately in lemon water to keep it from turning brown. Soak until ready to use.

2. Prepare meat filling. When it has cooled slightly, add crumbled feta and mix well. Lightly oil bottom of a large pot. Stuff each artichoke with about 2 to 3 tablespoons filling. Arrange artichokes in pot, layering if necessary. Add ¼ to ½ cup water. (See Note.) Cover and cook over medium heat for 50 minutes to 1 hour, or until artichokes are soft and rice tender. Serve warm with béchamel or *avgolemono* sauce.

Yield: 4 to 6 servings

Note: A little béchamel is sometimes spooned gently over each artichoke before cooking, to form a crust.

Serving Suggestion: I would recommend a deep Náoussa with stuffed artichokes, to match their strong flavor.

Imam Bayaldi

(ONION-STUFFED BAKED EGGPLANTS)

THIS is a classic throughout the Near East and Greece. Its name is a genial reference to the fact that this is, indeed, a filling dish, so filling that even the imam—or priest—gorged himself and swooned *(bayaldi)*, which is what its name means in translation.

---

1. Lightly oil a baking dish large enough to hold 8 eggplant halves.
2. Wash eggplants and cut off stems. Cut in half lengthwise. Sprinkle with ample salt and let stand 45 minutes to 1 hour. Rinse very well and pat dry.
3. In a large heavy skillet, heat 2 to 3 tablespoons olive oil. Sauté as many of the eggplants as will fit in the skillet, turning them on both sides, for 3 to 4 minutes, or until flesh is lightly golden in color. Remove eggplants from skillet, set aside, and cool slightly. Repeat with remaining eggplants, adding more oil each time.
4. With either a fork or a sharp knife, gently pull away flesh from inside of each eggplant half, discarding as many of the seeds as possible and leaving about $\frac{1}{4}$ inch of skin. Chop the flesh and set aside.
5. In a large heavy skillet, heat 3 to 4 tablespoons olive oil and sauté onion until translucent. Add chopped eggplant flesh, tomatoes, garlic, and wine. Reduce heat, cover, and simmer until liquid is absorbed. Stir in herbs a few minutes before removing mixture from heat. Season with salt and pepper. Set aside until ready to use.
6. Preheat oven to 350°F. Fill each eggplant half with onion mixture, shaping filling into a gentle mound (there should be ample filling to do this). Place eggplant halves in baking pan and bake for 30 to 35 minutes, or until eggplants are completely cooked. Serve hot or cold, sprinkled, if desired, with grated Parmesan cheese.

4 medium to large oval eggplants
Salt
Olive oil
8 medium onions, coarsely chopped
10 to 12 plum tomatoes, peeled, cored, and chopped
3 to 4 large garlic cloves, finely chopped
$\frac{1}{4}$ cup dry red wine
1 cup chopped fresh parsley
2 teaspoons dried oregano
Freshly ground pepper, to taste
Grated Parmesan cheese (optional)

Yield: 4 servings

Serving Suggestions: Dominated by onions, this dish needs a wine that's brisk and deep and complex. I would have with this a Náoussa Grande Réserve or a luscious Gouménissa red.

Melitzanes Papoutsakia

(EGGPLANT "SHOES" STUFFED WITH MEAT)

6 to 8 small to medium eggplants (not longer than 5 inches and preferably thin), washed and dried

Olive oil

¾ cup finely chopped onion

½ pound ground beef

3 large plump ripe tomatoes, peeled, cored, and chopped (or 4 to 5 plum tomatoes)

2 garlic cloves, finely chopped

½ cup chopped fresh parsley

Salt and freshly ground pepper, to taste

½ cup grated kefalotyri or Parmesan cheese

2 cups medium to thick béchamel (page 40)

½ cup plain bread crumbs

1. Cut off eggplant stems and discard. Cut eggplants in half lengthwise. With a teaspoon or a small sharp knife, very gently remove pulp, discarding seeds and being careful not to tear or puncture eggplant skin. (Leave shells about ⅛ inch thick.)

2. Chop the eggplant pulp. In a large heavy skillet, heat 2 to 3 tablespoons olive oil and sauté onion until it begins to turn translucent. Add eggplant pulp and stir with a wooden spoon for 2 to 3 minutes. Add ground meat and continue to sauté until meat is lightly browned. Add tomatoes, garlic, parsley, salt, and pepper. Reduce heat, add a little water to skillet, if necessary, cover skillet, and simmer until liquid has been absorbed, 7 to 10 minutes. Remove and cool slightly.

3. In another large skillet, heat 3 to 4 tablespoons olive oil and quickly sauté eggplant halves on both sides, just to soften. (Since eggplants absorb so much oil, you may need to replenish skillet with a little more.) Remove eggplant from skillet and drain on paper towels.

4. Preheat oven to 350°F. Place eggplant halves in a large ovenproof casserole dish. Sprinkle a little grated cheese into each, then spoon in meat mixture, until eggplants are heaping. Spoon a generous amount of béchamel sauce over eggplants (about 2 tablespoons per half). Sprinkle with bread crumbs and remaining grated cheese and bake until eggplants are soft and béchamel is pleasantly gold and thickened. Remove casserole from oven and serve warm.

Yield: 6 to 8 servings

Serving Suggestion: This is another robust dish that needs a wine that can stand up to it; a brisk Náoussa or a robust Nemea would do.

—LATHERA (STOVE-TOP VEGETABLE— STEWS AND RAGOUTS)

Bamyies Yiahni

(OKRA RAGOUT)

GREEKS call okra by its Arabic name, *bamya,* or *bamyies* in the plural. This is one of several dishes that fall under the category of *lathera,* literally "oily," although tastes have changed and the overuse of olive oil is in considerable decline. The *lathera* dishes usually refer to stove-top vegetable stews, and feta is usually on the table with all of them.

Greeks, not enamored of the gummy quality of okra, usually soak the vegetable in undiluted vinegar ($\frac{1}{2}$ cup vinegar per pound) before cooking it. When buying okra, look for the tender young pods with firm tips. Allow one hour of soaking time in the preparation.

---

1. Wash the okra thoroughly and cut off the stems with a small sharp knife. Place in a glass or clay bowl and douse with 1 cup vinegar. Let stand for 30 minutes to 1 hour.

2. Rinse okra thoroughly in a colander, so that all the gluey liquid washes away.

3. In a large heavy pot, heat olive oil and sauté onion until translucent. Add okra, reduce heat slightly, and stir gently with a wooden spoon for 2 to 3 minutes. Add tomatoes, garlic, salt, pepper, and enough water to cover okra. Taste sauce and add sugar, if necessary, as desired. Cover and simmer over low heat for about 45 minutes, or until okra is tender. Check and add water, if necessary, during cooking. Gently stir in parsley 10 minutes before removing from heat; 5 minutes before removing pot from heat, pour in remaining vinegar, a little at a time (taste it to make sure it's not too acidic). Serve hot or cold.

Yield: 4 to 6 servings

Note: If fresh okra is unavailable, frozen okra may be used, but be sure to defrost it before soaking it in vinegar.

Serving Suggestions: Retsina, feta, and hearty bread are the must here.

2 pounds fresh okra (see Note)
1 cup plus 2 to 3 tablespoons quality red wine vinegar
$\frac{1}{2}$ cup olive oil
2 to 3 medium to large onions, peeled, halved, and sliced
1 pound plum tomatoes, peeled, cored, and coarsely chopped (with juice)
2 to 3 garlic cloves, finely chopped (to taste)
Salt and freshly ground pepper, to taste
1 to $1\frac{1}{2}$ teaspoons sugar (optional)
$\frac{1}{4}$ cup chopped fresh parsley, packed

Aracas

(FRESH PEAS)

THESE appear at market in the spring, at the same time as artichokes and fresh broad beans, with which they frequently share space in a pot. But cooked alone, *aracas* make for a favorite springtime dish.

---

2 pounds fresh peas
¼ cup olive oil, or
    more, to taste
4 to 6 scallions,
    washed and thinly
    sliced
¼ cup finely chopped
    fresh fennel, packed
¼ cup finely chopped
    fresh dill, packed
¾ cup water
Salt and freshly
    ground pepper, to
    taste

1. Wash pea pods. Using a sharp paring knife, cut off tips and remove any fiber along seam of pod. If pods are large and tough, remove peas completely, and discard pods. Wash again.

2. In a medium saucepan, heat 2 tablespoons olive oil and sauté scallions until translucent. Add peas, fennel, and dill and sauté 2 to 3 minutes.

3. Add water, ½ cup first, and the remainder only if necessary. Cover and simmer over low-to-medium heat for 20 to 30 minutes, until peas are tender. Season with salt and pepper.

Yield: 4 servings

Serving Suggestions: Porto Carras Réserve, a medium dry white, would work well here, as well as Chateau Matsa.

Anginares me Koukia

(ARTICHOKE HEART AND BROAD BEAN STEW)

"BROAD beans need sugar," says my husband's grandmother with authority, and she's right. "Two teaspoons per kilo," she adds. This is a classic Greek dish, one that requires a little patience for the cleaning of the beans and artichokes, and a little care in making the sauce.

---

1. Have ready a large bowl of 2 cups cold water mixed with the juice of 2 lemons. Cut off all but 1 inch of artichoke stems. Cut away tough outer leaves and chop off 2 to 2½ inches from top of each artichoke. Open flowers and, using a teaspoon or a potato peeler, scrape out choke. Rub each artichoke with lemon as soon as you clean it and then submerge it immediately in lemon water to keep it from turning brown. Soak until ready to use.

2. Remove broad beans from pods and cut away black "eye" of beans. Wash and drain in a colander.

3. In a large heavy saucepan, heat 3 tablespoons olive oil and sauté scallions until just translucent. Add broad beans and sauté 2 to 3 minutes. Add artichokes, garlic, fennel, salt, pepper, sugar, juice of 1 lemon, and enough water to cover. Reduce heat, cover pan, and simmer 45 minutes to 1 hour, until artichokes and beans are tender. Add more water to pot during cooking, if necessary. When vegetables and beans are cooked, remove them from the pot with a slotted spoon and reserve liquid. Keep them covered on top of the stove so that they'll stay warm.

4. *To prepare sauce:* In a separate saucepan, heat 3 tablespoons of the olive oil. Add flour and whisk over low heat to make a roux—until the flour becomes pasty and starts to change color to a very light golden brown, 3 to 5 minutes. Don't burn the flour, however. Add lemon juice, pan liquids from the artichoke and beans, salt, sugar (if necessary), and water (if necessary) and whisk until sauce is thick and creamy, another 6 to 10 minutes. Remove at once and pour over vegetables. Serve warm, seasoned with freshly ground pepper.

Yield: 4 to 6 servings

Serving Suggestions: Any of Greece's notable dry (unresinated) whites—Santorini Boutari, Robola Calliga, Porto Carras Réserve, or Chateau Matsa—would do here. All else that should really accompany this dish is feta, in ample amount, and bread, of course.

2 cups water
3 to 4 lemons (reserve strained juice of 1 lemon for sautéing)
8 to 10 artichokes
2 pounds fresh broad beans
3 tablespoons olive oil
8 scallions, washed and thinly sliced
3 garlic cloves, finely chopped
½ cup finely chopped fresh fennel, packed
Salt and freshly ground pepper, to taste
1 to 1½ teaspoons sugar (or slightly less, to taste)
SAUCE
¼ cup olive oil
1 tablespoon plus 1 teaspoon all-purpose flour
Strained fresh juice of 1 lemon
Pan juices from artichokes and broad beans
Salt
½ teaspoon sugar (to taste, and if necessary)
1 to 1½ cups water (if necessary)
Freshly ground pepper

Anginares à la Polita

(ARTICHOKE STEW, CONSTANTINOPLE STYLE)

ARTICHOKES cooked in this way are a classic Greek dish. The artichokes should be tender and not too large.

---

2 to 3 cups cold water
3 lemons
6 to 8 artichokes
½ cup olive oil
2 medium-size white onions, finely chopped
4 to 6 scallions, chopped
4 medium-size potatoes, peeled and quartered
3 medium-size carrots, peeled and sliced into ¼-inch rounds
2 garlic cloves, finely chopped
½ cup chopped fresh dill
2 to 3 tablespoons chopped fresh fennel (optional)
Salt and freshly ground pepper, to taste
2 to 3 teaspoons all-purpose flour

1. Have ready a large bowl of 2 cups cold water mixed with the juice of 2 lemons. Cut off all but 1 inch of artichoke stems, but don't discard. Cut away tough outer leaves and chop off 1 to 1½ inches from the top of each artichoke. Open flowers and, using a teaspoon or potato peeler, scrape out choke. Cut away tough outer parts of stems leaving only tender white core. If desired, clean leaves away from entire artichoke so that only the heart remains (see Note). Rub each artichoke with lemon as soon as you clean it and then submerge it immediately in lemon water to keep it from turning brown. Soak until ready to use.

2. In a large pot, heat olive oil and sauté onion and scallions until translucent. Add potatoes and sauté 5 to 7 minutes. Add carrots, stir once or twice, and add artichokes and stems, garlic, herbs, salt, and pepper and stir.

3. Stir flour with strained juice of 1 remaining lemon and a little water. Pour over *anginares* and add enough water to cover vegetables. Cover pot and simmer over medium heat for 45 minutes to 1 hour until potatoes and carrots are tender and artichokes and stems are cooked. Serve warm, with fresh lemon on the side.

Yield: 6 to 8 servings

Note: Greeks generally eat only the heart of the artichoke, harboring an aversion for any part of the leaves. But some people do make this dish with the artichoke more or less intact. The choice is yours.

Serving Suggestions: This dish, like all stove-top meals, stands on its own, requiring little besides feta and bread. A fine white wine is required here, however. I'd suggest Santorini, with its mineral undertones and crispness, to underscore the artichokes. Robola Calliga or Porto Carras Réserve, though mellower, would also work here.

Anginares me Araca

(ARTICHOKE HEARTS AND PEA STEW)

1. Have ready a large bowl of 2 cups cold water mixed with the strained juice of 2 lemons. Cut off all but 1 inch of artichoke stems, but don't discard. Cut away tough outer leaves and chop off 1 to 1½ inches from top of artichoke. Open flowers and, using a teaspoon or potato peeler, scrape out choke. Cut away tough outer parts of stems leaving only tender white core. If desired, clean leaves away from entire artichoke so that only the heart remains. Rub each artichoke with lemon as soon as you clean it and then submerge it immediately in lemon water to keep it from turning brown. Soak until ready to use.

2. Wash and drain peas. If the pods are small and tender, keep the vegetable intact, but shell if the pods are too large or tough.

3. In a heavy stewing pot, heat ¼ cup plus 2 tablespoons of the olive oil. Add artichoke hearts and peas and turn gently in pot with a wooden spoon to coat with oil. Season with dill, salt, and pepper. Pour in ½ cup water. Cover the pot and cook over low heat until the artichokes and peas are tender, adding more water, if necessary, during cooking. About halfway through cooking, taste the pan juices and add sugar, if necessary. Remove pot from heat and add remaining 2 tablespoons olive oil. Serve warm.

2 cups cold water
12 medium fresh artichokes
2 pounds fresh peas
2 lemons
½ cup extravirgin olive oil
¼ cup chopped fresh dill, or 2 tablespoons chopped fresh mint
Salt and freshly ground pepper, to taste
½ to 1 cup water
1 teaspoon sugar (optional, and only if necessary)

Fassolakia Yiahni

(FRESH GREEN BEAN RAGOUT)

$1\frac{1}{2}$ to 2 pounds fresh
  green beans
$\frac{1}{4}$ cup olive oil
2 medium to large
  white onions, peeled
  and coarsely
  chopped
2 to 3 medium-size
  potatoes, peeled and
  quartered
1 garlic clove, finely
  chopped
4 to 5 plump ripe
  tomatoes, peeled and
  cored (not chopped)
1 to 2 small hot red
  peppers (optional)
$\frac{1}{4}$ cup water, or more
  if necessary
Salt and freshly
  ground pepper, to
  taste
Feta cheese (optional)

FRESH green beans come in several varieties in Greece, and all are suitable to this simple, earthy dish. Plain string beans work well, as do the thinner haricots (*ambelo fasoula* to the Greeks), and the large knobby beans known as *barbounia* to the Greeks and as "American beans" in other areas. Greeks usually eat this dish cold.

---

1. Wash and clean beans. Snap or cut off tips and remove stringy fiber along seams with a sharp small knife. Wash thoroughly.
2. In a large pot, heat olive oil and sauté onion until translucent. Add green beans and potatoes and stir with a wooden spoon for 2 to 4 minutes, until vegetables are coated with olive oil. Add garlic and stir once or twice.
3. Squeeze tomatoes into pot. Add hot pepper and $\frac{1}{4}$ cup water. Season with salt and pepper. Reduce heat to low, cover pot, and simmer for about $1\frac{1}{2}$ hours, adding a little water, if necessary, until beans are very tender and potatoes cooked.

Serve warm or cold, topped with feta, if desired.

Yield: 4 to 6 servings

Serving Suggestions: This dish is country fare at its best and calls out for feta, good bread, and retsina.

Kounoupithi Kapama

(CAULIFLOWER BAKED WITH TOMATO SAUCE AND FETA)

$\frac{1}{4}$ cup plus 2
  tablespoons olive oil
1 large onion, halved
  and sliced
2 garlic cloves, finely
  chopped

1. Preheat oven to 375°F.
2. In a large heavy skillet, heat 2 to 3 tablespoons olive oil and sauté onion and garlic over medium-low heat until slightly wilted. Add tomatoes, cinnamon, bay leaves, oregano, salt, and pepper; simmer, covered, for 5 minutes. Toss in cauliflower, cover, and simmer 10 to 15 minutes. Remove skillet from heat.

3. In a medium-large baking pan, preferably clay or glass, pour in cauliflower and tomato sauce. Pour remaining 3 tablespoons olive oil and lemon juice over mixture. Toss in pan to combine. Sprinkle with crumbled feta.

4. Place pan in oven and turn heat down to 350°F. Bake for 50 minutes to 1 hour, or until cauliflower is soft and feta melted. Add a little water during baking, if necessary.

Yield: 4 to 6 servings

Serving Suggestions: Try serving this with three-meat Cephalonian meat pie, or rabbit pie, *lagopitta*, to add some substance to the prosaic cauliflower. With the wine, be daring here, savoring Mavrodaphne from Cephalonia or Patras to blend with the cinnamon, with which this dish is redolent.

6 to 8 plum tomatoes, peeled, cored, seeded, and coarsely chopped (with juice)

$\frac{1}{4}$ teaspoon cinnamon

2 bay leaves

2 teaspoons dried oregano

Salt and freshly ground pepper, to taste

1 medium to large cauliflower (3 to 4 pounds), cut into florets

Strained fresh juice of 1 lemon

$\frac{1}{4}$ cup grated or crumbled feta cheese

Melitzanes Yiahni

(EGGPLANT RAGOUT)

1. Cut the stems off the eggplants and cut the eggplants crosswise into thick rounds, about 2 inches long. Place in a colander and douse with salt. Let stand 30 to 45 minutes; rinse and drain thoroughly.

2. In a large pot, heat olive oil over medium heat and sauté onion until wilted. Add the eggplants and turn in the pot to coat with oil. Add the garlic, tomatoes, and parsley. Season with salt and pepper and add a little water, if necessary. Simmer, covered, over low to medium heat until the eggplants are tender and the sauce thick, about 50 minutes.

Yield: 4 servings

Serving Suggestions: Like ragout of green beans, this dish stands alone save for some feta and bread. Serve it with a robust Nemea red.

$2\frac{1}{2}$ to 3 pounds long thin eggplants

Salt

$\frac{1}{3}$ to $\frac{1}{2}$ cup olive oil

2 large onions, peeled, halved, and sliced thin

4 to 5 garlic cloves, finely chopped

$1\frac{1}{2}$ pounds ripe plum tomatoes, peeled, seeded, and chopped (with juice)

2 to 3 tablespoons chopped fresh parsley

Salt and freshly ground pepper, to taste

Argyro's Ikarian Soufiko

(SKILLET MEDLEY OF EGGPLANTS AND ZUCCHINI, IKARIAN STYLE)

ARGYRO, cooking mate for all seasons, fellow villager, and diehard for old island ways, is at a distinct advantage when she makes this simple island vegetable medley. All her ingredients, down to the olive oil, are reaped from the garden she tends so lovingly. She's the village school teacher in Raches, Ikaria, and one of the few people I've ever known so enamored of old country ways that she had her husband build her a hearth for cooking in their recently remodeled kitchen. This recipe was inspired by her ample garden and blackened old skillet, and was savored on many occasions with a pitcherful of her potent Ikarian wine.

---

3 to 4 long thin eggplants, cut lengthwise into $\frac{1}{8}$-inch slices

Salt

$\frac{1}{2}$ cup olive oil

4 to 5 medium onions, peeled, halved, and sliced

2 to 3 medium zucchini, cut into $\frac{1}{4}$-inch rounds

3 to 4 plum tomatoes, peeled, cored, and sliced (with juice)

2 garlic cloves, finely chopped

Salt and freshly ground pepper, to taste

1 teaspoon dried oregano

1. Douse the eggplant slices generously with salt and let them sit in a colander to drain for 30 minutes. Rinse them thoroughly afterward, drain, and pat dry.

2. In a large heavy skillet, heat the olive oil and add the onion slices. Stir to coat and soften, 4 to 6 minutes. Add the eggplant and zucchini to the skillet and stir gently to coat with oil. Add the tomatoes and stir. Season with garlic, salt, and pepper. Cover the skillet, lower heat to low, and let the vegetables cook slowly until they are soft and have almost fallen apart, 45 minutes to 1 hour. Remove the cover, season with oregano, and cook the mixture down until pan juices have almost evaporated, another 10 to 12 minutes. Serve hot or cold.

Yield: 2 large servings or 4 side-dish servings

Serving Suggestions: This is wonderful with a plain bulgur pilaf. As for wine, my heart says to recommend dry Ikarian muscat, but you'll have to have an inside connection to find it in America. Try a pungent retsina instead with this soul-warming country dish.

— BEANS AND LEGUMES —

Fava

(PUREE OF SPLIT PEA)

FAVA in Italy and elsewhere in the Mediterranean refers to the broad bean, whether pureed or not. Greeks call *fava* a dish of creamy pureed green or yellow split peas. This is standard taverna fare throughout the country, as well as a winter staple on most household tables.

---

1. Place split peas in a medium-size pot with the cold water. Season with salt and pepper. Bring to a boil and simmer, covered, over low to medium heat for 50 minutes to 1 hour, or until beans are so soft they have disintegrated to a puree. Add water during cooking, if necessary. Stir occasionally to keep peas from sticking to bottom of pot.

2. Remove pot from heat and cover with a cloth for 15 to 20 minutes.

3. Before serving, mix in $\frac{1}{4}$ cup olive oil (more, if desired), and top with chopped scallions or red onions.

$\frac{1}{2}$ pound yellow or green split peas, rinsed

5 cups cold water

Salt and freshly ground pepper, to taste

$\frac{1}{4}$ to $\frac{1}{2}$ cup olive oil

4 to 5 scallions, coarsely chopped, or 1 large red onion, peeled and chopped

Yield: 4 servings

Serving Suggestions: I offer three here, but they're requisites more than suggestions—feta, bread, and retsina.

Clay-Baked Chick-Peas and Eggplants

TO ACHIEVE the special, earthy flavors in this dish, you'll need a two-quart ovenproof clay or earthenware casserole with cover. Substitute a Pyrex dish if a clay casserole is unavailable.

½ pound raw chick-peas

3 to 4 small to medium eggplants, sliced into ⅛-inch rounds

5 to 6 tablespoons olive oil

2 large onions, peeled, halved, and sliced

2 large garlic cloves, finely chopped

6 to 8 plum tomatoes, peeled and chopped (with juice)

1 large bay leaf, torn in half

Salt and freshly ground pepper, to taste

2 to 3 tablespoons dry red wine

1. Soak chick-peas according to package directions. Drain off water and place chick-peas in a medium-size pot with enough water to cover by several inches. Bring to a boil, lower heat, and simmer, uncovered, until chick-peas are softened but not cooked through, 20 to 25 minutes. In the meantime, place eggplants in a colander and salt them. Let drain for 20 to 25 minutes, rinse, and pat dry.

2. While chick-peas are simmering, heat 3 tablespoons olive oil in a large heavy skillet over medium to low heat and sauté onions 3 to 6 minutes, until coated with oil and wilted. Toss in eggplants and stir constantly until eggplants start to soften, 5 to 7 minutes longer. Add ¼ to ½ cup water to keep eggplants and onions from burning. Toss in chopped garlic and stir for 30 seconds. Remove mixture from heat and let cool slightly.

3. When chick-peas are softened, remove from heat and drain. Cool slightly.

4. Gently combine eggplants, onions, and chick-peas in a 2-quart clay casserole with cover. Add the tomatoes and their juice and place the halves of the bay leaf on either side of the dish. Season with salt and pepper; add ¼ cup water and 2 to 3 tablespoons olive oil to the mixture.

5. Cover the pan with its earthenware top and place in cold oven. Turn oven to 375°F and bake for 1¼ to 1½ hours, until chick-peas are tender and eggplants cooked. Ten minutes before shutting off the oven, add the wine to the pan and stir in gently. Shut off the oven, open the door, and let the eggplant and chick-pea ragout cool slighty inside the oven.

Yield: 4 servings

Serving Suggestions: Marry earth with earth in this dish by including a robust, *brusco*—or brisk—Náoussa red on the table.

Koukia Stifatho

(DRIED BROAD BEAN STEW)

BROAD beans have been known in Greece since antiquity. They were forbidden by Pythagoras to his students for fear that they contained the spirits of the dead. They were utilized as a token in ancient Athenian elections, and I presume they were even ingested as a food. Today, broad beans are mainly eaten fresh, partnered with artichokes and/or peas in a luscious green stew. They are often the subject of a morning reprimand at neighborhood farmers' markets as old women explain to young how to clean them. The dried beans, reddish brown and rather uninviting at first, have a dark ominous "eye" and the reputation for containing a toxin or two (actually they do, and the "eye" must be removed). They are nonetheless cooked up into a thick, hearty, and earthy stew.

---

1. Wash beans and place them in a large pot with enough water to cover. Bring water to a boil, reduce heat, and simmer, uncovered, for 10 minutes. Remove pot from heat and drain beans (water will be black). Fill pot once more with enough water to cover beans and bring to a boil. Simmer, uncovered, for about 25 minutes, until beans are almost cooked. Remove pot from heat, drain beans, and cool slightly.
2. With a small sharp knife, remove black "eye" and husks from beans.
3. In a large heavy skillet, heat 2 tablespoons olive oil over medium heat and sauté onion until translucent, 3 to 4 minutes. Add tomatoes, garlic, bay leaves, salt, and pepper. Bring to a boil, reduce heat, and simmer, uncovered, another 3 to 4 minutes. Add broad beans, sugar, and wine. Cover and simmer over low heat for 35 to 40 minutes, adding water if necessary, until beans are tender. Remove bay leaves and serve hot.

Yield: 4 to 6 servings

Serving Suggestions: Serve this with plain rice or bulgur pilaf, *horta*, feta, and a deep Nemea red wine.

1 pound dried broad beans
$\frac{1}{4}$ cup olive oil
4 medium to large white onions, peeled and sliced
8 to 10 plum tomatoes, peeled, seeded, and quartered
3 garlic cloves, finely chopped
2 large bay leaves
Salt and freshly ground pepper, to taste
$\frac{1}{2}$ to 1 teaspoon sugar, to taste
$1\frac{1}{3}$ cups dry red wine

Fassolakia Plaki me Spanaki

(BABY LIMA BEANS BAKED WITH SPINACH)

½ pound dried baby
  lima beans
1 pound fresh spinach,
  finely chopped
1 large Spanish onion,
  finely chopped
3 large ripe tomatoes,
  peeled, seeded, and
  coarsely chopped
  (with juice)
1 garlic clove, finely
  chopped
¼ cup olive oil
Salt and freshly
  ground pepper, to
  taste
Juice of ½ lemon, or
  more to taste

1. Wash and soak beans according to package directions. Preheat oven to 375°F.

2. Place beans in a large pot with enough water to cover. Bring water to a boil and cook beans for 10 to 15 minutes, until softened. They should be fairly soft before baking.

3. In a medium-size baking dish, combine beans, spinach, onion, tomatoes, garlic, olive oil, salt, pepper, and a little water. Bake, uncovered, for about 1 hour, or until beans are tender. Add a little water during baking, if necessary. Drizzle in lemon juice about 5 minutes before removing beans from oven. Remove baking dish from oven and serve warm or cold.

Yield: 2 servings

Serving Suggestions: I would recommend a bone-dry Zitsa wine from Epirus, whence this dish originates. Serve it with a *paximathi* and tomato salad, or a *tiganopitta* Epirou, or just plain feta and bread.

Macedonian Lima Bean Casserole

THIS recipe comes from Sithonia, in northern Greece, where hot pepper is incorporated into many foods—from meat dishes to a feta cheese spread—to give food just a bit of a bite.

---

1. Soak beans overnight and follow directions on package for boiling, but remove and drain when half done. Set aside.
2. Preheat oven to 375°F.
3. In a large heavy skillet, heat 3 tablespoons of the olive oil and sauté onion until translucent.
4. In a large baking pan, preferably clay, combine lima beans, onion, and sweet and hot peppers. Add tomatoes as well as remaining 5 tablespoons olive oil, garlic, cumin, oregano, salt, pepper, and water. Toss so that all ingredients are thoroughly mixed.
5. Cover and bake for 1 to 1½ hours, or until beans are soft. Add more water, if necessary, during baking.

Yield: 4 to 6 servings

Serving Suggestions: A strong Macedonian mountain wine to match this dish's heartiness is needed here. Try a Náoussa red or Cava Boutari. Serve this with feta, wild greens, and an ample *horiatiki salad.*

1 pound dried lima beans
½ cup olive oil
3 medium onions, peeled and chopped
4 to 5 medium-size green Italian peppers, cored and cut into thin rounds
1 to 2 small hot red peppers, seeded and chopped
1 pound fresh ripe plum tomatoes, peeled, cored, and chopped
2 garlic cloves, minced
1 teaspoon ground cumin (or less, to taste)
1 teaspoon dried oregano
Salt and freshly ground pepper, to taste
2 cups water (more, if necessary)

Chapter 12

Poultry, Fowl, and Rabbit

I've noticed a disparity in the attitudes of Greek men and women regarding the humble hen. For men, the six hundred or so servings of chicken they must endure over twenty months of mandatory army service color their attitude for a long time to come. For women, the versatile bird holds no such memories and so it continues to find its way to the table, just as it has done since about the second century B.C., when—according to Waverley Root—Greeks on the island of Kos were already fattening poultry for the table.

Chicken and other fowl (especially turkey) are almost sure to appear on the Greek Christmas table, and some dishes like the *missoura* (stuffed chicken enveloped by leeks and meat and slow-baked) have an almost symbolic presence on the table. Greek cookery boasts a rich variety of poultry dishes. Chicken is one of the few meats readily cooked with fruits—prunes or quinces or raisins—or adorned with nuts. The breast, deboned and simmered for hours, can become an Asia Minor pudding *(taouk kioksou)* that has been adopted by Asia Minor Greeks and can be found in some of the specialty bakeries in Phaleron, a suburb of Athens. And, of course, there is the ubiquitous chicken soup, augmented in Greece with lemon and egg, but still containing all the reputed salutary qualities afforded it by grandmothers the world over.

As for other birds and wildfowl, they, too, have been loved by Greek cooks since antiquity. Partridges, pigeons, quails, thrushes, and woodcocks are becoming more scarce each year, but if they can be obtained (from a gifted hunter), they will be eaten much the same as they've been for several thousand years—roasted, either on a spit or, more conveniently now, in the oven. Pheasant is mostly farm raised in

Greece. Duck, however, are still hunted with some regularity. Both, like the smaller birds, are considered best when simply grilled.

Rabbit is the most common of other game animals. It enjoys myriad preparations, and is something akin to a national dish on Crete. *Lagostifatho Cretis* (Cretan rabbit stew) is a well-known and revered dish in Greece; an interesting *meze*—pickled rabbit—also derives from Crete. While rabbit is readily found in Greek butcher shops, wild hare is not, since it is against the law to hunt it commercially.

—CHICKEN AND TURKEY—

Chicken Barthounikiotou

(STEWED CHICKEN WITH FETA AND GREEN OLIVES)

THIS dish is found in various forms throughout the Peloponnisos and is generally made with braised chicken, ample onions, and one of several varieties of Greek cheese—feta, kasseri, or kefalograviera. Sometimes it is prepared with olives, or, as is also common in the Peloponnisos, with raisins, since the region is a major producer of both. Its name comes from a small village called Barthouna, near Sparta.

1 medium-size frying chicken (3 to 4 pounds), washed and quartered

Flour seasoned with a bit of salt and pepper, for dredging

6 tablespoons olive oil

¾ pound small white stewing onions, peeled and whole

4 to 6 plum tomatoes, peeled, seeded, and chopped

½ to ¾ cup water

Salt and freshly ground pepper, to taste

¾ cup pitted, rinsed green olives

1 tablespoon quality red wine vinegar

¼ pound hard feta cheese, cut into thin slices

1. Dredge chicken lightly in seasoned flour. In a large heavy skillet or Dutch oven, slowly heat the olive oil. Brown the chicken by placing a few pieces at a time in the skillet and turning them frequently. Set the pieces aside until all of the chicken is browned.

2. Place onions in the skillet, reduce heat, and sauté until translucent. Add browned chicken to pan; pour tomatoes over mixture and add ½ cup water. Season with salt and pepper. Cover and simmer for 20 to 25 minutes over medium to low heat, until chicken is almost cooked, adding more water, if necessary, to keep the meat from drying out.

3. About 10 minutes before removing skillet from heat, add pitted green olives and vinegar. Carefully place feta slices over chicken. Keep skillet half covered and simmer another 10 minutes or so, until cheese has melted. Serve hot over rice.

Yield: 4 servings

Serving Suggestions: Serve with roasted potatoes, plain rice, or bulgur pilaf, a light salad such as zucchini and olive or plain lettuce, and a bottle of deep-scented Nemea red wine, also from the Peloponnisos.

Rithanathema

(BAKED FETA-STUFFED CHICKEN AND RICE)

THIS dish finds its roots in the northwestern reaches of Epirus (now part of Albania), in a village called Droziani. It comes from an Athenian philologist who traces her ancestry to the village and who claims the dish as a family specialty. Its name, she explains, derives from a simple transliteration from the ancient Greek word for bird, *ornitha,* and *ethesma,* an archaic word for food.

---

1 medium-size
  roasting chicken, 3½
  to 4 pounds
¼ cup plus 1
  tablespoon, olive oil
1½ cups finely chopped
  onion
1 cup chopped fresh
  parsley, packed
1 garlic clove, finely
  chopped
¾ pound feta cheese,
  crumbled
1 tablespoon oregano
2 cups long-grain rice
Salt and freshly
  ground pepper, to
  taste

1. Preheat oven to 450°F.

2. In a large pot, place chicken and enough salted water to cover. Bring water to a boil over medium heat and partially cook chicken for 15 to 20 minutes, occasionally skimming off the top of the pot. Remove chicken from pot and set aside. Do not discard the broth.

3. While chicken is cooking, heat 2 tablespoons of the olive oil in a large heavy skillet and lightly sauté onion and parsley until onions are translucent and parsley is wilted. Stir in garlic and sauté for about 30 seconds.

4. In a food processor or by hand, puree ¼ pound of the feta, 1 teaspoon oregano, and ¼ cup of the onion and parsley mixture until feta has "ignited," or has become really sharp in taste. Stuff the chicken with the feta and onion mixture. Sew closed and truss.

5. Place chicken in a medium-to-large baking dish. Distribute rice evenly around bird. Add 5 cups of the chicken broth to rice. Season with salt and pepper and dot with remaining feta and oregano. Drizzle with remaining 3 tablespoons olive oil. Place pan in hot oven and reduce temperature to 350°F. Bake uncovered for 40 to 50 minutes, until chicken is tender and rice cooked. Baste chicken with pan juices and toss rice every 10 to 12 minutes. Add a little more water during baking, if necessary, to keep rice from drying out. Remove, cool slightly, and serve.

Yield: 4 servings

Serving Suggestions: A heaping plate of fried green peppers or a platter of roasted sweet red peppers would be lovely with this chicken dish. As for wine, try a Porto Carras Réserve, a crisp Santorini Boutari, or a white wine from Zitsa to counter the pungency of the feta.

Kotopoulo me Kythonia

(CHICKEN WITH RED SAUCE AND QUINCE)

QUINCES come to the markets of Greece in mid–October. They are a fall and winter fruit in America, too. Greeks make quince jam and preserves and also use this fragrant cousin to the apple in various meat and poultry stews. The quince also had a substantial, but nonculinary role until not too long ago: appreciated for its perfume and its keeping power, women used to place it in their lingerie drawers.

---

2 medium to large quinces
Strained fresh juice of $\frac{1}{2}$ lemon
1 medium-size frying chicken ($3\frac{1}{2}$ to 4 pounds), cleaned and quartered
Flour seasoned with salt and pepper, for dredging
4 tablespoons lightly salted butter
1 large Spanish onion, peeled, halved, and sliced
1 cup peeled, cored, chopped plum tomato (about 10 tomatoes)
1 small cinnamon stick
$\frac{1}{4}$ to $\frac{1}{2}$ teaspoon sugar, depending on sweetness of quinces
Salt, to taste
1 heaping tablespoon finely chopped fresh mint
1 tablespoon tomato paste

1. Peel, halve, and core the quinces and let stand in enough cold water to cover plus the juice of half a lemon to keep from discoloring. When ready to use, drain and pat dry.

2. Lightly dredge chicken in seasoned flour. In a Dutch oven or large heavy skillet, slowly heat 2 tablespoons butter and brown the chicken by placing a few pieces at a time in the skillet, and turning frequently until rosy brown. Remove chicken from skillet with a slotted spoon and set aside.

3. Heat 1 more tablespoon butter in skillet and sauté quinces until lightly brown. Remove quinces from skillet with a slotted spoon and set aside.

4. In same skillet, heat remaining tablespoon butter and sauté onion slices until they start to become translucent. Add chicken to skillet. Pour in tomatoes, cinnamon, sugar, salt, and a little water ($\frac{1}{2}$ to $\frac{3}{4}$ cup). Reduce heat, cover, and simmer for 30 minutes. Add quinces and continue simmering until chicken is tender, 25 to 45 minutes. Stir in mint 10 minutes before chicken is cooked; 5 minutes before removing skillet from heat, add tomato paste and stir well with a wooden spoon. Remove cinnamon stick and serve hot.

Yield: 4 servings

Variation: Beef, veal, and pork may also be prepared using this recipe. Substitute $2\frac{1}{2}$ to 3 pounds lean meat for the chicken.

Serving Suggestions: Accompanying food should play second fiddle to this opulent dish. Serve it with a simple bulgur or rice pilaf, *horta*, or wild greens, a salty wedge of kefalograviera cheese to counter the sweetness of the dish, and a wine to equal it in richness: Náoussa Grande Réserve.

Kotopoulo Psito Lemonata

(CLASSIC ROASTED CHICKEN WITH LEMON AND HERBS)

1 medium-size roasting chicken (3 to 4 pounds)
¼ cup plus 2 tablespoons olive oil
Salt and freshly ground pepper, to taste
Strained fresh juice of 2 lemons
2 teaspoons dried thyme
½ teaspoon crushed rosemary
½ teaspoon marjoram
2 garlic cloves, finely chopped
6 to 8 large oval potatoes, peeled and quartered lengthwise

1. Preheat oven to 450°F.
2. Rub outside of chicken with 1 tablespoon olive oil and season with salt and pepper. In a bowl, combine remaining olive oil, lemon juice, thyme, rosemary, marjoram, garlic, and freshly ground pepper. Brush chicken generously with marinade.
3. Place chicken on a rack inside a medium-to-large baking pan and spread potatoes evenly around pan. Pour marinade and 1 or 2 cups water over potatoes. Season potatoes with salt and pepper, if desired. Place pan in hot oven and reduce heat to 350°F. Bake for 1 to 1½ hours, basting chicken with pan juices every 10 minutes, until meat is tender. Add water to potatoes during cooking, if necessary. Remove chicken from oven as soon as it's tender.
4. If potatoes aren't completely cooked by the time chicken is ready, remove the bird, turn up the oven to 450°F, add water if necessary, and roast another 15 to 20 minutes, or until potatoes are golden brown and tender. Serve warm.

Yield: 4 servings

Serving Suggestions: A simple, savory *pitta* such as spinach or leek, perhaps a fresh loaf of olive bread, and a simple tomato salad would all be nice additions here. Serve it with any of Greece's better white wines—Santorini Boutari, Robola Calliga, Porto Carras Réserve, or Chateau Matsa.

Kotopoulo Yiahni me Damaskina

(CHICKEN BRAISED WITH RED WINE AND PRUNES)

1. Dredge chicken in flour. In a large skillet or Dutch oven, heat ¼ cup of the olive oil and brown chicken, a few pieces at a time, turning them frequently. Remove chicken from skillet with a slotted spoon. Add remaining 1 tablespoon olive oil, if necessary and sauté onion until wilted.

2. Place chicken, tomatoes, cinnamon, cloves, nutmeg, salt, and pepper in skillet with sautéed onion. Stir with a wooden spoon once or twice over medium to high heat. Reduce heat, add ½ to ¾ cup water, if necessary, cover, and simmer for 25 to 30 minutes, adding more water if needed during cooking.

3. Add prunes and red wine, keep pot half covered, and simmer 25 to 40 minutes longer, or until chicken is tender. Stir in mint a few minutes before removing skillet from heat. Remove cinnamon stick and serve hot.

Yield: 4 servings

Serving Suggestions: Plain rice or mashed potatoes belong with this dish. As for wine, I'd try something daring—such as a sweet, aromatic Samos muscat to blend with the fragrance of the prunes.

1 medium frying or roasting chicken (3 to 4 pounds), rinsed and quartered

Flour, for dredging

¼ cup plus 1 tablespoon olive oil

1 large red onion, halved and sliced

4 to 6 plum tomatoes, peeled and chopped (with juice)

1 small cinnamon stick

5 to 6 whole cloves

Grating of whole nutmeg

Salt and freshly ground pepper, to taste

20 whole pitted prunes

¼ cup dry red wine

½ teaspoon dried mint

Kotopoulo Yemisto à la Polita

(CONSTANTINOPLE STUFFED CHICKEN WITH RICE, RAISINS, AND NUTS)

RAISINS, pine nuts, almonds, and rice, sometimes with a shredding of carrot and a little parsley, make for a classic pilaf, Constantinople style. Here it's used as a stuffing to make one of the most popular chicken dishes in Greek cookery.

$\frac{1}{4}$ *cup olive oil*
2 *medium onions, finely chopped*
1 *cup long-grain rice*
4 *whole plum tomatoes, peeled, cored, and chopped*
$\frac{1}{2}$ *cup coarsely chopped blanched almonds or whole pine nuts*
$\frac{1}{2}$ *cup dark seedless raisins*
1 *cinnamon stick*
1 *bay leaf*
Salt and freshly ground pepper, to taste
$2\frac{1}{2}$ *cups water*
3 *tablespoons finely chopped fresh parsley*
1 *medium roasting chicken (3 to 4 pounds)*
$\frac{1}{4}$ *cup dry red wine (optional)*
Plain yogurt

1. Preheat oven to 450°F.

2. In a large heavy skillet, heat 2 tablespoons of the olive oil and sauté onion until translucent. Add rice and sauté, stirring with a wooden spoon, until it begins to brown very lightly. Reduce heat and add 2 chopped tomatoes to mixture. Add almonds or pine nuts, raisins, cinnamon stick, bay leaf, salt, pepper, and $\frac{3}{4}$ cup water. Stir continuously with a wooden spoon until liquid is absorbed and rice softened but not cooked, about 10 minutes. Toss in parsley just before removing from heat.

3. Rub outside of chicken with salt and pepper and stuff loosely with rice mixture. Truss, if desired. Place in a glass baking dish and spread remaining rice around chicken. Spoon remaining chopped tomatoes over rice and add $1\frac{1}{2}$ cups water and $\frac{1}{4}$ cup red wine (or adjust accordingly if you opt against wine). Drizzle with remaining 2 tablespoons olive oil.

4. Place in hot oven. Reduce heat to 350°F and bake for 1 to $1\frac{1}{2}$ hours, or until chicken is tender and rice cooked. Add more water, if necessary, during cooking, and baste chicken every 10 to 15 minutes with pan juices. When chicken and rice are done, remove from oven, cover with a cloth, and let sit for 10 to 15 minutes. Serve hot.

Yield: 4 servings

Variation: The rice stuffing may be prepared alone to make a classic pilaf, *politiko* style. Sauté the onion in either olive oil or butter, then add 1 cup rice to skillet and sauté until very lightly browned. Add 3 cups water or light stock, the cinnamon stick, bay leaf, salt, and pepper. Bring to a boil and simmer, covered, over low heat until liquid is absorbed. Add almonds or pine nuts, raisins, and parsley 5 to 7 minutes before removing skillet from heat. Remove and cover with a cloth or towel for 10 minutes. Remove cinnamon stick and bay leaf before serving.

Serving Suggestions: A side dish of plain yogurt and a simple cabbage salad—red or green—would nicely accompany this main course. As for a wine, to blend with the sweetness of the raisins here, I'd suggest something sweet but daring, like an Achaia Claus Mavrodaphne.

Tsarouhia

(CHICKEN WITH PICKLED CABBAGE)

TSAROUHIA is the name for the pointy tassled shoes Greek soldiers wore during the Revolution. This dish comes from Kaválla and is a traditional Christmas meal in the northeastern parts of the country. Perhaps influenced by Russian and other Baltic cooking, the dish calls for pickled cabbage. Sometimes the cabbage leaves themselves are stuffed, as in *dolmades*. Here, they are simply layered and the chicken sandwiched between them. Try not to use sauerkraut. Look for *lahano toursi*, or pickled cabbage, sold loose in barrels in most Greek and Middle Eastern specialty food shops. If you pickle the cabbage yourself, that's even better.

---

1. In a large heavy stewing pot, heat olive oil and add chicken or turkey pieces, a few at a time, turning frequently until lightly browned. Remove with a slotted spoon and place on paper towels to drain.
2. Place half the cabbage leaves on bottom of stewing pot so that entire surface is covered. Add chicken or turkey, bay leaves, parsley, and chopped hot peppers. Cover with remaining cabbage leaves. Pour in water. Cover and simmer over low heat for 2 to 2½ hours, until chicken is tender and cabbage almost translucent. Carefully remove chicken and cabbage from pot and place on a serving platter. Sprinkle with paprika and serve hot.

¼ *cup olive oil*
1½ *to 2 pounds boneless chicken or turkey breast, cut into 2-inch cubes*
1 *to 1½ pounds whole pickled cabbage leaves, very well washed and drained*
2 *bay leaves*
1 *cup chopped fresh parsley*
1 *to 3 hot red peppers, finely chopped*
½ *cup water*
Paprika

Yield: 4 to 6 servings

Serving Suggestions: Serve over a bed of plain rice with a side dish of creamy strained yogurt and a loaf of hard-to-make *eptazymo*, or chick-pea bread. A difficult dish to match with wine, I'd try a simple table wine like Lac des Roches or, perhaps more fitting, would be an ouzo.

Kotopoulo Kavourmas or Kokkinisto

(BRAISED CHICKEN WITH TOMATO SAUCE)

KOKKINISTO means "reddened" and *kavourmas* means "seared." This dish gets its name from an older way of preparing chicken, braised first, not until lightly browned, but until bright red. Now, *kokkinisto* generally refers to any meat cooked in tomato sauce.

$\frac{1}{4}$ *cup olive oil*
1 medium-size frying or roasting chicken (3 to 4 pounds), rinsed and cut into serving pieces
Flour, for dredging
2 medium to large red onions, halved and sliced
10 to 12 plum tomatoes, peeled, cored, and chopped (with juice)
2 garlic cloves, finely chopped
1 bay leaf
Salt and freshly ground pepper, to taste
1 to 2 tablespoons quality red wine vinegar

1. In a large stewing pot, heat 2 to 3 tablespoons of the olive oil. Dredge chicken in flour; add a few pieces at a time to skillet and turn frequently until lightly browned. Remove chicken from pot with a slotted spoon and place on paper towels to drain.

2. Add remaining olive oil, if necessary, to pot and sauté onion until translucent. Place chicken back in pot and add tomatoes, garlic, bay leaf, salt, pepper, and a little water. Cover and simmer for 45 to 55 minutes over low heat, or until chicken is almost completely cooked. Check occasionally to make sure there is liquid in the pot and add more water, if necessary.

3. Add vinegar (to taste) about 7 minutes before removing chicken from heat and cook uncovered. Remove chicken from pot and serve hot.

Yield: 4 servings

Kotopoulo Kokkinisto me Bamiyes **(Chicken and Okra Stew):** Follow directions for cleaning and soaking 1 pound of okra on page 181. Prepare chicken *kokkinisto,* but do not dredge chicken in flour before browning. Add okra to pot along with lightly browned chicken and cook over low heat for 50 minutes to one hour, until okra and chicken are done.

Serving Suggestions: Serve this with plain rice, bulgur, or roasted or mashed potatoes and *horta.* As for wine, try a tannin-rich Náoussa or Nemea red, or even a mellower Páros or Gouménissa red.

Kotopoulo Yiaourtava

(CHICKEN BAKED IN YOGURT)

CREAMY, thick, strained yogurt of either sheep's or cow's milk is a
favorite ingredient in the cooking of northeastern Greece. Sometimes
it's served plain as a side dish, sometimes tangy sausage or ground meat
dishes are served on a bed of it, and sometimes, as here, it's baked into
a tart, stiff sauce.

1. Preheat oven to 450°F. In a heavy skillet, heat olive oil and sauté
onion until translucent. Lightly salt chicken breasts and place with
sautéed onion in a shallow (about 2 inches by 10 inches round) clay
or ceramic baking dish.

2. In a medium-size bowl, combine yogurt, flour, mint, garlic,
cumin, and pepper and mix well. Beat eggs until creamy and light and
pour into yogurt mixture to combine. Pour yogurt sauce over chicken
and sprinkle with grated cheese. Place dish in hot oven and reduce heat
to 350°F. Bake until yogurt has solidified and chicken is tender, about
one hour. Serve hot.

Yield: 6 servings

Serving Suggestions: Roasted potatoes, a simple green salad, and a
basic white wine are all you need to complete this dish. Try Lac des
Roches or a Santa Helena by Achaia Claus.

2 tablespoons olive oil
*1 medium-to-large red
   onion, finely
   chopped*
Salt, to taste
*4 large boneless
   chicken breasts,
   halved and
   quartered*
*2 cups strained yogurt
   (page 32)*
3 tablespoons flour
2 teaspoons dried mint
*1 garlic clove, finely
   chopped*
Pinch of cumin
*Freshly ground
   pepper, to taste*
2 eggs
*2 tablespoons grated
   Parmesan cheese*

Kotopoulo Giouvetsi

(SPICY CHICKEN AND ORZO CASSEROLE)

*1 medium-size
roasting chicken (3
to 4 pounds)
3 tablespoons olive oil
Salt and freshly
ground pepper, to
taste
1½ cups orzo
3 medium onions,
coarsely chopped
2 garlic cloves, minced
2 large bell peppers,
cored, seeded, and
finely chopped
1 cup peeled and
chopped plum
tomatoes
½ teaspoon ground
cumin
⅓ cup brandy
4 cups water
Grated Parmesan
cheese*

THIS dish gets its name from the clay casserole, the *giouvetsi*, that it's traditionally prepared in.

1. Preheat oven to 450°F.
2. Wash chicken and rub outside and inside with 1 tablespoon olive oil. Season skin with salt and pepper.
3. Place chicken in a medium-to-large baking pan, preferably glass or clay, and spread orzo evenly around chicken. Add remaining oil and other ingredients except cheese and toss in pan to combine. Place pan, uncovered, in hot oven and reduce heat to 350°F. Bake for 1 to 1½ hours, basting chicken every 10 to 15 minutes with pan juices, until chicken is tender and orzo cooked, adding more water, if necessary, during baking if orzo seems too dry. Sprinkle with grated cheese before serving.

Yield: 4 servings

Serving Suggestions: With this dish serve a simple green salad or a pan of spinach pie, perhaps a loaf of earthy olive bread, and a deep, velvety wine such as Gouménissa red, to match the strong flavors in the chicken.

Missoura

(SLOW-BAKED CHICKEN WITH LEEKS, RICE, RAISINS, AND MEAT)

THIS is the traditional Christmas dish in a small village some twenty kilometers outside Salonika. It's a time-consuming dish to prepare: chicken stuffed with rice and raisins and enveloped by leeks, pork, and beef. Traditionally, it's baked in a special clay dish with a bed of vines on the bottom, sealed with dough, and slowly baked in an outdoor wood-burning oven. Katerina Vahtsevani, from whom this recipe comes, says that in Melissohori most people still prepare it this way, outdoors and all. Its name comes from *messi,* or "middle," to refer to the chicken that is "wrapped" by leeks and meat, symbolic, Katerina thinks, of the baby Jesus wrapped in swaddling cloth. Although I could find no proof to substantiate her claim, so much of Greek food derives from religious ritual that it seemed quite likely. Regardless of the origin of its name, *missoura* is a great dish.

———————

1. Preheat oven to 300°F.
2. In a medium-size bowl, stir together flour and water and knead until a dough is formed. Set aside.
3. In a large heavy skillet, heat olive oil and sauté onion until translucent. Add liver, then rice, and stir constantly with a wooden spoon until both begin to brown. Pour in $\frac{1}{2}$ cup water, raisins, salt, and pepper. Reduce heat and simmer, uncovered, 5 to 10 minutes, adding another $\frac{1}{4}$ to $\frac{1}{2}$ cup water if necessary, until rice is softened but not cooked, and liquid is absorbed. Remove skillet from heat and cool slightly.
4. Season chicken with salt and pepper and carefully stuff with cooled rice mixture. Sew closed and truss.
5. Place a quarter of the chopped leeks on the bottom of a large, oval glass or earthenware casserole. Next place $\frac{1}{4}$ pound each of beef and pork over leeks. Season lightly with salt and pepper. Place chicken in center of dish, over meat layer. Arrange chopped celery all around chicken and continue with leeks and meats, in layers, until entire bird is covered. Season with salt, pepper, and paprika.
6. Cover baking dish with lid. Roll out dough into strips about 3 inches wide and press to baking dish to seal together lid and pan. Bake for $3\frac{1}{2}$ to 4 hours. Turn off oven, open door, and leave dish in oven for another 45 minutes to 1 hour. Remove dough with a sharp knife and serve *missoura* piping hot.

Yield: 4 to 6 servings

Serving Suggestions: Serve this complicated dish with a pungent bowl of *tzatziki,* a *pitta* of either spinach or leeks, hearty bread, and hearty wine such as a Náoussa Grande Réserve.

$\frac{3}{4}$ **cup all-purpose flour**
3 to 4 tablespoons water
2 tablespoons olive oil
2 medium red onions, finely chopped
Chicken liver and any other innards, finely chopped (optional)
$\frac{1}{2}$ **cup long-grain rice**
2 tablespoons light seedless raisins
Salt and freshly ground pepper, to taste
1 medium-size roasting chicken (3 to 4 pounds), washed inside and out
2 pounds leeks, thoroughly washed, cut in half lengthwise and then into $\frac{1}{8}$-inch slices
1 pound boneless beef, diced
1 pound boneless pork, diced
$\frac{3}{4}$ **cup chopped celery**
Paprika

Galopoula Yemisti

(STUFFED CHRISTMAS TURKEY)

TURKEY is the traditional Christmas meal in Greece.

---

1 pound chestnuts
3 tablespoons butter or
**   margarine**
2 large white onions,
**   peeled and finely**
**   chopped, or pureed**
**   in a food processor**
2 celery ribs, diced
1 turkey liver, chopped
1 pound ground beef
½ teaspoon cumin
Dash of ground cloves
1 small cinnamon
**   stick**
½ cup dark seedless
**   raisins**
1 cup chopped almonds
**   and pine nuts,**
**   mixed**
1 turkey, 10 to 12
**   pounds, washed**
**   inside and out**
4 tablespoons butter or
**   margarine, melted**
Salt and freshly
**   ground pepper**
½ cup dry white wine
**   (optional)**

1. Preheat oven to 325°F.

2. Make a small slit on flat side of chestnuts. Place chestnuts in a large pot with enough water to cover and boil until tender. Remove and peel off skin and fibers, being careful not to break or crumble.

3. In a large heavy skillet, heat 3 tablespoons of the butter and sauté onion for 2 to 3 minutes, until slightly wilted. Add celery, stir with a wooden spoon, and continue sautéing until both onion and celery are softened, 3 to 4 minutes. Add liver and chopped meat to skillet and stir until lightly browned. Pour ½ cup water into skillet, add spices, and lightly cook stuffing, uncovered, over low heat for 3 to 4 minutes. Stir in raisins, mixed nuts, and prepared chestnuts. Continue to simmer, uncovered, another 4 to 6 minutes, until liquid is absorbed. Remove skillet from heat and cool slightly. Remove cinnamon stick.

4. While stuffing cools, prepare the bird. Brush with melted butter and season lightly with salt and pepper. Fill the large cavity of the turkey with slightly cooled stuffing and sew closed. Add remaining stuffing to neck cavity and close. Brush outside of turkey with melted butter, place in a large shallow baking pan, and add ½ cup warm water or dry white wine to pan. Bake for 3½ to 4 hours, or until turkey is tender and cooked. Baste with pan juices every 10 to 15 minutes during baking. Remove pan from oven, cool turkey slightly, and remove stuffing from cavity. Serve on a large platter with stuffing on the side.

Yield: 6 servings

Variation: Replace ground meat with 1 to 1½ cups long-grain rice, or a combination of meat and rice. Sauté the rice to soften it before adding it to the other stuffing ingredients.

Serving Suggestions: This holiday dish would bring with it a host of side dishes, from *tyropittakia* (cheese and phyllo triangles), to spinach pie, to myriad dips and salads. Serve it forth with any of the better Greek wines—a crisp, white Santorini, a softer Robola Calliga, or even a rich dark red like Boutari Grande Réserve.

—GAME BIRDS—

Most of the game birds one finds now in meat shops are farm raised, but there is a long tradition of hunting in Greece, and most of the recipes for cooking wild birds simply call for charcoal grilling them and squeezing a generous amount of lemon over them afterward. Thrushes, partridges, quail, pigeons, and woodcocks are the most common small game birds in Greece, with quail being the most widely available. Any of them can be prepared skewered or grilled.

General Instructions for Grilling Game Birds

1. Pluck, remove innards, and thoroughly wash birds inside and out, then arrange them side by side in a baking dish.
2. Prepare enough marinade of the remaining ingredients (except tomatoes) to cover as many birds as you are cooking, adjusting proportions to your taste. Marinate cleaned whole birds for 2 hours, covered.
3. Skewer the birds, widthwise, and place a sliced tomato between each. Slit the skin lightly, if desired, and place a thin sliver of garlic in each bird. Brush with marinade and grill over slow-burning coals, turning every 2 to 3 minutes, and brushing liberally with marinade, until the birds are golden brown and thoroughly cooked.

Any small game birds
Olive Oil
Dry red wine
1 garlic clove, crushed
1 bay leaf
Oregano
Thyme
Plum tomatoes (same number as birds), sliced in half lengthwise

Serving Suggestions: Roasted potatoes, to be sure, a hearty loaf of olive bread, and any of the myriad Greek *mezedakia* might all be served with simple, grilled game birds. As for wine, the sun-colored Santorini dry white, Chateau Matsa, or Robola Calliga, could all accompany this dish.

Quail-Stuffed Eggplant, Klephtic Style

EGGPLANTS stuffed with quail make their appearance in some of the eastern Aegean islands and Cyprus. Klephtic refers to the Klephts, bands of Greek revolutionary outlaws who lived and fought in the mountains during the War of Independence and who were often forced to cook their meals in makeshift ovens underground—concealed, so that no steam would escape during the cooking process and thus disclose their position. Klephtic, in cooking, is a genial term for any number of dishes that are sealed and cooked, so that little of the flavor escapes. This is a rather unusual dish, and one that has never failed to impress company.

4 medium-size eggplants
½ cup extravirgin olive oil
10 to 12 scallions, finely chopped
4 whole quail, washed inside and out
2 garlic cloves, minced
½ pound ripe plum tomatoes, peeled and chopped
Salt and freshly ground pepper, to taste
1 teaspoon dried thyme
Pinch of allspice
1 bay leaf
¾ cup dry white wine
¾ cup grated kefalotyri or Parmesan cheese

1. Preheat oven to 350°F. Bring a large pot of salted water to a boil, drop in whole eggplants, and boil for about 5 minutes, to soften. Remove eggplants from pot and drop immediately into cold water. Drain.

2. In a large heavy skillet, heat 2 tablespoons of the olive oil and sauté scallions until wilted. Remove with a slotted spoon and set aside. Add 2 to 3 tablespoons olive oil and sauté quail until very lightly browned on all sides, 3 to 5 minutes. Add scallions, garlic, tomatoes, salt, pepper, thyme, allspice, bay leaf, and wine. Cover and simmer over very low heat until sauce is thick, 15 to 20 minutes. Remove skillet from heat.

3. While quail are cooking, prepare eggplants: Remove stems and cut in half lengthwise. Carefully remove pulp and seeds and discard, leaving the skin about as thick as two quarters. Be sure not to puncture skin.

4. Brush insides of each gutted eggplant half with olive oil and sprinkle with grated cheese. Place 1 quail inside each of the four of the eight halves (keep pairs together for a perfect fit). Dot each quail with a little of the tomato sauce, sprinkle with grated cheese, and cover with corresponding eggplant shell. Secure closed with a toothpick or needle and thread. Lightly oil a glass or clay baking dish and carefully place eggplants inside. Pour over remaining sauce and bake, uncovered, for about 30 minutes, or until eggplants and quail are tender.

Yield: 4 servings

Serving Suggestions: Serve this with roasted potatoes and a big, heaping tomato salad like *horiatiki*. Try a supple Páros red with it or a stronger Cava Red such as that produced by Boutari or Carras.

Fasiano

(PHEASANT)

BESIDES being the name of a famous Greek painter, *fasiano* is also the word for pheasant. It comes from Phasis, the river that in antiquity was the divider between Europe and Asia. (Its modern name is Rion, and it runs into the Black Sea from Soviet Georgia, which to the ancients was called Colchis. The bird's scientific name is *Phasianus colchicus.*) According to Waverley Root, and to legend, Jason and his Argonauts, after procuring the Golden Fleece, sailed toward home down the River Phasis, where they discovered the regal pheasant and brought it into Greece.

There is a stall in the central market of Athens—spanking white and quite an anomaly amid the general mayhem, the blood, and the incessant thud of cleavers—that sells the almost kingly, farm-raised pheasant, which is grown on Cephalonia. The hunted variety is by far superior, but difficult to find. Regardless of the origin of your pheasant, the meat will be tasty and is rarely enhanced by elaborate preparations. We are lucky to have a hunter in the family, and I agree with his philosophy of keeping the bird unadorned. The following method of simple roasting is an adaptation of his technique.

---

1. Tie a fresh pheasant in a cheesecloth sac and hang for 3 to 5 days in a cool, dry, airy place. Pluck the feathers, remove any meat around shotgun hole, and discard all innards. Wipe bird with a damp cloth and wait until just before you're ready to cook it to wash it thoroughly.

1 pheasant
Salt and freshly
*   ground pepper*
Salt pork

2. Preheat oven to 450°F. Season the bird with salt and pepper, inside and out (see Note). Truss, and place thin slices of salt pork around bird to cover all exposed areas. Tie salt pork to bird with thin kitchen twine to secure.

3. Place the bird on a rack in a shallow baking pan and put it in the hot oven. Lower temperature immediately to 350°F and roast pheasant for 20 to 25 minutes per pound. Baste with pan juices every 15 minutes. Remove from oven and discard salt pork. Serve warm.

Yield: About 1½ pounds per serving

Note: You may stuff the pheasant with the chestnut stuffing for turkey (page 206).

Serving Suggestions: Roasted potatoes and a stunning platter of roasted sweet red peppers would be excellent with this simple, regal dish. As for a wine, I think only the deep, strong Grande Réserve produced in Náoussa would do here.

— RABBIT —

Lagostifatho Cretis

(RABBIT STEW)

*1 medium-size rabbit
   (3 to 4 pounds), cut
   into serving pieces
1 cup dry red wine
2 bay leaves
1 teaspoon oregano
½ teaspoon thyme
4 to 5 whole cloves
5 to 6 whole allspice
   berries
1 cinnamon stick
Grating of nutmeg
2 teaspoons dried mint
½ medium-size onion,
   finely chopped
Salt and freshly
   ground pepper, to
   taste
¼ cup plus 2 to 3
   tablespoons olive oil
Flour, for dredging
2 pounds pearl onions,
   peeled and whole
6 to 8 plum tomatoes,
   coarsely chopped
   (with juice)
1 teaspoon grated
   orange rind
½ cup water, or more
   if needed*

THIS is probably the best-liked preparation for rabbit in Greece, and a kind of national dish in Crete.

1. Wash rabbit pieces well. Place them in a bowl large enough to hold them side by side.

2. Make marinade: In a small bowl, combine wine, bay leaves, oregano, thyme, cloves, allspice, cinnamon, nutmeg, mint, chopped onion, salt, pepper, and 2 to 3 tablespoons olive oil. Pour over rabbit and refrigerate, covered, for 8 to 12 hours.

3. When ready to cook, remove rabbit from marinade with a slotted spoon and dredge lightly in flour. In a heavy stewing pot, preferably enamel, heat 2 to 3 tablespoons olive oil. Add rabbit, a few pieces at a time, turning frequently until lightly browned. Remove rabbit from pot with a slotted spoon. Set aside until ready to use again.

4. Add remaining 2 tablespoons olive oil to pot, heat, and sauté onions until translucent. Place rabbit back in pot, add marinade, tomatoes, orange rind, and ½ cup of water. Season with salt and pepper. Cover and simmer over low heat for about 1 hour, or until rabbit is tender and sauce reduced. Check and stir occasionally, and add more water if pot juices seem too scant. Remove rabbit when done, and reduce sauce a bit more, if desired. Serve hot.

Yield: 3 to 4 servings (about 1 pound per serving)

Serving Suggestions: Mashed potatoes, or plain rice, or buttered noodles should accompany this dish. I'm inclined to recommend a strong Cretan wine as the logical choice here, but it's hard to come by in America. Try a stiff, robust bottle of Náoussa Grande Réserve.

Kounelli Yemisto me Feta

(RABBIT STUFFED WITH FETA CHEESE)

THE hare is considered superior to the rabbit by most Greeks in the know on such matters, but hare is difficult to find—even in the U.S.— unless you have a gifted hunter in the family. In Greece, hare is prohibited from sale in the markets; only farm-raised rabbit can be sold in butcher shops. Hare may be substituted readily for any of the following recipes.

---

1. Remove innards from rabbit and discard all but the liver, which should be covered and refrigerated until ready to use. Wash rabbit well inside and out. Place in a bowl large enough to hold it.

2. Make marinade: In a small bowl, combine juice of $2\frac{1}{2}$ lemons, wine, garlic, 3 tablespoons of the olive oil, salt, pepper, 1 teaspoon oregano or thyme, and marjoram. Pour over rabbit and refrigerate, covered, for 6 to 8 hours. Turn rabbit occasionally in bowl.

3. When ready to cook, preheat oven to 450°F and remove rabbit and liver from refrigerator. In a heavy skillet, heat 1 tablespoon olive oil and lightly sauté liver. Remove liver from skillet and set aside. In a food processor, combine feta, 1 teaspoon oregano or thyme, 2 tablespoons olive oil, liver, and chopped parsley. Process on and off for 3 to 4 minutes, until feta is a thick paste and pungent.

4. Fill stomach cavity of rabbit with feta cheese mixture. Sew closed. Season with salt and pepper and dredge lightly with flour (optional). Place on a rack in a shallow baking pan with potatoes (on the bottom of the pan), if desired. Pour marinade into pan along with 2 cups water and place in hot oven. Immediately reduce heat to 350°F. Baste rabbit every 10 to 15 minutes with pan juices. Turn it over halfway through baking and bake for about 2 hours total, or until rabbit is tender.

Yield: 3 to 4 servings (about 1 pound per serving)

Serving Suggestions: Roasted potatoes, perhaps little cheese triangles to pick up on the feta, and a simple green salad are what I'd serve with this. Try a Nemea or a Páros red wine.

1 medium-size rabbit (3 to 4 pounds)
Strained fresh juice of 3 lemons
$\frac{1}{2}$ cup dry red wine
3 garlic cloves, finely chopped
$\frac{1}{4}$ cup plus 2 tablespoons olive oil
Salt and freshly ground pepper, to taste
2 teaspoons dried oregano or thyme
$\frac{1}{2}$ teaspoon dried marjoram
$\frac{3}{4}$ cup crumbled feta cheese
$\frac{1}{3}$ cup chopped fresh parsley, packed
Flour, for dredging (optional)
2 to 3 pounds small white potatoes, peeled (optional)
2 cups water

Kounelli me Dendrolivano

(RABBIT BRAISED WITH WHITE WINE AND ROSEMARY)

*1 medium-size rabbit
(3 to 4 pounds), cut
into serving pieces
1 cup dry white wine
¼ cup plus 2
tablespoons olive oil
2 teaspoons crushed
dried rosemary
1 teaspoon dried
thyme
Salt and freshly
ground pepper
Flour, for dredging
2 pounds small white
stewing onions,
peeled and whole*

1. Wash rabbit pieces well. Place them in a bowl large enough to hold them side by side.
2. Make marinade: In a small bowl, combine white wine, 2 tablespoons olive oil, rosemary, thyme, salt, and pepper. Pour over rabbit and refrigerate, covered, for 6 to 8 hours.
3. When ready to cook, remove rabbit from marinade, pat dry, and dredge lightly in flour. In a large heavy pot or Dutch oven, heat 2 to 3 tablespoons olive oil and add rabbit, a few pieces at a time, turning frequently, until lightly and evenly browned, adding more oil, if necessary, for browning all the pieces.
4. Remove rabbit with a slotted spoon from pot. Add onions to pot and sauté until translucent. Place rabbit back in pot along with marinade and a little water, if necessary. Cover and simmer over low heat for approximately 1 hour, or until rabbit is tender.

Yield: 3 to 4 servings (about 1 pound per serving)

Serving Suggestions: Serve with plain rice or with roasted potatoes. I would drink a dry Santorini white or a Robola Calliga with this.

Braised Rabbit with Olives

*1 medium-size rabbit
(3 to 4 pounds), cut
into serving pieces
1 cup dry red wine
2 garlic cloves, finely
chopped
Salt and freshly
ground pepper
1 teaspoon oregano
¼ cup plus 2
tablespoons olive oil
3 plump ripe tomatoes,
peeled and chopped
½ cup water, or more
if needed
⅓ cup chopped parsley
¾ cup pitted, rinsed,
and drained
kalamata olives*

1. Wash rabbit pieces well. Place them in a bowl large enough to hold them side by side.
2. Make marinade: In a small bowl, combine wine, garlic, salt, pepper, oregano, and 3 tablespoons of the olive oil. Pour over rabbit and refrigerate, covered, for 6 to 8 hours.
3. In a heavy pot or Dutch oven, heat remaining 3 tablespoons olive oil. Remove rabbit from marinade with a slotted spoon and add to pot, a few pieces at a time, turning frequently to brown lightly. Add remaining marinade to pot, along with tomatoes and about ½ cup water. Reduce heat and simmer, covered, for about 1 hour, until rabbit is tender, adding more water if pot looks dry during cooking. Ten minutes before removing pot from heat, stir in parsley and olives.

Yield: 3 to 4 servings (about 1 pound per serving)

Serving Suggestions: Serve over plain buttered noodles *(hilopittes)* with a bottle of Náoussa red wine.

Chapter 13

Fish and Seafood

It is easier, by a million degrees, to get access to the
General Staff . . . than it is to approach the damned
fishmongers in the market. Whenever a purchaser
picks up one of their wares on display and addresses
to them a question, the dealer . . . crouches in silence
first . . . and as if he meant to pay no attention and
had not heard a word, he pounds a polyp. The
purchaser bursts into a flame of rage. . . .
—The Deipnosophists, Book III

These sentiments ring true even today, for Greeks, enamored of their luscious wine-dark sea and of its many creatures, hold little esteem for the fishmonger, who, they fear, is always trying to hawk something less than fresh. One learns to be fast and alert at the *psaragora,* or fish market: to recognize the curved gleaming sight of a fresh fish against the vapid one of an old or frozen specimen.

The fish market, whether it be the Central Agora in Athens, or the Piraeus Market, or the fish emporiums of Vólos or Salonika or Patras, is often the most graphic and bustling place in each city. One sees all sorts of picture-worthy sights at the old neoclassical markets: a politicized monger who has set red carnations between his wet lead-colored sardines; another who shouts that *his* mussels are gathered only by the light of the full moon; another who sells pigs' feet and tunny on the same block of ice.

But as fascinating as the fish market is, with its noise, its nonstop commotion, the constant cries of hawkers and buyers, and the cold gritty atmosphere, it is not evincing of Greeks' love of their sea. For that, one must go elsewhere.

At dusk, in any of Greece's tiny island ports, the sea is amethyst, like the sky. Local fishermen are just setting out for the night's fishing. Their bright wooden boats *(grigri),* strung together and lighted with lanterns, create a bouncing, eerie procession as they chug out of the harbor toward open water. By dawn, when they return, a cargo full of fish accompanies them. Snappers and bream, mackerel, red mullet, and porgies might still be smacking against the deck.

By late morning, the fishermen are on the wharf again, nimbly mending ochre nets, unbothered by flies or bees, noticing only the wind, the waves, the day's new weather. Other fishermen—free-divers who descend as deep as 35 meters, more than 100 feet—set out in dark rubber suits. For them, the gem of the sea is the fat blackfish *(rofos),* better known as sea bass. The patient divers float about like living shadows in the water, waiting for the sea bass to appear, then descend for ten, twenty, thirty interminable seconds until they can snap the trigger on their spearguns and snatch the unsuspecting creature. The divers also target octopus, spearing them, hauling them still sucking to the surface, slapping them limp on the wharf, and retreating again to the sea.

One has to love the salt-crusted scent of octopus grilling over hot coals, or the flat warm taste of seawater in a simple *kakavia*—a kind of soup—or the naked flavor of a sea urchin plucked from the rocks and eaten at that moment, astringent with lemon squeezed into it, to understand the Greek feeling for the sea and the life it holds.

The dishes that make up the seafood heading in Greek cookery might be many and diverse. But the simple grilled fish, unadorned save for a little dome of lemon, and plain but for its own immaculate flavor, is by far the way Greeks like Poseidon's bounty best.

—THE BASIC MEDITERRANEAN— FISH

—For Grilling *(Steen Skara)* —

barbouni (red mullet)
christopsaro (John Dory)
heli (eel)
htapothi (octopus)
kolios (mackerel)
palamitha (tunny or bonito)
pestrofa (trout)

rofos (sea bass)
sfiritha (pike)
skaros (parrotfish)
stira (grouper)
synagritha (red snapper)
tsipoura (porgy)
xifias (swordfish)

—For Frying *(Tiganito)* —

bakaliaros (cod, either salted or fresh)
barbouni (red mullet)
galeo (shark)
gavros (pilchard)
glossa (sole)
gopa (smelt)

kalamari (squid)
lithrini and *fagri* (bream)
maritha (pickerel)
salahi (skate or ray fish)
sarthela (fresh sardine)
tsipoura (porgy)
zargana (hornfish)

—For Baking and Stewing *(Plaki or Psito)* —

barbouni (red mullet)
christopsaro (John Dory)
freskos bakaliaros (fresh cod)
gavros (pilchard)
glossa (sole)
htapothi (octopus)
kalamari (squid)
kefalos (mullet)
kiprina (carp)

kolios (mackerel)
palamitha (tunny)
pestrofa (trout)
sarthela (fresh sardine)
synagritha (red snapper)
tonnos (tuna)
tsipoura (porgy)
xifias (swordfish)

—For Poaching *(Vrasto)* —

freskos bakaliaros (fresh cod or, in America, haddock)
hannos (sea perch)
heli (eel)
kiprina (carp)
lithrini and *faqri* (sea bream or shad)

rofos (sea bass)
salahi (skate or ray fish)
sfiritha (pike)
skorpina (scorpion fish)
stira (grouper)
synagritha (red snapper)

—GRILLED FISH—

Grilling or barbecuing are the most popular methods for cooking whole fish, as well as skewered chunks. To barbecue any whole fish (see list on the opposite page for the most commonly grilled fish), it's important to have a hand-held grid that opens and closes so that you may easily turn the fish. Gut and scrape off scales; have barbecue ready; brush fish with olive oil, lemon juice, and herbs; place fish on hand-held grid to grill. Turn several times as necessary to grill evenly. To broil fish, brush with seasoning and place in broiler pan 6 to 8 inches from heat. Turn over once to cook evenly.

Xifias Souvlaki

(SKEWERED, GRILLED SWORDFISH)

$\frac{1}{2}$ *cup olive oil*
Strained fresh juice of
  2 lemons, or more
  to taste
1 teaspoon dried
  thyme or oregano,
  or 1 tablespoon
  fresh, chopped
Salt and freshly
  ground pepper, to
  taste
1$\frac{1}{4}$ to 2 pounds
  swordfish steak,
  skinned and cut
  into 1$\frac{1}{2}$ to 2-inch
  cubes
3 to 4 firm ripe
  tomatoes, cored and
  quartered
2 to 3 large green bell
  peppers, seeded and
  cubed
2 to 3 medium-size
  onions, peeled and
  quartered
8 to 10 large firm
  mushrooms, halved
  (optional)
8 to 10 bay leaves

1. In a medium-size bowl, whisk together olive oil, lemon juice, thyme or oregano, salt, and pepper. Add swordfish chunks and marinate for 30 minutes.

2. Preheat broiler or barbecue.

3. Alternating fish, vegetables, and bay leaves, slide a wedge at a time onto skewers. Brush with marinade and broil 6 to 8 inches from heat or grill on a barbecue, dousing with marinade and turning to cook evenly, until done, 12 to 15 minutes. Serve hot over rice or with a crisp green salad.

Yield: 4 to 6 servings

Serving Suggestions: Serve with tomato and bulgur or barley toast salad, *horta*, and a dry Santorini white wine.

——FRIED FISH——

Refer to page 215 to see which fish are usually fried in Greek cookery. The basic preparation for any of these fish is as follows.

Clean fish by scraping off scales (as required, according to the type of fish you're using), then slit open gently on belly side and remove intestines, but leave head intact. Prepare seasoned flour (with salt and pepper), dredge fish, and fry in a skillet with olive oil until lightly golden brown. Drain on paper towels and sprinkle with lemon juice as desired. Serve hot.

Bakaliaro/Galeo Skordalia

(BATTER-FRIED SALTED COD OR FRESH SHARK WITH GARLIC AND POTATO PUREE)

BAKALIARO or *galeo* with *skordalia* is a classic Greek meal, one of the staple combinations on the Greek table. In Greek food stores here, salt cod is sold in neat, pliable strips, generally already cleaned. In Greece, it's stiff as board, stacked upright, and sold in crates, most often at the central markets.

---

1. Place salted cod (whole or cut in half) in a large basin and fill with ample cold water. Soak fish for 10 to 12 hours at room temperature, changing the water three or four times.

2. When the fish is ready to be cooked, prepare batter: In a medium-size bowl, combine $1\frac{1}{4}$ cups of the flour, salt, pepper, and baking powder. Make a well in center and add cold water or beer. Stir with a fork until a thick batter is formed, adding more flour if necessary. Cover and set aside.

3. Remove cod from water and rinse very well. Cut either cod or shark into wedges about 2 inches square, removing any bones. Pat dry and sprinkle with lemon juice (optional). If cod disintegrates, remove any bones and shape fish into balls about $1\frac{1}{2}$ inches in diameter. Dredge cod or shark in remaining $\frac{3}{4}$ cup flour and dip into batter.

4. In a medium-size pot or deep-fryer, heat 3 to 4 inches of oil and deep-fry the fish, a little at a time, for a few minutes, until batter turns a light golden brown and becomes crisp. Remove fish and drain on paper towels. Serve hot and squeeze lemon over fish as desired.

Yield: 4 to 6 servings

Note: Sometimes the cod is boiled for 2 to 3 minutes and then deboned. Also, plain or seasoned flour may be used in lieu of a batter.

Serving Suggestions: *Lahanosalata,* or shredded cabbage salad, *skordalia,* and retsina are the three classics that almost always accompany this dish.

$1\frac{1}{4}$ to 2 pounds salted cod, preferably filleted (see Note), or fresh shark fillets, preferably boneless

2 cups all-purpose flour

Salt and freshly ground pepper, to taste

1 scant teaspoon baking powder

$\frac{2}{3}$ cup cold water or flat beer

2 tablespoons strained fresh lemon juice (optional)

Olive or vegetable oil, for frying

Skordalia *(page 85)*

2 to 3 lemons

Kalamarakia Tiganita

(BATTER-FRIED SQUID)

THIS is another classic of the Greek table, a *meze* and main course alike, and a favorite summer meal.

---

2 to 2½ pounds fresh squid, preferably small

Flour

Salt and freshly ground pepper, to taste

Olive or vegetable oil, for frying

Lemons

1. Clean squid: Wash, remove and discard mouth and eyes, and soft, cartilagelike strip on inside. Cut squid into small round rings, about 1 inch wide, but leave tentacles whole. Dry thoroughly.

2. In a paper or plastic bag, combine flour, salt, and pepper and dredge squid completely.

3. In a saucepan, deep-fryer, or heavy skillet, heat ample oil—2 to 3 inches—and fry squid a little at a time until crisp and golden brown. Serve piping hot and douse with lemon juice.

Yield: 4 to 6 servings

Variation: An interesting variation of this dish is grilled or barbecued squid. You'll need large squid. Wash and clean as above. Cut the squid in half lengthwise and marinate in lemon juice for 30 minutes. Grill lightly. Serve with lemon and a crisp green salad. Squid may also be batter-dipped: Dredge in flour and prepare batter as for *bakaliaro* (see page 217).

Serving Suggestions: Serve with *skordalia* or *tzatziki,* shredded cabbage salad, and any of a number of white wines—retsina, Lac des Roches, Chateau Matsa, Robola, or Porto Carras Réserve.

Trout

TROUT *(pestrofa)* and frogs' legs *(vatrahakia)* are specialties of Ioannina and other regions of northern Greece. Generally, trout is simply grilled or fried.

Season cleaned, gutted trout with salt, pepper, and oregano. Heat olive oil or butter in a large, heavy skillet. Add fish. Flatten fish slightly in the pan with a spatula as it cooks. Sauté until browned and tender. Serve with lemon wedges.

Vatrahakia Ioanninas

(DEEP-FRIED FROGS' LEGS)

Frogs' legs
Semolina flour
1 to 2 eggs, slightly
  beaten
Olive or vegetable oil,
  for frying

WASH the frogs' legs and wipe dry. Dip them in semolina flour and toss back and forth between the palms of your hands so that excess flour falls away. Dip in the slightly beaten egg and then back in the semolina. Let them stand for 20 minutes before frying. Deep-fry in very hot oil.

Psari Marinata

(PAN-COOKED FISH WITH VINEGAR, TOMATOES, AND ROSEMARY)

*1½ to 2 pounds small
    fish (red mullet,
    fresh sardines,
    smelts, etc.)*
*Flour for dredging,
    plus 1 scant
    tablespoon*
*Olive oil for frying,
    plus ¼ cup for sauce*
¼ cup red wine vinegar
*1 cup peeled, chopped
    tomato (with juice)*
*1½ teaspoons dried
    rosemary*
*1 large bay leaf,
    ripped*
*1 scant teaspoon dried
    oregano*
*1 large garlic clove,
    finely chopped*
*Salt and freshly
    ground pepper*
1 to 2 teaspoons sugar

1. Wash and clean fish. If using fresh sardines, remove the heads as well. Dredge fish lightly in flour. In a large heavy skillet, heat enough olive oil to come up about ¼ inch in pan. Fry dredged fish until golden brown. Remove with a slotted spoon to a serving platter. Pour off oil from skillet, but don't scrape it clean.

2. Heat ¼ cup olive oil in skillet. Add 1 tablespoon flour and stir vigorously with a wooden spoon until flour turns a light golden brown. Add vinegar, tomatoes, rosemary, bay leaf, oregano, and garlic. Stir once or twice, reduce heat, and season with salt, pepper, and sugar. Cover and simmer over low heat for 15 to 20 minutes, checking occasionally to be sure sauce doesn't cook down too much, or burn; add water if necessary to keep it liquid. The sauce should, however, be thick. Pour over fish and serve warm.

Yield: 4 servings

Serving Suggestions: I'd serve plain rice and *horta* and a simple salad of shredded cabbage or lettuce, coupled by one of two wines—risky though it seems, a Nemea red to balance the piquancy of this dish, or a rosé demi-sec.

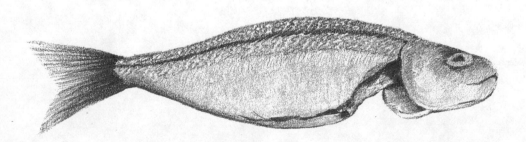

—BAKED FISH AND FISH STEWS—

Psari Plaki

(CLASSIC BAKED FISH)

COULD *plaki* be the original planked fish? Who knows. The word comes from the ancient Greek *plax,* a stone plaque on which bread was grilled. The term now refers to a simple baked fish, usually with vegetables and a tomato or two.

———

1. Sprinkle the fish with lemon juice, salt, and pepper; let stand 1 hour before baking.
2. In the meantime, heat the 2 tablespoons olive oil in a heavy skillet or stewing pot and sauté onion and celery until almost translucent. Remove pot from heat, let mixture cool, then stir in garlic and parsley.
3. Preheat oven to 350°F. Spread 2 tablespoons olive oil in a clay or glass baking dish and place fish in pan. Top with onion and celery mixture, then with tomatoes, strewn all around it. Season with salt and pepper. Pour in wine and remaining 2 tablespoons olive oil. Bake uncovered until fish is fork-tender, 25 to 30 minutes (filleted fish will take less time). (Add water, if necessary, to keep pan moist during baking.) Remove from oven and serve on a platter garnished with fresh parsley sprigs.

Yield: 4 servings

Serving Suggestions: Serve with *rossiki salata* (potatoes and mayonnaise) or simple potato salad with olive oil and vinegar, *horta,* and any of a number of good white wines—Porto Carras Réserve, Santorini Boutari, or Robola Calliga.

2 to 2$\frac{1}{2}$ pounds fresh seasonal fish, washed, cleaned, and either sliced or whole
2 to 3 tablespoons strained fresh lemon juice
Salt and freshly ground pepper, to taste
$\frac{1}{4}$ cup plus 2 tablespoons olive oil
1 large onion, halved and sliced
1 celery rib, cut into thin rounds
1 to 2 garlic cloves, peeled and sliced paper-thin
3 tablespoons finely chopped fresh parsley
3 to 4 medium-size ripe tomatoes, peeled, cored, and sliced across the width into rounds about $\frac{1}{8}$ inch thick
$\frac{1}{3}$ cup dry white wine
Fresh parsley sprigs, for garnish

Sartheles Psito se Klimatofilla

(SARDINES BAKED IN GRAPE LEAVES)

FRESH sardines are cooked everywhere in Greece—usually fried in a skillet and served in a heaping mound with plenty of fresh lemon wedges. They are also a regional specialty of the northeastern parts of Macedonia, especially regions populated by Pontian Greeks. This dish is a specialty of the *Pontiyoi*, but can be made with any fresh whole baking fish (see page 215).

2 pounds large fresh sardines, washed and gutted, with heads removed (or any fresh whole fish, washed and gutted, but with head intact)

¼ cup plus 2 tablespoons olive oil

Strained fresh juice of 2 lemons

1 tablespoon dried thyme or oregano

Fresh or brine-preserved grape leaves (as many as there are fish, plus 4 to 6 for layering the bottom of the pan)

Salt and freshly ground pepper, to taste

1. Place fish in a large dish. In a small bowl, whisk together 2 to 3 tablespoons olive oil, juice of 1 lemon, and thyme or oregano. Pour mixture over fish and marinate for 30 minutes.

2. Rinse and parboil the grape leaves in ample boiling water for 2 to 4 minutes, to soften. (If using preserved leaves—the fresh are seasonal and difficult to find outside of ethnic markets—rinse them very thoroughly to rid them of their briny taste before parboiling.) Cut off the hard stems.

3. Preheat oven to 350°F. Brush 1 tablespoon olive oil on bottom of a clay or glass baking dish and cover the bottom of the pan with 4 to 6 grape leaves. Remove fish from marinade, season with salt and pepper, and wrap carefully and individually in grape leaves. Place in the pan, seam side down. Pour remaining 2 tablespoons olive oil and lemon juice over fish rolls and bake for 25 to 30 minutes, until grape leaves are very soft and fish is fork-tender. Serve on a platter garnished with lemon wedges.

Yield: 4 to 6 servings

Serving Suggestions: Serve with plain rice, cabbage salad, or steamed zucchini, *skordalia* or *taramosalata*. I would try a soft Robola Calliga or Chateau Matsa to counter the pungency of this dish.

Psari Psito me Domates kai Stafithes

(FISH BAKED WITH RAISINS AND TOMATOES)

1. In a large dish, marinate fish in $\frac{1}{2}$ cup of the wine for 30 to 40 minutes. Preheat oven to 350°F.

2. In a large heavy skillet, heat 2 tablespoons of the olive oil and sauté onions until translucent. Add tomatoes, raisins, remaining $\frac{1}{4}$ cup wine, salt, and pepper. Simmer, uncovered, over low heat for about 10 minutes, stirring frequently with a wooden spoon until sauce is slightly thickened. (There should be enough liquid to cover fish. Add a little water, if necessary.) Sprinkle in mint at the end and remove from heat.

3. Lightly oil a glass baking dish. Add fish and top with sauce. Bake until fish is fork-tender, about 20 minutes. Remove pan from oven and place fish on a serving platter. Pour sauce over fish and serve hot.

Yield: 2 to 4 servings (about 1 pound per serving)

Serving Suggestions: Serve with plain rice, *horta,* and either a soft Robola Calliga, a demi-sec rosé, or dry white Santorini by Boutari.

2 to 4 pounds fresh
  whole fish or fish
  fillets
$\frac{3}{4}$ cup dry white wine
$\frac{1}{4}$ cup olive oil
$1\frac{1}{2}$ cups pearl onions,
  peeled and whole
2 cups peeled, seeded,
  and chopped fresh
  tomatoes
$\frac{1}{2}$ cup light seedless
  raisins, soaked for
  several hours in
  water until plump
Salt and freshly
  ground pepper, to
  taste
2 teaspoons dried mint

Heli Psito

(BAKED EEL)

WE FIRST tried this dish in Ioannina, on the Nissaki, or small island that stands in the middle of the city's lake. In northern Greece, freshwater trout, frog, and eel are all considered local specialties. This eel dish is called *heli sto keramithi,* or "eel in clay," for the way it's traditionally prepared in a wood-burning oven inside a makeshift pan—a U-shaped ceramic roof tile enclosed at both ends with dough.

2 to 2½ pounds fresh live eel

4 to 6 garlic cloves, thinly sliced

2 large bay leaves, ripped

¼ to ½ cup quality red wine vinegar

Salt and freshly ground pepper, to taste

1. First, kill and clean the eel: Give it a sharp blow to the head in order to kill. Then, tie a noose around the eel's head and hang the other end of the cord on a hook. Cut the skin 3 to 3½ inches below the head and peel it back. Tug it downward until the skin slips off like a glove. Remove the eel from the hook and clean it: Slit the eel with a sharp knife from the vent to the gill and turn it over to slice through the backbone. Remove the intestines and head with one motion. Scrape out either side of the backbone, where the kidneys are, rinse the eel well, then cut it into 2- to 3-inch pieces.

2. Place eel in a large dish. In a small bowl, combine garlic, bay leaves, vinegar, salt, and pepper. Pour mixture over eel and marinate for 2 hours before baking.

3. Preheat oven to 375°F, then bake eel with its marinade—preferably in a clay dish—for 20 to 25 minutes, or until tender. Baste with marinade during cooking and turn the eel frequently. Serve hot.

Yield: About 4 servings

Serving Suggestions: Ouzo stands up nicely to this rich, heavy dish, but so does a crisp retsina.

Psari à la Spetsiota

(BAKED FISH WITH BREAD CRUMBS AND TOMATO)

2 to 2½ pounds large baking fish, washed and cleaned, or fish steaks

1½ cups finely chopped fresh tomato, peeled and seeded (with juice)

THIS baked fish dish, named for Spétsai, the posh island off the eastern shores of the Peloponnisos, is considered fancy fare and is a standard on the menus of good Greek restaurants and Aegean cruise ships. Its versions are plentiful. Some make a sauce thickened with bread crumbs and pour it over the fish before baking; some spread several layers of bread crumbs and tomato over the fish; and some prepare it rather simply, as below.

1. Lightly salt cleaned fish and let stand 30 minutes. In a medium-size bowl, combine tomatoes, garlic, parsley, and wine and let stand 30 minutes as well. Preheat oven to 350°F.

2. Season fish with salt and pepper. Place in a lightly oiled clay or glass baking dish. Pour marinade over fish, sprinkle with bread crumbs, and drizzle with olive oil. Bake for 20 to 25 minutes, basting several times, until fish is fork-tender and bread crumbs are baked to a golden crust. Serve warm.

2 to 4 garlic cloves, chopped
⅓ cup chopped fresh parsley
½ cup dry white wine
Salt and freshly ground pepper, to taste
¾ cup plain bread or toast crumbs
¼ cup olive oil

Yield: 4 servings

Serving Suggestions: Serve with a traditional Greek potato salad, spinach pie, and any of a number of white wines: Boutari's Santorini, Porto Carras Réserve, Tsantalis Aghioritiko, or Chateau Matsa.

Pehti

(LEEK AND SARDINE CASSEROLE)

THIS is an old and interesting dish, a specialty of the Pontian Greeks, that utilizes some of their most revered ingredients, namely the leek and the fresh sardine.

------

1. Wash and clean the sardines: Cut off the heads and slit open the undersides to remove the guts. Wash well, sprinkle with the juice of 1 large lemon and set aside, covered, until ready to use.

2. Preheat oven to 375°F. Slit leeks lengthwise and wash thoroughly, being sure to remove any sand or dirt between layers. Chop into thin rounds and pat dry. In a heavy skillet, heat 3 tablespoons olive oil over medium heat and sauté leeks until wilted and soft.

3. Lightly oil a large clay or glass casserole with 1 to 2 tablespoons olive oil. Spread half the leeks on the bottom of the dish and place the sardines over them. Cover with remaining leeks. Season with salt and pour in lemon juice and remaining olive oil. Bake for about 20 minutes, or until sardines are fork-tender and done. Serve hot.

2 pounds fresh sardines
Strained fresh juice of 1 large lemon plus ⅓ cup strained fresh lemon juice
2 to 3 leeks, white part only
¼ cup plus 3 tablespoons olive oil
Salt, to taste
Several thin slices of lemon, for garnish

Yield: 4 to 6 servings

Serving Suggestions: Try retsina, Porto Carras Réserve, or a dry white Santorini with this and serve with plain rice and *maroulosalata* (lettuce salad).

Psari Bianco

(FISH STEW WITH VEGETABLES AND GARLIC)

¼ cup plus 2
  tablespoons olive oil
1 large yellow onion,
  peeled, halved, and
  sliced
2 to 3 pounds small
  white potatoes,
  peeled and cut into
  ½-inch rounds
2 medium-size carrots,
  pared and cut into
  1-inch chunks
1 to 2 celery ribs, cut
  into ¼-inch pieces
Freshly ground
  pepper, to taste
4 to 6 garlic cloves,
  chopped
Salt, to taste
2½ pounds fresh fish
  fillet, cut into
  2-inch squares
¼ cup strained fresh
  lemon juice

THE predominant flavor in this dish from Corfu is garlic, and plenty of it.

1. In a large heavy stewing pot, heat ¼ cup olive oil and sauté onion until translucent. Add potatoes, carrots, celery, and pepper and sauté for 3 to 4 minutes, stirring constantly with a wooden spoon until coated with oil. Add garlic and enough water almost to cover vegetables. Bring to a boil, reduce heat, season with salt, cover, and simmer for 10 to 15 minutes, until vegetables are about halfway cooked.

2. Add fish to pot and stir gently, so as not to break pieces apart. Simmer, covered, for another 10 to 15 minutes, adding a little water if necessary to keep pot moist, until fish is tender, vegetables are cooked, and most of the liquid is absorbed. Remove lid and pour in lemon juice 3 to 5 minutes before taking the pot off the heat. Season with remaining 2 tablespoons olive oil and freshly ground pepper and serve hot.

Yield: 4 to 6 servings

Serving Suggestions: *Horta* and hearty bread are all that are needed to complete this dish. As for wine, probably a fellow Ionian Island variety—Robola Calliga from Cephalonia—would work best.

3 tablespoons olive oil
1 bay leaf, ripped
¼ cup water, or more
  if necessary
2 medium-size red
  onions, peeled and
  sliced into rings
½ cup dry white wine
2 pounds stewing fish
  (cod, carp, whiting,
  mackerel, etc.),
  washed and cut into
  large chunks

Psari Bourtheto

(PEPPERY FISH STEW)

1. In a large heavy stewing pot, bring olive oil, bay leaf, and water to a boil. Add onion and simmer until slightly translucent. Pour in wine, bring to a boil, and add fish and remaining ingredients except for the lemon juice and paprika. Reduce heat and simmer with pot lid on but slightly ajar for about 8 minutes (adding a bit more water if necessary to keep stew from drying out), until fish is almost tender. Add lemon juice and simmer another 2 to 5 minutes, or until fish is flaky and fork tender.

2. Remove fish carefully with a slotted spatula. Continue to heat the pan liquids until they are reduced and thickened slightly. Pour over fish and serve warm, garnished with paprika and fresh parsley, if desired.

Yield: 4 to 6 servings

Serving Suggestions: Serve with roasted potatoes, wild greens *(horta)*, any of a range of Greek dips, and for wine, a Boutari Santorini, Robola Calliga, or Porto Carras Réserve.

½ cup finely chopped fresh parsley
1 heaping teaspoon dried thyme
1 teaspoon crushed dried rosemary
Freshly ground black and green peppercorns, to taste
Dash of cayenne or ½ small hot red pepper (optional)
Salt, to taste
2 to 3 tablespoons strained lemon juice
1 scant teaspoon paprika

Htapothi me Maratho kai Prasines Elies

(OCTOPUS COOKED WITH FENNEL AND GREEN OLIVES)

THIS is a tangy, exotic dish that's as beautiful to look at—with plump, purplish pieces of octopus and tender green fennel leaves and olives—as it is to eat.

1. Wash octopus and cut away ink sac and mouth. Beat against a marble slab to soften.

2. Place octopus in a large heavy pot without any liquid, cover, and cook over low heat until the octopus discards its juices and is bright pink and tender, about 30 minutes. Check occasionally to be sure it doesn't burn, adding a little water if there is no liquid in pot.

3. Add olive oil to the octopus, stir in scallions, and simmer until slightly wilted. Pour in the wine and season with fennel and pepper. Cover and simmer over low heat for another 1½ to 2 hours, until octopus is very tender. Check during cooking to be sure there's ample liquid in the pot, and add water, if necessary. About 5 minutes before removing octopus from heat, add green olive halves and season with salt.

Yield: 4 servings as a main course

Serving Suggestions: Serve hot over rice or cold, alone. This can be either main course or meze and is best had with a refreshing ouzo.

1 medium-size octopus (2 to 2½ pounds)
½ cup olive oil, or slightly more if desired
4 to 6 scallions, coarsely chopped
1 cup dry white wine
½ cup fresh chopped fennel leaves, packed
Freshly ground black and green peppercorns, to taste
½ cup pitted, halved green olives, rinsed thoroughly
Salt, to taste

1 medium-size
  octopus, 2 to 3
  pounds
$\frac{1}{4}$ cup olive oil
1$\frac{1}{2}$ cups stewing or
  pearl onions, peeled
  and whole
1$\frac{1}{2}$ cups coarsely chopped
  fresh peeled tomato
1 garlic clove, finely
  chopped
1 cinnamon stick
$\frac{1}{2}$ cup dry red wine
$\frac{1}{2}$ cup water
2 small bay leaves,
  ripped
Salt and freshly
  ground pepper
$\frac{1}{2}$ teaspoon grated
  orange rind
1 tablespoon quality
  red wine vinegar

Htapothi Stifatho or Krasato

(OCTOPUS STEWED IN RED WINE)

1. Wash octopus and remove mouth and ink sac. Pound to tenderize, if desired.

2. Place octopus in a large heavy pot without any liquid, cover, and cook over low heat until the octopus discards its juices and is bright pink and tender, about 30 minutes. Check occasionally to be sure it doesn't burn. Remove octopus from pot, cool slightly, and cut into chunks about 1$\frac{1}{2}$ inches long.

3. In the same pot, heat olive oil and sauté onions until they begin to turn translucent. Add tomatoes, garlic, cinnamon stick, octopus, wine, water, bay leaves, salt, and pepper. Bring to a slight boil, reduce heat, and simmer, covered, for about 2 hours, or until octopus is tender. Add the orange rind about halfway through the cooking. Stir in the vinegar about 5 minutes before removing pot from heat. Keep pot covered until ready to serve. Remove cinnamon stick.

Yield: 4 servings

Serving Suggestions: Serve over plain rice with a heady bottle of Náoussa or Náoussa Grande Réserve to match.

2 to 2$\frac{1}{2}$ pounds
  cuttlefish
Ink sac from fish (if
  available)
4 cups water
$\frac{1}{4}$ cup plus 2
  tablespoons olive oil
1 cup finely chopped
  red onion
1$\frac{1}{2}$ cups chopped fresh
  tomato, with juice
$\frac{3}{4}$ cup dry white wine
1 to 2 large garlic
  cloves, finely
  chopped (to taste)

Soupies Pilafi

(INK OR CUTTLEFISH PILAF)

1. Wash and clean cuttlefish very well. Pull out the eyes and mouth. If the ink sacs are intact, carefully remove them so as not to break, and reserve. Cut the cuttlefish into equal-size rings about 2 inches long.

2. In a large heavy stewing pot, heat olive oil and sauté onion until almost wilted. Add cuttlefish and sauté until lightly browned. Add tomatoes, water, wine, garlic, crushed red pepper, and black pepper. If available, break ink sacs into pot, discarding sacs. Cover, bring to a boil over low heat, and simmer for 1$\frac{1}{2}$ to 2 hours, until cuttlefish are almost tender. Stir in parsley 5 minutes before removing pot from heat.

3. In the meantime, make rice: Bring 3 cups of salted water to a boil. Add remaining 2 tablespoons olive oil and the rice. Bring to a boil and

simmer over medium heat until rice is tender and liquid is absorbed. Serve cuttlefish over rice.

Yield: 4 to 6 servings

Serving Suggestions: This is a meal onto itself, needing little else but feta, bread, and wine. I'd suggest a dry white to match the flavors here—Chateau Matsa or Robola Calliga.

Soupies me Spanaki

(CUTTLEFISH AND SPINACH STEW)

CUTTLEFISH—or squid if cuttlefish aren't available—and spinach combine to make another common, much-loved Greek family dish. The trick to making cuttlefish tender is to cook them slowly and for a long time.

1. Wash and clean cuttlefish very well. Pull out the eyes and mouth and if the ink sacs are intact very carefully remove them, so as not to break, and reserve. Cut the cuttlefish into equal-size rings about 2 inches long. If available, break ink sacs, discarding sacs, and combine ink with the water; set aside.

2. In a stewing pot, heat 3 to 4 tablespoons olive oil and sauté onion until translucent. Add cuttlefish and brown slightly. Add garlic, dill, parsley, and spinach and toss with a wooden spoon for several minutes. Pour in ink and water mixture. Season with salt and pepper, cover, and simmer over low heat, adding more water, if necessary, to keep mixture moist, for $1\frac{1}{2}$ to 2 hours, or until cuttlefish is tender and liquid is absorbed. When done, toss with lemon juice and remaining olive oil. Serve warm or cold.

Yield: 4 servings

Serving Suggestions: Nothing more than feta, bread, and good white wine should go with this. Boutari Santorini, Porto Carras Réserve, or Robola Calliga would all do.

---

1 to 2 hot red peppers, crushed (optional)
Freshly ground black pepper, to taste
$\frac{1}{2}$ cup fresh chopped parsley, packed
1 cup long-grain rice
Salt

2 pounds cuttlefish
Ink sac from fish (if available)
1 cup water
$\frac{1}{4}$ cup plus 2 tablespoons olive oil
1 cup finely chopped red onions or scallions, packed
1 to 2 garlic cloves, finely chopped
3 tablespoons chopped fresh dill
$\frac{1}{4}$ cup chopped fresh parsley, packed
2 to $2\frac{1}{2}$ pounds spinach, washed, drained, and chopped
Salt and freshly ground pepper, to taste
Strained fresh juice of 1 lemon

Mihali's Shrimp with Feta Cheese

SHRIMP cooked in the skillet in a tangy feta cheese sauce is a Salonika specialty, but it's also found in one or two Athenian kitchens.

$\frac{1}{2}$ *cup olive oil*

3 to 5 scallions, finely chopped, including the greens

2 green Italian peppers, finely chopped

1 small red chile pepper, finely chopped (optional)

1 bunch parsley, finely chopped

Freshly ground pepper, to taste

Oregano, to taste

1$\frac{1}{2}$ pounds medium-size shrimp, washed and deveined, but with shell intact

4 medium-size ripe tomatoes, peeled and chopped

$\frac{1}{2}$ *to 1 teaspoon sugar*

$\frac{1}{2}$ *pound feta cheese, crumbled or grated*

3 to 4 tablespoons milk

1. In a large heavy skillet, heat the olive oil and sauté scallions until translucent. Add the peppers, parsley, black pepper, and oregano and continue sautéing for another 5 to 6 minutes.

2. Reduce heat, add the shrimp, and cook, uncovered, for about 30 minutes, stirring occasionally with a wooden spoon. Add the tomatoes and sugar and simmer for another 5 minutes. Finally, add the feta and milk to the skillet and simmer, uncovered, over low heat for another 20 to 25 minutes, until feta is melted.

Yield: 4 servings

Serving Suggestions: Serve this hot over plain rice and drink ouzo with it.

Calamaria Gemista

(STUFFED SQUID)

1. Wash and clean squid: Grasp the head just below the eyes, pull it off from the rest of the body, and set it aside. Cut away the thin purplish membrane on the outside of the tail section. Using your index finger, scoop out and discard the guts and the thin cartilage "icicle" on the inside of the tail section. Rinse tail sections inside and out and set aside in a colander to drain. Take the head section in one hand and put pressure with your thumb and forefinger around the mouth and eyes, to squeeze them out. Discard mouth and eyes.

2. Chop the squid tentacles and have them ready, as they will be used in the stuffing.

3. In a large heavy skillet, heat $\frac{1}{4}$ cup of the olive oil and sauté onion until wilted. Add rice, tentacles, and pine nuts and sauté over medium-low heat for 2 to 3 minutes. Add garlic and currants to rice and stir quickly with a wooden spoon. Pour in $\frac{1}{4}$ cup wine and $\frac{1}{4}$ cup water. Season with salt and pepper. Reduce heat to low and simmer, covered, until liquid is almost completely absorbed and rice is soft but only about half cooked, about 15 minutes. About 5 minutes before removing skillet from heat, add parsley, dill, and mint. Remove and let cool enough to be able to handle.

4. Using a small teaspoon or a butter knife, carefully fill about three quarters of each squid with the rice mixture. Use toothpicks to secure closed. Pour remaining $\frac{1}{4}$ cup olive oil into a large stewing pot. Place squid carefully in pot. Pour in remaining $\frac{1}{2}$ cup wine and enough water to cover. Bring to a boil, reduce heat to low, and simmer, covered, for about $1\frac{1}{2}$ hours, or until rice is cooked and squid fork-tender. Twenty minutes before removing squid from heat, add chopped tomatoes to pot and adjust seasoning with salt and pepper. Check throughout cooking to see if more water is necessary so that mixture doesn't dry out. Serve squid hot or cold with a simple green salad.

Yield: 4 to 5 servings

Serving Suggestions: This dish needs a delicate white wine such as Robola Calliga or Santorini Boutari. Serve with wild greens *(horta)*, *horiatiki salata,* and a beautiful olive bread.

2½ to 3 pounds large fresh squid

½ cup olive oil

1 cup coarsely chopped onion, packed

⅓ cup long-grain rice

¼ cup pine nuts

2 large garlic cloves, chopped

¼ cup currants

¾ cup dry white or red wine

Salt and freshly ground pepper, to taste

¾ cup chopped fresh parsley, packed

¼ cup chopped fresh dill, packed

3 to 4 tablespoons chopped fresh mint

2 cups peeled, seeded, and chopped fresh tomatoes

Astakos/Karavitha Latholemono

(LOBSTER OR CRAYFISH WITH OLIVE OIL
AND LEMON)

THE *karavitha,* or crayfish, is a more common—and less expensive—treat than the lobster for most Greeks, unless there's a lucky fisherman in the family. Both, though, are generally poached and served with a bowl of *latholemono* (page 41).

For the lobster: Be sure the lobster is alive when you buy it. To clean it, hold it from the topside under the faucet and rinse its claws, body, and back with cold water. In a large pot, bring enough water to more than cover the lobster to a rolling boil. Immerse lobster head first in boiling water. When the water resumes boiling, reduce the heat and simmer, partially covered, until lobsters are done (about 7 minutes per pound). Their shells should be bright orange. Remove the meat from the tail and claws. Cut into chunks, season with salt and pepper, and mix as a salad with *latholemono.*

For the crayfish: To clean it, give a good, strong pull to the tail fin, then remove the stomach and intestinal vein. Immerse a few at a time in salted boiling water and cook for 5 to 7 minutes, until bright pink and tender. Serve with *latholemono.*

Serving Suggestions: Serve with wild greens *(horta),* tomato salad, and any good, dry white wine. Chateau Matsa and Santorini go well here.

— POACHED FISH —

Psari Vrasto

(POACHED FISH)

1. Wash, scrape, and gut fish. Keep whole (including the heads). Sprinkle with the juice of 1 lemon and set aside, covered, until ready to use.

2. In a large pot or poacher, bring about 2 to 3 quarts water to a rolling boil and add the onion and olive oil. Add the potatoes, carrots, and celery and bring back to a boil. Season with bay leaf, parsley, salt, and pepper. Simmer, partially covered, for about 20 minutes, or until vegetables are a bit more than half done. Add the fish and lemon juice to taste, and simmer gently, partially covered, for another 15 minutes or so, until fish is tender.

3. Remove fish and vegetables carefully with a slotted spoon and arrange on a serving platter. Strain the remaining stock and reserve, if desired, for *psarosoupa avgolemono* (page 132).

Yield: Allow ½ pound per serving

Psari Mayonnaisa: Debone the fish completely after removing it from pot. Save the head. Place the head at one end of an oblong, oval, or fish-shaped platter. Arrange the cleaned meat in a gentle mound behind it and form the shape of a fish. Cover the entire surface with mayonnaise (page 41). Garnish around sides with boiled vegetables, and decorate with capers, pickles, and fresh parsley sprigs.

Serving Suggestion: Serve with a pungent retsina.

2 to 4 pounds poaching fish (see page 215)
Strained fresh juice of 3 lemons
1 large onion, peeled and whole
½ cup olive oil
5 to 6 medium potatoes, peeled
2 to 3 carrots, scraped and cut into 1½-inch wedges
2 celery ribs, halved lengthwise
1 large bay leaf
4 to 5 fresh parsley sprigs
Salt, to taste
¼ teaspoon crushed black peppercorns
Latholemono (page 41) or mayonnaise (page 41)

—SNAILS—

Born in the wood, yet having no thorns and
no blood, moving in a slimy trail.
                        —*Conundrum,* The Deipnosophists, *Book I*

Crates of snails can be seen in the better markets of Athens; tavernas
list them on the menu in the spring and fall; they've been found at
archeological sites of the Minoan ruins on Santorini; and on Crete,
they're akin to a national dish and called by a special, local name—
cochli. (In the rest of Greece, they're known as *salingaria.*)

The snail certainly makes for some of the more exotic dishes in
Greek cookery, and Cretans, after feeding them tenderly on a diet of
barley and thyme, do just about everything to the sauntering mollusk:
they fry them to make *bourbourista;* they turn them into pies and pilafs
and even *moussaka;* and they serve them in innumerable stews and
casseroles.

Cretan snails are free-roaming, not farm raised, and big business for
a few of the island's exporters. Some export nearly 150 tons annually
to Belgium and France. *"Les petits gris de Crete,"* they're called.

Snails are easy to catch after the first fall rains, but they're best in
the summer, when they're at their plumpest. Here are three recipes for
what were once in Greek called the "dinner-delayers."

Cochli me Pligouri

(SNAIL AND BULGUR PILAF)

1. Brush or scrub snail shells to scrape away any debris. With a small sharp knife, carefully remove the operculi (paperlike covering over the opening). Rinse in cold water and discard any snails that aren't alive. Place snails in a large, wide-bottomed pot. Add just enough warm water to cover over them and sprinkle liberally with salt (3 to 4 tablespoons). Bring snails to a boil over medium heat, reduce heat, and simmer for 20 minutes, uncovered, skimming off foam and muck frequently. Remove snails from pot, drain, and rinse in cold water three to four times, or until water comes away completely clean.

2. In a medium-size pot, bring $1\frac{1}{2}$ cups water to a boil and add salt to taste. Add bulgur and dribble in 2 tablespoons olive oil. Stir once or twice, lower heat, cover the pot, and let bulgur simmer until it has completely absorbed the water and has softened and expanded, about 45 minutes.

3. In the meantime, prepare snails. In a stewing pot, heat remaining 2 tablespoons olive oil and sauté scallions until wilted. Add snails and sauté for 2 to 4 minutes. Add tomatoes, garlic, parsley, oregano, mint, salt, and pepper. Reduce heat and stir with a wooden spoon. Cover and simmer 12 to 15 minutes, adding a little water to keep mixture moist.

4. When bulgur is done, mix in snails and serve, or turn bulgur onto a platter and pour snails and their sauce over the grain. Serve hot.

1 pound large snails
Salt
1 cup water, or more if necessary
$\frac{1}{2}$ cup bulgur
$\frac{1}{4}$ cup olive oil
4 to 5 scallions, finely chopped
5 to 6 plum tomatoes, peeled and chopped
2 garlic cloves, crushed
$\frac{1}{4}$ cup finely chopped fresh parsley, packed
1 teaspoon dried oregano
1 teaspoon dried mint, or 1 tablespoon chopped fresh mint
Freshly ground pepper, to taste

Yield: 2 servings

Serving Suggestion: If Cretan wine is unavailable, try a Páros red.

Cochli or Salingaria Stifatho Cretis

(CRETAN CLASSIC SNAIL STEW)

THIS is a wonderfully aromatic stew, sweet with onions and rich with wine. It's a classic of the Cretan table, but is also found in infinite variation in tavernas and home kitchens throughout the country.

1 pound large snails
Salt
$\frac{1}{4}$ cup extravirgin olive
    oil
$\frac{3}{4}$ pound small white
    stewing or pearl
    onions, whole
8 to 10 plum tomatoes
2 to 3 garlic cloves,
    finely chopped
1 large bay leaf,
    ripped
1 cinnamon stick
Freshly ground
    pepper, to taste
$\frac{1}{2}$ to $\frac{3}{4}$ cup water
$\frac{1}{2}$ cup finely chopped
    fresh parsley,
    packed
$\frac{1}{4}$ cup dry red wine

1. Follow step 1 on page 235 for cleaning and preparing snails.
2. In a large heavy skillet, heat olive oil and sauté onions until translucent, 3 to 5 minutes, stirring frequently with a wooden spoon. Add snails and sauté 2 to 3 minutes, stirring occasionally.
3. Add tomatoes, garlic, bay leaf, cinnamon, salt, pepper, and $\frac{1}{2}$ cup water to skillet. Cover and simmer over low heat for 25 to 30 minutes, adding more water during cooking, if necessary. About 5 minutes before removing snails from heat, add parsley and wine and continue to simmer, covered. Remove from heat and serve hot over rice, if desired.

Yield: 2 to 4 servings

Serving Suggestions: This dish really needs a heady Cretan red wine. You might try it, however, with a robust Nemea red.

Snails Bourbourista

BOURBOURISTA is an onomatopoeia for the crackling sound the snails make upon contact with the salt, then oil. This is a classic Cretan preparation, excellent as both main course and *meze;* serve it with a crusty loaf of bread and plenty of good strong red wine.

1 pound large snails
3 tablespoons plus 2
    teaspoons salt
$\frac{1}{2}$ cup extravirgin olive
    oil
$\frac{1}{4}$ cup red wine
    vinegar

1. Follow step 1 on page 235 for cleaning and preparing snails, but use 3 tablespoons salt in first boiling to clean.
2. In a large, heavy, nonstick skillet, heat 2 teaspoons salt over medium heat, making sure that it's spread evenly around pan.
3. Place snails, open side down, in skillet. Reduce heat and cook, uncovered, for 3 to 4 minutes, stirring with a wooden spoon. Add olive oil to skillet and continue stirring for another 5 to 7 minutes. Pour in vinegar, cover skillet, and continue to cook over low to medium heat for 5 to 7 minutes longer. Serve snails piping hot, in a deep dish, with all their pan juices.

Yield: 2 to 4 servings

Serving Suggestions: Serve this exotic, salty dish with a fiery *raki* (page 16) or a robust red wine.

Chapter 14

Meats

There is a dubious claim to fame among late twentieth-century Greeks and that is that they are the largest consumers of red meat in the European Community. Meat dishes occupy an indispensable column on restaurant and taverna menus, and not a small place on the daily dinner table.

But the everyday eating of meat is a phenomenon Greeks have enjoyed for only a brief time—about the last twenty years. Much more customary—and still very much the case in the countryside—is to limit the preparation of meat to holiday and festive tables.

—A NOTE ON BASIC— PREPARATIONS

One might notice in the following pages that most of the meat dishes are prepared on top of the stove, not baked. There's a simple reason for the prevalence of stews and braised meats in the country's cookery. Most Greeks didn't own an oven—except outdoor wood-burning ovens specifically for bread making—until fairly recently. Large roasts were reserved for the Sunday meal or for holidays, and taken to the village oven to be baked.

—BEEF AND VEAL—

Beef is a meat for all seasons in Greece. Ground, it finds its way into the stuffed vegetables so popular in summer; grilled, it becomes the standard taverna fare of *souvlaki* and *brizoles;* and stewed, it makes for some of the country's best winter dishes. Dried beef seasoned with a pungent, spicy paprika spread is called *pastourma*. Although there are no recipes calling for it, it is frequently chopped into omelettes or used as a flavoring in peinirli.

Beef was certainly known to the ancients. The Minoans had their minotaur and bullfights; and Homer's heroes preferred oxen to any other meat for the truly great feasts. In modern Greece, one day a year—*Tsiknopempti,* which is hard to translate but roughly means "Aromatic Thursday," for the scent of sizzling meat that wafts through the air—is set aside before Lent for purposely indulging in meat. It is a day on which tavernas are packed.

Beef and veal are at least as widely eaten as lamb and goat, and perhaps more so given the dubious claim at the start of this chapter. *Moscharaki* and *moschari* (veal and beef, respectively) have always been expensive, and sometimes reserved just for the Sunday table. As in other cuisines, each lends itself to a great variety of preparations.

Kyria Mylona's Sofrito Kerkireiko

(CORFU VEAL STEW SEASONED WITH VINEGAR)

2 pounds veal shoulder, cut into slices about $\frac{1}{2}$ inch thick
Flour, for dredging
$\frac{1}{2}$ cup olive oil
$\frac{1}{2}$ cup finely chopped fresh parsley, packed
3 to 4 garlic cloves, minced
3 to 4 tablespoons quality red wine vinegar
Salt and freshly ground pepper, to taste

1. Lightly dredge meat in flour. In a large heavy skillet or stewing pot, heat olive oil and lightly brown meat. Remove meat immediately from pot and set aside; spoon out any flour residuals that might burn, but don't discard the oil.

2. Lightly sauté parsley and garlic. Add veal and enough hot water to cover; bring to a boil. Pour in vinegar, cover, and simmer over very low heat until meat is fork tender, $1\frac{1}{2}$ to 2 hours. Add more water, if necessary, to keep mixture moist during cooking. Season with salt and pepper.

Yield: 4 to 6 servings

Variation: Some versions of this dish call for chopped fresh tomato. Add 1 cup, if desired, along with water in step 2, and cook as indicated.

Serving Suggestions: Serve hot with mashed potatoes. If you can get hold of a white Corfiot wine called Theotoki, serve it forth with this; otherwise, settle for a noble Náoussa dry red.

Kerkireiki Pastitsada

(CORFIOT VEAL AND PASTA)

1. In a large heavy stewing pot, heat olive oil. Add meat a little at a time and cook, turning frequently on all sides to brown evenly. Remove meat with a slotted spoon and set aside. Add onions and sauté, stirring constantly with a wooden spoon, until wilted.

2. Stir in tomatoes, garlic, bay leaves, cinnamon, cloves, sugar, salt, and pepper. Return meat to pot and bring to a boil. Cover and simmer over very low heat until meat is fork-tender, about 2 hours. Five to 7 minutes before removing pot from heat, add paprika, wine, and vinegar and simmer uncovered. Remove cinnamon sticks.

3. Add drained spaghetti to sauce, stirring once or twice to combine well. Serve at once, topped with grated cheese.

Yield: 4 to 5 servings

Serving Suggestions: A bold Nemea, rich, deep Náoussa, or a Cava Carras would all work well with this luscious dish.

$\frac{1}{2}$ *cup olive oil*
1$\frac{1}{2}$ pounds boneless
  veal or beef, cut
  into 2-inch cubes
1 cup coarsely chopped
  white onion, packed
4 cups fresh chopped
  peeled tomato, with
  juice
3 to 4 garlic cloves,
  finely chopped
2 small bay leaves,
  ripped
2 small cinnamon
  sticks
5 to 7 whole cloves
1 scant teaspoon sugar
Salt and crushed black
  peppercorns, to taste
1 heaping teaspoon
  paprika
3 tablespoons dry red
  wine
1 teaspoon strong red
  wine vinegar
1 to 1$\frac{1}{2}$ pounds very
  thick spaghetti,
  cooked
Grated kefalotyri or
  Parmesan cheese

Tas-Kebab

(SIMPLE, OVEN-BAKED VEAL OR BEEF)

1½ pounds boneless veal or beef, cut into 1½-inch cubes
1 cup coarsely chopped onion, packed
1 cup coarsely chopped fresh parsley
1½ cups chopped fresh peeled tomato
2 teaspoons dried oregano
Salt and crushed black peppercorns, to taste
¼ cup olive oil

1. Preheat oven to 450°F.
2. In a medium-size bowl, toss together all ingredients. Let stand, covered, about 1 hour before baking.
3. Place all ingredients in a clay or glass baking dish. Cover with aluminum foil. Place in hot oven and immediately reduce heat to 350°F. Bake for 2 to 2½ hours, or until meat is tender and juicy.

Yield: 4 to 5 servings

Serving Suggestions: Serve over plain rice with a tall, pungent glass of ouzo.

Moschari Kokkinisto

("RED" VEAL STEW)

THIS dish is really nothing more than a tomato-based veal stew. *Kokkinisto* is a classic preparation of meat in Greek cooking. Round-sliced carrots, celery, okra, and peas are commonly added to the stew about halfway through cooking.

---

2 to 2½ pounds veal, cut into stewing pieces
2 cups dry red wine
1 large garlic clove, minced
1 large bay leaf, ripped
½ cup olive oil
2 medium-size onions, peeled, halved, and sliced thin
3 cups chopped fresh peeled tomato
¼ cup chopped fresh parsley
1 teaspoon dried oregano (optional)
Salt and freshly ground pepper, to taste

1. Place meat in a large dish. In a small bowl, make a marinade of wine, garlic, and bay leaf. Pour over meat and let stand for 2 hours. Remove meat from dish and pat dry. Do not discard marinade.
2. In a large heavy stewing pot, heat olive oil and add meat, turning frequently to brown all sides evenly. Remove meat with a slotted spoon and set aside. Add onion to pot and sauté until wilted.
3. Place meat back in pot, add tomatoes, and bring to a boil. Pour in marinade, cover, and simmer for 1½ to 2 hours, or until meat is tender. Add parsley and oregano 15 minutes before removing pot from heat, and stir well with a wooden spoon to blend. Season with salt and pepper.

Yield: Serves 5 to 6

Kokkinisto me Prasines Elies: To make a more exotic version with tart green olives, thoroughly rinse, drain, and pit 1 cup green olives. Keep them whole and add them to the pot about 15 minutes before removing from heat.

Kreas Kokkinisto me Melitzanes: Eggplants, sliced long and thin, salted, rinsed, dredged in flour, and fried lightly are another favorite addition. Add the fried eggplants 20 to 25 minutes before removing the meat from heat. Mix the stew very gently after adding the eggplants, being careful not to tear them apart.

Serving Suggestions: Serve with roasted potatoes and a heady wine like Boutari Grande Réserve or Náoussa.

Moschari me Melitzanes Poure, Smyrneika

(BEEF STEW WITH EGGPLANT PUREE, SMYRNA STYLE)

1. Preheat oven to 375°F. Puncture eggplants slightly with a fork and place in an ungreased pan in hot oven. Remove eggplants from oven when skin begins to shrivel and eggplants are soft. Let cool. Reduce oven to 350°F.

2. In a large heavy skillet or stewing pot, heat $\frac{1}{4}$ cup of the butter and add meat, turning frequently on all sides to brown evenly. Remove meat from skillet with a slotted spoon. Add onions and sauté until wilted. Return meat to the pan and add tomato, wine, garlic, allspice, sugar, mint, salt, and pepper. Bring to a boil; lower flame immediately, and simmer, covered, for 10 minutes.

3. While meat is simmering, cut off eggplant stems, and skin carefully, leaving as much of the pulp as possible and discarding the skins. Puree the eggplant pulp either by pulverizing it manually with a mortar and pestle or by whipping it in a food processor or blender. Season with salt and pepper and slowly add milk and cream as you puree the pulp. Melt the remaining butter and add to the eggplants and milk. Stir in $\frac{1}{4}$ cup of the walnuts or almonds (optional).

4. Spread eggplant puree on the bottom of a clay or glass casserole. Spread the meat and tomato mixture evenly over the puree. Sprinkle with remaining walnuts (optional). Bake, covered, at 350°F, for about 1 to $1\frac{1}{2}$ hours, or until meat is tender. Serve warm.

Yield: 4 to 5 servings

Serving Suggestion: This is a perfect winter dish that needs a strong red wine such as a deep, dark Nemea.

1$\frac{1}{2}$ to 2 pounds eggplant
$\frac{1}{2}$ cup lightly salted butter
1$\frac{1}{2}$ to 2 pounds veal or boneless beef, cut into stewing pieces
$\frac{3}{4}$ cup finely chopped onion
1 cup fresh peeled, chopped tomato, with juice
$\frac{1}{4}$ cup dry red wine
2 garlic cloves, finely chopped
6 to 10 allspice berries, crushed
$\frac{1}{2}$ teaspoon sugar
$\frac{1}{2}$ teaspoon dried mint
Salt and freshly ground pepper, to taste
$\frac{1}{2}$ cup milk
$\frac{1}{2}$ cup heavy cream
$\frac{1}{4}$ cup plus 2 tablespoons ground walnut meats or almonds (optional)

Three-Meat Oven-Baked Stew

$\frac{1}{2}$ *cup all-purpose flour*
$\frac{1}{4}$ *cup water*
$\frac{3}{4}$ *pound veal shoulder,*
cut into stewing
pieces
$\frac{3}{4}$ *pound lamb,*
preferably leg, cubed
for stew
$\frac{3}{4}$ *pound boneless pork,*
cubed for stew
2 celery ribs, cut into
$\frac{1}{2}$*-inch pieces*
3 to 4 medium carrots,
scraped and cut into
$\frac{1}{2}$*-inch rounds*
4 to 6 medium
potatoes, peeled and
quartered
3 large onions, peeled,
coarsely chopped
4 garlic cloves, minced
1 heaping tablespoon
dried oregano
Strained fresh juice of
2$\frac{1}{2}$ lemons
$\frac{1}{2}$ *cup extravirgin olive*
oil
Salt and freshly
ground pepper

FOR a real taste of old-country Greek food, try baking this dish *steen hovoli,* literally, in ashes or embers. The *hovoli* is a makeshift oven in the ground made by digging a hole about two feet in diameter and two feet deep. Ignite within it ample charcoal and wood, enough to surround the entire baking dish. (Use a wrought iron casserole and cover or a Dutch oven with a wrought iron lid.) Wait for the fire to die down—the coals, though, should be smoldering. Seal the lid of the casserole with a three-inch strip of dough pressed all around its edge. Place the dish on top of the embers and surround it with embers and hot coals. Cover the hole with soil and leave it to bake slowly for four hours. If desired, wrap some potatoes and onions individually in tin foil and bake in the *hovoli* alongside the pot.

---

1. Preheat oven to 275°F. To make dough, place flour in a medium-size bowl and make a well in center. Add water and stir with a fork to form a dough. Knead until smooth and set aside, covered.

2. In a large glass or clay casserole dish, combine remaining ingredients. Roll out dough so that it is large enough to fit over top of casserole. Carefully seal dough around dish by pressing it over the sides. Bake for 3$\frac{1}{2}$ to 4 hours. Turn off the heat and let the dish cool in the oven for about 20 minutes before unsealing. Serve hot.

Yield: 4 to 6 servings

Serving Suggestion: This rich county preparation requires a simple wine like retsina.

Stifatho

(CLASSIC VEAL OR BEEF STEW)

1. In a large stewing pot, heat olive oil over medium to high heat. Add meat in batches, turning frequently to brown evenly and lightly on all sides. Add onions and stir several times with a wooden spoon.

2. Reduce heat, add tomatoes, garlic, bay leaf, and 1$\frac{1}{2}$ tablespoons vinegar. Stir in sugar a little at a time and season with salt and pepper.

Stir mixture several times with a wooden spoon. Cover and simmer over low heat for $1\frac{1}{2}$ to 2 hours, or until meat is very tender. Add water, if necessary, during cooking to keep the stew moist. About 3 minutes before removing pot from heat, uncover and stir in remaining $\frac{1}{2}$ tablespoon vinegar. Adjust seasoning and serve warm.

Yield: 4 to 5 servings

Glossa Stifatho (**Tongue Stew**): Beef tongue, which can so often be found dangling from hooks in neat rows at the Athens Central Market, is preferred to any other. To prepare the tongue: Scrub it well and soak it in cold water for 10 minutes. Drain. Bring enough water to a boil to barely cover the tongue and submerge tongue. Skim off any scum. Simmer, uncovered, until tender, 45 to 50 minutes. Remove tongue from pot, drain, and skin and trim off the gristle, roots, and small bones. Prepare the *stifatho* as above, without browning the tongue. Simmer the sauce for 45 minutes, then add tongue and continue cooking another 45 minutes, or until tongue is tender.

Serving Suggestion: I'd serve this dish with a velvety Gouménissa red.

Souvlaki

(SKEWERED MEATS SUCH AS LAMB, PORK, AND VEAL)

THIS is one Greek food known to most non-Greeks. Use about five chunks of meat per skewer/serving.

Marinate meat in either red wine or lemon juice, olive oil, and oregano for several hours before grilling. Reserve marinade. Slip chunks of meat onto 8-inch skewers, alternating onion, tomato, or pepper between each piece. Season with salt and pepper. Brush with marinade and broil 8 inches from heat, or barbecue over slow-burning coals. Brush with marinade several times during cooking.

Serving Suggestions: Serve with warm *pitta* bread and generous dollops of garlicky *tzatziki*. For wine, I'd go with a hearty Náoussa red here.

$\frac{1}{2}$ cup olive oil

2 to $2\frac{1}{2}$ pounds boneless veal or beef, cut into $1\frac{1}{2}$- to 2-inch cubes

2 pounds small white or pearl onions, peeled and whole

$1\frac{1}{2}$ to 2 cups peeled, cored, and chopped fresh tomato (with juice)

2 to 3 garlic cloves, minced

1 large bay leaf, ripped

2 tablespoons quality red wine vinegar

1 to 2 scant teaspoons sugar

Salt and freshly ground pepper

Boneless lamb, pork, or veal, cut into $1\frac{1}{2}$-inch cubes

Red wine or strained fresh lemon juice

2 to 3 tablespoons olive oil

Oregano or thyme

Several whole medium-size white or red onions, quartered

Several tomatoes, cored and quartered

2 to 3 green peppers, seeded and cut into $1\frac{1}{2}$-inch squares

Salt and freshly ground pepper

Exohiko Thessalias

(VEAL BAKED IN BREAD)

1 loaf (2 pounds)
 white or whole
 wheat French or
 Italian bread,
 unsliced
1½ pounds veal, diced
2 leeks or large white
 onions, peeled and
 coarsely chopped
2 large green bell
 peppers, finely
 chopped
2 to 3 garlic cloves,
 minced
¼ teaspoon crushed red
 pepper
2 teaspoons dried
 oregano
1 teaspoon cumin
Salt and freshly
 ground pepper
¼ cup plus 2
 tablespoons
 extravirgin olive oil
¼ cup grated kefalotyri
 or Parmesan cheese

EXOHIKO means "countryside-style." The term refers to dishes baked either *en papillote* or *en croûte,* similar to the following recipe. The *exohiko* style also falls into the general category of *klephtica* foods—"of thieves"—referring to the Klephts, or mountain fighters who, during the Greek War of Independence, often cooked their foods in makeshift ovens in the ground so that aromas and smoke wouldn't escape to disclose their positions. The Klephtic cooking of Greece has come to refer to any means in which the food being prepared is hidden or sealed, then slowly cooked.

────────────

1. Preheat oven to 275°F.
2. Cut bread in half lengthwise and scoop out a cavity in both halves, being careful not to rip bread or leave too thin a crust. It should be ½ to ¾ inch thick.
3. In a large bowl, combine veal, leeks or onions, peppers, and garlic. Add hot red pepper, oregano, cumin, salt, pepper, and 2 tablespoons of the olive oil. Toss thoroughly.
4. Brush insides of bread with remaining 4 tablespoons olive oil and sprinkle with grated cheese. Fill bottom half of bread cavity with the meat and carefully place top half over it, securing tightly. Wrap with aluminum foil and bake for 3½ to 4 hours. Slice crosswise and serve warm.

Yield: 6 servings

Serving Suggestions: Prepare a simple green salad to accompany this dish, and serve any country or table wine.

——PORK, LAMB, AND GOAT——

In the countryside, where life still follows the pattern of the seasons, winter marks the time of the hog slaughter, or *hirosfagi,* and the event is reason to celebrate in most country homes. It also takes place conveniently when the year's new wines are just about ready. What happens is more or less an *ad hoc* party. During the day of the slaughter—this is a family, not a community, event—friends and neighbors trickle in.

Brizoles (steaks) are usually smoking in the fire, or drying over it; *pihti,* or jellied pork, sits in a huge bowl in the center of the table; and a cabbage and pork stew, sometimes made from the lungs of the hog, sometimes with other, more savory parts, simmers gently on the stove. There is plenty of rough country wine.

The ancient Greeks were adept at preserving pork and other meat through drying, salting, and smoking. They also left little to waste, consuming snouts and ears and tongues and brains of swine, as well as the unlikely womb. Their modern brethren, though more discerning, remain equally skillful and economy minded. Little of the pig is left to waste. Its fat become *gleena,* a substitute for butter in times of paucity; its trotters and head become gelatinous *pihti;* and its meat in all its cooked and cured forms will see a family through until the end of winter.

Pork (as well as turkey) makes up the Christmas meal, and wild boar, which roam the mountains of Epirus and Macedonia, albeit in dwindling numbers, is also savored, especially if there's a gifted hunter in the family.

If pork is the meat of choice for winter, and beef is savored year round, then lamb and goat are preferred to no other animal in the spring.

Between lamb and goat, lamb is probably the commoner choice for the Easter table, although spit-roasting it is a practice more favored by mainlanders than by islanders. Islanders, too, have taken up the custom, to be sure, in the last few years, probably seeing in it a good reason to start the Easter fete early. (Motorized rotisseries are not part of most villagers' culinary outfit, and the labor of turning the rotisserie *(souvla)* must start in the morning if the meal is to be ready for the afternoon table. It's a labor shared by friends and relatives and punctuated by a steady stream of kitchen (and cellar) goodies.

In the Eastern Aegean islands, Samos, Mitilini, and Ikaria among them, a whole goat, stuffed with tender spring herbs and rice and roasted in the communal village oven, makes up the traditional Easter meal.

Lamb, at other times of the year, is just as versatile as veal or beef. It's baked in parchment or phyllo to make the dish known as *exohiko;* its chops and ribs are grilled over coals; it is stuffed into savory pies; and it is roasted into classic *giouvetsi* with orzo and tomatoes.

Goat, less versatile than lamb but more mouthwatering to many (I among them), is spit-roasted, stewed, and baked. Sometimes the goat is blamed for wreaking havoc on the country's greenery. Goats, in many parts of Greece and especially in the islands, are left to pasture freely. They have the unfortunate ability to denude even the plushest of slopes, devouring everything green in sight—and some things not so green. We've shared an empty beach with them more than once, our attention turned from the smacking waves (and other pleasures of the senses) to gape at the goat's insatiable appetite for seaweed.

The goat's meat is much leaner than the lamb's, and A. J. Liebling, whom Waverley Root quotes, was right in advising that it should be eaten young because "in late life it grows muscular through overactivity." Greeks call old goats *gida* (pronounced *yeetha*), and generally eat them boiled.

Kiskeki

(PORK AND WHEAT)

THIS is an interesting, simple, and quite old dish that comes from the eastern Aegean islands, namely Mitilini and Samos, but variations can be found in many rural areas of Greece. No doubt the dish originated during the time when families would slaughter a hog once a year, around Christmas, and consume virtually every part of the animal throughout the year. Until fairly recently, one common butter substitute—although it was really a food unto itself—was the *gleena,* or lard from the hog, and this dish was probably made with more fat than I have used in the following recipe. Here, olive oil replaces *gleena.*

¼ cup olive oil
2 pounds pork, cut into large stewing pieces
Salt, to taste
2 to 3 whole hot red peppers
1 cup whole wheat
4 tablespoons butter
2 medium onions, coarsely chopped
Ground cumin, to taste
Plain yogurt or sour cream

1. In a large stewing pot, heat olive oil and add pork, turning frequently on all sides to brown evenly. Add enough water to cover and bring to a boil. Reduce heat to very low, add salt and whole hot peppers, and simmer, covered, for about 2 hours, or until meat is very tender and falls away from the bone.

2. While meat is cooking, prepare whole wheat. In a medium-size saucepan, place whole wheat in enough salted water to cover by three inches. Bring to a boil, stir, and reduce heat. Simmer, covered, for 1½ to 2 hours, or until tender. Remove and drain.

3. In a medium-size skillet, melt butter slowly and sauté onion until wilted. Remove skillet from heat.

4. Remove pork from pot with a slotted spoon, debone, and shred. In a medium-size bowl, combine pork with whole wheat, then pour over butter and onions. Sprinkle with cumin to taste and serve topped with yogurt, preferably strained, or sour cream.

Yield: 6 servings

Hirino me Selino kai Prassa

(BRAISED PORK WITH CELERY AND LEEKS)

1. In a large heavy stewing pot, heat olive oil over medium-high heat. Add pork, a little at a time, and cook, turning frequently on all sides to brown evenly.

2. Add leeks and celery to pot and stir with a wooden spoon until wilted. Pour in water and wine and bring to a boil. Reduce heat, season with salt and pepper, cover, and simmer for about 1 hour and 45 minutes, or until pork is fork-tender, adding more water if necessary. Add lemon juice just before removing pot from heat. Serve warm with potatoes or plain rice.

Yield: 4 servings

Variation: This recipe is also commonly made with *avgolemono* sauce. To prepare *hirino me selino and avgolemono,* beat two eggs with the juice of $1\frac{1}{2}$ to 2 lemons. Very slowly add 2 to 3 ladlefuls, one at a time, of pot liquids to egg until the egg and lemon mixture is warm. Pour *avgolemono* into pot, stir well, and remove from flame before it boils. Serve hot.

Serving Suggestions: Serve this dish with plain rice and a dry white wine such as Robola Calliga from Cephalonia or a dry white from Santorini.

$\frac{1}{3}$ cup olive oil
$1\frac{1}{2}$ pounds boneless pork, cut into stewing pieces
$2\frac{1}{2}$ cups thoroughly washed, coarsely chopped leeks
$2\frac{1}{2}$ cups coarsely chopped celery (including leaves)
2 cups water
$1\frac{1}{2}$ cups dry white wine
Salt and freshly ground pepper, to taste
Strained fresh juice of 1 lemon

Afelia Kypriaka

(SUCCULENT BRAISED PORK WITH WINE AND CORIANDER, FROM CYPRUS)

2 pounds lean boneless pork, cut into stewing cubes

2 cups dry, full-bodied red wine, or more as desired

2 heaping tablespoons coriander seeds, crushed with a mortar and pestle

⅓ cup olive oil

Salt and freshly ground pepper, to taste

1. Place pork in a large bowl with cover and add 1 to 1½ cups wine and 1 heaping tablespoon crushed coriander seeds. Cover and marinate in refrigerator for 24 hours.

2. Remove pork from marinade and pat dry. Do not discard the marinade. In a large heavy stewing pot, heat olive oil over medium-high heat. Add pork chunks, a few at a time, and turn frequently on all sides so that they brown evenly and lightly.

3. Pour in marinade with coriander seeds, ½ cup more of red wine, and enough water to cover meat. Bring to a gentle boil. Reduce heat, add salt and pepper, cover pot, and simmer for about 2 hours, or until pork is very tender but not dry. Add more wine and water throughout cooking, if necessary, to keep mixture moist. About 20 minutes before removing pork from heat, add remaining tablespoon coriander. Sauce should be reduced and thick; it may be necessary to remove pork and to continue simmering the wine sauce until thick. Serve hot.

Yield: 4 to 6 servings

Serving Suggestions: Hearty olive bread and *patates antinaktes kyprou*, seasoned with coriander, would complement this simple, luscious meat dish perfectly. Try any of the robust Greek reds with this meal; the Náoussa or the Nemea wines would be perfect.

Arni me Diosmo kai Fascomilo

(SPICY LAMB STEW WITH MINT AND SAGE)

THIS dish has its roots among the Greeks of Asia Minor, where the addition of nuts like pignoli and almond, and sweeteners like carrot and mint, were common in many meat and pilaf dishes. I love to look at this dish, with its gold and treacle-colored raisins dotting the rice, and its orange carrots cut up between the simple brown of the lamb.

---

1. In a large heavy stewing pot, heat olive oil. Add lamb pieces, a few at a time and cook, turning frequently on all sides so that they brown evenly and lightly. Add onion and carrots and stir once or twice with a wooden spoon. Sauté, stirring constantly, until onion is wilted, about 5 minutes. Add wine, salt, and pepper and bring to a boil. Reduce heat to low. Cover and cook for about 10 minutes.

2. While meat is cooking, lightly toast the nuts in a heavy skillet over medium heat, stirring constantly so that they don't burn. This will take 2 to 3 minutes. Remove skillet from heat and set aside.

3. Add water to stew and continue simmering another 30 minutes, checking and stirring occasionally. Add rice, raisins, nuts, sage, and mint to stewing pot and season, if necessary, with a little more salt. Bring to a gentle boil and simmer, covered, over low heat, for another 25 to 30 minutes, or until rice is cooked and lamb is tender. Add water, if necessary, during cooking.

Yield: 4 servings

Note: Beef or veal may also be used in this dish.

Serving Suggestions: Serve a demi-sec rosé with this warming stew.

1/4 cup olive oil
2 pounds lean lamb, preferably shoulder or leg, cut into stewing pieces (see Note)
1/2 cup coarsely chopped onion
1/2 cup chopped pared carrots
1/2 cup dry white wine
Salt and freshly ground pepper, to taste
1/2 cup blanched almond slivers or pignolis (or 1/4 cup each)
3 cups water
1 cup long-grain rice
1/2 cup light and dark seedless raisins
1/2 teaspoon dried sage
1 teaspoon dried mint

Arni Steen Stamna

(LAMB BAKED IN A SEALED CLAY DISH)

½ cup all-purpose flour
¼ cup water
2½ pounds lean lamb, preferably leg, cut into 1½- to 2-inch cubes
12 small white onions, peeled and whole
6 medium potatoes, peeled and quartered
2 celery ribs, cut into ¼-inch pieces
4 to 5 hot pickled green peppers, seeded and chopped
3 garlic cloves, finely chopped
½ cup chopped fresh parsley
⅓ cup chopped fresh dill
Strained fresh juice of 2 large lemons
¼ cup plus 2 tablespoons extravirgin olive oil
1 tablespoon dried thyme
2 teaspoons dried rosemary
½ teaspoon dried sage
Salt and freshly ground pepper, to taste
¼ pound feta cheese, crumbled, chopped, or grated

THE method of roasting meat in a *stamna,* a clay water jug, was used by women during the Greek War of Independence to surreptitiously bake and bring food to their soldiers in the mountains. In Epirus, the technique has become a local specialty, especially with lamb, and the *stamna* can be found in pottery and cookery shops throughout Greece.

1. Place flour in a small bowl and make a well in center. Add water and stir to form a dough. Knead for 3 to 5 minutes, until dough is smooth, then set aside, covered, until ready to use.

2. In a large clay or glass baking dish (clay is preferable), combine lamb, onions, potatoes, celery, and peppers. Add garlic, parsley, dill, lemon juice, olive oil, dried herbs, salt, and pepper. Toss together so that all ingredients are thoroughly combined. Top with crumbled feta.

3. Roll out dough on a lightly floured surface to a sheet large enough to fit securely over baking dish. It should be about 2 inches larger than the dish. Carefully place the dough over the dish and seal by dipping your fingers in water and pressing dough tightly around rim.

4. Place baking dish on lowest rack in cold oven and turn heat to 275°F. Bake for 3½ to 4 hours. Turn off oven, open door, and allow dish to cool for at least 20 minutes before removing from oven. Place on a towel or meat and carefully cut open dough with a sharp knife. Serve hot.

Yield: 6 servings

Serving Suggestions: This dish doesn't need very much besides bread and wine. Try a crisp, fragrant demi-sec rosé with this dish.

Arni/Katsikaki Fricassee

(LAMB OR GOAT FRICASSEE)

WHAT most Greeks refer to as fricassee is really braised or stewed meat with a tangy *avgolemono* sauce. Here, in a variation on this simple and classic recipe, wild greens are used. The flavors are tart and succulent, with the tanginess of the *avgolemono* balancing especially well with the almost musty flavor of lamb and earth-bound flavors of the wild greens.

---

1. In a large heavy stewing pot, heat olive oil. Add lamb pieces, a few at a time, turning frequently on all side so that they brown evenly and lightly. Stir in the chopped onion and reduce heat. Sauté, stirring constantly with a wooden spoon, until the onion is wilted. Add garlic, salt, pepper and enough water to cover lamb. Bring to a boil and simmer, covered, over low heat for about 35 minutes.

2. While meat is simmering, bring a large pot of ample water to a rolling boil and add greens. Simmer, partially covered, for about 15 minutes. Drain well. Add the drained greens and dill to the lamb and continue cooking, covered, for another 30 to 35 minutes, or until lamb and greens are tender. Add water, if necessary, during cooking.

3. Just before lamb is done, make *avgolemono* sauce: In a medium-size bowl, beat together egg and lemon until frothy. Very slowly add 4 to 5 ladlefuls (2 to 3 cups) of lamb broth to egg mixture, beating vigorously with a whisk to keep egg from curdling. Remove pot from heat and pour in egg mixture. Place pot back on heat and stir sauce well, but do not allow it to boil. Remove pot from heat and serve immediately. It's best to make *avgolemono* just before serving.

1/4 cup olive oil
2 1/2 pounds boneless lamb or goat, cut into stewing pieces
1 1/2 cups coarsely chopped onion
2 to 3 garlic cloves, finely chopped
Salt and freshly ground pepper, to taste
3 pounds wild greens (dandelion, Swiss chard, spinach, etc.)
1/3 cup chopped fresh dill
2 to 3 eggs, at room temperature
Strained fresh juice of 1 to 2 large lemons

Yield: 4 to 5 servings

Serving Suggestions: I'd have little else besides tart feta and crisp white or rosé wine—Santorini Boutari, Porto Carras Réserve or demi-sec rosé, also by Boutari—with this.

Arni/Katsikai me Anginares kai Anithon (**Lamb or Goat with Artichokes and Dill**): Cut away the tough outer leaves and choke of 6 to 8 artichokes and rub with lemon juice to keep from discoloring. Sauté 1/2 cup chopped dill together with the onions in step 1. Add the artichokes, in place of the greens, about halfway through cooking. Cover and simmer about 35 more minutes. Serve with *avgolemono* sauce (see step 3).

Oven-Baked Lamb Stew

*4 pounds lean lamb
  shanks, or 2½
  pounds lean
  boneless lamb*
Flour, for dredging
½ cup olive oil
*1 large white onion,
  finely chopped*
*3 to 4 garlic cloves,
  minced*
*2 cups chopped peeled
  tomato, with juice*
2 bay leaves, ripped
*5 to 6 medium
  potatoes, peeled and
  quartered*
*1½ pounds small white
  onions, peeled and
  whole*
*3 large carrots, pared
  and cut into 1-inch
  rounds*
*2 celery ribs, cut into
  ½-inch pieces
  (optional)*
*¼ cup chopped fresh
  parsley, packed*
*¼ cup chopped fresh
  dill*
*1 teaspoon dried
  thyme or oregano*
*Salt and freshly
  ground pepper, to
  taste*
*1 to 2 tablespoons
  quality red wine
  vinegar*

1. Preheat oven to 350°F. Dredge lamb lightly in flour.
2. In a large heavy ovenproof pot, heat ¼ cup of the olive oil over medium-high heat. Add the lamb, a few pieces at a time, and brown lightly on all sides. Add the chopped onion, reduce heat slightly, and sauté until wilted.
3. Add 2 to 3 minced garlic cloves and sauté, stirring several times with a wooden spoon. Add tomatoes, enough water to cover lamb, and bay leaves. Bring to a boil. Cover the pot and transfer it to preheated oven. Bake for 1 hour.
4. While meat is baking, heat remaining ¼ cup olive oil in a large heavy skillet and sauté potatoes, whole onions, carrots, and celery, a little at a time, if necessary. Stir around pot for several minutes with a wooden spoon until all vegetables are coated with olive oil. Reduce heat to low and stir in remaining minced garlic and herbs. Season with salt and pepper and gently mix the vegetables into the lamb.
5. Cover and continue baking for about 25 minutes, or until vegetables and lamb are tender. About 5 minutes before removing from oven, uncover and sprinkle in vinegar.

Yield: 4 to 6 servings

Serving Suggestion: This is a meal by itself save for some wine. Have any of the dark bold Greek reds. Those from Nemea, Náoussa, or Gouménissa would be best.

Arni Kapama

(LAMB IN A SPICY TOMATO SAUCE)

KAPAMA is a classic preparation in Greek cooking that refers to any kind of meat or vegetable cooked in a slightly sweetened and spicy tomato sauce. Allspice, cinnamon, cloves, and nutmeg are all flavored and exotic additions to the tomato, and here, an extra delight is served up as well—grapes.

1. In a large heavy stewing pot, heat olive oil and cook lamb, turning it frequently on all sides to brown evenly and lightly. Add the onion and sauté, stirring with a wooden spoon, until wilted.

2. "Extinguish" the pot, as the Greeks say, with the brandy by pouring it into the pot. Add the tomatoes, allspice, bay leaves, cinnamon, salt, and pepper. Stir well with a wooden spoon to blend. Add, if necessary, enough water just to cover meat. Bring to a boil, then reduce heat to low. Cover and simmer for about 1 hour 15 minutes, or until meat is almost cooked. Add more water, if necessary, during cooking to keep mixture moist and sauce from reducing too much.

3. About 10 minutes before meat is cooked, gently stir in grapes. Adjust seasoning if necessary.

Yield: 4 to 6 servings

Variation: Chicken, beef, and veal may also be prepared as above, *kapama* style, but omit the grapes. Add, if desired, a bit of hot pepper to the sauce.

Serving Suggestions: Serve over macaroni or with rice or mashed potatoes. Choose any dry red Greek wine with this exotic dish.

$\frac{1}{4}$ cup olive oil
$2\frac{1}{2}$ pounds lean lamb, preferably leg or shoulder, cut into stewing cubes
2 large white onions, peeled and finely chopped
$\frac{1}{4}$ cup brandy
2 cups peeled, seeded, and finely chopped tomatoes (with juice)
6 to 8 allspice berries, crushed with a mortar and pestle
2 medium bay leaves, ripped
1 cinnamon stick
Salt and freshly ground pepper, to taste
2 cups seedless white grapes

Classic Roast Leg of Lamb or Goat

3 to 6 garlic cloves, to
  taste
$\frac{1}{3}$ cup olive oil, or
  more to taste
2 tablespoons or more
  crushed dried
  rosemary or dried
  oregano, or both, to
  taste
Strained fresh juice of
  4 lemons, or more
  to taste
1 cup dry red wine
1 leg of lamb,
  trimmed, about 5
  pounds
Salt and freshly
  ground pepper, to
  taste
Small new potatoes,
  whole or halved
  (optional)

1. Finely chop 2 garlic cloves and combine them in a large bowl with 1 tablespoon olive oil, 1 tablespoon of the dried rosemary and/or oregano, juice of 2 lemons, and dry red wine to make a marinade. Marinate lamb in mixture, covered and refrigerated, for 6 to 12 hours, turning lamb every few hours.

2. Remove lamb from refrigerator. Preheat oven to 450°F and lightly oil a large baking pan.

3. With a mortar and pestle, crush together all but 1 of the remaining garlic cloves and remaining herbs. Remove lamb from marinade and reserve liquids. With a sharp knife, make $\frac{3}{4}$-inch slits all around leg of lamb and stuff garlic and herb mixture inside slits. Reserve a small amount of the mixture for step 4.

4. Rub lamb with olive oil and 1 whole garlic clove, salt, pepper, and remaining herb mixture. Place lamb in prepared baking pan and arrange potatoes around it, if desired. Season potatoes with salt, pepper, and juice of remaining 2 lemons. Pour marinade over lamb. Place uncovered in oven and reduce heat immediately to 350°F. Bake for about $2\frac{1}{2}$ hours (about 30 minutes per pound), or until lamb is tender and slightly rare, and potatoes fork-tender. Baste every 10 to 15 minutes with pan juices. If potatoes need more liquid, add a little water to the pan during cooking.

Yield: About 6 servings

Variations: For a slight variation, especially in winter, try lamb or goat oven-roasted as above, but with chestnuts. Puncture 2 pounds of chestnuts with a fork or a sharp knife. Place chestnuts in a large pot with enough water to cover, and simmer them until tender. Drain in a colander, cool slightly, and peel. Sprinkle around the lamb or goat about halfway through baking.

Lamb Yuvetsi (baked with orzo) was the usual Sunday meal in our house. Add 4 cups chopped fresh tomatoes (with juice) and 2 cups water to the baking pan about 1 hour after placing the roast in the oven. Spread $1\frac{1}{2}$ cups orzo (*kritharaki* to the Greeks) in the pan. Season with salt and pepper and bake alongside lamb, basting the meat as above throughout baking. Serve the orzo alongside lamb on a large platter and top with grated cheese.

Greeks also roast lamb (and other meats) inside *lathoharto*, or parchment paper. This preparation is also called *exohiko*, or countryside-style. To roast it this way, season the lamb as above and fold a double piece of parchment paper around lamb, as though it were a package, tucking in both ends. Tie with string and bake, uncovered, in a slow oven for 2 to 2$\frac{1}{2}$ hours. Serve in paper with potatoes on the side.

Chops and stewing meat may also be baked *exohiko*, with parchment paper. Marinate the meat first for several hours. As with a proper roast, make several slits in the chops and press in herbs and spices. Spoon a tablespoon or two of marinade over the meat and top with a wedge of either feta or graviera cheese. Seal like a package, securing with string if necessary, and bake at 350°F until tender, about 1 hour. Serve in packet, with potatoes on the side, if desired.

Serving Suggestions: *Mageiritsa* soup, *kokkoretsi*, spinach pie, *maroulosalata*, and *tsoureki*, would go well with this dish, along with a bold. dry red wine.

Arni/Katsikaki Souvlas

(SPIT-ROASTED WHOLE BABY LAMB OR GOAT)

ALTHOUGH this preparation has come to be known as the classic Greek Easter meal, it's a more common sight on the mainland than on the islands. In the Aegean, generally, the classic Easter lamb or goat dish is stuffed whole with rice and herbs, and baked slowly, usually in the village wood-burning bread oven.

1 whole lamb or goat,
*   all innards removed*
Salt and freshly
*   ground pepper*
Ample strained fresh
*   lemon juice*
Ample olive oil
Oregano or thyme

1. Have the butcher remove all innards from lamb or goat. Reserve them, if desired, for making *mageiritsa* soup (page 132) or *kokkoretsi* (page 264). Rub the inside of the lamb or goat with salt and pepper.

2. Pass the skewer (it should be 8 to 12 inches longer than the animal on both sides) between the animal's hind legs, tying them, too, to the rod, then carefully through the stomach cavity and through its chin and mouth. Tie the front and back legs to the skewer and be sure that the back of the animal is straight on the skewer. The skewer should come out exactly through the middle of the animal's mouth. Tie the middle of the animal to the skewer and sew the stomach cavity closed. Rub the entire surface of the lamb or goat with lemon juice, olive oil, salt, pepper, and oregano or thyme.

3. Roast lamb or goat over slow-burning coals—the fire should be started at least 2 hours before cooking the animal—by turning slowly and steadily for several hours. Brush intermittently during roasting with a mixture of lemon juice, olive oil, and oregano or thyme. When the skin on the shoulders and legs begins to burst and the lamb or goat becomes the color of deep redwood or chestnut, the meat should be fork-tender. This will take at least 4 hours of slow spit-roasting. Carefully remove lamb or goat from skewer and carve.

Yield: Allow about 1 pound per serving

Serving Suggestions: Roasted potatoes, *mageiritsa* soup, *kokkoretsi,* spinach pie, *maroulosalata,* and *tsoureki* would complete this feast. Drink a heady, robust wine with it—a dry red from Náoussa or Gouménissa or Nemea. My choice with this meal would be Náoussa Grande Réserve.

—GROUND MEATS, ORGANS,— AND INNARDS

Ground meat, mostly beef but sometimes lamb and pork, finds its way into Greek cookery in myriad ways. It's turned into meatballs of every sort and flavor, stuffed into sausages, used in pie fillings and meat loaves, and simmered into sauce.

The eating of organs and innards, on the other hand, has been guided by economy, frugality, and a predilection for those parts of the animal most Americans would consider unsavory at best. The ancients enjoyed fried liver wrapped in caul (pig's stomach), and womb (not unlike haggis). The moderns enjoy *tsigerosarmathes,* lamb's liver wrapped in the *skepi,* or second stomach; and *sheftalia,* a sausagelike dish from Cyprus made of ground pork wrapped in the stomach lining of lamb or beef and grilled. Brains and sweetbreads are poached, breaded, and braised; tripe becomes the famous *patsas,* a soup; and lamb's innards, including the lungs, work themselves into *mageiritsa,* also a soup.

Surmising an innate dislike among most Americans for stuffed spleen or two pancreas on a plate, or for marinated testicles (*ameletitha,* to the Greeks), I've left the diehards' recipes out. But brains and sweetbreads and grilled and stuffed *skepi* are here for the brave at heart—or hearts, which are also eaten.

Rolo

(MEAT LOAF)

MY husband's grandmother has a way with meat loaf. She cooks it gently, stuffed with whole boiled eggs as is the tradition, and cuts it into thick wedges that she then sautés in more olive oil than I have ever learned to care for. She then carefully binds the pieces together again with string and bakes them once more. The result is a luscious, dark loaf of meat and eggs that brings her three grandchildren running to lunch. This is a toned-down version, with much changed except the egg, but I think Kyria Ioanna would approve.

---

1 pound ground beef ($\frac{3}{4}$ pound beef, $\frac{1}{4}$ pound pork, if desired)

$\frac{1}{4}$ cup minced onion

2 garlic cloves, minced

2 to 3 tablespoons finely chopped parsley

3 teaspoons dried oregano

1 egg

Salt and freshly ground pepper, to taste

3 ounces thinly sliced Italian bread

$\frac{1}{2}$ cup dry red wine

1 to 2 hard-boiled eggs, peeled

4 to 6 medium-size potatoes, halved and sliced

1 red onion, halved and sliced thin

1 tablespoon olive oil

$1\frac{1}{2}$ cups chopped peeled tomato

1. Preheat oven to 350°F and lightly grease a large glass baking dish.
2. In a large bowl, combine meat, onion, garlic, parsley, 2 teaspoons of the oregano, raw egg, salt, and pepper. In a separate bowl, crumble the bread and knead or mix with $\frac{1}{4}$ cup of the red wine. Add to meat mixture and knead well. Shape into one large or two small loaves, with a hard-boiled egg in the center of each. Place in baking pan.
3. In a large bowl, lightly mix potatoes, red onion, olive oil, remaining $\frac{1}{4}$ cup wine, remaining 1 teaspoon oregano, and tomatoes. Pour mixture over and around meat loaf in baking dish. Bake for 45 minutes to one 1, until meat loaf is cooked and tender but not dry. Baste every 10 to 12 minutes while baking and add water to pan, if necessary to keep liquids from drying out.
4. Remove baking dish from oven and place meat loaf on a large serving platter. If the potatoes are not yet cooked and pan liquids evaporated, add a little more water, if necessary, and continue baking them until tender. Arrange potatoes around meat loaf and serve warm.

Yield: 4 to 6 servings

Serving Suggestion: Anything from ouzo to beer to simple table wine would match this prosaic dish.

Yuverlakia

(GROUND MEAT AND RICE BALLS IN AVGOLEMONO)

"LITTLE spheres"—these fall somewhere between soup and stew, depending on how much and how thick your *avgolemono* is.

---

1. In a medium-size bowl, combine ground meat, rice, onion, garlic, herbs, and orange rind. Add egg yolk and season with salt and pepper. Knead well until all ingredients are thoroughly blended. Shape into balls 1½ to 2 inches in diameter, and, if desired, dredge with flour.

2. In a large stewing pot, bring olive oil and enough water or stock to cover meatballs to a boil. Add *yuverlakia*, cover, and simmer over medium heat for 35 to 40 minutes, or until meat and rice are tender. Add more liquid, if necessary, to keep mixture covered with liquid during cooking.

3. Just before meat and rice are done, make *avgolemono* sauce: In a medium-size bowl, beat together egg and lemon until frothy. Very slowly add 2 to 4 ladlefuls (1 to 2 cups) of broth to egg mixture, beating vigorously with a whisk to keep egg from curdling. Remove stewing pot from heat and pour in egg mixture. Place pot back on heat and stir sauce well, but do not allow it to boil. Remove pot from heat and serve immediately. It's best to make *avgolemono* just before serving.

Yield: 4 to 6 servings, or about 2 dozen meatballs

Variations: *Yuverlakia* may also be served with yogurt sauce, Smyrna style, or with tomato sauce—both in place of *avgolemono*.

With yogurt: Cook meatballs as in above recipe. Have yogurt—preferably goat's milk or sheep's milk—at room temperature. When *yuverlakia* are done, remove with a slotted spoon from pot and serve with yogurt and a generous sprinkling of cumin.

With tomato sauce: Add 1½ cups finely chopped peeled and cored tomatoes to water, so that all together there is enough liquid to cover *yuverlakia*. Season with ¼ cup olive oil, 1 crushed garlic clove, salt, and pepper, and cook as above until rice and meat are tender and sauce thick. Add more water, if necessary, to keep pot liquids from drying out during cooking.

Serving Suggestion: Try a simple white table wine such as Lac des Roches or a crisp demi-sec rosé with this.

---

1 pound ground beef or lamb
⅓ cup long-grain rice
½ cup finely chopped or grated white onion
2 garlic cloves, crushed
⅓ cup very finely chopped parsley, packed
1 to 1½ tablespoons finely chopped fresh dill
1 tablespoon chopped fresh mint (optional)
1 teaspoon dried oregano
Pinch of finely grated orange rind (optional)
1 egg yolk
Salt and freshly ground pepper, to taste
Flour (optional)
2 to 3 tablespoons olive oil
2 to 3 eggs, at room temperature
Strained fresh juice of 1 to 2 large lemons

Koubepia

(MEATBALLS COOKED WITH PRUNES AND WALNUTS, KOZANI STYLE)

I DON'T know if the word *koubepia* is a transliteration of the Eastern "kebab," but it certainly sounds as though it may be. In Cyprus, a dish by the same name refers to grape leaves stuffed with meat. In northern Greece, *koubepia* are sometimes cooked this exotic way, with walnuts and prunes, and sometimes in a fashion similar to *soutzoukakia smyrneika,* but with a thick, peppery tomato sauce. This sweetened version, luscious and filling, is perfect for warming a cold winter's day.

---

15 to 20 whole pitted prunes

15 to 20 walnut halves or blanched whole almonds

½ cup dry red wine

1 pound ground veal or beef

⅓ cup very finely chopped white onion

⅓ cup finely chopped fresh parsley, packed

½ cup finely ground walnut meats (or a combination of walnuts, pine nuts, and almonds, finely ground)

Salt and freshly ground pepper, to taste

3 large ripe tomatoes, peeled, cored, and chopped (with juice)

1. Stuff prunes with walnuts or almonds and marinate in red wine for 1 hour before using. Preheat oven to 450°F and lightly butter a clay or glass baking dish.

2. In a medium-size bowl, combine ground meat, onion, parsley, ground nuts, salt, and pepper and knead well until all ingredients are thoroughly blended. Shape into medium-size meatballs, about 1½ inches in diameter. (They shouldn't be much larger than the prunes.)

3. Arrange tomatoes in bottom of prepared baking dish, add a little water, and place meatballs on top of tomatoes. Put the dish in hot oven and lower temperature immediately to 350°F. Bake for about 1 hour, basting every 15 minutes or so, until meat is tender and cooked but not dry. About 20 minutes before removing dish from oven, add prunes and marinade to pan. Serve hot.

Yield: 4 to 6 servings

Serving Suggestions: Serve this dish with plain rice. I might try, daringly, a sweet Mavrodaphne with this to enhance the sweetness of the prunes, or use one of the robust Gouménissa or Náoussa red wines.

Soutzoukakia Smyrneika

(MEATBALL SAUSAGES, SMYRNA STYLE)

THIS is one of the few dishes in Greek cookery in which cumin is used generously. Its name translates literally as "little sausages, Smyrna style," but it is prepared with ground meat, not sausages.

2 wedges (2 inches thick) Italian bread, white part only
$\frac{1}{3}$ cup dry red wine
$1\frac{1}{2}$ pounds ground beef
$\frac{1}{2}$ cup plus 2 tablespoons finely chopped onion
1 to 3 garlic cloves, finely chopped
$\frac{1}{3}$ cup finely chopped fresh parsley, packed
2 scant teaspoons ground cumin
1 tablespoon plus 1 teaspoon quality red wine vinegar
Salt and freshly ground pepper, to taste
Olive oil, for frying

1. In a medium-size bowl, soak bread in red wine and set aside until ready to use.

2. In a medium-size bowl, combine ground beef, onion, garlic, parsley, cumin, and vinegar. Add wine-soaked bread, season with salt and pepper, and knead well until all ingredients are thoroughly mixed. Take 1 heaping tablespoon at a time and shape into oval nuggets about 2 inches long. Carefully place in a dish or bowl, cover, and let stand in the refrigerator for 1 hour before cooking.

3. When ready to cook *soutzoukakia,* heat olive oil in a large heavy skillet and brown *soutzoukakia* lightly, turning on all sides to cook evenly. Remove from skillet with a slotted spoon and drain on paper towels.

4. *To prepare sauce:* In a separate large heavy pot, heat olive oil and butter and add flour. Stir vigorously with a wooden spoon until flour browns very lightly. Add tomatoes, wine, sugar, salt, and pepper and bring to a boil. Add *soutzoukakia* to sauce. Reduce heat, cover, and simmer until meat is tender and sauce thick, about 50 minutes. Add a bit of water during cooking to keep the sauce from reducing too much.

SAUCE
$\frac{1}{4}$ cup olive oil
2 to 3 tablespoons butter
2 tablespoons all-purpose flour
$2\frac{1}{4}$ cups finely chopped peeled tomatoes, with juice
$\frac{1}{2}$ cup dry red wine
$\frac{1}{2}$ teaspoon sugar
Salt and freshly ground pepper, to taste

Yield: 4 to 6 servings

Serving Suggestions: Plain rice or mashed potatoes go nicely with this dish. Also serve with a side of creamy plain yogurt and a wine robust enough to counter the strong flavors in the dish. I would choose any of the earthy Náoussa, Nemea, or Gouménissa vintages.

Sheftalies

(STUFFED STOMACH LININGS)

SHEFTALIES are a Cypriot delicacy not unsimilar to the stuffed pigs' stomachs and metra (womb) delicacies held in such high regard by the ancients. A similar dish, *tsigerosarmades,* that is stuffed with lamb's entrails is a favorite among Macedonians. *Sheftalies* are grilled over charcoal.

¾ pound stomach lining of lamb or beef

1 pound ground pork

½ cup very finely chopped onion

2 to 3 garlic cloves, crushed

½ cup very finely chopped parsley

½ cup finely chopped, peeled, and seeded tomato

1 egg

Salt and freshly ground pepper, to taste

1. Allow stomach lining to soak in ample water either at room temperature or refrigerated for at least 8 hours before using. Wash carefully and thoroughly, trying not to tear it.

2. In a medium-size bowl, combine ground pork, onion, garlic, parsley, tomatoes, egg, salt, and pepper. Knead until all ingredients are thoroughly combined.

3. Gently lay the stomach lining on a large flat surface. With sharp scissors or kitchen shears, cut out 12 to 15 squares about 4 inches on all sides. Taking a heaping tablespoon or so at a time of pork mixture, roll in the palms of your hands into the shape of a sausage about 2½ inches long. Place on bottom center of a square of the lining. Fold over two sides to cover meat and roll up as one does a dolma (see page 171), so that each *sheftalia* is securely closed. Repeat until all the meat is used. Let stand until ready to use.

4. Heat charcoal and let fire simmer down for at least 45 minutes before grilling *sheftalies.* Grill evenly on all sides until crisp and browned. Serve hot with *pitta* bread and tomato.

Yield: 12 to 15 *sheftalies,* or about 4 servings as a main course

Serving Suggestions: Serve these with *patates antinaktes* and a pungent plate of *tzatziki.* Ouzo would accompany this nicely, as would any robust red Greek wine.

Myala Vrasta

(BOILED BRAINS)

PREPARE brains immediately after buying since they are quite perishable.

1. Soak the brains in enough cold water to cover, along with 2 tablespoons of the lemon juice and 1 teaspoon salt, for 1 hour. Remove the membrane, or skin, around the brains and soak again, in fresh water, with another 2 tablespoons lemon juice and 1 teaspoon salt, for another half hour.

2. In a medium pot, bring enough water to cover brains, along with 2 tablespoons lemon juice, vinegar, and salt to a slow simmer. Add brains to water, cover, and simmer slowly for 20 to 25 minutes. Remove brains from pot, place on a serving plate, and sprinkle with olive oil and lemon juice to taste. Refrigerate, covered, for several hours before serving. Serve at room temperature or cold.

1 pound lamb brains
6 tablespoons strained fresh lemon juice
Salt
1 tablespoon vinegar
Olive oil

Yield: 4 to 6 meze servings

Variation: For fried brains: Prepare as above and remove from water, once cooked, with a slotted spoon. Beat 1 egg and 2 tablespoons water together. Dip the brains in the egg mixture, then dip in plain bread crumbs. Sauté in ample butter until golden brown. Drain briefly on paper towels and serve with lemon, usually as an accompanying dish with lamb.

Glykathia

(SWEETBREADS OR THYMUS)

1. Soak sweetbreads in enough cold water to cover, along with 2 tablespoons of the lemon juice and 1 teaspoon of the salt, for 1 hour. Pour off water, soak again in fresh water, with another 2 tablespoons lemon juice and 1 teaspoon salt, for another half hour.

2. In a medium pot, bring enough water to cover sweetbreads, along with 2 tablespoons lemon juice and salt to taste, to a boil. Add sweetbreads to pot, reduce heat, and simmer, uncovered, for about 5 minutes. Remove sweetbreads with a slotted spoon and plunge immediately into cold water to firm them. Cool in the water, remove, and carefully remove cartilage, connective tissue, membrane, etc. Sauté, if desired, in a little butter, or dip sweetbreads in egg mixture, then bread crumbs, and sauté in butter. Serve hot with lemon wedges on the side.

1 pound sweetbreads
6 tablespoons strained fresh lemon juice
2 teaspoons salt plus salt to taste
Butter (optional)
1 beaten egg plus 2 tablespoons water (optional)
Bread crumbs (optional)
Lemon wedges

Yield: 4 to 6 servings

Kokkoretsi

(SKEWERED, GRILLED MIXED INNARDS)

KOKKORETSI, together with *mageiritsa* and roasted lamb or goat, make up the troika of classic Greek Easter savory dishes. It is part of the Easter table, served with the lamb, and vegetables and *pittas* that make up a typical Easter spread. It can also be eaten, however, as a prelude to the meal, a meze to keep those who are doing the spit roasting of the lamb sated—at least temporarily.

Liver, spleen, heart, sweetbreads, kidneys, intestines, and stomach lining from one spring lamb or goat

½ cup olive oil

½ cup strained fresh lemon juice

2 teaspoons dried oregano, or more to taste

2 to 3 cloves garlic, minced

Salt and freshly ground pepper

½ cup red wine vinegar

1. Cut all the organ meats except the intestines and stomach lining into cubes or bite-size pieces and place in a large bowl. In a small bowl, combine olive oil, lemon juice, oregano, garlic, and salt and pepper to taste. Pour marinade over meat, cover, and refrigerate for at least 1 hour.

2. While meat is marinating, wash the intestines and stomach lining thoroughly. To clean the intestines, attach one opening to the faucet and hold with one hand to keep it from popping off. Turn on cold water and let it run gently. Carefully squeeze intestine from top to bottom many times, with water running, so as to clean out all residue thoroughly. Turn inside out, if desired, to clean even more. Wash the stomach lining thoroughly. In a medium-size bowl, combine vinegar and 1 tablespoon salt. Place lining and intestines in vinegar mixture and let stand for about 30 minutes. Rinse well again and let drain in a colander before using.

3. Slide marinated organ meats onto a skewer, alternating the different types. Brush with marinade. Wrap stomach lining around meat, carefully and securely (it should be fairly tight). Pierce the intestine at one end of the skewer to secure and begin wrapping it tightly around enveloped meats. It shouldn't be so tight that it bursts, but it should be secure. Again, pierce at other end of skewer once all of the meats have been wrapped. Tie in several knots to keep from unwinding.

4. Brush with marinade and either roast on a spit over slow coals or barbecue. Brush liberally and frequently with marinade. (Add more lemon juice, oregano, and olive oil, if necessary.) Roast slowly until the *kokkoretsi* is deep reddish brown in color and fork-tender.

5. To serve, carefully slip meat off skewer onto a large serving platter. Cut into thick rounds—about 1½ inches per piece—and serve hot.

Yield: About 8 servings

Braised Liver with Rosemary and Laurel

1. Season flour with salt and pepper and dredge liver strips in it. In a large, heavy-bottomed stewing pot, heat 2 tablespoons of the olive oil and the butter. Cook the liver, turning on all sides to brown evenly, until very lightly browned. Remove the liver and set aside.

2. Add remaining 6 tablespoons olive oil, tomatoes, vinegar or wine, and 1 cup water to the pot. Bring to a boil, then reduce heat and simmer, uncovered, stirring with a wooden spoon, for 5 to 7 minutes. Add bay leaf, rosemary, salt, and pepper and simmer for another 3 to 4 minutes. Add the liver, stir gently to coat with sauce, and simmer, covered, over low heat until the liver is tender and the sauce thick, 15 to 20 minutes. Serve warm over plain rice.

Yield: 4 servings

Flour, for dredging
Salt and freshly ground pepper, to taste
$1\frac{1}{2}$ to 2 pounds lamb or calf's liver, cut into long strips about 1 inch wide
$\frac{1}{2}$ cup olive oil
2 tablespoons butter
$\frac{3}{4}$ cup peeled, seeded, and chopped tomato (with juice)
3 tablespoons red wine vinegar, or $\frac{1}{3}$ cup dry white wine
1 to 2 cups water
1 large bay leaf, ripped
1 teaspoon dried rosemary

—— SAUSAGES ——

Though traditionally country fare, prepared after the *hirosfagi* (hog slaughter) anywhere from the middle of November to New Year's Day, sausages *(loukanika)* for the most part are now commercially made. *Spetsofai,* a sausage and pepper recipe from Mount Pelion, is probably the best known sausage dish in the country's cookery. Ideally, one should use fresh and, if possible, homemade sausages for the dish, but there are many commercially made regional sausages that might be used instead:

Horiatika. Also known as village sausages, these are the most common sausages in *spetsofai.* They're fresh, long, and fat, seasoned with orange and sometimes with wine and oregano.

Loukanika Nissiotika. These are island sausages, similar to *horiatika,* but long and thin.

Loukanika Thessalias. From Thessaly, these are fresh pork sausages seasoned and stuffed with leeks.

Maniatika. These are from Mani, in the Peloponnisos. Like their Vólos cousins, these are half pork and half beef but are seasoned with oregano and mint.

Soutzoukaki Politiko. This is a dried black sausage sometimes tinged (or singed) with hot pepper.

Voliotika. From Vólos, these are small, fresh, fat sausages—half pork, half beef, and seasoned with allspice.

To make your own sausages, try the following recipe for *horiatiko loukaniko makedonitiko.*

Horiatiko Loukaniko Makedonitiko

(MACEDONIAN PORK SAUSAGE WITH LEEKS AND ORANGE)

$1\frac{1}{2}$ *pounds ground lean pork*
$\frac{1}{2}$ *pound ground pork fatback*
1 to 2 leeks, steamed until translucent and very well drained, then finely chopped (white part only)
1 teaspoon salt (or more to taste)
1 to 2 teaspoons coarsely ground pepper
1 heaping teaspoon dried oregano or thyme
Grated rind of 1 orange
1 teaspoon ground cumin
1 teaspoon powdered allspice
$\frac{1}{3}$ *cup red wine vinegar*
Pork casings

1. In a large bowl, combine the ground pork, fatback, cooked and chopped leeks, and remaining ingredients except the casings. Knead until everything is well blended. Refrigerate until ready to use (see Note).

2. Prepare the casings, which are usually salted: Place casings in a large bowl and rinse thoroughly under cold water 5 to 6 times. Drain on a lint-free towel.

3. Put the bowl of sausage stuffing in a larger bowl filled with ice cubes, to keep it cool while filling cases.

4. Using either a pastry bag or a sausage stuffer, attach the casing at one end and fill with the ground pork mixture. Pinch or gently twist the casing at intervals of 4 to 6 inches, allowing some space in between to form the links. If the casing breaks, discard the cut part and knot the end of the last sausage to close. When all the filling has been used, knot both ends of the link to secure closed.

5. To cook sausages, bring enough water in a skillet to cover them to a boil, drop them in, and simmer, covered, for 1 hour. Drain thoroughly. Fry, grill, or cook them in *spetsofai,* or in omelets (pages 270–271).

Yield: 6 to 8 servings

Note: Raw sausage meat should not be stored for more than 1 or 2 days in the refrigerator. To freeze, store uncooked sausages in portion-size batches. Wash your hands and any utensils used very thoroughly afterward, to avoid trichinosis.

Spetsofai

(SAUSAGE AND PEPPER STEW)

SPETSOFAI is a regional specialty of Mount Pelion in Thessaly. The dish is served in both country taverns and in homes, and is often made in individual clay bowls and baked. The following is a stove-top version.

1. In a heavy skillet, heat olive oil and brown sausages lightly on all sides. Remove sausages with a slotted spoon and drain on paper towels. Add onions and peppers and cook over medium heat until wilted. Add tomatoes, garlic, bay leaf, and oregano and bring to a boil.

2. Add sausages and wine to pot. Season with salt and pepper, and, if desired, hot pepper. Reduce heat to low and simmer, covered, until sausages are thoroughly cooked, 50 minutes to 1 hour. Add water during cooking, if needed, to keep mixture moist.

Yield: 4 to 6 servings

Serving Suggestion: *Tsipouro,* a drink similar to ouzo, is perfect with this dish.

3 tablespoons olive oil
$1\frac{1}{2}$ pounds fresh pork sausage
2 large onions, peeled and sliced into rings
$1\frac{1}{2}$ to 2 pounds Italian peppers, washed, seeded, and cut lengthwise into $\frac{1}{2}$-inch strips
$1\frac{1}{2}$ pounds tomatoes, peeled, cored, and cut into thick round slices (with juice)
2 garlic cloves, finely chopped
1 large bay leaf, ripped
1 heaping teaspoon dried oregano
$\frac{1}{3}$ cup dry red wine
Salt and freshly ground pepper to taste
1 to 2 small hot red peppers, crushed (optional)

Chapter 15

Eggs

*Bulbs, snails, eggs and the like are supposed to
produce semen . . .*
                    —*Athenaeus,* The Deipnosophists, Book I

The heavenly egg, the perfect egg, the beautiful brown egg that is choice among Greeks, glorifies their cooking in ways both obvious and obscure. Whipped into naked white sauce, the egg turns the sauce thick and helps it swell in the oven; hugged, hard-boiled, between walls of ground beef, it exalts the lowly meat loaf; plunged in a crimson bath, it sits, a ruby, on a crown of plaited Easter bread; and, beaten, with a stream of lemon and a ladling of broth, it becomes the famed *avgolemono,* a sauce, a soup, a savor for all and any season.

The egg *(avgo)* has been esteemed since ancient times, when it was thought to be aphrodisiac. Egg cookery was highly developed in antiquity. According to Waverley Root, there was a special pan for preparing eggs, "with three concentric oval-shaped indentations to hold three kinds of eggs," most likely the peacock egg, the goose egg, and perhaps the ostrich egg, all equally regarded. Fish eggs were also prized in antiquity. The eggs of the gray mullet were used much as they are now to produce *avgotaraho,* a kind of roe paste that today sells for nearly fifty dollars a pound.

But fish eggs hardly count here, because they're generally not poached or boiled—in Greek cookery, at least—and are not given the status enjoyed by the eggs of the humble hen. It is with her that we take up in the next few pages—poaching, boiling, frying, and baking her unassuming output.

Dyed Eggs for the Easter Feast

HOW (AND WHY) TO DYE AN EGG

HOLY Thursday is the day that the preparations for the Easter feast begin, and the dying of the eggs is a vital part of the ritual. In fact, the day is sometimes called *Kokkinopefti,* or the day on which the red falls. Greek Easter eggs are dyed the color of blood, deep red, a practice that began in Byzantium, and then polished with a rag dipped in olive oil. The color symbolizes the blood of Christ, although the egg itself is, of course, the symbol of life, regeneration, and spring. Until not very long ago, the eggs were dyed with a certain red wood, or sometimes tinted bright yellow with the leaves of the almond tree. The custom begins on Holy Thursday, when they are dyed, and ends when they are cracked and eaten to break the fast, along with *mageiritsa* soup (page 132), after the midnight Mass on Holy Saturday.

In Kozani, in the north, and in other parts of Greece, eggs are not only dyed but also painted with delicate designs, usually of birds—and called *perthikes,* or partridges—perhaps to symbolize the Resurrection. Wings, birds, beaks, and other motifs are stuck onto the eggs, which are then wrapped in a dyed cloth and boiled, a method similar to batik. Sometimes, dough is used to make beaks and wings, and the "birds" are hung as ornaments around the house.

---

1. Wash eggs very well and dry them. Dissolve dye in vinegar.

2. In a large pot, place enough water to cover one layer of eggs. Bring water to a boil and pour in vinegar and dye mixture. Skim off the top.

3. Add just enough eggs to cover the bottom of the pot (layering the eggs will create uneven color) and boil gently for 15 to 20 minutes. Remove eggs with a slotted spoon, drain well, and dry thoroughly. Repeat with remaining eggs and polish each boiled egg with a cloth dipped in olive oil. See *tsoureki* (page 60) for using eggs to decorate Greek Easter bread.

Yield: 2 dozen

2 dozen eggs
1 envelope red dye
1 cup white vinegar

Sfoungato

(BAKED OMELET)

3 tablespoons olive oil
3 to 4 scallions, finely
    chopped
2 small- to medium-
    size zucchini,
    washed and diced
3 tablespoons finely
    chopped fresh dill
1 tablespoon finely
    chopped fresh mint
    (optional)
4 to 5 eggs
2 to 3 tablespoons
    milk
3 tablespoons grated
    kefalotyri or
    Parmesan cheese
Salt and freshly
    ground pepper, to
    taste

SFOUNGATO—a transliteration of *sfoggos,* or sponge—is just another word for omelet in Greek, and one that dates to Byzantium. *Sfoungato* typically includes green vegetables such as zucchini or lettuce, and is traditionally baked, although the skillet will serve just as well if you're in a rush.

---

1. Preheat oven to 400°F. Lightly oil a small glass casserole dish with 1 tablespoon olive oil.
2. Heat 2 tablespoons olive oil in a skillet and sauté scallion until translucent. Add zucchini, dill, and mint and sauté over low heat until zucchini softens and liquid is cooked off, 7 to 10 minutes. Remove skillet from heat and drain any excess juices.
3. In a large bowl, beat eggs and milk very well. Fold in vegetables and grated cheese. Season with salt and pepper. Pour mixture into prepared casserole dish, place in oven, turn down temperature to 250°F, and bake for 30 to 40 minutes, or until eggs are golden and as firm as pudding. Serve warm.

Yield: 2 servings

Kayianas

(TOMATO, PEPPER, AND SAUSAGE OMELET)

$\frac{1}{4}$ to $\frac{1}{2}$ pound (to taste)
    dried sausage, sliced
    into $\frac{1}{4}$-inch rounds
4 large plum tomatoes,
    peeled and chopped
1 large green bell
    pepper, seeded and
    chopped (optional)
4 eggs
$\frac{1}{2}$ cup grated kefalotyri
    or Parmesan cheese
Salt and freshly
    ground pepper, to
    taste

KAYIANAS is the name given to an omelet in the Peloponnisos, where it is usually prepared with tomato and homemade sausage.

---

1. In an ungreased skillet, heat sausage slices until browned, turning frequently. Add tomatoes and green pepper and simmer, uncovered, 2 to 3 minutes over medium-low heat.
2. In a small bowl, beat together eggs and cheese. Pour egg mixture into skillet, stir, and simmer, uncovered, for 3 to 5 minutes, or until eggs are done and liquid is cooked off. Season with salt and pepper to taste and serve hot.

Yield: 2 servings

Strapatsatha

(SCRAMBLED EGGS WITH TOMATOES)

THIS recipe for scrambled eggs and tomatoes is very similar to *kayianas* (opposite page), but is prepared without the sausage and with a little olive oil.

---

1. In a large skillet, heat olive oil over medium heat. Add tomatoes, garlic, and herbs and simmer for 2 to 3 minutes, stirring with a wooden spoon.
2. In a small bowl, beat together eggs and cheese. Pour egg mixture into skillet and cook, stirring with a wooden spoon, for 3 to 5 minutes, or to desired doneness. Serve warm, garnished with parsley and seasoned with salt and pepper.

Yield: 2 servings

2 tablespoons olive oil
4 plump ripe tomatoes, peeled, cored, and chopped
1 garlic clove (optional), finely chopped
2 teaspoons finely chopped fresh mint or oregano
4 eggs
½ cup grated kefalotyri or Parmesan cheese
Parsley, for garnish
Salt and freshly ground pepper

Froutalia

(POTATO AND SAUSAGE OMELET)

THIS omelet is a specialty of the island of Andros, where it is made with potatoes, pork sausage, smoked ham, and, traditionally, *gleena,* or lard. In this more healthy version, the lard has been omitted.

---

1. In a large skillet, heat butter and sauté potatoes until lightly browned. Add sausage and smoked ham and cook, stirring with a wooden spoon, over medium heat until potatoes are cooked.
2. Beat eggs with mint, salt, and pepper. Pour into skillet with sausage and potatoes and tilt frying pan from one side to another so that all liquid in eggs is cooked evenly. Carefully flip omelet and continue cooking until both sides are golden brown. Serve hot.

Yield: 2 to 3 servings

2 to 3 tablespoons butter
3 to 4 medium potatoes, washed, peeled, and sliced into ⅛-inch rounds
1 medium pork sausage link (¼ to ½ pound), sliced into ⅛-inch rounds
2 to 3 thick slices smoked ham or Canadian bacon, cut into 1-inch strips
4 to 6 eggs, well beaten
2 teaspoons chopped fresh mint or basil
Salt and freshly ground pepper

Poached Eggs with Yogurt Sauce

THIS goes by the name *xoufota* among Pontian Greeks from the northeastern parts of the country. Greeks poach eggs the old-fashioned way, by bringing a skillet full of water to a rolling boil and dropping the eggs carefully within, regardless of "streamers." The yogurt sauce, really *tzatziki*, replete with cucumber and plenty of garlic, is a condiment common to the northern parts of the country.

Eggs
Tzatziki *(page 84; see*
  Note); strained,
  plain yogurt; or
  sour cream
Paprika
Salt, to taste

Bring a skillet full of water to a rolling boil. Reduce heat to medium and gently break and drop in as many eggs as desired, one at a time, to poach. Remove eggs with a slotted spoon and serve on a bed of *tzatziki*, yogurt, or sour cream, sprinkled with paprika and seasoned with salt.

Note: When making *tzatziki* for this dish, disregard the vinegar and dill.

"Jailed" Eggs

Large, firm tomatoes
  and peppers
Olive oil
Grated kefalotyri or
  Parmesan cheese
1 scallion per
  vegetable, very
  finely chopped
½ teaspoon thyme per
  tomato or pepper
Eggs (as many as you
  have tomatoes and
  peppers)
Salt and freshly
  ground pepper, to
  taste

THIS is a really simple baked egg dish shown to me by a woman on Crete.

1. Preheat oven to 375°F.
2. Wash and cut off the tops of tomatoes and peppers. Discard pepper seeds and inside of tomatoes, but be careful not to tear shells when scooping out insides.
3. Rub about ½ teaspoon olive oil on inside of peppers and tomatoes. Sprinkle insides of each evenly with about 1 teaspoon of grated cheese. Add scallion and thyme. Carefully crack open each egg, being sure not to break yolk, and pour into tomatoes and peppers. Season with salt and pepper and cover each vegetable with its top. Bake for about 45 minutes, or until egg has set. Serve warm.

Feta Cheese Omelet

1. In a large skillet, heat 1 tablespoon of the olive oil and sauté scallions for 3 to 4 minutes, until wilted. Remove scallions from skillet with a slotted spoon.

2. In a medium-size bowl, beat together eggs and milk until frothy.

3. Add remaining olive oil to skillet, heat, then pour in eggs. Sprinkle scallions, feta, and thyme over eggs. Fold over carefully and flip to cook on other side. Place lid on skillet, reduce heat, and cook for 2 to 3 minutes, until eggs are done and feta is soft. Serve warm, seasoned with salt and pepper.

Yield: 2 to 3 servings

*2 to 3 tablespoons
  olive oil
2 to 3 scallions, finely
  chopped
4 eggs, well beaten
2 to 3 tablespoons
  milk
$\frac{1}{2}$ to $\frac{3}{4}$ cup crumbled
  or grated feta cheese
1 scant teaspoon dried
  thyme or oregano
Salt and freshly
  ground pepper, to
  taste*

Part IV

THE SWEETS

Sweets are not the stuff of desserts in Greek cookery. What follows a meal—even in restaurants—is usually a piece of luscious, seasonal fruit. Apples, oranges, pears in winter; strawberries, loquats, cherries, apricots in spring; plums, peaches, and melons of all sorts in summer; grapes, figs, pomegranates, and persimmons in fall. Sweets are the stuff of a separate meal, almost on equal footing with the *meze,* and their preparation generally is the domain of women.

Up until not too long ago, before women worked outside the home, the household tasks were performed with almost ritualistic importance. Everything was done in its time and season. Not least among the tasks was the making of sweets, whether they be the myriad fruit preserves and jams; the honeyed holiday specialties; or simply the replenishing of everyday sweets such as breakfast *koulourakia.*

Like embroidery, sweet and pastry making became the showcase for the woman's skill, intelligence, and creativity, and even of her control over what was, indeed, her realm—the home.

Store-bought sweets for one's own household, except for *loukoumia,* or Turkish delights, was something unheard of, anathema, to any *nikokyra* (housewife) worth her salt—or sugar. They were considered the sign of an unkempt house. A few years ago I visited the home of a woman in Crete to collect recipes for some local sweets. Her mother-in-law was also visiting, much, it seemed, to the daughter's-in-law chagrin, for the woman spent the whole evening deriding her son's young wife about the bakery-made *koulourakia* in her cupboard. "I've never stepped into a pastry shop to buy a sweet for *my* home," she declared. "Every sweet I've ever served came from my own hands."

Although such absolute adherence to old household ways doesn't really exist anymore, and boxes of pastry-shop sweets are certainly a common sight on kitchen counters, there still is a sense of ritual and accomplishment and pride in the domain of the sweets.

Syrups—their consistency and sweetness and proper quantity—take home cooks years to perfect. A friend and avid cook calls in her mother every time there's a syrup to be poured. Although baking and sweet making are exacting labor, accurate recipes are scarce. *To mati*—the eye—is the cook's most reliable gauge, and most recipes requiring syrup—whether they be the fruit preserves or the honeyed delights like *baklava*—instruct one to simmer it until it binds. A sense of method and patience and perhaps intuition—rarely a thermometer—let the sweet maker know just when her work is done.

There is ritual, too, for the presentation of sweets, and a rhythm to the way they are served. There is special small dishware, often of porcelain, dainty and gold rimmed, decorated with pastoral scenes or intricate motifs. There are small spoons and separate, ornate trays and tall water glasses set aside for the serving of sweets, especially of the spoon sweets, or *glyka tou koutaliou.*

When a guest—whether male or female—arrives for a visit, one spends ten, fifteen minutes at most, chatting before offering a sweet. If the hostess offers a sweet too quickly, it's considered impolite—as though she's trying to rush her guest out; if she's too slow in the serving, it's as though she's been caught unprepared. Perhaps the cupboard is lacking in something sweet, the guest might think—a reflection of her own lack of care in presiding over the household duties. After the requisite period of conversation, the spoon sweets are brought out on a tray. There will be a small plate for each person, with a spoonful of syrupy *kythoni* (quince), *karythaki* (walnut), *nerantzi* (bitter Seville orange), or whatever, oozing in the center of each dish. Cold water accompanies each serving, and sometimes a demitasse full of thick Greek coffee, or a shot glass of *tsipouro* (a clear, fiery spirit), or brandy are also on the tray.

Spring, summer, and early fall mark the times that the *glyka tou koutaliou,* as well as the fruit preserves, are made. For the truly adept, spring roses are cultivated lovingly to make the *triantafyllo glyko,* a delicate rose-petal preserve; *vissina,* or sour cherries bathed in sugar, become one of the gems of the spoon sweets; watermelon rind, cleaned and cubed and firmed up in a wash of lime water, also expresses the nimbleness and skill of the preparer. Baby eggplants, cherry tomatoes, pistachios, walnuts, and quince, to name a few, all find their way into syrups, to be preserved for the winter months. Several unusual ingredients are used to preserve the color or the firmness of the fruits. *Alisiva,* a wood ash, and *asvestonero,* a calcium wash made from ground stone, are the traditional methods. Sometimes slaked lime is also used. (Most of the spoon sweet recipes that follow call for simple blanching.) Ammonium bicarbonate is also sometimes used in baking, in lieu of baking powder and soda.

The holiday sweets, especially those for Christmas and New Year's, are prepared with equal care and attention to detail. A week before Christmas, the dining room buffet begins to clutter with trays of honeyed delights. *Baklava, melomakarona* or *phoenikia* (sweet small honey cakes), *thiples* (crisp, fried bubbly dough dipped in honey and scattered with nuts), and a blinding array of powdered-sugar specialties including *kourambiethes* (Christmas shortbread) are piled high on trays, dishes, and serving platters.

Folklore and ritual are alive and well in these preparations, too. Many of the Christmas specialties are doused in a shower of confectioners' sugar, their whiteness representing hopes or wishes or prayers for a happy new year. Many of the specialties require nuts and sesame seeds, which are sometimes toasted. Their scent, delicious and inviting, is supposed to please—and appease—any mischievous imp or spirit lingering about the household. The scent of fried dough in the making of *thiples* or *xerotygana,* and *lalangia,* a Peloponnesian dough specialty, is supposed to have the same effect on naughty-minded spirits.

Sweets play an important part in another, fast-dying custom—the *Meloma tis Nifis,* or sweetening up of the bride by her mother-in-law. When the new bride first entered the home of her husband's family, she would sometimes dip her fingers in honey and make the sign of the cross—a prayer for mutual goodwill between mother-in-law and daughter-in-law. Sometimes the mother-in-law treated the bride to red sweets—grapes, roses, pomegranates—so that she might retain the colors of her youthful beauty. And sometimes the bride herself would throw a pomegranate with all her might into her new family's home; the seeds that broke out were counted as the happiness and wealth the newlywed couple would share.

The sweets in Greek cookery fall into several categories: confections, creams, and puddings; spoon sweets and preserves; cakes and biscuits; and honeyed fried doughs and stuffed or rolled phyllo pastries.

Fresh fruit is probably the only real dessert, in that it's almost universally served after a meal. If serving only fruit for dessert seems too plain, yet you still want to maintain a Greek flavor to the entire meal, try chopping the fruit and mixing it with yogurt, a few nuts (usually walnuts), and honey for a satisfying finish to your meal.

Chapter 16

Confections, Creams, and Puddings

Toula's Amigthalota

(ALMOND CONFECTIONS)

AMIGTHALOTA is sometimes the name given to almond macaroons, or, like below, to a delectable answer to the jellied *loukoumia* of the East.

_____

6 cups whole blanched
   almonds
6 cups sifted
   confectioners' sugar
2 to 3 tablespoons
   water, brandy, or
   rosewater

1. In a food processor, grind almonds to a mealy consistency. Reserve ½ cup of sugar and gradually add the remainder. Process until a smooth, malleable mass forms.

2. Place mixture in a medium-size bowl and work in liquid, a little at a time. Knead for several minutes until the paste is smooth and the flavor of the liquid is evenly distributed.

3. Place remaining sugar in a large tray or plate. Break off about 1 tablespoon at a time of almond paste and shape into balls or cigar shapes about ¾ inch wide. Roll in confectioners' sugar. Continue until all of the almond paste is used. To store, place in covered tins or boxes and keep in a cool dry place.

Yield: About 4 pounds

Variation: Two or three tablespoons cocoa may be added to the paste or to a portion of it during processing to make chocolate *amigthalota*.

Pastelli Androu

(WALNUT-HONEY CANDY, FROM ANDROS)

THIS dessert is simple to make yet always draws a rave review.

---

*2 cups coarsely ground
    walnuts*
*1 cup coarsely ground
    melba toast or
    toasted bread (not
    store-bought bread
    crumbs)*
Orange-blossom water
Sesame seeds
¼ cup sugar
¾ cup good honey

1. In a medium-size bowl, combine walnuts and bread crumbs and set aside until ready to use. Sprinkle the bottom of a 10-inch round pan with orange-blossom water and enough sesame seeds to cover the entire bottom surface.

2. In a medium-size saucepan, bring sugar and honey to a boil over medium heat and cook to the hard-ball stage (250–256°F on a candy thermometer). Remove pan from heat and immediately mix in walnut mixture, stirring somewhat vigorously with a wooden spoon.

3. Spread the mixture into the prepared pan either with your fingers or with a spatula dipped frequently in orange-blossom water. Douse the top with a layer of sesame seeds and let cool. This is best served the day after it's made. Store, covered, in a cool, dry place, and serve at room temperature.

Yield: One 10-inch round pan of candy

Pastelli me Sousame

(SESAME SEED–HONEY CANDY)

*Equal weight of
    sesame seeds and
    honey*
*Finely grated orange
    rind (1 scant
    teaspoon per 2 cups
    sesame seeds)*
Orange-blossom water

1. Spread sesame seeds on a baking sheet and toast in a 350°F oven for 5 to 10 minutes, or until lightly browned, being very careful not to burn. Seeds may also be toasted in an ungreased skillet over medium heat. When lightly toasted, toss seeds with orange rind in a small bowl. Sprinkle orange-blossom water on the bottom of a baking pan.

2. In a saucepan, boil honey to the hard-ball stage (250–256°F on a candy thermometer). Remove pan from heat and quickly stir in sesame seed mixture. Spread into prepared pan and pat down. Sprinkle with more orange-blossom water, if desired. Let stand, covered, 1 day at room temperature before serving. Store in a cool, dry place and break off as desired.

Soutzouk Loukoum

(STRUNG, CANDIED WALNUTS)

1. With a needle and thread, thread the walnuts together carefully, as many as desired, and set aside.

2. Prepare *moustalevria*. When the *moustalevria* comes to a boil and begins to thicken, dip the strung walnuts into the mixture several times until they are well coated. Let them cool. Gently remove walnuts from thread and serve as candy. Store in a box or wrapped in plastic in a cool, dry place.

Whole shelled walnuts
Moustalevria *(page 284)*

Rizogalo

(CREAMY RICE PUDDING)

1. In a large saucepan, combine rice, milk, sugar, and butter. Cook over low heat, stirring frequently, for 1 to 1½ hours, or until mixture is thick and creamy and the rice has absorbed the liquid and is soft. Add cinnamon stick about halfway through.

2. Just before removing the rice pudding from heat, beat egg yolks until creamy in a medium-size bowl. Discard cinnamon stick and stir in grated lemon rind. Remove the pudding from heat and stir in vanilla. Add a little pudding at a time to the egg yolks, stirring all the while, then pour egg yolks into pudding and stir well with a wooden spoon.

3. Pour the pudding into a large serving bowl or into individual bowls and refrigerate. Sprinkle with cinnamon before serving.

Yield: 10 to 12 servings

1 cup long-grain rice
6 cups milk
¾ cup sugar
1 tablespoon butter
1 small cinnamon stick
2 egg yolks, at room temperature
¼ teaspoon finely grated lemon rind
1 teaspoon vanilla extract
Ground cinnamon, for garnish

Halva Tis Rinas

(GOLDEN SEMOLINA PUDDING)

3 cups granulated
  sugar
4½ cups water
2 teaspoons strained
  fresh lemon juice
¼ cup pine nuts
  (optional)
¾ cup coarsely chopped
  blanched almonds
  or almond slivers
¼ pound unsalted
  butter
¼ cup olive oil
2 cups coarse semolina
  flour
2 teaspoons cinnamon,
  plus cinnamon and
  whole blanched
  almonds for garnish

1. In a medium-size pot, bring sugar and water to a boil over medium heat. Simmer, uncovered, for 10 minutes. Add lemon juice and simmer another minute. Remove pan from heat and cool slightly.

2. In an ungreased skillet over medium heat, toast pine nuts and almonds, stirring constantly, until very lightly browned, 1 to 2 minutes. Remove skillet from heat and cool.

3. In a large skillet or saucepan, heat butter and olive oil until they just begin to sizzle. Slowly add semolina, stirring constantly with a wooden spoon over low heat until semolina is lightly browned, about 10 minutes.

4. Add the toasted nuts and syrup very slowly to the semolina mixture, stirring with a wooden spoon. (Be careful not to burn yourself, as the mixture will bubble up rapidly). Sprinkle in 2 teaspoons cinnamon and stir over very low heat until the syrup is absorbed by the semolina and the mixture is thickened, 7 to 10 minutes. It should be congealed but grainy and honey colored. Remove the skillet from heat and pour the *halvah* into a gelatin mold. Cover with a cloth and cool until it's completely set. Unmold it, garnish by placing whole blanched almonds decoratively between the grooves, and sprinkle with cinnamon.

Yield: 10 to 12 servings

Halva Farsalon

(CARAMELIZED SUGAR AND RICE FLOUR PUDDING)

THIS sweet comes from Fársala in Thessaly. It is sold in huge round trays in bakeries in Vólos and in the streets of touristy towns on nearby Mount Pelion. It's a difficult sweet to make. If the rice flour is under-cooked, the halvah will taste raw and starchy; an overcooked mixture will not spread well and will be uneven in the pan. It takes a bit of practice.

---

1. In a large bowl, dissolve rice flour in warm water and stir to keep from clumping. Set aside, on top of the stove, to keep slightly warm.

2. In a large heavy pot, heat $\frac{1}{2}$ cup of the sugar over medium-low heat until it's a chestnut brown color and caramelized. Stir continuously while doing this. When the sugar has caramelized, slowly add the rice flour and water mixture, remaining 3 cups sugar, butter, and $\frac{1}{2}$ cup of the almonds. Beat with a wooden spoon and keep stirring the mixture over very low heat until it thickens and begins to have a rubbery consistency. Remove pot from heat immediately and spread into a 10-inch round pan. Sprinkle with remaining almond slivers and additional sugar, if desired. Let it set, covered, at room temperature. Store covered at room temperature.

5 cups warm water
2 cups rice flour (see Note)
3$\frac{1}{2}$ cups granulated sugar
$\frac{1}{4}$ pound plus 3 tablespoons unsalted butter
$\frac{3}{4}$ cup blanched almond slivers

Yield: 6 to 8 servings

Note: Rice flour may be found in Asian and Greek specialty food shops.

Moustalevria

(GRAPE MUST PUDDING)

7 cups strained must (see step 1)

1 cup fine semolina flour

Chopped walnuts or almonds or sesame seeds (optional)

Cinnamon

1. Follow the directions for making *petimezi* (page 293), disregarding the last step—the boiling of the grapes must to the large-thread stage. The grape juice should just be clarified (with wood ash or dry bread), allowed to stand overnight, strained, and cool.

2. In a medium-size bowl, mix 2 cups of the must with the semolina. Set aside. In a large pot, bring the remaining 5 cups must to a boil, reduce heat to low, and slowly add the semolina mixture, stirring constantly with a wooden spoon. Simmer the mixture until it reaches the soft-ball stage (234°F on a candy thermometer), stirring all the time. Remove pot from heat and pour into small, shallow bowls or into a shallow tray. Let it cool and set at room temperature. Serve sprinkled with either nuts or sesame seeds, and cinnamon.

Yield: 4 to 6 servings

Chapter 17

Spoon Sweets and Preserves

Verikoko Glyko Tou Koutaliou

(APRICOT SPOON SWEET)

2 teaspoons slaked
lime (available in
pharmacies or
specialty food stores)
1 quart cold water
2½ pounds firm, ripe
unblemished
apricots, washed,
peeled, halved, and
pitted
4 to 5 cups sugar
2 cups water
Strained fresh juice of
1 lemon

1. In a large bottle, combine slaked lime and water and shake very well. Allow lime to settle on bottom of bottle.

2. Place apricots in a large bowl and, using a strainer, pour lime water mixture over them, discarding the lime that is caught in the strainer. Let stand for 1 hour. Rinse apricots thoroughly in several washes of cold water and drain in a colander.

3. In a large pot, combine sugar and water. Bring to a boil over medium-low heat and simmer, uncovered, for 10 minutes. Add the drained apricots to the mixture and continue simmering for another 10 minutes. Remove pot from heat. Cover and let stand for 24 hours at room temperature.

4. The next day, remove apricots from syrup with a slotted spoon. Place pot back on burner and simmer syrup over medium-low heat until it reaches the large-thread stage (230°F on a candy thermometer). Add apricots and lemon juice to syrup and simmer another 3 to 4 minutes, or until the syrup binds with the fruits. Cool, place in airtight jars, and store in a cool, dark place. Serve like all other spoon sweets— on a small plate with a glass of ice water on the side.

Yield: About 1 quart

Karpouzi Glyko

(WATERMELON RIND SPOON SWEET)

1 pound watermelon rind, from a thick-skinned melon, cut into 1¼-inch square pieces (see Note)
Boiling water and ice water
Blanched almonds (as many as you have pieces of watermelon)
1 cup granulated sugar
1 cup honey
1 cup water
1 tablespoon lemon juice
2 tablespoons vanilla extract

1. Wash watermelon rind. Peel off tough outer green skin and cut away any of the fruit, to keep only the white part of the rind.

2. Add watermelon rind to boiling water to blanch for 3 to 4 minutes. Remove and drop pieces immediately into ice water. Drain the rind thoroughly in a colander, then wrap it in lint-free towels so that all the moisture can be absorbed. Let stand, wrapped, for 2 to 3 hours.

3. Remove the rind from the towels. Make a little slit in each piece and slip in one whole blanched almond.

4. In a large pot, combine the rind, sugar, and honey. Pour in the water. Bring the mixture to a boil, lower heat, and simmer, uncovered, until the rind is pearly and translucent and the syrup is thick, about 1 hour. Remove pot from heat, stir in lemon juice and vanilla, cool, and store in airtight jars.

Yield: About 1½ quarts

Note: The watermelon should be the early, thick-skinned ones. As a general rule, use an equal weight of rind and sugar or honey. Serve as with all spoon sweets—a few pieces dripping in their syrup offered on a plate with cold water or coffee on the side.

Kerasi Glyko

(CHERRY SPOON SWEET)

2½ pounds cherries
4 cups sugar
1 cup water
2 tablespoons strained fresh lemon juice

1. Wash cherries well and remove stems. Using either a cherry pitter or a sewing needle, remove pits, being careful to keep cherries intact.

2. In a large pot, bring sugar and water to a boil over medium heat and simmer for 5 minutes. Add cherries and simmer over medium heat for another 5 minutes. Remove pot from heat and let stand, covered with a cloth, for 24 hours at room temperature.

3. The next day, remove the cherries with a slotted spoon and place pot back on flame. Simmer syrup until it reaches the large-thread stage (230°F on a candy thermometer), and add cherries and lemon juice. Simmer for several more minutes, until the fruit and syrup bind.

Remove pan from heat, cool, and spoon cherry mixture into airtight jars. Store in a cool, dark place. To serve, pour several heaping teaspoons onto a small plate and serve with ice water on the side.

Yield: About 1 quart

Melitzanaki Glyko

(BABY EGGPLANT SPOON SWEET)

1. Wash eggplants thoroughly and remove stems. Using a sharp knife make a small slit lengthwise in each of the eggplants.

2. Place eggplants in a large bowl or basin with enough water to cover and 2 tablespoons of the lemon juice. Cover with a plate to keep the eggplants submerged and let stand for 1 hour. Rinse well and drain thoroughly.

3. Scald eggplants in a large pot with enough boiling water to cover. Remove eggplants from pot, drain immediately, and plunge into ice water. Drain and dry thoroughly on lint-free towels.

4. Gently slip 1 blanched almond into each of the eggplants.

5. In a large pot, combine sugar, honey, and 2½ cups water and heat over medium heat until sugar is dissolved. Add the cinnamon, cloves and orange peel; bring mixture to a boil, and simmer uncovered, over low heat for 15 to 20 minutes, until the syrup is heavy and thick. Add the eggplants and continue simmering another 5 to 7 minutes. Remove from heat, cool, cover, and let stand at room temperature for 24 hours.

6. The next day, remove the eggplants with a slotted spoon. (The almonds will be secured inside.) Heat the syrup over low to medium heat until it reaches the large-thread stage (230°F on a candy thermometer). Put the eggplants back into the syrup and simmer over low heat until syrup and eggplants bind, 20 to 25 minutes. The syrup should be thick enough to keep the eggplants suspended within it. Remove pot from heat, cool, and spoon mixture into airtight jars. Store in a cool dry place. As with all spoon sweets, serve several pieces and syrup on a small plate with a glass of ice water on the side.

2½ pounds firm baby eggplants (2 to 3 inches in length)
3 tablespoons strained fresh lemon juice
Blanched whole almonds
3½ cups sugar
¾ cup honey
2½ cups water
1 cinnamon stick
5 to 7 whole cloves
2 strips thin orange peel

Yield: About 2 quarts

Kythoni Glyko

(QUINCE SPOON SWEET)

3 pounds firm, sweet
  quince
4 cups water
Strained fresh juice of
  1 large lemon
6 cups sugar
4 to 5 rose geranium
  leaves (see Note), or
  2 teaspoons vanilla
  extract

1. Wash, peel, and grate quinces. In a large saucepan, bring grated quince, water, and 1 tablespoon lemon juice to a boil. Simmer for several minutes until quince is slightly softened.

2. Stir in sugar and simmer, uncovered, over low to medium heat until syrup thickens and binds with the fruit, about 1 hour. (It will be at the large-thread stage on a candy thermometer.) Add the remaining lemon juice, remove pot from flame, and stir in rose geranium leaves or vanilla. Cool and remove geranium leaves. Seal in airtight jars and store in a cool dark place. To serve, pour several teaspoons onto a small plate for each serving. Serve with ice water on the side.

Yield: About 1½ quarts

Note: If using scented geranium leaves, make sure they are free of pesticides and other chemicals.

Syko Glyko Tou Koutaliou

(FIG SPOON SWEET)

40 dried figs
⅓ cup brandy
3 cups water
2 cups sugar
6 to 7 whole cloves
Strained fresh juice of
  1 lemon
1 teaspoon vanilla
  extract (optional)

1. In a large bowl, soak the figs in brandy and 1 cup of the water for 3 to 4 hours at room temperature.

2. In a large pot, bring sugar and 2 cups water to a boil. Add cloves and simmer, uncovered, for 10 minutes. Remove the figs from marinade with a slotted spoon and add to the syrup. Simmer, uncovered, another 10 minutes. Remove pot from heat, cool, and let stand, covered with a cloth, overnight at room temperature.

3. The next day, bring the syrup and figs to a boil and simmer until the syrup reaches the large-thread stage (230°F on a candy thermometer). Add lemon juice 3 to 4 minutes before removing pot from heat. As soon as the pot is removed from the heat, stir in vanilla. Cool and store in a cool, dry place. To serve, spoon out a little onto a small plate and serve with ice water on the side.

Yield: About 1 quart

Pergamonto Glyko

(BERGAMOT RIND SPOON SWEET)

1. Gently grate the bergamots to release the oils from their skins.
2. Cut each bergamot lengthwise into four or six equal wedges. Remove and discard the fruit, keeping the rind intact. Cut each rind wedge in half lengthwise to form thin strips, about $\frac{1}{2}$ inch wide.
3. Place the rind in a large pot, cover with cold water, and bring to a boil. Remove rind from heat immediately, drain, and repeat the procedure two to four times more with fresh water to wash away all of the rind's bitterness. Measure the rind and measure out an equal volume of sugar and half as much water (e.g., 4 cups rind, 4 cups sugar, 2 cups water).
4. Curl each strip of rind into a little coil, and with a clean sewing needle and thread, sew through the center of each coil and string them together. (Make sure the ends of the chain are knotted.)
5. In a large saucepan, bring sugar and water to a boil and simmer, uncovered, for 10 minutes over medium heat. Add the rind chains and simmer for about another 10 minutes, until they're softened but not mushy, and a needle pierces them easily. Remove the rind from the syrup with a slotted spoon and set aside, but continue to simmer the syrup until it reaches the large-thread stage (230°F on a candy thermometer). Remove syrup from the heat and add the rind, still strung. When mixture has cooled completely, gently pull the strings from the rinds and store the sweet in airtight jars in a cool dark place. As with all spoon sweets, serve several pieces and syrup on a small plate with a glass of ice water on the side.

12 medium bergamots (pear-shaped oranges; see Note)
Sugar
Water
Strained fresh lemon juice

Yield: About 1 quart

Note: Bitter Seville oranges, *nerantzi* to the Greeks, or large thick-skinned navel oranges may be substituted for bergamot. The rind may also be grated with a zester into thin strips, in which case it wouldn't need to be strung together with thread.

Domatouli Glyko

(CHERRY TOMATO SPOON SWEET)

2½ *to 3 pounds firm*
  ripe cherry tomatoes
  (see Note)
Boiling water
Ice water
Blanched almond
  slivers (as many as
  there are tomatoes)
5 cups sugar (see
  Note)
4 to 5 whole cloves
1 small cinnamon
  stick
2 thin wedges of
  lemon rind
1 tablespoon strained
  fresh lemon juice
1 teaspoon vanilla
  extract

1. Wash tomatoes thoroughly. Scald in boiling water, drain, and drop immediately into ice water. Peel off skins and place tomatoes in a large bowl. With a sharp knife, make an incision in the underside of each tomato and squeeze gently to push out the seeds. Try not to push out too much of the pulp. Slip an almond sliver into each tomato.

2. Layer tomatoes alternately with sugar in a large bowl. Cover and let stand overnight at room temperature. The next day, drain off the sugar (it will be liquid) into a large saucepan. Bring to a boil, lower heat, add cloves, cinammon, and lemon rind, and simmer uncovered for about 15 minutes, until syrup falls in large droplets from a spoon.

3. Add the tomatoes to the syrup and continue simmering, uncovered, for 5 to 7 minutes. Stir in lemon juice, remove pot from heat and gently stir in vanilla. Cool in pot, spoon into an airtight jar, and store at room temperature in a cool, dry place. As with all spoon sweets, serve with syrup on a small plate with a glass of ice water on the side.

Yield: About 3 cups

Note: Tomatoes and sugar should be used in equal weight, should you wish to reduce or make more of this recipe.

Fistiki Aeginis Glyko

(PISTACHIO SPOON SWEET FROM AEGINA)

5 cups sugar
2½ *cups water*
2 thin (1-inch-wide)
  strips orange peel
2½ *to 3 cups shelled,*
  cleaned, unsalted
  pistachios
2 teaspoons strained
  fresh lemon juice
1 teaspoon rose water
  or orange-blossom
  water (optional), or
  1 teaspoon vanilla
  extract (optional)

1. In a medium-size pot, bring sugar, water, and orange peel to a boil. Lower heat and simmer, uncovered, for 10 minutes. Add pistachios, bring to a boil, and simmer, uncovered, over low heat for 3 minutes. Remove pot from heat, cover, and let stand at room temperature overnight.

2. The next day, bring the syrup and nuts to a boil and simmer, uncovered, until the syrup reaches the large-thread stage (230°F on a candy thermometer). Add lemon juice a minute or two before removing pot from heat. Remove pot from heat and add either rose water or vanilla, if desired. Cool and store in airtight jars in a dark, dry place. As with all spoon sweets, serve with syrup on a small plate with a glass of ice water on the side.

Yield: About 1 quart

Vissino

(SOUR CHERRY SPOON SWEET)

VISSINO probably reigns supreme among the spoon sweets. It's a treat most women will still go to the painstaking trouble to make each year in early summer when the luscious trees bear their succulent, tart berries.

---

1. Wash cherries very well. Using a cherry pitter or, for nimble hands, a sewing needle, push the pits out of the cherries.

2. In a large basin or bowl, arrange the cherries and sugar in alternate layers. Sprinkle with the water, cover, and refrigerate for at least 12 hours.

3. The next day, pour syrup and cherries into a large pot and bring to a boil over medium heat. Add the lemon juice and simmer, skimming off the foam at the top of the pot frequently, until the mixture is thick and at the large-thread stage. This will take 30 to 35 minutes over medium-low heat. Remove pot from heat, cool, and store in airtight jars. Serve *vissino* as with all spoon sweets, on a small plate in a sea of syrup with a glass of ice water on the side. *Vissino* is also wonderful over vanilla ice cream.

2½ pounds sour cherries
5 cups sugar
2 cups water
2 tablespoons lemon juice

Yield: About 1 quart

Variation: To make *vissinada,* or cherry cordial, just add 1 teaspoon of the sour cherry preserves and their syrup to a glass of ice water. It will turn a transparent dusty pink and is more than refreshing on a hot summer day.

Aunt Mary's Karythaki Glyko

(WALNUT SPOON SWEET)

THIS is among the most difficult and time-consuming of the spoon sweets to prepare. You'll need fresh English walnuts, unripe and green, and about ten days' patience. The dark greenish brown—almost black—color of this sweet might seem unsavory at first, but its taste is unforgettable. This is an Ikarian recipe from an aunt who lives by her garden's bounty.

---

*150 immature green
    English walnuts
Whole cloves
    (optional)
5 cups sugar
5 cups honey
1 to 3 cups water*

1. With a small sharp knife, remove the outer green husks of the walnuts. Using a clean heavy sewing needle, make a hole through the center of each walnut (through its length, from point to point). In a large pot, soak the walnuts in enough cold water to cover them by 3 or 4 inches for 8 days at room temperature. Change the water twice a day (once in the morning, and once at night). It will be black.

2. At the end of 8 days, drain the walnuts. Place them in a large enamel pot with enough cold water to cover them by 3 or 4 inches. Bring to a boil and simmer until the walnuts are soft enough to slip off a fork when punctured. Drain and lay the walnuts to dry on a lint-free towel for 24 hours. Stud the walnuts, if desired, with a whole clove at one end, after drying and before boiling them in syrup.

3. Place the walnuts, sugar, honey, and water in a large enamel pot and bring to a boil. Reduce the heat and simmer the mixture, uncovered, until the syrup reaches the large-thread stage (230°F on a candy thermometer). Remove pot from heat and let the walnuts stand overnight in the syrup. If the syrup is still thick the next day, the walnuts are ready to be stored in jars. But they will most likely have oozed some more of their own liquid overnight and the syrup will be loose. If this is the case, bring to a boil again and simmer to the large-thread stage. Let the walnuts sit overnight again and retest. Reboil if necessary. Cool the walnuts and syrup and store in airtight jars. As with all spoon sweets, serve on a small plate with a glass of ice water on the side.

Yield: About 2 quarts

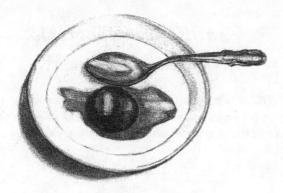

Petimezi

(GRAPE MUST SYRUP)

To make *petimizi,* use a minimum of 10 pounds of sweet grapes (with or without seeds). The grapes will yield about half their volume in juice. Ideally, you will also need wood ash or any clean ash (from the fireplace), *stahti* to the Greeks, a standard albeit disappearing component in many of the country's sweets. A piece of firm, very dry bread may also be used.

Wash grapes thoroughly and remove the stems, discarding any grapes that are bruised. Push the grapes through a food mill and place the milled grapes in a colander with a container underneath to catch the juice. When the grapes have drained, discard the pulp and seeds. To clarify the grapes, use 1 tablespoon wood ash or 1 piece very dry bread for every 5 cups must or juice. Tie either the ash or bread in a piece of muslin or white cotton cloth. Place the must and the sac in a large saucepan and bring to a boil. Simmer, uncovered, for 10 to 15 minutes. Remove the cloth from the pot and let the must stand, covered, overnight at room temperature. Pour out the juice very carefully the next day, discarding any ash residue that may have settled on the bottom of the pot.

In a separate clean pot, bring the must to a boil and simmer over medium heat until it reaches the large-thread stage (230°F on a candy thermometer). Remove pot from heat, cool, and pour must into jars. Store in a cool, dry place. Use *petimizi* in place of honey, if desired, and for making *moustalevria,* a pudding (page 284).

Yield: About 1 quart

Vanillia Yia Ipovrihio

(VANILLA SPOON SWEET)

IPOVRIHIO means submarine in Greek, and both *vanillia* and *mastiha* get their names because they're immersed in cold water, softened a bit, then sucked off the spoon. These are sweets for kids—and orthodontists.

---

6 cups sugar
3 cups water
1 tablespoon strained
   fresh lemon juice
2 teaspoons vanilla
   extract

1. In a large heavy saucepan, combine sugar, water, and lemon juice. Heat over low heat, stirring with a wooden spoon until sugar is dissolved. Cover pot and simmer for 3 minutes.

2. Remove cover and let syrup simmer for another 15 to 20 minutes, until it reaches the soft-ball stage (234–238°F on a candy thermometer).

3. While the syrup simmers, it's important to clean away the granules that accumulate on the side of the pot or that foam up at the top. To do this, wrap a small damp cloth carefully around a spoon or fork and continuously wipe clean the sides of the pot. Rinse and wet the cloth frequently. The sweet should be very smooth and pastelike, not in any way grainy or crystallized.

4. Once the syrup reaches the soft-ball stage, remove pan from heat and cool. (If you cover and submerge the pot in cold water, cooling will go faster.)

5. When the mixture is cooled but still slightly warm, work it with a wooden spoon until it whitens. Add the vanilla and work it in. Knead the mixture on a marble or nonstick surface until it's soft and malleable. It should be like a smooth thick paste. Place in a large airtight jar and let stand 24 hours before using. To serve an *ipovrihio,* take a spoonful of the paste and submerge it in ice water. The water will take on the faint scent of either vanilla or, as in *mastiha chiou,* mastic and the paste will soften slightly. Suck it slowly off the spoon. Store in a cool, dark place.

Yield: About 3 cups, or 25 to 30 heaping soup-spoon-size servings

Mastiha Chiou: Substitute 1 teaspoon finely ground mastic (available in crystal form in Greek and Middle Eastern food shops) for the vanilla in step 5.

Chapter 18

Biscuits and Cakes

Koulourakia me Kimino kai Sousami

(OLIVE OIL BISCUITS WITH CUMIN AND SESAME)

THIS recipe comes from Crete. The biscuits should be a comfortable size for dipping into morning coffee, the standard breakfast for most Greeks.

---

4 to 4½ cups
   all-purpose flour
2 teaspoons baking
   powder
2 teaspoons ground
   cumin
2 tablespoons finely
   grated orange rind
¼ teaspoon ground
   cloves
½ cup olive oil
½ cup sugar
3 eggs
½ cup strained fresh
   orange juice

1. In a medium-size bowl, stir together 4 cups flour, baking powder, cumin, orange rind, and cloves and set aside until ready to use.

2. In a large bowl and using an electric mixer set at high speed, beat the olive oil and sugar until creamy. Add 2 of the eggs, one at a time, and beat well with electric mixer after each. Pour in the orange juice and whip until all ingredients are well blended and mixture is smooth and creamy.

3. Add the flour mixture to the liquid in three separate batches, stirring well with a wooden spoon after each addition, until a dough mass begins to form. Turn the dough out onto a lightly floured surface and knead, using remaining ½ cup of flour if necessary, until smooth and soft, 7 to 8 minutes. Cover and refrigerate for 1 hour before using.

4. Remove the dough from the refrigerator and let stand at room temperature for about 30 minutes before using. Preheat oven to 350°F and lightly grease two cookie sheets.

5. Take a little piece of dough about the size of an unshelled walnut and roll it into a rope about 6 inches long and ⅓ inch wide. Repeat with remaining dough. It's important for all the *koulourakia* to be the same size to ensure even baking. Shape dough ropes as indicated in the illustration on page 295 and place about 1½ inches apart on the cookie sheets. Lightly beat remaining egg and brush over *koulourakia* as a glaze. Bake for 15 to 20 minutes, or until *koulourakia* are a light golden yellow. Remove sheets from oven and place on a wire rack to cool. Store completely cooled *koulourakia* in a cookie jar or in sealed containers.

Yield: 5 to 6 dozen

Koulourakia Methysmena

("INEBRIATED" BISCUITS)

1. In a medium-size bowl, sift together flour, baking powder, and salt; set aside.

2. In a large bowl and using an electric mixer set at high speed, beat the butter or margarine and sugar until creamy. Add 2 of the eggs, one at a time, and beat well with mixer after each addition. Drizzle in the ouzo and mix at low speed. Add the fennel seeds and ground mastic.

3. Add the flour mixture to the liquid in three separate batches, stirring well with a wooden spoon after each addition, until a dough mass begins to form. Turn the dough out onto a lightly floured surface and knead by hand until smooth and soft, 7 to 8 minutes. Cover and refrigerate for 1 hour before using.

4. Remove the dough from the refrigerator and let stand at room temperature for about 30 minutes before using. Preheat oven to 350°F and lightly grease two cookie sheets.

5. Take a little piece of dough about the size of an unshelled walnut and roll it into a rope about 6 inches long and $\frac{1}{3}$ inch wide. Repeat with remaining dough. It's important for all the *koulourakia* to be the same size to ensure even baking. Shape dough ropes as indicated in illustration (see page 295), and place about $1\frac{1}{2}$ inches apart on prepared cookie sheets. Lightly beat remaining egg and brush over *koulourakia* as a glaze. Bake for 15 to 20 minutes, until *koulourakia* are a deep golden yellow. Remove sheets from oven and place on a wire rack to cool. Store completely cooled in a cookie jar or in sealed containers. Serve with coffee.

$3\frac{1}{2}$ to 4 cups
  all-purpose flour
1 tablespoon baking
  powder
$\frac{1}{2}$ teaspoon salt
4 tablespoons unsalted
  butter or margarine
$\frac{1}{2}$ cup sugar
3 eggs
$\frac{1}{3}$ cup ouzo
$\frac{1}{2}$ teaspoon crushed
  fennel seeds
$\frac{1}{2}$ teaspoon ground
  mastic (optional)

Yield: 5 to 6 dozen

Moustokouloura

(GRAPE SYRUP BISCUITS)

THESE spicy, dark cookies come to market or are made at home in the fall, during the grape harvest, when the fruit is pressed for wine and there is plenty of grape must to spare for making *petimezi,* the thick syrup that is a component of these tangy, generally O-shaped delights.

4 to 5 cups all-purpose
   flour
1 scant teaspoon
   baking powder
$\frac{1}{2}$ teaspoon cinnamon
$\frac{1}{2}$ teaspoon ground
   cloves (or slightly
   less to taste)
$\frac{1}{2}$ teaspoon grated
   nutmeg
$\frac{1}{2}$ cup olive oil
2 tablespoons sugar
$\frac{3}{4}$ cup **petimezi** (page
   293; see Note)
$\frac{1}{3}$ cup water

1. Lightly grease several cookie sheets. Preheat oven to 350°F.
2. In a large bowl, sift 4 cups flour, baking powder, and spices and set aside until ready to use.
3. In a large bowl and using an electric mixer set at high speed, beat the olive oil and sugar until creamy. Slowly add *petimezi* and beat with electric mixer for about 10 minutes. Add the water and beat another 5 minutes.
4. Add the sifted flour mixture to the liquid and stir with a wooden spoon until a dough begins to form. Knead the dough in the bowl until it is soft and malleable.
5. Take a little dough at a time, a bit smaller than an unshelled walnut, and roll it into a thin rope, 4 to 6 inches long. Form a circle with it, or shape as desired into braids, curls, or mounds (see illustration, page 295). Place on prepared cookie sheets, about $1\frac{1}{2}$ inches apart, and bake for 12 to 15 minutes, until crisp. Cool on racks and store completely cooled in jars or tins in a cool, dry place.

Yield: About 4 dozen

Note: *Petimezi* may be found in Greek and Middle Eastern food shops.

Koulourakia Lambriatika

(EASTER BISCUITS)

WITH *tsoureki* (page 60) and some of the sweet cheese specialties, these are a staple on the Easter table, and are dunked into breakfast coffee for weeks after the holiday.

---

1. Preheat oven to 350°F.
2. In a medium-size bowl, sift together flour, baking powder, and salt.
3. In a large bowl and using an electric mixer set at high speed, beat the butter and sugar until light and fluffy. Add eggs, one at a time, beating well with electric mixer after each, then beat in milk. Slowly add the orange and lemon rinds and vanilla and continue to beat. Slowly add flour to the liquid and beat until a dough mass begins to form. Remove to a lightly floured surface, and knead until a smooth soft dough forms. Let the dough rest 10 minutes before shaping the *koulourakia*.
4. Break off a heaping tablespoon at a time of dough. Roll into ropes about 6 inches long. Braid, or shape as desired into "S" curves, rings, twists, or mounds. All *koulourakia* should be about the same size to ensure even baking. Place on an ungreased baking sheet. Lightly beat egg yolk with orange juice and brush over *koulourakia* to glaze. Sprinkle with sesame seeds and bake for 15 to 20 minutes, until golden. Cool on wire racks and store sealed in a jar or airtight container in a cool, dark place.

Yield: About 4 dozen

3½ cups bread flour
1 tablespoon baking powder
½ teaspoon salt
¼ pound plus 4 tablespoons butter, at room temperature
¾ cup sugar
2 eggs
½ cup milk
1 teaspoon grated orange rind
1 teaspoon grated lemon rind
1 teaspoon vanilla extract
1 egg yolk, plus 1 to 2 tablespoons strained fresh orange juice for glaze
Sesame seeds

Kostia's Kourambiethes

(CHRISTMAS SHORTBREAD)

KOURAMBIETHES are the traditional Greek Christmas shortbread. They should melt in your mouth and leave a lingering taste of fresh sweet butter and almonds. They're dusted heavily with powdered sugar, the whiteness representing wishes for good fortune and happiness in the coming year. Experience will teach you the exact silky feel of the dough for the cakes to turn out just short of the crumbling point. They should be fragile enough to disappear in your mouth, but firm enough to stay intact when holding them. The butter is one part of the secret. Some cooks whip it for nearly 45 minutes for the proper texture to result. Here, pre-whipped butter is used, and the whipping time is decidedly shorter, but the results just as delicious.

---

10 ounces blanched
  almonds
1 pound prewhipped
  sweet unsalted
  butter
2 egg yolks
3 to 4 cups plus $\frac{1}{4}$ cup
  sifted confectioners'
  sugar
$\frac{1}{2}$ teaspoon baking
  powder
1 shot glass of scotch
  and cognac or
  Bristol cream
2 to $2\frac{1}{2}$ cups sifted
  all-purpose flour

1. Preheat oven to 350°F. Lightly toast the almonds either in an ungreased skillet over low heat or in the oven. They should be a very light golden brown. Do not burn. Chop well and set aside.

2. In a large bowl and using an electric mixer set at high speed, beat butter, egg yolks, $\frac{1}{4}$ cup of the confectioners' sugar, and baking powder until smooth and creamy, 6 to 9 minutes. Add almonds and scotch mixture and beat for another 4 to 5 minutes, until smooth.

3. Add $1\frac{3}{4}$ cups of the sifted flour to the butter mixture and knead by hand. Add remaining flour in $\frac{1}{4}$-cup increments until just enough flour has been added to make a silky, smooth dough that doesn't stick to your hands. Knead for 5 to 8 minutes.

4. Take a little piece of dough about the size of an unshelled walnut and shape it into a mounded conical round, oblong, or oval. Repeat with remaining dough. Place on an ungreased cookie sheet about 1 inch apart and bake for 10 to 12 minutes, or until *kourambiethes* are a pale yellowish golden color. They should not be golden brown or chestnut-hued.

5. Remove cookie sheet from oven and place *kourambiethes* on a wire rack. Cool slightly, then sift 3 to 4 cups confectioners' sugar over *kourambiethes* until they are completely doused. Store *kourambiethes* in tins.

Yield: About 4 dozen

Melomakarona or Phoenikia

(SYRUP-DUNKED SEMOLINA AND NUT COOKIES)

1. In a medium-size bowl, sift together 2½ cups flour and baking powder; set aside.

2. In a large bowl and using an electric mixer set at high speed, beat butter and shortening until soft and creamy. Add olive oil, beating all the while, and slowly beat in sugar. Slowly add wine and orange juice and continue beating with mixer. Sprinkle in spices and orange rind, beating with mixer to combine. Add the flour mixture to the liquid in three separate batches, stirring vigorously with a wooden spoon after each addition, until a dough mass forms. Turn the dough out onto a lightly floured surface and knead, adding more flour, if necessary, until dough is soft and malleable. Cover and let the dough rest for 30 minutes before using.

3. Prepare filling, if desired, by combining chopped walnuts and honey. Preheat oven to 350°F.

4. Knead dough for 3 to 5 minutes longer before using. Take a little piece of dough about the size of a small egg and shape it into a conical oblong about 2½ inches long by 1 inch high. The top should be gently rounded. Repeat with remaining dough. If desired, fill *melomakarona* with walnut filling: Flatten each oblong and press the center gently to make a small well. Add a scant teaspoon to center and press dough around it to seal. Adjust the shape to make it a smooth rounded oblong again. Place *melomakarona* on an ungreased cookie sheet and bake in the center of the oven until golden, 20 to 25 minutes. Remove cookie sheet from oven and place on a wire rack to cool (see Note).

5. *To prepare syrup:* While *melomakarona* are cooling, in a medium-size saucepan, combine the sugar, honey, and water and bring to a boil. Add orange zest and simmer for 10 to 12 minutes. Remove saucepan from heat and add lemon juice. Dip the *melomakarona* in the syrup with a slotted spoon and allow the cakes to soak up the syrup and to moisten. Remove and place on a serving dish or tray. Sprinkle when still wet with ground walnuts. *Melomakarona* may be made in advance and dipped into piping hot syrup just before serving. Store in tins or cookie jars at room temperature.

Yield: About 2 to 3 dozen

2¼ to 3 cups all-purpose flour, sifted, or an equal measure of semolina and all-purpose flour
1¼ teaspoon baking powder
4 tablespoons butter
6 tablespoons shortening
2 to 3 tablespoons olive oil
¼ cup sugar
¼ cup dry white wine
¼ cup strained fresh orange juice
1 teaspoon cinnamon
½ teaspoon ground cloves
Grating of nutmeg
Chopped grated rind of 1 orange
⅓ pound walnuts, chopped (optional)
½ cup honey (optional)
½ cup ground walnuts

SYRUP
2 cups sugar
½ cup honey
2¼ cups water
1 strip orange zest
2 teaspoons strained fresh lemon juice

Revani Verrias

(RICH SEMOLINA AND SYRUP CAKE FROM VERRIA)

THIS recipe stands in humble deference to the real thing: *revani Hohliourou,* which is a specialty of Kyrios Hohliouros, proprietor of a small, plain shop in the old part of Verria, one of Greece's better-preserved northern cities. The shop sells nothing but trays and trays of *revani,* which the proprietor cuts into long thin rows and wraps in a nondescript parcel of wax paper for the lines of people who are always waiting, inside and out.

SYRUP
3 cups water
1½ cups sugar
1 cinnamon stick
1 tablespoon brandy

CAKE
½ pound butter
1½ cups sugar
6 eggs, separated
1 tablespoon cognac
1 tablespoon strained
    fresh orange juice
2 cups coarse semolina
    flour
1 tablespoon baking
    powder
½ cup finely ground
    blanched almonds

1. *To prepare syrup:* In a medium-size saucepan, bring water and sugar to a boil. Add cinnamon stick and brandy and simmer for 5 to 7 minutes over medium heat. Remove pan from heat and let stand until cool.

2. Preheat oven to 375°F and lightly butter either a 10-inch round springform or 9 × 12 × 3-inch cake pan.

3. *To prepare cake:* In a large bowl and using an electric mixer set at high speed, beat butter until creamy. Gradually add sugar and continue beating. Add egg yolks, one at a time, and beat well after each addition. Beat in cognac. Gradually sift semolina and baking powder into mixture and add ground almonds, beating all the while, until all ingredients are well blended.

4. In a separate bowl and using an electric mixer, whip egg whites until soft peaks form. Gently, rapidly, and thoroughly fold the egg whites into the semolina mixture. Pour into prepared baking pan and bake for 30 to 35 minutes, or until *revani* is dark golden brown and a thin, soft spongy layer has formed on top.

5. Remove pan from oven and place on a wire rack. Gently score the cake by drawing a sharp knife first vertically down the length of the pan and then diagonally in order to form diamonds. Pour cooled syrup over *revani* immediately, distributing it evenly. Cool in pan and serve warm or at room temperature. Store sealed in a cool, dry place, or in the refrigerator.

Yield: 8 to 12 servings

Karythopitta

(RICH WALNUT TORTE)

ALTHOUGH it's not customary in Greece to serve wine with dessert, this cake is wonderful washed down with fragrant Samos muscat.

---

1. *To prepare syrup:* In a heavy saucepan, heat the sugar, honey, and water over medium heat. When the sugar is dissolved, add cloves and simmer uncovered for 5 minutes. Stir in lemon juice just before removing from heat. Remove cloves, remove pan from heat, and cool completely.

2. Preheat oven to 350°F. Lightly butter a 9- or 10-inch round springform pan.

3. *To prepare cake:* In a medium-size bowl, stir together walnuts, zwieback crumbs, flour, baking powder, cinnamon, cloves, and orange rind and set aside until ready to use.

4. In a medium-size bowl and using an electric mixer set at high speed, beat butter and sugar until light and fluffy. Add 1 egg yolk at a time and beat well after each addition. Beat in half the nut mixture. Beat in milk, a tablespoon at a time, using only enough to keep the mixture moist.

5. Using an electric mixer set at high speed, beat egg whites (including the 2 additional whites) until firm peaks form and egg whites are stiff. Quickly fold egg whites and remaining nut mixture into batter so that all ingredients are evenly and rapidly blended. This is best done by hand. Pour the mixture into prepared springform pan and bake for about 40 minutes, or until the *karythopitta* is dark golden brown and a cake tester inserted in its center comes out clean.

6. Remove pan from oven and place on a wire rack. Pour the cool syrup over the hot cake, cover it with a cloth, and let it cool in pan. Cut into diamonds or wedges and serve. Store either refrigerated or at room temperature, covered.

Yield: 8 to 10 servings

SYRUP
¾ cup sugar
½ cup honey
1 cup water
4 to 5 whole cloves
1 tablespoon strained fresh lemon juice

CAKE
2¼ cups finely ground walnuts
¾ cup finely crushed zwieback biscuits
¼ cup sifted, all-purpose flour
2 teaspoons baking powder
1 teaspoon cinnamon
½ teaspoon ground cloves
1 teaspoon grated orange rind
5⅓ tablespoons butter
¼ cup sugar
4 eggs, separated, plus 2 egg whites
¼ cup milk

Keik me Tahini

(LENTEN CAKE WITH SESAME PASTE)

$1\frac{3}{4}$ *cups all-purpose flour*
2 *scant teaspoons cinammon*
1 *teaspoon ground cloves*
Grating of nutmeg
Pinch of salt
2 *tablespoons grated orange rind*
2 *teaspoons baking powder*
$\frac{1}{4}$ *teaspoon baking soda*
$\frac{1}{2}$ *cup tahini (sesame paste)*
1 *cup strained fresh orange juice*
$\frac{1}{2}$ *cup water*
$\frac{1}{4}$ *cup honey*
$\frac{1}{2}$ *teaspoon vanilla extract*
Confectioners' sugar (optional)

1. Preheat oven to 350°F. Lightly grease a 10-inch springform pan.
2. In a large bowl, sift together flour, cinnamon, cloves, nutmeg, salt, orange rind, baking powder, and soda and set aside. Place tahini in a large bowl and with an electric mixer set at high speed, alternately and slowly add half of the orange juice, then half of the water, then half of the honey and vanilla. Repeat with remaining liquids and vanilla, and continue whipping at high speed until ingredients are thoroughly mixed. (Since there are no eggs in this Lenten cake, beating it very well will add some volume.)
3. Slowly add flour to tahini mixture (in increments of about $\frac{1}{4}$ cup) and beat well with electric mixer after each addition. Batter will be thick but liquid. Pour into prepared baking pan and bake for 40 to 45 minutes, until cake is golden and a tester inserted in center comes out clean. Remove pan from oven and let cake cool in pan before serving. Sprinkle, if desired, with confectioners' sugar.

Yield: 8 to 10 servings

Bobota

(CORNMEAL CAKE FROM EPIRUS)

$1\frac{3}{4}$ *cups fine yellow cornmeal*
$1\frac{1}{4}$ *cups all-purpose flour*
2 *heaping teaspoons baking powder*
$\frac{1}{2}$ *teaspoon baking soda*
Pinch of salt
$\frac{1}{2}$ *cup olive oil*
$\frac{1}{4}$ *cup sugar*

1. Preheat oven to 350°F. Lightly grease a 10-inch springform pan.
2. In a large bowl, sift together cornmeal, flour, baking powder, baking soda, and salt. In a medium-size bowl and using an electric mixer set at high speed, beat together olive oil and sugar until creamy. Slowly add orange juice and continue beating with electric mixer. Add raisins, rinds, and vanilla and continue beating. Spoon in flour mixture slowly, beating with electric mixer until a thick batter forms. It should be as thick as pudding, but grainy from the cornmeal. Pour into prepared pan, smooth out the top with a spatula or cake icer, and bake for 35 to 40 minutes, until cake is deep golden yellow and a cake tester inserted in its center comes out clean.

3. *To prepare syrup:* While cake is baking, in a medium-size saucepan, bring sugar and water to a boil. Lower heat and simmer, uncovered, for 12 to 15 minutes, adding lemon juice during last 5 minutes. Remove cake from oven when done. Syrup will be slightly cooled by then; slowly pour it over cake in pan. Cover with a cloth and let sit for about 1 hour before removing from pan.

Yield: 8 to 10 servings

$1\frac{1}{2}$ cups orange juice
$\frac{1}{2}$ cup light raisins
2 tablespoons grated
  orange rind
1 to 2 teaspoons grated
  lemon rind
1 teaspoon vanilla
  extract
SYRUP
$1\frac{1}{4}$ cups sugar
$1\frac{1}{2}$ cups water
1 teaspoon strained
  fresh lemon juice

Olive Oil Cake

1. Preheat oven to 350°F. Lightly grease a 9-inch bundt pan.
2. In a medium-size bowl, sift together flour, baking powder, soda, and salt. Set aside.
3. In a large bowl and using an electric mixer set at high speed, beat the olive oil and sugar until creamy. Slowly add the orange juice, grated rinds, and vanilla; continue beating with electric mixer. Beat in raisins. Slowly add the flour to the liquids, mixing with a wooden spoon until a thick batter forms. Beat egg whites in a separate bowl until stiff and fold into batter. Pour batter into prepared baking pan and bake for 50 minutes to 1 hour, or until cake is golden and springy. Remove pan from oven. Cool in pan for 10 minutes, then remove cake from pan and cool on a rack. Dust with confectioners' sugar before serving.

Yield: 8 to 10 servings

$2\frac{1}{2}$ cups all-purpose
  flour
1 teaspoon baking
  powder
$\frac{1}{2}$ teaspoon baking
  soda
Pinch of salt
$\frac{1}{2}$ cup light olive oil
$\frac{3}{4}$ cup sugar
1 cup strained fresh
  orange juice
2 teaspoons grated
  orange rind
1 teaspoon grated
  lemon rind
1 teaspoon vanilla
  extract
$\frac{1}{2}$ cup raisins
3 egg whites
Confectioners' sugar

Yiaourtini

(YOGURT CAKE WITH ORANGE LIQUEUR)

$1\frac{3}{4}$ cups all-purpose
  flour
2 teaspoons baking
  powder
$\frac{1}{4}$ teaspoon baking
  soda
Pinch of salt
$\frac{1}{4}$ pound plus 4
  tablespoons unsalted
  butter
$\frac{1}{3}$ cup honey
$\frac{1}{4}$ cup granulated
  sugar
2 eggs, separated
3 tablespoons strained
  fresh orange juice
2 tablespoons orange
  liqueur (or brandy)
1 tablespoon grated
  orange rind
1 cup plain yogurt
  (sheep's-milk
  yogurt, if available)
Confectioners' sugar

1. Preheat oven to 350°F. Lightly butter and dust with flour a 9-inch bundt pan.

2. In a medium-size bowl, sift together flour, baking powder, soda, and salt.

3. In a large bowl and using an electric mixer set at medium to high speed, beat the butter until light and fluffy. Add the honey and sugar and continue beating until creamy. Add the egg yolks, one at a time, beating well with electric mixer after each addition. Slowly add orange juice, liqueur, and rind and beat well with mixer at medium–high speed after each addition.

4. Continuing with electric mixer, gradually beat flour mixture and yogurt into the butter mixture, alternating between each until well blended.

5. In a separate bowl, beat egg whites with electric mixer at high speed until stiff. Fold into batter.

6. Pour batter into prepared baking pan and bake for 45 minutes to 1 hour, or until cake is golden and springs back when pressed. Remove pan from oven and place on a wire rack to cool for a few minutes in pan, then turn out cake onto rack to cool. Dust with confectioners' sugar when completely cool.

Yield: 8 to 10 servings

Samali

(SEMOLINA, ALMOND, AND ORANGE CAKE WITH SYRUP)

THIS semolina and syrup cake is similar to *revani* (page 302) but is generally not as fluffy.

---

1. Lightly butter a 9- or 10-inch springform pan. Preheat oven to 350°F.

2. In a large bowl and using an electric mixer set at high speed, beat butter and sugar together until smooth and creamy, at least 5 minutes. Add the eggs, one at a time, beating well with electric mixer after each addition. Gradually add semolina, almonds, cinnamon, and orange rind to the butter mixture, alternating among each until well blended. The batter should be fairly thick.

3. Pour batter into prepared pan and bake for 30 to 40 minutes, or until a cake tester inserted into the center comes out clean.

4. *To prepare syrup:* While cake is baking, in a small saucepan, bring the sugar and water to a boil and simmer for 5 minutes over medium heat. Add the lemon juice about 2 minutes before removing pan from heat. Cover to keep hot.

5. When cake is done, remove pan from oven and pour the warm syrup over the hot cake in the pan. Cover with a cloth until completely cooled. Score it into diamonds and serve.

Yield: 8 to 10 servings

$\frac{1}{4}$ **pound plus 3 tablespoons unsalted butter**
$\frac{1}{3}$ **cup sugar**
4 large eggs plus two whites
1 cup fine semolina flour
1 cup finely ground blanched almonds
1 teaspoon cinnamon
Grated rind of 1 orange
SYRUP
1$\frac{1}{2}$ cups sugar
1$\frac{1}{4}$ cups water
1 teaspoon strained fresh lemon juice

Chapter 19

Stuffed and Rolled Pastries and Phyllo Specialites

——HONEY-DIPPED FRITTERS——

Xerotygana or Thiples

(CRISP, FRIED, HONEY-DIPPED DOUGH)

IF there's anything that evokes childhood memories for me, it's the mountainous platters of *xerotygana* my dad used to fry up every Christmas Eve. These are a holiday specialty.

_____

1. *To prepare dough:* In a medium-size bowl, sift together 2 cups of the flour, baking powder, and baking soda and set aside until ready to use.

2. In a large bowl and using a wire whisk (or an electric mixer set at low speed), beat eggs until frothy and pale yellow in color, 2 to 4 minutes. In a small bowl, stir together sugar, orange juice, and vanilla. Slowly add the sugar mixture to the eggs, beating all the while. Add the butter last, still beating until mixture is fluffy.

3. Add the flour mixture to the egg mixture and beat gently until a dough mass begins to form. Turn the dough out onto a lightly floured surface and knead, adding more flour if necessary, until dough is smooth and elastic, about 10 minutes. Let dough rest, covered, for a few minutes.

4. *To prepare syrup:* In the meantime, combine water, sugar, and honey in a large saucepan. Bring to a boil over medium heat; reduce heat and simmer, uncovered, for 15 minutes.

5. Using a sharp knife, divide the dough into three equal balls and roll each, one at a time, into a thin sheet. There should be some weight to the dough sheets; they shouldn't be paper-thin and translucent, but about as thick as noodles.

6. Cut each sheet into strips $1\frac{1}{2}$ to 2 inches long. (The length may be cut diagonally to make trapezoid or diamond shapes; see Note.) Keep them covered with a towel to prevent them from drying out while you heat the oil. In a deep heavy pot, heat 4 to 5 inches of pure, light olive oil. When the oil reaches 360°F, add the *xerotygana,* one or a few at a time. It's important that the oil maintain a steady temperature of about 360°F. Fry them for only a few seconds and remove with either a slotted spoon or tongs. They'll bubble immediately in the hot oil and should still be yellow in color—not too brown—when they are removed from the oil. Drain on paper towels and cool on wire racks. Dip in warm syrup and sprinkle generously with nuts and cinnamon or sesame seeds, or dust with sifted confectioners' sugar. Pile them high and eat them for days on end.

Yield: 4 to 5 dozen

Note: *Xerotygana* can be made in several shapes: bows, knots, rolls, plain strips, and folds.

DOUGH

2 to $2\frac{1}{2}$ cups
    all-purpose flour
$\frac{1}{2}$ teaspoon baking
    powder
$\frac{1}{2}$ teaspoon baking
    soda
4 eggs, at room
    temperature
1 to 2 tablespoons
    granulated sugar
$\frac{1}{4}$ cup strained fresh
    orange juice
1 teaspoon vanilla
    extract
2 tablespoons butter

SYRUP

$1\frac{1}{2}$ cups water
$2\frac{1}{4}$ cups sugar
$\frac{3}{4}$ cup honey

Light olive oil, for
    frying
Coarsely ground
    walnuts
Ground cinnamon,
    sesame seeds, or
    confectioners' sugar
    (optional)

Loukoumathes

(SPONGY, HONEY-DIPPED BATTER-FRITTERS)

ACCORDING to folk wisdom, if *loukoumathes* aren't made for St. Andrew's Day, on November 30, St. Andrew may retaliate by making holes in your skillet!

DOUGH
3 cups bread flour
½ teaspoon salt
1 envelope active dry yeast
1 to 1½ cups warm water
SYRUP
1 cup water
1½ cups sugar
½ cup honey

Vegetable oil, for frying
Ground cinnamon

1. *To prepare dough:* In a medium-size bowl, sift together flour and salt and make a well in center. Dissolve yeast in ½ cup warm water and add to flour. Stir with a wooden spoon until a thick batter forms, adding a little more water, if necessary. This should not be a dough, but a thick batter that falls off the tip of a spoon. Cover and let rise for about 2 hours, until doubled in bulk.

2. *To prepare syrup:* About 30 minutes before frying *loukoumanthes,* combine water, sugar, and honey in a saucepan. Bring to a boil. Lower heat and simmer for 15 minutes.

3. In a large heavy pot, heat 4 to 5 inches of oil to 360–365°F. Take 1 heaping teaspoon of the dough at a time and push it into the hot oil with another teaspoon. The *loukoumathes* will expand and puff up and rise to the surface of the oil. Remove with a slotted spoon when light golden brown in color. Drain on paper towels and douse, while still warm, with syrup. Sprinkle with cinnamon and serve warm as a snack.

Yield: 2 to 3 dozen

Sfiggoi

(DOUGH PUFFS)

SFIGGOI (pronounced sveengy) are the Greek equivalent to French *beignets*. They're similar to *loukoumathes* (opposite page), except that the dough recipe is the basic one for *pâte à choux*. Serve them with warmed honey or dust with confectioners' sugar.

---

1. In a medium-size saucepan, bring water, salt, and butter to a rolling boil. All at once, pour in flour.

2. Stir the mixture constantly with a wooden spoon until the paste pulls away from the sides of the pot in one mass or ball.

3. Remove pan from heat and let it cool for several minutes, until the paste reaches about 140°F. Once the paste is 140°F, beat each egg slightly and add, one at a time, to the paste. Stir rapidly after adding each egg until it is completely absorbed. Beat until the dough is shiny.

4. In a deep heavy pot, heat 2 to 3 cups vegetable oil to 375°F. Break off rounded teaspoons of the *choux* paste and drop into the hot oil. Fry until deep golden brown and puffed. Remove *sfiggoi* with a slotted spoon and drain on paper towels. Sprinkle with confectioners' sugar or dip in honey before serving.

1 cup water
¼ teaspoon salt
¼ pound unsalted butter
1 cup sifted bread flour
4 eggs
Vegetable oil, for frying

Yield: About 2½ dozen

—NUT-STUFFED PASTRIES—

Thaktyla Kypriaka

(CYPRUS LADY FINGERS)

SYRUP
2 cups sugar
$\frac{1}{4}$ cup honey
$1\frac{1}{2}$ cups water
2 pieces lemon zest
2 tablespoons rose water
2 teaspoons strained fresh lemon juice
DOUGH
$2\frac{1}{2}$ to 3 cups all-purpose flour
$\frac{1}{4}$ teaspoon salt
$\frac{1}{4}$ cup butter
2 tablespoons vegetable shortening
4 to 6 tablespoons water
1 egg yolk
FILLING
1 egg white
2 tablespoons sugar
$\frac{1}{2}$ pound almonds, coarsely ground
2 teaspoons cinnamon
$\frac{1}{2}$ teaspoon crushed whole cloves

Vegetable oil
$\frac{1}{2}$ cup ground blanched almonds combined with 1 teaspoon cinnamon

1. *To prepare syrup:* In a medium-size saucepan, dilute the sugar and honey with water and bring to a gentle boil over medium heat. Add lemon zest and rose water. Simmer for 1 to 5 minutes. About 1 minute before removing pot from heat, stir in lemon juice. Set aside to cool completely, uncovered.

2. *To prepare dough:* In a large bowl, sift together flour and salt and make a well in center. Work in butter and vegetable shortening with your fingers until dough is mealy. Add 2 tablespoons of the water and egg yolk and mix with your fingertips until the mixture begins to form into a dough mass. Add remaining water, a little at a time, until a soft dough begins to form. Turn the dough out onto a lightly floured surface and knead until it's silky and malleable. Cover and let rest for 1 hour before using.

3. *To prepare filling:* Just before rolling out dough, in a medium-size bowl, whip together the egg white and sugar until a stiff meringue forms. Fold in the almonds, cinnamon, and cloves with a fork so that all ingredients are well blended.

4. To make the *thaktyla,* roll out the dough to a thin, almost translucent sheet. (A pasta maker would expedite this.) Cut it into long strips about 2 inches wide and cut each strip at $3\frac{1}{2}$-inch intervals to make little rectangles. Have ready a small bowl of water and a fork. Dot the bottom center of dough, on its 2-inch side, with about $\frac{1}{2}$ teaspoon of filling. Roll up, lengthwise, as shown in the illustration on the opposite page. Dip the fork in water and use it to press the ends of the dough closed, pulling it gently with your fingers as much as possible to stretch the *thaktyla.* They should be about the length of a woman's forefinger. Press closed with the prongs of a fork to make serrated edges.

5. Heat the oil to 360°F and fry the *thaktyla.* Remove with a slotted spoon and drain briefly on paper towels; dip immediately in the syrup and sprinkle with additional chopped almonds. Serve warm or at temperature.

Yield: 30 to 40

Folding thaktyla Kypriaka (page 312) and tourtes Karpathou (page 320).

Patoutha

(NUT- AND HONEY-FILLED PASTRIES FROM CRETE)

PATOUTHA, a specialty of Crete, are similar to other stuffed pastries, especially *skaltsounia karpathou* (page 316), except that the filling is fairly moist.

DOUGH

3 cups all-purpose flour
½ teaspoon salt
½ teaspoon baking soda
¼ cup pure olive oil
6 tablespoons butter
2 tablespoons strained fresh lemon juice
⅓ cup strained fresh orange juice
¼ cup brandy

FILLING

½ cup honey
¼ cup water
1 cup ground blanched almonds
1 cup chopped walnut meats
½ teaspoon nutmeg
1 teaspoon cinnamon
½ teaspoon ground cloves

Sifted confectioners' sugar

1. *To prepare dough:* In a medium-size bowl, sift together flour, salt, and baking soda. In a large bowl, beat together oil and butter. Slowly add juices and brandy. Slowly add flour mixture, beating with an electric mixer until dough begins to form. Knead in bowl or on a floured surface until soft and malleable; set aside to rest for ½ hour. Preheat oven to 350°F.

2. *To prepare filling:* In a small saucepan, bring honey and water to a boil, reduce heat, and simmer for 3 to 5 minutes. In a large bowl, combine nuts and spices and pour in warm honey mixture. Stir with a wooden spoon so that the honey is distributed evenly among all the nuts. The mixture should be fairly loose.

3. Break off little pieces of dough—about the size of an unshelled walnut—and roll them into 3- or 4-inch squares or circles. Place a heaping teaspoon of nut mixture in the center of each dough segment. If making circles, fold over to form crescents, press the edges together with dampened fingers, and use a pastry wheel to seal decoratively (see illustration on page 317). If making squares, fold the four corners of the square toward the center as shown in the illustration on page 315. Press gently with dampened fingers to seal.

4. Bake on ungreased cookie sheets for 15 to 20 minutes, or until pastry is golden brown. Remove cookie sheets from oven and place on a wire rack. Cool *patoutha* slightly and dust with confectioners' sugar before serving. Serve warm or at room temperature.

Yield: 3 to 4 dozen

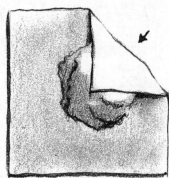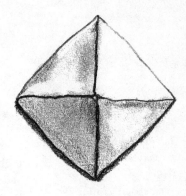

Folding squares, for patoutha (page 314) and skaltsouria Karpathou (page 316).

Irini's Skaltsounia Karpathou

(NUT- AND SESAME-FILLED PASTRIES FROM KARPATHOS)

DOUGH
4 cups all-purpose flour
2 teaspoons baking powder
Pinch of salt
$\frac{1}{4}$ teaspoon cinnamon
$\frac{1}{4}$ teaspoon grated nutmeg
1 teaspoon finely grated orange rind
$\frac{1}{2}$ cup vegetable oil
$\frac{1}{2}$ cup strained fresh orange juice
$\frac{1}{2}$ cup granulated sugar
2 to 3 tablespoons brandy
$\frac{1}{4}$ to $\frac{1}{2}$ cup water, if necessary

FILLING
$\frac{1}{4}$ pound sesame seeds
$\frac{1}{4}$ pound walnuts, coarsely chopped
$\frac{1}{2}$ teaspoon cinnamon
$\frac{1}{2}$ teaspoon grated nutmeg
$\frac{1}{2}$ teaspoon grated orange rind
5 to 10 whole cloves, crushed to a coarse powder
$\frac{1}{4}$ to $\frac{1}{3}$ cup honey

Butter
Confectioners' sugar
Rose water

1. *To prepare dough:* In a medium-size bowl, sift together flour, baking powder, salt, cinnamon and nutmeg. Add orange rind. Set aside until ready to use. In a large bowl and using an electric mixer set at high speed, beat the vegetable oil, orange juice, and sugar until smooth and creamy. Add brandy and continue beating. Slowly add flour mixture to liquids, beating with electric mixer until a soft dough mass begins to form. If dough appears too stiff, work in a little water and knead some more until it is silky to the touch. Cover and let the dough rest for 1 hour before using.

2. *To prepare filling:* While dough is resting, if you have a large mortar and pestle at your disposal, use it to lightly crush sesame seeds. In an ungreased skillet over low heat, toast whole or crushed seeds until lightly browned and aromatic. Remove skillet immediately from heat.

3. In a large bowl, toss together chopped walnuts, cinnamon, nutmeg, orange rind, cloves, and toasted sesame. Transfer the nut mixture to a large saucepan and add honey. Cook the mixture over medium heat for just a few minutes, stirring constantly with a wooden spoon. Cook for no longer than 3 to 4 minutes—just enough to dampen the mixture. There shouldn't be drippings of honey; the mixture should be fairly dry. Remove pan from heat and set aside to cool.

4. Lightly butter two baking sheets and preheat oven to 375°F.

5. Break off a piece of dough about the size of an unshelled walnut and roll it into a 5-inch circle. Place about 2 teaspoons of filling in center of dough and fold over to make a crescent (see illustration on page 317). Press the edges together with dampened fingertips to seal; trim with a serrated pastry wheel to form a decorative rim. Repeat with remaining dough and filling. Place crescents on prepared baking sheets and bake until lightly browned, about 20 minutes.

6. Remove baking sheets from oven and cool *skaltsounia* slightly on the baking sheets, enough so that they can be handled easily. Sift confectioners' sugar over a large plate or tray. Sprinkle *skaltsounia* with rose water and dredge in confectioners' sugar before serving. Store in tins or pastry boxes in a cool, dry place.

Yield: About 3 dozen

——SWEET CHEESE PASTRIES——

A wide variety of sweet cheese specialties are prepared all over Greece, but of special note are the types found at Easter on Crete and some of the Aegean islands. It's spring, and the milk—hence cheese—is at its best, with goats and sheep feeding only on tender spring herbs. What's used is a soft, fresh, saltless cheese, usually mitzithra or anthotiro, which is combined with eggs, sugar, sometimes flour or mastic, baked in homemade dough, the shapes of which vary from place to place, and devoured with alacrity.

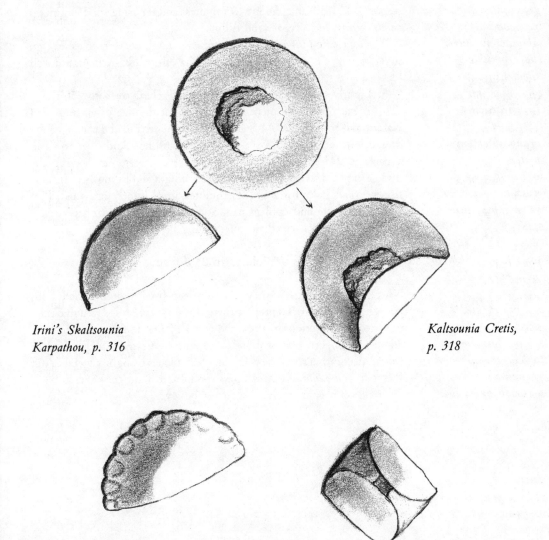

Irini's Skaltsounia
Karpathou, p. 316

Kaltsounia Cretis,
p. 318

Kaltsounia Cretis

(SWEET CHEESE PASTRIES FROM CRETE)

DOUGH

2 to 2½ cups sifted
   all-purpose flour
1 teaspoon baking
   powder
2 tablespoons
   granulated sugar
¼ teaspoon salt
4 tablespoons butter
¼ cup vegetable
   shortening
2 eggs, at room
   temperature
2 teaspoons
   orange-blossom
   water
1 to 2 tablespoons
   milk or water, at
   room temperature

FILLING

2 cups fresh, saltless
   mizithra, anthotiro,
   or farmer's cheese
1 egg
⅓ cup granulated
   sugar
2 tablespoons honey
½ to 1 teaspoon
   cinnamon
½ teaspoon dried mint

Confectioners' sugar

1. *To prepare dough:* In a medium-size bowl, sift together 2 cups flour, baking powder, sugar, and salt. Cut in butter and shortening and work them in with a pastry blender or your fingers, until the mixture is mealy. Add eggs and stir with a fork until a dough mass begins to form. Add orange-blossom water, then milk or water, but only enough to make a soft, elastic dough. Knead on a lightly floured surface until smooth and malleable, about 10 minutes, and set aside for 10 minutes or so, while you prepare the filling.

2. *To prepare filling:* In a medium-size bowl, combine cheese, egg, sugar, honey, cinnamon, and mint and mix until all ingredients are well blended.

3. Lightly butter a large baking sheet. Preheat oven to 350°F.

4. Break off a little piece of dough about the size of an unshelled walnut and roll it into a 4-inch circle or square. Fill the center of the dough with a rounded teaspoon of cheese filling. Fold over to form a package, folding each side in toward the center, but leaving the middle exposed. Repeat with remaining dough and filling (see illustration p. 317). Bake for 20 to 25 minutes, until lightly browned. (See Note.) Remove and cool in pan. Sprinkle with confectioners' sugar, if desired. Store, covered, in refrigerator.

Yield: 2 to 2½ dozen

Note: *Kaltsounia Cretis* may also be deep-fried and sprinkled with confectioners' sugar. To prepare them this way, fold filled dough circles over to make a crescent. Press the edges of the dough together with dampened fingertips to seal and trim with a serrated pastry wheel to form a decorative rim. Deep-fry in 4 to 5 inches of light vegetable oil. Remove *kaltsounia* with a slotted spoon and drain on paper towels. Sprinkle with confectioners' sugar or honey.

Melitinia Santorinis

(SWEET CHEESE TARTLETS FROM SANTORINI)

MELITINIA are similar to other sweet cheese pastries except that the filling is thickened with flour. These should look like little tartlets.

---

1. *To prepare filling:* In a medium-size bowl, combine cheese, sugar, whole egg, mastic, and 1 cup flour. Mix so that all ingredients are thoroughly blended. The mixture shouldn't be pasty, but it shouldn't be watery either. If the mixture is very loose, add more flour. In a large bowl and with an electric mixer set on high speed, beat egg whites until stiff but not dry and quickly but gently fold cheese mixture into egg whites.

2. Preheat oven to 350°F. Lightly butter a large baking sheet.

3. Break off a small piece of dough (a bit larger than an unshelled walnut) and roll it into a 4-inch circle. The dough should be at least as thick as a quarter. Place a rounded teaspoon of cheese filling in the center of the dough and pinch the edges of the dough together to make an ersatz tartlet (see illustration below). Repeat with remaining dough and filling. Place *melitinia* on prepared baking sheet and bake for 20 to 25 minutes, or until cheese mixture has solidified and dough is a light golden brown. Remove baking sheet from oven and place on a wire rack to cool. Sprinkle *melitinia* with cinnamon before serving. Store covered in the refrigerator.

Dough for kaltsounia Cretis *(page 318)*

FILLING

2 cups unsalted soft cheese, such as mizithra, anthotiro, ricotta, or farmer's cheese

1½ cups granulated sugar

1 whole egg, plus 2 egg whites

½ teaspoon finely ground mastic (see Note)

1 to 1½ cups all-purpose flour

Ground cinnamon

Yield: 2 to 2½ dozen

Note: Mastic crystals can be found in Greek specialty shops.

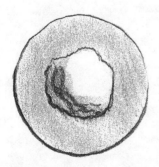
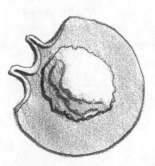

Irini's Tourtes Karpathou

(CHEESE-FILLED LITTLE TARTS FROM KARPATHOS)

THIS recipe most probably got its start after one inventive housewife had a little leftover *tsoureki* (sweet Easter bread) dough she didn't want to waste. The *tourtes* are now an Easter specialty of the island of Kárpathos, and this recipe comes from a passionate Karpathian in Neapoli, a neighborhood in Piraeus.

$\frac{1}{2}$ recipe **tsoureki dough (page 60)**

FILLING

3 cups soft unsalted mitzithra cheese (see Note)

3 whole eggs

2 tablespoons butter, melted

$\frac{1}{2}$ **cup sugar**

1 teaspoon finely ground mastic (see Note)

$\frac{1}{2}$ **teaspoon grated nutmeg**

Milk and 1 to 2 eggs, for brushing surface

Blanched almond slivers, for garnish

1. Make *tsoureki* dough, but wait until after the first rising of the dough before you use it.

2. *To prepare filling:* In a medium-size bowl, combine mitzithra, eggs, butter, sugar, mastic, and nutmeg and mix until all ingredients are thoroughly blended.

3. Lightly butter two large baking sheets. Take a little piece of dough about the size of an unshelled walnut and roll it out to a thin 4- to 5-inch square. Place a heaping teaspoon of cheese filling in the center of the dough. Fold two sides to the center, overlapping to close, and press the ends of the dough together with a moist fork to make a serrated design (similar to *thaktyla kypriaka;* see illustration on page 313). Repeat with remaining dough and filling. Place the *tourtes* on prepared baking sheets, cover with a cloth, and let rise until almost doubled in bulk, 35 to 40 minutes.

4. While dough is rising, heat oven to 400°F. Just before baking, brush *tourtes* with a mixture of 1 to 2 eggs beaten with 2 to 3 tablespoons milk. Sprinkle with almond slivers and bake for 15 to 20 minutes, or until golden brown. Remove baking sheets from oven and place on a wire rack to cool. Store sealed in the refrigerator.

Yield: about 3$\frac{1}{2}$ dozen

Note: Mitzithra and mastic can be found in Greek and Middle Eastern food shops.

Flaounes Kyprou

(PUNGENT CHEESE FLUTES FROM CYPRUS)

THESE are traditional Easter pastries from Cyprus.

---

1. *To prepare dough:* In a medium-size bowl, sift together flour, baking powder, and salt and set aside. In a large bowl and using an electric mixer set at high speed, beat the butter, shortening, eggs, and 1 tablespoon of the sugar until creamy. With a mortar and pestle, pulverize the mastic, mahlepi, and remaining 1 tablespoon sugar together. Add mastic mixture to the butter and continue beating. Slowly pour in warm milk and beat to combine. Add the flour mixture, a little at a time, and beat with electric mixer until a dough mass begins to form. Continue kneading either in bowl or on a lightly floured surface by hand for 5 to 10 minutes, until the dough is silky smooth and elastic. Cover dough and set it aside for 1 hour.

2. *To prepare filling:* In a large bowl, combine cheeses, raisins, mastic, sugar, semolina, and mint. Pour in 2 slightly beaten eggs and work into mixture so all ingredients are well blended. The filling should be thick.

3. Preheat oven to 350°F and lightly grease a large baking sheet.

4. Break off a piece of dough about the size of an unshelled walnut and roll it into a thin circle 5 to 6 inches in diameter. Place 1 tablespoon of filling in the center of the dough and fold the sides of the circles over to make either a square or a triangle, leaving the filling exposed. Repeat with remaining dough and filling. Place *flaounes* on prepared baking sheet. Brush with remaining eggs and sprinkle with sesame seeds. Bake for 20 to 25 minutes, or until *flaounes* are a light golden brown. Remove baking sheet from oven and peace on a wire rack to cool. Store *flaounes,* sealed, in the refrigerator.

Yield: About 2 to 2½ dozen

Note: Mastic, mahlepi, and the cheeses can be found in Greek and Middle Eastern food shops.

DOUGH

2½ *to 3 cups*
  all-purpose flour
1 *teaspoon baking*
  powder
¼ *teaspoon salt*
¼ *pound butter*
2 *tablespoons vegetable*
  shortening
2 *eggs*
2 *tablespoons sugar*
½ *teaspoon finely*
  pulverized mastic
¼ *teaspoon mahlepi*
¼ *cup warm milk*

FILLING

1 *cup soft, unsalted*
  mizithra or far-
  mer's cheese
½ *cup grated kefalotyri*
  or hard mizithra
  cheese
2 *cups grated haloumi*
  cheese
½ *cup golden seedless*
  raisins
½ *teaspoon finely*
  ground mastic
1 *teaspoon sugar*
2 *to 4 tablespoons fine*
  semolina flour
1 *heaping teaspoon*
  crushed dry mint or
3 *tablespoons*
  chopped fresh mint
3 *to 4 whole eggs,*
  slightly beaten

Sesame seeds

—— PHYLLO PASTRIES ——

In all the nut-filled phyllo pastries *(baklava, saraigli, floyeres)*, any combination of walnuts and almonds may be used. Sesame seeds are also a popular addition to the filling.

Argyro's Baklava

BLATANTLY absent from this version of Greece's most famous dessert are the cinnamon and cloves that commonly flavor most renditions. Here, butter, plenty of it, is the shameless protagonist, and if it comes from a sheep, that's all the better.

---

*1 pound very good
   quality unsalted
   butter (preferably
   sheep's-milk butter)*
½ pound margarine
*10 cups coarsely
   chopped walnuts or
   blanched almonds,
   or a mixture of
   both*
*3 cups zwieback
   biscuit crumbs*
*2 pounds commercial
   phyllo or strudel
   pastry*
*Whole cloves
   (optional)*
SYRUP
4 cups sugar
4 cups water
*2 tablespoons strained
   fresh lemon juice*

1. Clarify butter and margarine: Place butter and margarine in a small saucepan and heat slowly over low heat. Remove pan from heat and cool for 2 to 3 minutes. With a spoon, skim the milky foam from the top of the butter and discard foam. Pour the remaining clarified butter in a bowl and set aside until ready to use.

2. Preheat oven to 400°F. Lightly butter a 15×18×3-inch baking pan.

3. In a large bowl, combine nuts and zwieback. Add ¼ to ⅓ cup clarified butter/margarine to the mixture—enough to moisten it.

4. Layer 6 phyllo sheets on bottom of prepared baking pan, one at a time, brushing each one generously with butter and margarine mixture. Sprinkle about a third of the nut mixture over the sixth phyllo sheet and spread it evenly. Drizzle 1 to 2 teaspoons more butter and margarine over nuts.

5. Layer 4 phyllo sheets over the nuts, one at a time, buttering each generously. Spread another third of the nut mixture on top and drizzle, as before, with a teaspoon or two of butter and margarine. Layer and butter another 4 phyllo sheets, top with remaining nut mixture, and drizzle with clarified butter and margarine. Top the pan with 5 to 6 sheets of phyllo, each brushed generously with butter and margarine. With the tips of your fingers, sprinkle the top phyllo with a little water, and brush again. Score into diamond shapes, first cutting gently with a sharp knife vertically, then horizontally, making sure the knife cuts all the way down through the very bottom phyllo. Press a whole clove into each piece of *baklava,* if desired, before baking to make the tray more decorative.

6. Bake for 10 to 12 minutes, or until the phyllo begins to crisp-and brown slightly. Reduce heat to 325°F and bake for $1\frac{1}{2}$ to 2 hours, or until *baklava* is golden brown. Five minutes before removing baking pan from oven, brush *baklava* with one more ample dousing of butter and margarine.

7. *To prepare syrup:* While *baklava* is baking, in a large saucepan combine sugar and water and bring to a boil. Reduce heat and simmer, uncovered, for 12 to 15 minutes, until syrup is heavy and lusciously thick. Remove pot from heat and immediately stir in lemon juice.

8. Remove baking pan from oven and pour hot syrup over the *baklava.* Place the *baklava* back in the oven—which has been turned off but is still hot—and let stand until all the syrup is absorbed, about 20 minutes. Serve *baklava* warm or at room temperature and store at room temperature, sealed in a tin.

Yield: About 30 pieces

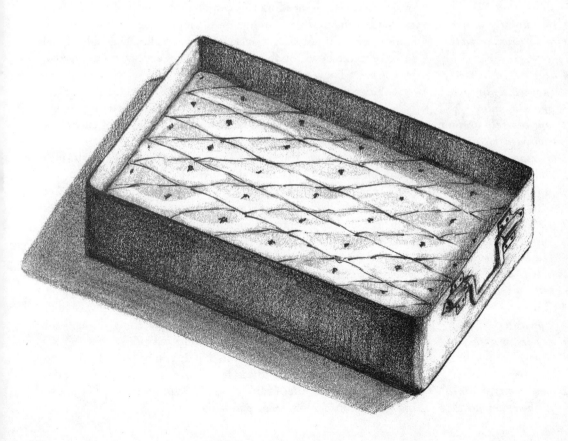

Chocolate Baklava

I LOVE this sweet. I first encountered it in a small, unassuming pastry shop called Karavan in the center of Athens. The shop specializes in the exquisite sweets of the Poli (Constantinople), and chocolate baklava was one of the most sublime—if difficult to make—confections of the little store. Melted baker's chocolate is worked into the dough before kneading and the labor and patience needed to stretch the phyllo thin is painstaking. I recommend a manual pasta maker as a special tool for this recipe.

PHYLLO

2 ounces dark, semisweet baker's chocolate

$4\frac{1}{2}$ to 6 cups all-purpose flour

$\frac{1}{2}$ teaspoon salt

4 tablespoons butter

2 tablespoons vegetable shortening

1 egg, slightly beaten

1 to $1\frac{1}{2}$ cups ice water

FILLING

4 cups mixed, coarsely chopped walnuts and almonds

2 cups coarsely ground zwieback biscuits

2 tablespoons cinnamon

$\frac{1}{4}$ cup melted butter

ASSEMBLY

2 sticks unsalted butter, melted, to brush phyllo

Whole cloves

SYRUP

3 cups sugar

3 cups water

1 cinnamon stick

1 large piece lemon zest

2 tablespoons strained fresh lemon juice

1. *To prepare phyllo:* In a double boiler melt chocolate. In a large bowl, combine $4\frac{1}{2}$ cups of the flour and the salt. Using a pastry knife or your fingers, cut butter and shortening into flour until the mixture is mealy. Make a well in center. Add egg, melted chocolate, and $\frac{3}{4}$ cup of the ice water. Using a fork and working from the center of the well outwards, combine flour into liquid. Add more water as you go along, and more flour if necessary to make a stiff but malleable dough. Knead mixture in the bowl for about 5 to 8 minutes and set aside, covered, to rest for $\frac{1}{2}$ hour.

2. *To prepare filling:* While dough is resting, combine nuts, zwieback crumbs, cinnamon, and the $\frac{1}{4}$ cup melted butter in a large bowl. Mixture should be damp, somewhat mealy, and redolent of butter. Set aside until ready to use.

3. Lightly grease a $12 \times 15 \times 3$-inch baking pan or two 10-inch round springform tart pans. Preheat oven to 450°F.

4. Have ready a large floured work surface and the pasta maker. Cut the dough into thick slices, each a little larger than a fist. Pat both sides with flour and run it gently through the No. 2 or 3 (wide) gauge on the pasta maker. Do this several times, sprinkling with flour after each passage if dough seems too moist. (Be careful, however, not to make it overly dry with too much flour.) After running the strip through the No. 2 or 3 gauge about three times, run it through a narrower gauge, such as No. 6. Do this several times, sprinkling after each roll with flour if necessary. Finally, run the dough strip very carefully through the narrowest gauge, probably No. 7, several times and sprinkling with flour as necessary, until the dough is paper-thin. It will be pinkish beige and almost transparent. Set it gently aside and cover with a cloth; repeat this procedure for fistful after fistful of dough. Be prepared to spend at least one hour, probably longer, preparing the dough.

5. Melt remaining 2 sticks of butter. Clarify, if desired, by skimming the foam off the top of the melted butter.

6. Place enough strips side by side, with a little overlap, to cover bottom of pan. Brush gently with butter and repeat until you have at least three, but preferably four, layers of chocolate phyllo, each brushed gently with melted butter. Spread half the nut filling over last phyllo sheet and pat down gently. Dot, if desired, with a little melted butter. Place three layers of phyllo (thin strips side by side to cover width of pan, layered three times) over filling. Spread remaining filling over phyllo. And spread remaining sheets side by side, buttering between each, to form three or four layers on top. Cut away any excess phyllo hanging over side of pan. Using a sharp knife, cut vertical, then diagonal incisions in phyllo, making sure knife reaches the bottom of the pan and forms diamonds. Stud each diamond with a whole clove.

7. Place in hot oven. After 5 minutes, lower heat to 350°F; continue baking for 45 minutes to one hour, until phyllo is crisp and baked thoroughly. If any melted butter remains, pour it over *baklava* halfway through baking.

8. *To prepare syrup:* While *baklava* is baking, in a large saucepan combine sugar and the water and bring to a boil. Add cinnamon stick and lemon zest, reduce heat, and simmer for 10 minutes. Stir in lemon juice 2 minutes before turning off heat.

9. When *baklava* is done, turn off oven, pull out oven rack, and pour hot syrup evenly over the *baklava,* making sure it gets into all the rows. Return *baklava* to turned-off oven, shut oven door, and let sit for at least 30 minutes before serving. Serve warm or at room temperature.

**Yield: One 12×15×3-inch tray should satisfy at least 20
people**

Saraigli

(COILED, NUT-FILLED PHYLLO PASTRY)

THIS dessert is similar to *baklava*, except that it's rolled and turned into a sleek coil in the pan, then baked.

¾ pound butter

2 cups granulated sugar

1 cup honey

2 cups water

Strained fresh juice of ½ lemon

2 cups finely chopped walnuts

1 cup sesame seeds

1 package (6 ounces) zwieback biscuits, ground to a coarse crumb

2 to 3 teaspoons cinnamon

2 to 3 tablespoons granulated sugar

1 pound thin commercial phyllo pastry

1. Clarify butter: Place butter in a small saucepan and heat slowly over low heat. Remove pan from heat and cool for 2 to 3 minutes. With a spoon, skim the milky foam from the top of the butter and discard foam. Pour the remaining clarified butter into a bowl and set aside until ready to use.

2. In a medium-size saucepan, combine sugar, honey, and water and bring to a boil over medium heat. Reduce heat to medium low and simmer, uncovered, for 5 to 7 minutes. Add lemon juice about 1 minute before removing saucepan from heat. Cool completely.

3. Preheat oven to 350°F. Lightly butter a 12-inch round baking pan.

4. In a large bowl, combine chopped walnuts, sesame seeds, zwieback, cinnamon, and sugar and toss so that all ingredients are evenly distributed. Unroll phyllo pastry and cover it with a slightly damp cloth to keep it moist. Take 1 sheet of phyllo and brush with clarified butter. Place another phyllo sheet over it, and also brush with butter. Spread a little of the nut filling in a 1½-inch-wide strip across the long side of the phyllo. Using a pastry brush, brush the nuts with clarified butter. Roll gently along the length of the phyllo to make a cylinder that is tight enough so as not to open but loose enough so as not to break when bent into a curved shape. This takes a bit of practice. Repeat this procedure with remaining phyllo and filling.

5. Starting from the outside and working toward the inside of the prepared baking pan, carefully curve and arrange the phyllo rolls so that they form a continuous coil, spiraling to the center of the pan, as shown in the illustration. Score the rolls gently every 2 or 3 inches. Brush remaining butter over coil and bake for about 25 minutes, or until the phyllo is a light golden brown and crisp.

6. Remove the baking pan from the oven and immediately pour the cooled syrup over the *saraigli*. Let cool in pan and serve. Store in pan covered with plastic wrap at room temperature.

Yield: About 2 dozen servings

Kataifi

(SHREDDED WHEAT PASTRY)

1. Clarify butter: Place butter in a small saucepan and heat slowly over low heat. Remove pan from heat and cool for 2 to 3 minutes. With a spoon, skim the milky foam from the top of the butter and discard foam. Pour the remaining clarified butter into a bowl and set aside until ready to use.

2. Preheat oven to 350°F. Lightly butter a baking sheet.

3. In a medium-size bowl, combine almonds, zwieback, cinnamon, orange rind, sugar, and orange juice and toss so that entire mixture is lightly dampened. Add a little more orange juice, if necessary. Set aside until ready to use.

4. Unwrap the raw kataifi pastry and cut it lengthwise into three long sections. Cut each section lengthwise, every 6 inches. There will be about 24 in total. Brush each small section, one at a time, very lightly with clarified butter and place about 1 tablespoon of nut filling at the bottom center of the pastry strip. Roll up to form a log about 3 inches long and place seam side down on prepared baking sheet. Repeat with remaining pastry and filling. Brush *kataifi* rolls with half of remaining butter and bake for about 20 minutes. Spoon remaining butter over *kataifi* and continue baking another 10 to 15 minutes, or until golden brown on top.

5. *To prepare syrup:* While *kataifi* is baking, in a medium-size saucepan, combine sugar and water and bring to a boil. Simmer uncovered over low to medium heat for 15 minutes. Remove pan from heat and add lemon juice. Cover until ready to use.

6. When *kataifi* are done, remove baking sheet from oven and spoon warm syrup over the pastry rolls. Cover with a cloth or towel and let cool. Store covered either at room temperature or in the refrigerator. Serve with vanilla ice cream or topped with whipped cream, if desired.

Yield: 2 dozen

Note: Kataifi pastry may be found in Greek and Middle Eastern food shops.

Kataifi may also be made as a whole pie. When unwrapping the shredded wheat pastry, divide it into two equal sections. Spread one section on the bottom of a 10-inch round buttered baking pan. Brush with butter and fill with nut filling. Spread remaining pastry on top. Pour remaining butter over top of pie and follow baking and syrup directions above. Cut like a pie from the center outward.

¾ pound unsalted butter

1½ cups blanched almonds, coarsely chopped

¼ cup chopped or ground zwieback biscuits

1 scant teaspoon cinnamon

½ to 1 teaspoon grated orange rind

1 tablespoon sugar

2 to 4 tablespoons strained fresh orange juice

1 pound **kataifi** *(shredded wheat) pastry (see Note)*

SYRUP

4 cups sugar

5½ cups water

2 teaspoons strained fresh lemon juice

Kataifi Yianniotiko

(SHREDDED WHEAT PASTRY, IOANNINA STYLE)

$\frac{3}{4}$ *pound unsalted
    butter*
$\frac{1}{2}$ *pound blanched
    almonds or walnuts,
    coarsely chopped*
$\frac{1}{2}$ *cup ground
    zwieback biscuits*
*1 teaspoon grated
    orange rind*
1 teaspoon cinnamon
*2 to 3 tablespoons
    granulated sugar*
1 pound **kataifi**
    *(shredded wheat)
    pastry (see Note)*
$\frac{1}{2}$ *pound thin
    commercial phyllo
    pastry*
SYRUP
4 cups sugar
5 cups water
*2 teaspoons strained
    fresh lemon juice*

1. Clarify butter: Place butter in a small saucepan and heat slowly over low heat. Remove pan from heat and cool for 2 to 3 minutes. With a spoon, skim the milky foam from the top of the butter and discard foam. Pour the remaining clarified butter in a bowl and set aside until ready to use.

2. Preheat oven to 350°F. Lightly butter a 9×12×3-inch baking pan.

3. In a medium-size bowl, stir together nuts, zwieback, orange rind, cinnamon, and sugar and set aside until ready to use.

4. Unwrap the raw kataifi pastry and the phyllo and divide each in half. Keep both covered so they will not dry out. Layer half the phyllo pastry, 1 sheet at a time, on bottom of prepared baking pan, brushing each sheet generously with clarified butter. Spread half the kataifi pastry over the phyllo and brush with butter. Spread the nut mixture over the kataifi and dot with butter. Cover nuts with remaining kataifi and brush again with butter. Layer remaining phyllo over kataifi, brushing each layer generously with butter. Tuck the phyllo neatly into the sides of the pan. Pour remaining butter over phyllo. Score lightly—$\frac{3}{4}$ to 1 inch deep—at first vertically, then horizontally, to form diamonds. Bake for about 1 hour 10 minutes, or until phyllo is golden brown.

5. *To prepare syrup:* While the pastry is baking, in a medium-size saucepan, combine sugar and water and bring to a boil. Simmer, uncovered, over low to medium heat for 15 minutes. Add lemon juice and remove pan from heat.

6. When pastry is done, remove baking pan from oven and spoon warm syrup over the pastry. Cool pastry in pan before serving.

Yield: 8 to 12 servings

Note: Kataifi pastry may be found in Greek and Middle Eastern food shops.

Galaktoboureko

(CUSTARD-FILLED PHYLLO)

1. Clarify butter: Place butter in a small saucepan and heat slowly over low heat. Remove pan from heat and cool for 2 to 3 minutes. With a spoon, skim the milky foam from the top of the butter and discard foam. Pour the remaining clarified butter into a bowl and set aside until ready to use.

2. *To prepare syrup:* In a large saucepan, combine sugar and water and heat over medium heat until sugar is dissolved. Add cinnamon stick and cloves. Bring mixture to a boil and simmer for 10 to 12 minutes, stirring slowly and constantly with a wooden spoon. Remove the saucepan from the heat and immediately pour in brandy, lemon juice, and orange juice. Set aside and let cool.

3. Preheat oven to 350°F. Lightly butter a 9×12×3-inch baking pan.

4. *To prepare filling:* In a large saucepan, combine sugar, semolina, and milk and cook, stirring constantly with a wooden spoon, over medium-low heat for 15 to 20 minutes, until mixture is thick and creamy. It should not appear gelatinous and should still be relatively liquid, although very thick. Two to 3 minutes before removing pan from heat, stir in brandy. Remove pan from heat and cool slightly.

5. In a medium-size bowl and using an electric mixer set at high speed, beat the eggs until pale and creamy. Quickly pour the eggs into the semolina mixture, along with the orange rind, and stir vigorously with a wooden spoon. Let the semolina cool to tepid before using it.

6. Layer 6 to 8 sheets of phyllo pastry on bottom of prepared baking pan, brushing with ample butter between each layer. Spread semolina and milk mixture evenly over phyllo and top with 5 to 6 more pastry sheets, brushing generously with butter between each.

7. With a very sharp knife, gently score the top phyllo layers to form either squares or diamonds. Don't score the filling. Bake for about 45 minutes, or until phyllo is golden brown and semolina filling is set.

8. Remove baking pan from oven and immediately pour the cooled syrup over the pastry, making sure it's evenly spread. Let cool and serve sprinkled, if desired, with ground cinnamon.

Yield: 8 to 10 servings

*4 to 8 tablespoons
unsalted butter*
*1 pound commercial
phyllo pastry*
*Ground cinnamon
(optional)*
SYRUP
2 cups sugar
1 cup water
1 cinnamon stick
5 to 6 whole cloves
1 tablespoon brandy
*1 tablespoon strained
fresh orange juice*
*2 teaspoons strained
fresh lemon juice*
FILLING
1 cup sugar
*1 cup fine semolina
flour*
6 cups milk
1 tablespoon brandy
*3 whole eggs, at room
temperature*
½ teaspoon orange rind

Some Classic Greek Meals

EASTER

Main Course:
Maroulosalata (Fresh Lettuce Salad, page 96)
Spanakopitta (Classic Spinach Pie Filled with Fresh Spring Herbs such as Dill and Fennel and Parsley, page 117)
Mageiritsa (Lamb's Head and Innard Soup, page 132)
Dyed Eggs (page 269)
Kokkoretsi (page 264)
Classic Roast Leg of Lamb or Spit-Roasted Lamb or Goat (pages 254 and 256)
Roasted Potatoes (page 105)
Fresh Spring Cheese such as Manouri (page 32) or Anthotiro (page 30)

Bread: *Tsoureki* (Easter bread, page 60)

Dessert: *Tourtes Karpathou* (page 320), *Kaltsounia Cretis* (page 318), or *Melitinia Santorinis* (page 319)

Wine: For this special, classic meal, a deep, full-bodied wine such as the Boutari Grande Réserve or Náoussa would be a perfect foil to the rich, strong flavors of *mageiritsa* and *kokkoretsi,* and an excellent accompaniment to the roasted spring lamb. Samos Muscat goes well with the sweet cheese desserts.

CHRISTMAS

An array of appetizers such as olives, cheese (feta, kasseri, or haloumi), *dolmadakia yialantzi* (stuffed grape leaves, page 82), *tyropittakia* (page 70), and *keftedes* (pages 72–75) usually fills the table.

Main Course:
Prassopitta (Savory Leek Pie, page 120)
A Traditional Chicken or Turkey Dish such as *Missoura* (Stuffed Chicken with Leeks, Pork, and Beef, page 204); Stuffed Christmas Turkey (page 206); or *Kotopoulo Yemisto à la Polita* (Stuffed with Rice, Pine Nuts, and Raisins, page 200)
Or a Pork Dish such as *Afelia Kypriaka* (Braised Pork with Red Wine and Coriander, page 248)
Roasted Potatoes (page 105) or *Patates Antinaktes Kyprou* (Pan Cooked and Seasoned with Coriander, from Cyprus, page 106)
Boiled *Horta* (Wild Greens) with Olive Oil and Vinegar (page 96)

Bread: *Christopsomo* (page 62) and *Vassilopitta* (page 62)

Dessert: The Christmas table is laden with sweets, generally as a boding for a good, healthy year. Among the classics would be some of the deep-fried dough fritters, confectioners' sugar-coated delights, and nut-filled specialties: *xerotygana* or *thiples* (page 308), *kourambiethes* (page 300), *baklava* (page 322), *melomakarona* (page 301), and *skaltsounia Karpathou* (page 316)

Wine: Calliga Robola or Chateau Matsa best accompanies the poultry dishes; the pork requires a full-bodied wine such as a Náoussa.

THE LENTEN TABLE

Pickled Onions (page 103) and Pickled Small Green Peppers (available
   in Greek specialty food shops)
Olives
Fresh Garlic Stalks and Spring Onions or Scallions
Taramosalata (page 87), Hummus (page 90), and *Tahinosalata* (page 90)
Htapothi Xithato (page 79)
Horta with Olive Oil and Vinegar or Lemon (page 96)
Revithokeftethes (Chick-pea Patties, page 75) or *Revithatha* (Tangy
   Chick-pea Soup, page 138)

Bread: Lagana (page 58)

Dessert: *Halvah tis Rinas* (page 282) and/or *Keik me Tahini*
(page 304)

Wine: Retsina would be the most compatible wine with this
menu. A light white table wine such as Lac des Roches would also
be a welcome choice.

WINTER FISH MENU

Main Course:
Tzatziki (page 84) and Lima Bean *Skordalia* (page 86) or
   Makedonitiki Skordalia (page 85)
Lahanosalata (Shredded Red or Green Cabbage Salad, page 98)
Patzaria (Beets) and *Patzarohorta* (Beet Greens) with Olive Oil,
   Garlic, and Vinegar
Feta
Bakaliaro (Salt Cod), *galeo* (Shark), or *Marithes* (Smelts, page 217),
   Floured, Battered, and Deep-Fried

Bread: *Horiatiko* (page 48) or *Eptazymo* (page 56)

Dessert: Fresh Fruit such as Pears, Apples, or Grapes

Wine: Retsina or a mild white wine

A FAVORITE SUMMER MEAL

Main Course:
Vassilis's Paximathia and Tomato Salad (page 94) or *Horiatiki Salata* (page 93)
Horta (Wild Greens, page 96)
Tzatziki (page 84)
Saganaki (page 81)
Pseftokeftedes Santorinis (Mock *Keftedes,* Santorini Style, page 74)
Piperies Florinis (Roasted Red Peppers with Olive Oil, Vinegar, and Garlic, page 102)
Xifias Souvlaki (Skewered, Grilled Swordfish, page 216)
Tiganopitta Epirou (Grilled Feta Cheese *Pitta* from Epirus, page 125)

Bread: *Horiatiko Psomi* (page 48), Whole Wheat *Pitta* (page 53), or Olive Bread (pages 54 and 55)

Dessert: *Kataifi* with Vanilla Ice Cream (page 327)

Wine: A dry, crisp Santorini white

Mail Order Sources for Greek Food

Titan Foods Retail, 25–50 31st Street, Astoria, NY 11102; telephone: 718–626–7771

Athena International Foods, 77 Legion Parkway, Brockton, MA 02401; telephone: 508–588–9731

Athens Grocery, 324 South Halsted Street, Chicago, IL 60606; telephone: 312–454–0940

C & K Importing, 2771 Bico (corner of Normandy), Los Angeles, CA 90005; telephone: 213–737–2970

Peloponnese & Rockbridge Trading Co., 2227 Poplar Street, Oakland, CA 94607; telephone: 415–839–8153 (wholesalers of upscale Greek food and wine and a good source for information)

Glossary

Arni (ar-née) Lamb

Avgolemono (av-gho-lé-mo-no) Egg and lemon sauce

Bakaliaros (bak-a-lee-ár-os) Cod

Baklava (bak-la-vá) Layered, syruped phyllo and nut dessert

Boureki (boo-ré-kee) Baked or fried dumpling-like mini, stuffed savory doughs

Diosmo (thee-ós-mo) Mint

Dolmades (dol-má-thez) Stuffed leaves such as grape or cabbage

Elliniko (el-een-ee-kó) Greek, but also refers to thick Greek coffee

Feta Sharp goat cheese

Giouvetsi (yui-vé-tsee) Baked meat, usually lamb or chicken, with orzo and tomato in a special clay pan by the same name

Goudi (ghoo-theé) Mortar

Kafe (ka-féh) Coffee

Kali orexi (ka-leé ór-e-xee) *Bon appétit*

Keftedes (kef-té-thes) Little meatballs

Kima (kee-má) Ground meat

Kourambiethes (kou-ra-mbié-thes) Powdered butter cookies, like shortbread

Krasi (kra-seé) Wine

Kreas (kré-as) Meat

Lathera (la-theh-rá) A group of stove-top stews in which olive oil is a main flavoring

Lathi (lá-thee) Oil. Greeks use the word *oil* generically to mean *olive oil.*

Latholemono (la-tho-léh-mo-no) Oil and lemon dressing or marinade, usually made with oregano

Lathoxitho (la-thó-xee-tho) Oil and red wine vinegar dressing

Melitzanosalata (mel-eetz-an-o-sa-lá-ta) Eggplant puree, one of the classic Greek dips

Meze (me-zéh) Appetizer

Mezedaki(a) (me-ze-thá-kee, singular) or (me-ze-thá-keea, plural) Diminutive of meze

Mezedes (me-zé-thes) Plural of meze, appetizers

Moussaka (moo-sa-ká) Eggplant, ground meat, and béchamel casserole

Nero (neh-ró) Water

Orektiko (or-e-ktee-kó) Appetizer

Orexi (ór-e-xee) Appetizer

Orzo (ór-zoh) Rice-shaped pasta, also known as *kritharaki*

Ostraka (ós-tra-ka) Shellfish

Ouzo (oó-zo) Anise-flavored liqueur

Pastitsio (pa-stée-tseeo) Macaroni baked with ground meat and béchamel

Pitta (peé-ta) Savory pie

Psari (psá-ree) Fish

Psito (psee-tó) Baked

Psomi (pso-meé) Bread

Rigani (rheé-gha-nee) Oregano

Skordalia (skor-tha-lee-áh) Garlic and potato or bread puree

Skordo (skór-tho) Garlic

Skordostoumbi (skor-tho-stóom-bee) Red wine vinegar and garlic dressing

Souvla (sóov-la) Spit roast

Spanakopitta (spa-na-kó-pee-ta) Spinach pie

Steen skara (stéen ská-ra) Grilled or barbecued

Tarama (ta-ra-má) Fish roe, usually of the carp, sometimes of the gray mullet

Taramosalata (ta-ra-mo-sa-lá-ta) Fish roe spread

Tiganito (tee-gha-nee-tó) Fried

Tiri (tee-reé) Cheese

Tzatziki (dza-dzeé-kee) Yogurt, cucumber, and garlic dip

Vrasto (vra-stó) Boiled or poached

Xithato (xee-thá-to) Flavored with vinegar, or briny

Xithi (xée-thee) Vinegar

Yiahni (yee-ach-neé) Stew

Zesto (zes-tó) Hot

Zoumi (zou-meé) Broth

Conversion Tables

—TEMPERATURES—

	Fahrenheit	Centigrade
Water freezes	32°F	0°C
Water boils	212°F	100°C
Soft ball	234°F	112°C
Firm ball	244°F	117°C
Hard ball	250°F	121°C
Very low oven	250°–275°F	121°–133°C
Low	300°–325°F	149°–163°C
Moderate	350°–375°F	177°–190°C
Hot	400°–425°F	204°–218°C
Very hot	450°–475°F	232°–246°C
Extremely hot	500°–525°F	260°–274°C

To convert Farenheit to Centigrade, subtract 32, multiply by 5, and divide by 9. To convert Centigrade to Farenheit, multiply by 9, divide by 5, and add 32.

Dry Measures
1 ounce = 28.35 grams = 16 drams (a measure still used in Greece)
1 pound = 16 ounces = 454 grams
1 gram = .565 dram = .032 ounce = .002 pound = .001 kilo
1 kilo = .000032 ounce = 2.2 pounds = 1000 grams

Liquid Measures

1 teaspoon = 5 milliliters

1 tablespoon = 3 teaspoons = 15 milliliters

1 fluid ounce = 6 teaspoons = 2 tablespoons = 29.56 milliliters = .030 liter

1 cup = 16 tablespoons = 8 fluid ounces = 236 milliliters = .236 liter

1 U.S. pint = 2 cups = 473 milliliters = .473 liter

1 quart = 32 ounces = 4 cups = 946 milliliters = .946 liter

1 liter = 2.113 cups = 1.057 quarts = .264 gallon = 1000 milliliters

Water: 1 cup = 115 grams

       1 pound = 2 cups

Linear Measures

1 centimeter = .394 inch

1 inch = 2.54 centimeters

1 meter = 39.37 inches

Bibliography

Allen, H. Warner, *History of Wine*. London: Faber & Faber, 1962.

Andrioti, N. P., *The Etymological Dictionary of Common Greek*. Third edition. Thessaloniki, Greece: Institute of Modern Greek Studies, 1983.

Athenaeus, *The Deipnosophists*. English translation by Charles Burton Gulick, Ph.D. The Loeb Classical Library. Cambridge, Mass.: Harvard University Press, 1961.

Biris, Kostas, "Ti Etrogan kai ti Epinan oi Palaioi Athinaioi," *Ios—Epitheorisis Touristiki, Aeroporiki, Ypaithrou*. January 10, 1939.

Brothwell, Don and Patricia, *Food in Antiquity*. London: Thames and Hudson, 1919.

Calzolari, Silvana Bevilacqua, *Olive Oil*. Rome: Lucarini Editore s.r.l., 1986.

Chantiles, Vilma Liacouras, *The Food of Greece*. New York: Atheneum Publishers, 1975.

Chatto, James and Martin, W. L., *A Kitchen in Corfu*. New York: New Amsterdam Books, 1987.

Clarke, Oz, *The Essential Wine Book*. New York: Viking Press, 1985.

Crane, Eva, *A Book of Honey*. Oxford: Oxford University Press, 1980.

Farah, Adelaide P., "The Good Oil," *Health*, June 1986.

Foxhall, Lin, "Greece Ancient and Modern—Subsistence and Survival," *History Today*, July 1986.

Frazier, Greg and Beverly, *Aphrodisiac Cookery Ancient and Modern.* San Francisco: Troubador Press, 1979.

Freiman, Jane Salzfass, "Making the Most of Your Liquid Assets—Olive Oil," *Cuisine,* February 1984.

Garnsey, Peter, *Famine and Food Supply in the Graeco-Roman World: Responses to Risk and Crisis.* Cambridge: Cambridge University Press, 1989.

Gold, Alec H., *Wines and Spirits of the World.* Chicago: Follett Publishing Co., 1972.

Goldberg, Howard, "Premium Wines of Greece No Longer Taste of Resin," *The New York Times,* October 26, 1988.

Goode, John and Wilson, Carol, *The World Guide to Cooking with Fruits and Vegetables.* New York: Dutton, 1974.

Grace, Virginia R., *Amphorae and the Ancient Wine Trade.* Princeton: American School of Classical Studies, 1979.

Gunyon, R. E. H., *The Wines of Central and Southeast Europe.* London: G. Duckworth & Co., 1971.

Hallgarten, Peter and Olney, Bruce, *Liqueurs, Aperitifs, and Fortified Wines.* London: Hills and Boon, 1972.

Hatzipetros, Emmanuel, "Sweetly Syros," *The Athenian,* April 1984.

Heiser, C. B., *Seed to Civilization—The Story of Food.* Second Edition. San Francisco: W. H. Freeman, 1981.

Hillman, Howard, *The Cook's Book.* New York: Avon Books, 1981.

Jacob, H. E., *Six Thousand Years of Bread.* New York: Doubleday, 1944.

Jenkins, Nancy Harmon, "In the Pantheon of Olive Oils, the Extra-Virgins are at the Top," *The New York Times,* April 13, 1988.

Jenkins, Nancy Harmon, "The Virtues of Olive Oil," *The New York Times,* April 16, 1986.

Jobe, Joseph, *Le Grand Livre du Vin.* New York: World Publishing Company, 1970.

Johnson, Hugh, *The World Atlas of Wine.* New York: Simon and Schuster, 1985.

King, Helen, "Food as Symbol in Classical Greece," *History Today,* September, 1986.

Kochilas, Diane, "From Greek Outlaws, Underground Food," *The New York Times,* November 2, 1988.

Koukoule, Phaedon I., *Ta Laographika, Tomos A'.* Athens: Center for Macedonian Studies, 1950.

Kourakou-Dragona, Stavroula, *Wine in Greece* (in Greek). Athens: The Hellenic Export Promotion Organization, 1987.

Kyriakidou-Nestoros, Alkis, *Laographika Meletimata.* Athens: Ekdosis Nea Synora.

Makrides, Nika, *Neotaton Ellinoaglicon Lexicon,* Athens: Elefteroudakis Press.

Manus, Willard, "The Mastic Towns of Chios," *The Athenian,* August 1987.

McConnell, Carol and Malcolm, *The Mediterranean Diet.* New York: W. W. Norton and Company, 1987.

McGee, Harold, *On Food and Cooking—The Science and Lore of the Kitchen.* New York: Charles Scribner's Sons, 1984.

Megas, G. A., *Ellinikes Yiortes kai Ethyma tis Laikis Latreias,* Athens: Odysseus Publishers, 1988.

Melidou, Glykeria, "To Psomi stin Halkidiki," *Makedoniki Zoi,* July 1972.

Miha-Lambraki, Aspasia, *Y Diatrophe ton Arhaion Ellinon kata tous Arhaious Komothiographous.* Athens, 1984.

Nelson, James, *The Poor Person's Guide to Great Cheap Wines.* New York: McGraw-Hill Publishers, 1977.

Nikolaos, Nearhos, *Mageiriki Apo Tin Kyprou.* Cyprus: Ekdoseis Vrakas-Kypros, 1987.

Paradeisi, Chryssa. *Mageiriki, Zaharoplastiki.* Athens: Biblioekdotiki, 1958.

Penner, Lucille, *The Honey Book.* New York: Hastings House, 1986.

Perry, Charles, "The Oldest Mediterranean Noodle: A Cautionary Tale," *Petits Propos Culinaires 9.* London: Prospect Books, October 1981.

Petropoulos, Elias, *Turkish Coffee in Greece.* Athens: Grammata Press, 1979.

Reid, Diana, trans. *Traditional Greek Cooking.* Athens: Aegean Eva Fytrakis, 1981.

Rodd, Rennell, *The Customs and Lore of Greece.* Chicago: Argonaut, Inc., 1892.

Root, Waverley, *Food.* New York: Simon & Schuster, 1980.

Root, Waverley, ed., *Herbs and Spices—A Guide to Culinary Seasoning.* New York: Alfred van der Marck Editions, 1985.

Seltman, Charles, *Wine in the Ancient World.* London: Routledge and Kegan, 1957.

Seward, Desmond, *Monks and Wine.* New York: Crown Publishers, 1979.

Skoura, Sofia A., *Greek Cooking.* Athens: Aegean, Eva Fytrakis Publishers, 1979.

Soler, J., *Food and Drink in History*. Baltimore: Johns Hopkins Press, 1979.

Sparkes, Brian A., and Talcott, Lucy, *The Pots and Pans of Classical Athens*. Princeton, New Jersey: The American School of Classical Studies, 1977.

Spoerri, Daniel, *Mythology & Meatballs—A Greek Island Diary/Cookbook*. Berkeley: Aris Books, 1982.

Stathaki-Koumari, Rodoula, *To Rethymniotiko Paradosiako Psomi*. Rethymnon, Crete: Ekdosi Istoriko kay Laographiko Museo Rethymnis, 1983.

Stavroulakis, Nicholas, *Cookbook of the Jews of Greece*. Athens: Lycabettus Press, 1986.

Stenzel, Samantha B., "Wine: Dionysos' Legacy to Man . . . and Woman," *The Athenian,* October 1984.

Tannahill, Reay, *Food in History*. New York: Stein and Day Publishers, 1973.

Thursby, J. M., "The Salepi Season," *The Athenian,* Athens, December, 1983.

Tzartzanos, Achilles, "To Ouzo, Istoria mias Lexeos," *Imerologion tis Megalis Ellados*. Athens: Ekdotis I.N. Sideris, 1932.

Wolfert, Paula, "Olives, the Treasure of Greece, Yield an Array of Flavors," *The New York Times,* June 3, 1987.

Yannoulis, Anne, *Greek Calendar Cookbook*. Athens: Lycabettus Press, 1988.

Index